The Original
WORD GAME
DICTIONARY

The Original WORD GAME DICTIONARY

Thurston Moore

STEIN AND DAY/ *Publishers*/ New York

First published in 1984.
Copyright ᶜ 1984 by Thurston Moore Country, Ltd.
All rights reserved, Stein and Day, Incorporated
Designed by Louis A. Ditizio
Printed in the United States of America
STEIN AND DAY/*Publishers*
Scarborough House
Briarcliff Manor, N.Y. 10510

Library of Congress Cataloging in Publication Data

Moore, Thurston, 1926–
 The original word game dictionary.

 1. Word games—Terminology. 2. Word games.
I. Title.
GV1507.W8M58   1983   793.73   83-42631
ISBN 0-8128-2926-3
ISBN 0-8128-6191-4 (pbk.)

To Earl and Sue
who, during an evening of BOGGLE® playing,
inspired the idea that developed
into this volume.

Acknowledgments

I want to thank everyone who encouraged this project and assisted in making it a reality. I am particularly indebted to each of the game manufacturers for their help.

To my editor at Stein and Day, Benton M. Arnovitz, I owe a special thanks for his understanding and faith in the concept of this dictionary. To Sydona M. Young for her valued criticisms and to my wife, Georgianna, who did far more than I can repay, I offer my deepest gratitude.

Contents

The Original
WORD GAME
DICTIONARY

Introduction

All word game players who use this dictionary will find it beneficial to become acquainted with its features and read this introduction.

This new dictionary has been compiled for the millions of word game addicts who want to save time while playing games and who want to improve their playing skills.

Words are often challenged in word games as being invalid or misspelled. Because many dictionaries differ, it is often difficult to draw a clear line between words that are admissable in a game and those that are not. Now the *Original Word Game Dictionary* will help you quickly determine whether the challenged word is acceptable or not. You can set your own "house rules" with respect to all your word games and let the *Original Word Game Dictionary* be your "final word" authority.

Remember, too, that you always have the option of changing game rules. Therefore, even if the published rules that come with a particular game allow the use of proper nouns, for example, you still can use this dictionary.

Dictionaries can be daunting. They are often hard to carry and impossible to read without glasses. They are crammed full of 6-part definitions, derivatives, explanations of parts of speech, pronunciation keys and other features most such reference works included. This dictionary is different. It eliminates those frustrating symbols, descriptions, and signs found in standard dictionaries: it also dispenses with etymologies, most of the labels given to words, and those words not acceptable in most word games: abbreviations, contractions, proper nouns, hyphenated words, and the like.

The units of any language are collected for reference in dictionaries. These units are words, which are (1) the names of things or referents of any kind, about which information is conveyed to a reader; and (2) any other separable parts of a sentence by which that information is conveyed.

This dictionary contains selected entries compiled in a handy quick-reference format that allows you to look up words during a game in the least possible amount of time; it also provides concise, simple definitions for those words. With this special dictionary you no longer have to wade through a large volume with thousands of very common and standard derivatives—as well as thousands of words the average word game player probably will never use.

This little volume is not intended to be a scholarly dictionary of English usage. The structure and importance of the *Original Word Game Dictionary* will be obvious to word game enthusiasts: it is designed to stimulate thinking and creativity and, most importantly, to help you master these games.

While the *Original Word Game Dictionary* will be used primarily by adult game enthusiasts, it has been compiled with young people also in mind. Authorities have determined that the average preschool child has a vocabulary of 3,000 to 4,000 words. By the time he leaves college he will have a vocabulary of 10,000 to 30,000 words. While a dictionary of the English language frequently contains as many as 100,000 entries, and some more than 500,000, there are not more than 60,000 words with which anyone but a specialist is likely ever to be concerned. But of these 60,000 words only about 20,000 occur frequently in general reading materials.

On the other hand, scholars have compiled a mere 850 words to form what is known as Basic English—a simple form of English to be used as an international language. These 850 words cover the requirements of everyday communication with a minimum of grammatical and structural apparatus. Of the 850 words in the Basic vocabulary, 600 are names of things or events (nouns), 150 are names of qualities or properties (adjectives), and the remaining 100 put the system into operation.

Standard dictionaries vary greatly in the selection of words they include. Several of those reference works, both time-honored and contemporary, were consulted in the preparation of the *Original Word Game Dictionary*. Since this vocabulary was prepared *solely* for word game players, this selection—more than 27,000 entry words—should fill the need.

The *Original Word Game Dictionary* includes only words containing up to nine letters. (Any challenged words containing more letters can be looked up in a standard dictionary.) It is rare, of course, for even very skilled players to make words of more than eight letters in most popular word games. One exception is Parker Brothers' PROBE®; it permits words of up to twelve letters and allows participants to consult a dictionary before play to find a word. (*The Official SCRABBLE® Players Dictionary*, published for SCRABBLE® tournaments, contains two-to-eight letter words.)

All lexicographers have to make decisions about which words to include. The preparation of this volume raised a number of questions about what constitutes "good usage" and what constitutes "bad usage."

Dr. Samuel Johnson (1709–1784) was concerned about speech corrupting the language when he compiled his epochal volume, *A Dictionary of the English Language*, in 1775. In his preface Dr. Johnson wrote, "Tongues, like governments, have a natural tendency to degeneration; we have long preserved our constitution, let us make some struggle for our language. . . . [Yet] pronunciation will be varied by levity or ignorance, and the pen must at length comply with the tongue."

Noah Webster (1758–1843), a Connecticut farm boy with a Yale education, recognized the fact that speech, and not writing, must in the end command the usage of words. He said, "Several customs must be the rule of speaking and it is always better to be vulgarly right than politely wrong."

VULGAR WORDS

Whether or not one agrees with Mr. Webster's statement, the selection process for this *Original Word Game Dictionary* has focused on the overall purpose of the book and the audience who will use it. Therefore, certain words that are generally termed vulgar, or coarse, often are socially taboo and are not included.

In this area the scholarly editors of the *Webster's New World*

Dictionary, Second College Edition, offer sound judgment. Many people object to certain well-known vulgate terms for sexual and excretory organs and functions. Players can easily dispense with those obscenities as well as with terms of racial or ethnic opprobrium. In any case those words are so well known that they need not be included in *any* dictionary, but it is certainly the prerogative of word game players to permit vulgar words if they wish.

SLANG WORDS

Slang words are indicative of a style of language, as opposed to vulgarity, and therefore most words commonly referred to as slang are included. Because some word games state that "slang words cannot be used," those words are labeled as slang.

OBSOLETE WORDS

In vocabulary (i.e., not only words but also meanings) changes take place constantly. So whether or not to include words that are generally labeled "obsolete," "archaic," "rare," and "poetic" in most standard dictionaries constituted another problem in compiling this dictionary. Cultural changes necessarily alter our language; old words and expressions fall out of use or have their meanings changed while new words are introduced. Taking their frequent appearance in crossword puzzles as a guide, many obsolete words have been included. They are not labeled as such, since word games generally do not prohibit their usage.

REGIONAL WORDS

This dictionary also includes words that are used primarily in only one area (or another) of the United States. An example is the word *goober*, meaning peanut, used chiefly in the South.

Besides geographical dialects, there are also social dialects. Persons of different social groups, classes, and occupations often develop special ways of speaking, and thus form words of their own. Many of these words, too, have found their way into this reference book.

FOREIGN WORDS

Many words that are foreign origin, such as *señorita*, *crepe*, and *garçon*, have been incorporated into our vocabulary too, and although most word game rules state that foreign words are not acceptable, many such words are found in most of the standard English dictionaries, and are also included here.

BRITISH WORDS

Some standard dictionaries label words that are of chiefly British usage. Many of those words, such as *telly* (television), are included in this book but are not labeled.

MAIN ENTRIES

The entry words (those to be looked up) are in **boldface** type for quick sighting. The words are not divided into syllables, and only brief, condensed definitions of the words are provided.

In nearly all word games, the only relevant factors are the authenticity of the words and their spelling. Multiple meanings are irrelevant.

The main purpose of the *Original Word Game Dictionary* is to show whether or not a challenged word is valid and usable in your game, and to do so as quickly as possible. A word game player must only justify the validity and correct spelling of the word he has selected, not its correct meaning or usage. If the complete meaning of a word is desired you can always refer to a standard dictionary.

Some words can be used as more than one part of speech; *grate,* for example, can be used as both a noun and a verb. Since this dictionary does not define the parts of speech of the entry words, only one choice and one meaning is shown.

RUN-ON ENTRIES

Run-on entries are derivatives of the main entry, and are shown in all standard dictionaries:

> *itchy -ier, -iest*
> *rely -lied, -lying, -lies*

Simple run-on entries such as those shown above are not included in this dictionary. Even the youngest word game player who may need to check the spelling of a word like *itchiest* or *relying,* and who finds the main entry words, *itchy* and *rely,* will be able to confirm the correct spelling.

PLURALS

Neither does this dictionary include the most obvious plural forms of main entry words such as those words that add only an *s*, *es*, or those in which the *y* changes to *ies* or *s*. However, the less common plural forms are shown, and in most cases these are shown immediately after the main entry word. But in some instances, such as "ovum" and "talus" in the following examples, plural words are also listed as main entries alphabetically.

custos, pl custodes   *mahzor, pl mahzorim*
houri, -ris   *nebula, -lae*
hyrax, -raxes or -races   *ovum, -ova*
lavabo, -boes   *talus, pl tali*
leaf, pl leaves

PARTS OF SPEECH AND LABELS

The parts of speech of main entry words are not indicated, and as stated before, the only words labeled are *slang* words.

As explained under *plurals*, uncommon plural forms of the main entry words are included; these are labeled *pl* and are listed immediately after the main entry words.

WORDS NOT INCLUDED

For the sake of compactness, in order to produce an easy-to-use and affordable dictionary for word game players this dictionary does not show the simple run-on entries and inflected forms. In addition, certain words are not included when the spelling is obvious from the main entry word shown, and where the spelling should be familiar to the vast majority of those who play word games.

Example:
rest -ed, -ing, -s   *restive*
rester   *restless*
restful

Rest is included as a main entry word without including the run-on entries *ed*, *ing*, and *s*. Neither does this book include words like *restful* and *restless*. However, included are *rester* and *restive* because they are not common words.

UNDEFINED WORDS INCLUDED

Where a main entry word is followed by a number of words that contain the main entry word as the first syllable, the meanings of which are self-explanatory to most word game players, those words are listed after the main entry without definition.

Example:

day—The time between dawn and nightfall

daybook	dayroom
daybreak	dayside
daydream	dayspring
dayglow	daystar
daylight	daytime
daylong	daywork
daymare	

Also listed without definition are compound words formed with the more common prefixes, such as *non-*, *pre-*, *re-*, and *un-*. This technique is consistent with that followed by a number of high-priced, multipurpose dictionaries.

I

Increase Your Vocabulary and Word Game Skills

"Words are easy, like the wind."

Richard Barnfield
English Poet
(1574–1627)

The Original Word Game Dictionary

A skilled word game player must be a good speller, and must be able to understand and use a wide variety of words. This isn't difficult if you want to improve your vocabulary and are willing to use this book. Many people are amazed at how fascinating a dictionary can be. Wilfred Funk, the noted lexicographer, wrote, "I can only wish that the reader might be encouraged to walk among words as I do, like *Alice in Wonderland*, amazed at the marvels they hold."

Make your dictionary your friend. Either read it, or simply browse through it at random, and when your friends ask what good book you've read lately, answer, "The dictionary."

Some words are difficult to spell; others seem inordinately complicated. George Bernard Shaw, the famous playwright, once offered a dramatic proposal to reduce England's taxes. "Eliminate unnecessary letters from our unwieldy spelling," he said, "and you'll save enough money in paper and printing to cut everyone's tax rate in half."

Many words do have unnecessary letters, but that's unlikely to change in our lifetime. What else is there to do, then, but meet the challenge and improve our spelling? This chapter isn't meant to be a mini-textbook on grammar and language. However, some of the more common rules of spelling are included to help word game players; you should find that especially useful since the simple run-on entries and inflected forms have not been included in this dictionary.

SPELL CORRECTLY

Remember the vowels—*a, e, i, o, u,* and sometimes *y*—when you're playing word games. All other letters are consonants. The majority of words require a vowel but, like many spelling rules, there are exceptions: *cwm, nth, crwth,* and *pht,* for example.

In monosyllabic words ending in a single consonant preceded by a single vowel, the final consonant is usually doubled before a termination that begins with a vowel: *jog, jogging.*

The final consonant is not doubled in monosyllables in which it is preceded by a digraph (*ea* in bread): *bread—breaded, breading;* or a diphthong (*oi* in spoil): *spoil—spoils, spoiled.*

When a monosyllable ends in a double consonant, the double

final consonant is retained: *fill—filling, filled; gross—grossly, grosses.*

When polysyllables are accented on the last syllable and end in a single consonant (with the exception of *h* and *x*) preceded by a single vowel, the final consonant must be doubled before adding a termination that begins with a vowel: *admit—admitted, admitting.*

Remember, the final consonant is not doubled in those words that aren't accented on the last syllable, nor in the words in which the single consonant is preceded by more than one vowel: *congeal—congealed, congealing; shovel—shoveled, shoveling.*

The final silent *e* is usually dropped before a suffix beginning with a vowel: *amaze—amazing.* But the silent *e* is usually retained before a suffix beginning with a consonant: *taste—tasteful, tastefully.*

Also, some words ending in silent *e* immediately preceded by a vowel other than *e*, always drop the *e* when forming derivatives: *true—truly.*

Though exceptions exist, remember the rule of *i* before *e* except after *c* or when sounded as *a*, as in *weigh.*

> Examples:
> *fierce, grieve, relief*
> *conceit, perceive, receipt*
> *eight, deign, sleigh*

The general rule in American usage, when adding *-ing* to a word ending in *-ie*, the vowel *e* is dropped, and the vowel *i* is changed to *y*: *caddie—caddying; lie—lying.*

When the termination *-y* is preceded by a consonant, the *y* is usually changed to *i* before adding the termination (other than the vowel *i*): *mercy—merciful, merciless; pushy—pushiest.*

Plurals often confuse even the best word game players, so remember that *sound* is the key. Generally, nouns become plural by the simple addition of *-s*, if the singular ending of the word contains a sound with which *s* can be combined and easily pronounced: *brake—brakes; cow—cows; doe—does; stove—stoves.*

On the other hand, when a noun singular ends in a sound with which *s* cannot be combined in pronunciation without the formation of a separate syllable, add the vowel *e* before the *s*, unless a silent *e* with which you can form the extra syllable *es* is already there: *cross—crosses; gape—gapes; hose—hoses; loathe—loathes; perch—perches; rush—rushes.*

While a noun ending in *o* usually forms a plural by only adding *-s* (*dittos, jockos*), some nouns ending in *o* preceded by a consonant, add *-es* (*vetoes, tomatoes*).

Generally, nouns ending in the vowel *i* have plurals formed by the addition of *s*: *ghibli—ghiblis.*

A noun plural ending in *y*, preceded by a consonant, is formed by changing the *y* to *i* and adding *-es*: *frivolity—frivolities.*

Many confusing endings exist in English. Here are some common endings along with tips on how to overcome these spelling pitfalls.

-cede, -ceed or *-sede?*

There's only one word ending in *-sede*: *supersede*. Only three words end in *-ceed*: *exceed, proceed,* and *succeed*. All other words with this phonetic sound end in *-cede*: *precede, recede,* and *secede.*

-ar, -er, or *-or?*

The ending *-ar* is uncommon. Therefore, all you need to learn are the common *-ar* words, such as *beggar, cedar, dollar, liar, scholar,* and *similar.*

The more confusing endings are *-er* and *-or*. For the simple, more common words, *-er* is generally the right ending. Remember that the Latin *-or* goes with arcane unusual words, and that *-re* is uncommon. Knowing these six *-re* words could help you win your next game: *acre, lucre, ogre, macabre, massacre,* and *mediocre.*

-efy or *-ify?*

The ending *-ify—beautify, clarify, falsify,—*is more common than *-efy*. Some *-efy* words: *liquefy, putrefy, rarefy,* and *stupefy.*

-ary or *-ery* ?

Though most words with these two endings sound alike, remember that several hundred words end in *-ary—canary, contrary, ordinary—*while only a few end in *-ery*. Some words to learn with the *-ery* ending are: *artillery, bakery, bindery, celery, ceme-tery, fishery, flowery, millinery, monastery,* and *refinery.*

  -ise, -ize, or *-yze?*

The most common suffix is *-ize.* Only two common words end in *-yze: analyze* and *paralyze.* Only a few dozen words end in *-ise;* among them are: *advertise, comprise, despise,* and *exercise.*

  -ily or *-ally?*

When the original word ends in *-ic,* the adverb-making suffix sometimes is —*ally* instead of *-ly,* as in *clinically.* A good example of the *-ly* ending is public; it becomes an adverb—*publicly*—by adding *-ly.*

WORDS COMMONLY MISSPELLED

If you use your dictionary and commit to memory those words that you usually misspell, your scores will improve remarkably. The following list is composed of 100 often misspelled words that contain no more than nine letters. Test yourself. If you can spell the majority of these words, you're on your way to word game victories.

absence	career	eighth	luxury
absurd	cemetery	exceed	marriage
achieve	column	existence	medieval
acquire	committee	expense	merely
allotted	competent	feasible	murmur
amateur	conceit	foreign	necessary
analysis	condemn	grammar	neither
analyze	conqueror	grievous	newsstand
apparent	conscious	harass	nucleus
appetite	coolly	height	obstacle
arctic	dealt	inoculate	occurred
argument	decision	insistent	oscillate
ascend	desirable	irritable	pamphlet
assistant	dilemma	jealousy	panicky
balloon	disappear	judgment	parallel
beginning	disease	laid	paralyze
believe	dissipate	leisure	persuade
benefited	ecstasy	license	plebeian

possess	receive	sheriff	tendency
prejudice	recommend	siege	tragedy
privilege	rhythm	succeed	usually
professor	safety	supersede	vacillate
pursue	scene	suppress	vacuum
quizzes	seize	syllable	vicious
really	sergeant	tariff	weird

LETTER Q

Concerning *q* words many people say, "You can't make a word beginning with *q* without a *u*." Several dictionaries reveal twenty-two words (of nine letters or less) that *don't* need a *u* following the *q*. They aren't proper nouns, either. Granted, these aren't words in common use, but they are contained in standard English dictionaries and are officially included in the *Original Word Game Dictionary*.

qabbala	qantar	qere	qiviut
qadarite	qarmatian	qeri	qiyas
qadi	qashqai	qibla	qoph
qaf	qasida	qinah	qoran
qaid	qat	qindar	
qaimaqam	qazaq	qintar	

LETTERS OF THE ALPHABET

Avid crossword puzzlers know that each letter, except the vowels, has a definitive word. The vowels have only the speech sound of the letter; also note that the word for *w*—*double-u*—is hyphenated and therefore not admissable in word games. These are listed as a matter of interest and to further aid you in extending your vocabulary.

A	*a*	H	*aitch*	O	*o*	V	*vee*
B	*bee*	I	*i*	P	*pee*	W	*double-u*
C	*cee*	J	*jay*	Q	*cue, kue*	X	*ex*
D	*dee*	K	*kay*	R	*ar*	Y	*wye*
E	*e*	L	*el, ell*	S	*ess, es*	Z	*zee, zed*
F	*eff, ef*	M	*em*	T	*tee*		
G	*gee*	N	*en*	U	*u*		

GENERIC FORENAMES

Personal forenames (including nicknames) are not permitted, per se, in most word games. There are some, however, that are often thought of as *only* proper names, but also bear a generic meaning for which a capital initial is not required. The following generic forenames are listed to call your attention to a rarely tapped word and point source that will both extend your vocabulary and boost your word game scores.

abbe	charity	eve	heather	joy	matilda
abigail	charlotte		hector	judas	matt
alan	chastity	faith	henry	julienne	maud
alec	christie	fanny	herby		mavis
alexander	christy	fay	holly	kay	maxwell
alma	cicely	flora	homer	kelvin	may
amber	clarence	florence	hope	ken	mel
angel	clay	flossy		kit	melody
anna	clement	foster	iris	kitty	merlin
ava	cliff	frank			mickey
	colleen	franklin	jack	lambert	midge
basil	cornel		jane	lance	mike
belle	crystal	gale	jasper	lane	moira
ben		garth	jay	laura	molly
benedict	daisy	gay	jean	laurel	myrtle
benjamin	dale	gene	jenny	lee	
bertha	daphne	georgette	jerry	lewis	nana
beryl	dawn	gigot	jess	lily	nick
beth	dean	gilbert	jewel	logan	noel
bill	deke	ginger	jezebel	louis	
billie	derrick	glen	jill		olive
billy	devon	gloria	jimmy	mae	opal
bob	dick	grace	jo	magdalene	otto
bobby	dolly	graham	job	mamie	
bonita	don	grant	joe	marc	page
brad	donna	guy	joey	margarita	pam
			john	margarite	pat
carl	earl	hank	johnny	maria	patsy
carol	eddy	harry	jordan	mark	patty
celeste	erica	hazel	joseph	martin	pearl

peg	regina	rosemary	sonny	toby	victoria
perry	rex	ruby	spencer	tom	viola
peter	reynard	ruth	sterling	tommy	violet
phoebe	rick		sue	tony	
	robin	sally			wade
randy	rod	sandy	tammy	vera	wally
ray	roger	saul	terry	veronica	will
reed	rose	sibyl	timothy	victor	willy

An old English textbook chapter on building one's vocabulary cautions students not to overuse their newly acquired words, especially those long and uncommon. The book advises that the *best* word is always the simplest and most common word that will *exactly express your thought and feeling*; and to use your words to express your ideas, not to "decorate" composition.

In its proper context that advice is sound. But when you're playing word games, forget it: find the word that gives you the highest score—and if your opponent isn't familiar with it, so much the better. Keep employing new words and you'll not only impress your opponent, you'll beat him, too.

IMPROVING YOUR WORD GAME SKILLS

To further aid you in building your vocabulary and improving your word game skills, here are some general tips, strategies, and word exercises. Analyze your word games to determine which of these tips are the most helpful for your particular games. Then develop your own strategy for creating more challenging and exciting game-playing.

RHYMING

Rhyming readily reveals additional playable words. For example, if you have the letters *l, a, i, f, n, s, b*, and make the word "*snail*," you will immediately discover *bail, fail,* and *nail*. With the letters *g, l, b, o, d, c, f*, you may see the word "*log*" first, and then *bog, cog, dog,* and *fog*.

WORDS-WITHIN-WORDS

Words-within-words are often overlooked.

Examples:

crust—*rust*

mangonel—*man, mango, go, gone, on, one.*

spare—*pare, are*

trail—*rail, ail*

ADD-A-LETTER

By adding letters, other than an *s* or *y*, etc., to certain words you can oftentimes make additional words.

Examples:

grip*(e)*   patter*(n)*

bee*(f), (n), (p), (r), (t)*   plan*(e), (k), (t)*

moral*(e)*   van*(e), (g)*

EXTRA ENDINGS

To save precious time in games in which you are playing against time limits and writing down words, don't waste time writing out each additional word. For example, don't write both *chain* and *chains*; merely add an *s*: *chain-s*.

Don't overlook "extra endings." They give you longer words, when that's advantageous, and in some games they yield additional words.

Examples of extra endings:

ABLE	— eat: *eatable*	IEST	— hand: *handiest*
ABLY	— honor: *honorably*	ING	— eat: *eating*
ARY	— honor: *honorary*	LE	— crack: *crackle*
D	— cage: *caged*	LY	— crack: *crackly*
ED	— team: *teamed*	NESS	— mild: *mildness*
ER	— coax: *coaxer*	OR	— may: *mayor*
ERY	— eat: *eatery*	ORY	— access: *accessory*
ES	— coax: *coaxes*	OUS	— valor: *valorous*
EST	— mild: *mildest*	R	— rove: *rover*
FUL	— doubt: *doubtful*	S	— chain: *chains*
IER	— hand: *handier*	Y	— hand: *handy*

ANAGRAMS

There are literally thousands of anagrams in the *Original Word*

27

The Original Word Game Dictionary

Game Dictionary. Using the anagrammable variations and learning
to recognize transposable words will vastly improve your skills in
word game playing.

Examples:

ARE	— *ear, rea*	PESTER	— *preset*
EAT	— *ate, tea*	RATE	— *tare, tear*
HARE	— *hear, rhea*	SAVIOUR	— *various*
INKS	— *kins, sink, skin*	TIME	— *item, mite*
KISS	— *skis*	WAISTER	— *waiters, wariest*

REVERSE WORDS

How many words do you know that make *another* word when
the letters are reversed? (All reverse words also fall into the category of anagrams.) Being aware of the words in these categories
will automatically give you additional words.

Examples:

BAN — NAB	ERA — ARE
BAT — TAB	GAB — BAG
CRAM — MARC	PART — TRAP
DAM — MAD	SAG — GAS
DECAL — LACED	TAR — RAT
DOG — GOD	TON — NOT

REPEATED FIRST SYLLABLES

As explained in the introduction, certain groups of words containing the same first syllables are listed in this dictionary but
without their meanings. Familiarize yourself with those compound
words (and words in similar groups).

Examples:

BED — *bedfast, bedpost, bedroom, bedtide,* etc.
BLUE — *bluebell, bluefin, bluenose,* etc.
DEAD — *deadbeat, deadeye, deadpan, deadwood,* etc.
EYE — *eyecup, eyelid, eyewash,* etc.
FOOT — *football, footmark, footrace, footstool,* etc.

THE TIMER

The number of words or letters you see at a single fixation is referred to as "the span of recognition," and your span of recognition is particularly important when you're using a timer, since you must form words quickly. Remember, too, that worrying too much about the time limit can create tension that might interfere with your thinking. Relax and let your opponent watch "the sands of time" running out; let him or her shout, "It's through!" While your opponent is watching the timer, *you* can be making words.

VARIATIONS

Many word games offer challenging variations not indicated in the official rules. With some creative thinking you may discover a whole new approach to word game playing.

The main reason you play word games probably is to have fun; but whether or not you're aware of it, when you play these games they become your tools for learning and for vocabulary expansion.

The desire to win makes a successful player, but if you can't always make *long* words, don't worry. One of Winston Churchill's favorite sayings was, "Short words are best, and the old words when short are best of all."

II

More than 40 Fascinating Word Games to Play

"Good words are worth much, and cost little."

George Herbert
English Poet
(1593–1633)

The Original Word Game Dictionary
AN INDEX OF GAMES

Game	Number of Players	Ages	Manufacturer
Addiction	1 or more	8 to adult	Waddingtons Games, Inc.
BALI®	1 to 4	8 to adult	The Avalon Hill Game Company
BITS & PIECES™	1 or more	All ages	Samuel Ward Company
BOGGLE® (3 editions)	2 to 6	8 to adult	PARKER BROTHERS
Campbell's® Alphabet SCOOP and SPELL™	1 to 4	6 and up	Warren Industries, Inc.
CATCHWORD™	2 to 6	8 to adult	International Games, Inc.
CROSS CUBES™	1 or more	8 to adult	BARON SCOTT/ Enterprises, Inc.
CROSSWORD BINGO™	2 to 6	All ages	SKOR•MOR/ A Samuel Ward Company
Scrabble® Brand Crossword Cubes Game	1 or more	10 to adult	Selchow & Righter Company
Scrabble® Brand Crossword Dominoes™	2 to 4	10 to adult	Selchow & Righter Company
CROZZLE®	2 to 4	8 to adult	Cadaco, Inc.
Dig-It!®	2 to 10	All ages	Cadaco, Inc.
DIXIT	2 to 4	8 to adult	Waddingtons Games, Inc.
GARFIELD™° KITTY LETTERS™	2 to 4	6 to 10	PARKER BROTHERS
GRID WORD	1 to 6	10 to adult	Waddingtons Games, Inc.
HANGMAN™	2	8 to adult	Milton Bradley Company
KEEP QUIET®	1 or more	7 to adult	Kopptronix Company

KEEP QUIET® REWORD™	1 to 6	7 to adult	Kopptronix Company
Kontrast™	2 to 8	7 to adult	Matthews & Marshall Inc.
LEXICON®	2 to 4	8 to adult	Waddingtons Games, Inc.
LINGO^T.M.	2 or more	8 to adult	Lingo Games
My Word	1 to 6	10 to adult	Waddingtons Games, Inc.
OPTION™	2 to 4	8 to adult	PARKER BROTHERS
Perquackey®	2 or more	8 to adult	Lakeside Games, Division of Leisure Dynamics, Inc.
PROBE®	2 to 4	8 to adult	PARKER BROTHERS
Quadtriple™	2 to 4	8 to adult	Eltron Game Company
RAZZLE®	2	8 to adult	PARKER BROTHERS
Royalty®	1 or more	9 to 90	S.J. Miller Co.
Scrabble® Brand RSVP®	2 or 4	8 to adult	Selchow & Righter Company
Scrabble® Brand Scoring Anagrams	1 or more	8 to adult	Selchow & Righter Company
Scrabble® Brand Crossword Game (various editions)	2 to 4	8 to adult	Selchow & Righter Company
Spelling and Counting Wheel^T.M.	1 or more	4 to 9	Pressman Toy Corporation
SPILL and SPELL®	1 or more	8 to adult	PARKER BROTHERS
SUM-WORDS™	1 to 5	All ages	MPH Games Company
THAT'S INCREDIBLE!®	2 to 6	All ages	MPH Games Company
The Perfect 10 Word Game	2	6 to adult	Smethport Specialty Company
TUF•ABET	1 to 4	8 to adult	The Avalon Hill Game Company

The Original Word Game Dictionary

Scrabble® Brand Upper Hand™	2 to 4	12 to adult	Selchow & Righter Company
UPWORDS™	2 to 4	10 to adult	Milton Bradley Company
WORDMASTER™	2 to 4	8 to adult	Invicta Plastics Ltd.
WORD YAHTZEE®	1 or more	8 to adult	E.S. Lowe, A Milton Bradley Company
ZIG-ZAG™	2	10 to adult	Xanadu Leisure, Ltd.

Word Games are very popular today because people realize that they're often more entertaining and stimulating than television and that it's more fun to be a participant than a spectator.

In reviewing the following word games, you'll likely discover exciting new ones to add to your game library. Whichever word games you play, remember above all: enjoy yourself. Don't take the results too much to heart. As Shakespeare wrote, they're only "words, words, mere words."

Addiction

In this frustratingly addictive crossword game, thirteen wooden letter cubes are tumbled one at a time from the top of a plastic platform and the player gambles to form words with the highest score. It is totally "addictive" for the whole family.

BALI®

The intrigue and challenge of both card and word games are combined into one. Players build words on their own cards displayed in seven columns or by stealing cards to disrupt their opponent's strategy. Fascinating for solitaire or it can be expanded for group participation.

BITS & PIECES™

Bits and Pieces of words are juxtaposed on cubes totalling a baker's dozen. Some cubes have single letter *bits*, others have two and three letter *pieces* of words. The myriad possibilities make for a challenging game. Players race against time; the level of competition depends on their wits and speed.

BOGGLE®

Trying to beat the clock, players scramble to find more words than their opponents do, listing as many words as can be found among the random assortment of 16 letters in the cube tray. Acute scrutiny and quick thinking are the keys to success in "the BOGGLE® zone."

BIG BOGGLE® comes with 25 letter cubes, providing a greater challenge for longer words and higher scores.

POCKET BOGGLE™ is a compact edition, using letter strips instead of cubes.

Campbell's® Alphabet SCOOP and SPELL™

An activity word game for children and/or adults. Everyone competes to form words, scooping piles of letters out of the Campbell's®-styled soup carton.

CATCHWORD™

A word game of letter cards, identifying chips, and cubes. 54 cards show consonants and six dice cubes bear the vowels. Hold the cards, throw the dice, catch a word, and shout it out. Variations can be played by youngsters and advanced players.

CROSS CUBES™

This crossword game with 19 letter cubes and 6 black cubes provides players with hours of excitement and fun. A stimulating game, the constantly changing crossword puzzle can also be played as a solitaire game.

CROSSWORD BINGO™·M·

Two of America's favorite pastimes inspired this game of word play containing bingo cards and 240 letter tiles. Words must be formed before tiles can be placed on the bingo cards. Each round is a test of skill and nerves.

Scrabble® Brand
Crossword Cubes Game

A challenging word game created for the most demanding crossword fans as well as for those players who enjoy a simple, fast-moving game. Shake the 14 hardwood playing cubes and race the timer while forming words in crossword fashion.

Scrabble® Brand

Crossword Dominoes™

Dominoes with a challenging difference, letters instead of dots turn this popular classic into a two-dimensional game. Players build crosswords in the domino pattern with 50 tiles, each with two letters arranged horizontally on one side and vertically on the other.

CROZZLE®

A competitive crossword-puzzle game combining strategy and word power, **CROZZLE®** is a variation of the crossword puzzle. Words are formed on each player's individual playing board. A game for travel or at-home family fun.

Dig-It!®

An action word game with 378 alphabet letters. No need to be a genius or a word expert to play this—just quick and eager. Players are dealt subject cards and everyone digs into the letter pile for letters. Object: to spell words that describe the subject.

DIXIT

This game is an invigorating battle of words. Make interconnecting words by clever use of the letter tiles and colored frames and score high points. *Collins' Minigem Dictionary*, a bestseller in England, is included with the game.

GARFIELD™° KITTY LETTERS™

America's favorite cat has his own spelling game. Young players pick up "letter sticks" and use them to spell 2-, 3-, or 4-letter words. A combination of fun and learning, it improves manual dexterity and encourages interaction among players. It's a CAT-chy game.

GRID WORD

This is a deluxe version of the regular My Word game. It challenges players' thinking powers by using words of four letters only. The 48 miniature letter cards are played in crossword fashion on a rigid grid made of a rich flocked material.

HANGMAN^T.M.

In this brainteasing game, each player's word is presented backwards to the opponent. The game continues until one of the words is guessed—or until a player is "hanged." A game for youngsters that adults will have fun sharing.

KEEP QUIET®

This crossword game teaches the alphabet *sign language* (manual alphabet) when played. Players make words from the sign language symbols printed on the cubes. This game helps to break down the barrier between the deaf and those whose hearing is normal, and it motivates players to learn and enjoy a new and useful language.

KEEP QUIET® REWORD™

This game teaches the alphabet used by the deaf, while the manual alphabet is taught to the hearing. The game can be played either way—a deck of 60 cards contains letters of the sign language alphabet on one side and the equivalent alphabet on the opposite side. Those who know sign language can play it with those who do not.

Kontrast™

In this family word/card game, the object is to be the first player to remove all the cards from his or her hand by forming valid words. The 112 alphabet cards make this game easily adaptable and fun for all ages.

LEXICON®

A fascinating word game, originally launched in 1933. It is played with 52 letter cards, crossword fashion, and the player with the *low* score wins. Two packs (two complete games) can be used together for games with up to eight people.

LINGO™·M·

A zigzag word game to play with friends and family or it can be a game of solitaire. Fill a 25-card square by building words, either horizontally, vertically, or diagonally (in any direction).

My Word

The last word in crossword card games for the whole family.

The Original Word Game Dictionary

There are no rules to make; just use this dictionary as a referee. There are forty-eight cards, each containing 8 letters in two-letter combinations.

OPTION™

A double-sided word game with twice the challenge. Players form words using letter prisms; each prism has two sides and two colors from which to choose. Words formed on the grid of all one color double the point value; or flip a prism and form a new word.

Perquackey®

Racing against the clock, this challenging word game builds and tests vocabularies. Players form as many single words as possible from 10 letter cubes. When someone reaches 2,000 points, add three cubes—and the first to reach 5,000 is the winner.

PROBE®

An exercise in concentration and logic, this word pursuit game allows the use of the dictionary *before* the game. Form a word, disguise it, keep it a secret; then use deductive skills to guess opponent's word, letter by letter.

Quadtriple™

Can be played two ways—hence the name of the game: a combination of the words "quad" and "triple." Three letters inspire players to write as many words as they know containing those letters.

RAZZLE™

A fast and furious activity word game where players place the carriage in the center of the platform, drop the letter cubes in, and the race for the words is on. The first person to spot a word calls it out loud and spells it. Each time the carriage is moved a new letter combination appears.

Royalty®

Using a single or double deck of letter cards, the game's objective is to form and/or capture words; "Coalitions" are partnerships and "Monarchy" is solitaire. Meld the word "Royalty" and tradition dictates that all players stand in tribute.

Scrabble® Brand
RSVP®

This three-dimensional crossword game challenges players to think backwards. Words are formed crossword-fashion on a stand-up grid, while blocking opponent's words on the opposite side. It creates an intriguing form of concentration and can be played by two teams.

Scrabble® Brand
Scoring Anagrams

Here, quick thinkers make and capture words. Each of the 180 hardwood tiles has a letter and point value. Players form words by combining letters drawn at random or by adding to and rearranging letters. This is a new scoring version of the classic Anagrams.

Scrabble® Brand Crossword Game

The original crossword game on a playing board. The object is to form words on the board, crossword style, from the letter tiles on each player's rack. An ingenious combination of strategy and luck makes this game a favorite for word game fanatics.

The Scrabble® Brand Crossword Game is also available in the following Foreign Language Editions: German, French, Spanish, Italian, Russian, and Hebrew. The rules are printed in both English and in the foreign language.

The Travel Edition comes in a compact carrying case so **Scrabble®** buffs can play on land, sea, and air. This edition is also available with the hardcover volume of *The Official Scrabble® Players® Dictionary.*

The Scrabble® Pocket Edition, also for players on the go, is available singly and also comes packaged with the softcover edition of the *Scrabble® Dictionary.*

The Scrabble® Brand Duplicate Edition is a different version of the game. A new twist has been added: all players play the same letters on each turn.

The Original Word Game Dictionary

Large-Type Edition of Scrabble® is for those people who are more comfortable playing on a larger board with bigger, more legible letters.

Scrabble® Crossword Game for Juniors (for ages 6 through 10) is available in three language editions: English, Spanish, and French.

Spelling and Counting Wheel^T.M.

The wheel combines playing and skill to teach children reading, spelling, and arithmetic. A colorful, reversible wheel with letters on one side and numbers on the other stimulates young minds and develops hand–eye coordination.

SPILL and SPELL®

Either crossword buffs or youngsters spill out the 15 wooden letter cubes and make crosswords before the timer runs out. Several variations are given, including a challenging game of solitaire.

SUM-WORDS™

The word game that stimulates the unlimited memory powers of word gamesmen. It features a unique handicapping system: a beginning speller can play competitively with an aggressive wordmonger. The 54 playing cards contain consonants only; vowels are free.

THAT'S INCREDIBLE!®

A series of nine "incredible" card games combining memory, lady luck, masterful strategy, and devilish gambling. Game #1, *Zenith*, is a crossword game using 81 letter cards; players build an actual 9 x 9 (81 piece) letter crossword puzzle.

The Perfect 10 Word Game

This little **Hip Hugger®** word game is designed like a wallet so you can carry it with you. The letter tiles used for making words are magnetized to adhere to the squares marked on the vinyl playing surface. No time limit—but you need a partner.

TUF•ABET

This game builds vocabulary and reinforces spelling ability. Concentration and logic are essential. All players play at once, constructing interlocking words into individual crosswords against 3 time levels to shout: "Tuf!", "Tuffer!", or "Tuffest!"

Scrabble® Brand
Upper Hand™

A contract word game combining the bidding feature of bridge with the challenge of word play. Players compete for high score by forming words, crossword-style, on the board while taking advantage of letter values, suit values, and bonus squares.

UPWORDS™

A 3-dimensional word strategy game in which words are formed crossword style with letter tiles on a board. The words can then be changed by stacking new letters on top, up to five levels.

WORDMASTER™

An action crossword game with a difference. Black tiles are inserted at random for each game so that no two games are ever the same. Words are formed between the black spaces in crossword fashion. The instruction sheet is printed in eight languages.

WORD YAHTZEE®

An absorbing fast-paced version of the classic **Yahtzee®** game, in which careful choices and shrewd strategy play a greater role than ever before. Players use their own judgment for possible combinations—winning by outsmarting opponents.

ZIG-ZAG™

Player attempts to discover opponent's secret words by using test words with letters that not only appear in the secret word, but that also fall into a matching position. By the last turn of each round, he or she should be able to correctly name opponent's secret word.

III

The Dictionary

The *Original Word Game Dictionary* is not a standard reference book for general use, but is a dictionary compiled and edited specifically for word game players. To better understand how the selections of words (and exclusions of others) and their meanings were determined, please read the introduction.

aa Solidified lava
aah Surprise
aalii A tropical tree
aardvark A burrowing mammal
aardwolf, *pl*-**wolves** Hyenalike mammal
aba Garment worn by Arabs
abaca A Philippine plant
aback Backward
abacus, *pl*-**cuses** or **-ci** Part of a column
abaft Toward the stern
abalone A species of gastropod
abamp An abampere
abampere Electromagnetic unit
abandon To forsake
abase Humiliate
abash To make uneasy
abate Lessen
abattoir Slaughterhouse
abaxial Away from the axis
abba Father
abbacy Office of an abbot
abbatial Pertaining to an abbey
abbe Ecclesiastical figure
abbess Female superior of a convent
abbey A monastery
abbot Superior of a monastery
abcoulomb Electromagnetic unit
abdicate To relinquish high office
abdomen Belly
abduct To kidnap
abeam At right angles to the keel of a ship
abed In bed
abele A tree
abelmosk A species of plant
aberrant Deviation from the norm
abet To incite
abetter, abettor One who abets
abeyance Suspension

abfarad Electromagnetic unit
abhenry Electromagnetic unit
abhor To regard with loathing
abhorrent Loathsome
abidance Compliance
abide To await
abigail Lady's maid
ability Natural or acquired talent
abject Wretched
abjure To renounce under oath
ablation Amputation of any part of the body
ablaut A change in words to show changes in meaning
ablaze On fire
able Especially capable
ablegate Papal envoy
abloom Flowering
abluent A cleansing substance
ablution Cleansing of the body
abnegate To renounce
abnormal Not normal
aboard On board a passenger vehicle
abode Past tense of abide
abohm Electromagnetic unit
abolish Do away with
abomasum, *pl*-**sa** Part of the stomach in certain animals
abominate To detest
aboral Away from the mouth
aborigine Earliest known inhabitant of a region
aborning Getting under way
abort To terminate
aboulia Variant of abulia
abound To be great in number
about Approximately
above Overhead
abrade To erode
abrasion Process of wearing away
abreact To release tension

abreast Aware of
abri Bomb shelter
abridge To condense
abroach Moving about
abroad In a foreign country
abrogate To annul
abrupt Suddenly
abscess A localized collection of pus surrounded by inflamed tissue
abscise To cut off
abscissa, pl **-sas** or **-scissae** A mathematical measurement
abscond To avoid arrest
absence The time one is away
absent Missing
absentee One who is absent
absinthe, absinth A bitter liquid prepared from herbs
absolute Complete
absolve To pardon a sin
absorb To soak in or up
abstain To refrain from something
absterge To clean
abstract Not easily understood
abstruse Difficult to understand
absurd Ridiculous
abulia Loss of ability to act independently
abundant Ample
abuse To misuse
abut Be next to
abutilon A species of plants
abuttal The parts that abut against other parts
abuzz Buzzing
abvolt Electromagnetic unit
abysm An abyss
abysmal Extreme
abyss Bottomless pit
abyssal Resembling an abyss
acacia A species of trees
academe The world of higher education
academy School
acajou Mahogany
acaleph, pl **-lephae** or **-lephs** A species of animal
acanthoid Horn or spine shaped
acanthus, pl **-thuses** or **-thi** A species of plant

acariasis An infestation with mites
acaricide Substance deadly to mites
acarid A species of insects
acaroid A gum from Australian trees
acarpous Sterile
acarus, pl **-ri** A mite
acaudate, acaudal Having no tail
accede To consent
accent A characteristic pronunciation of words
accentor A species of bird
accentual Pertaining to accent
accept To receive something
acceptor, accepter One who accepts
access The right to enter
accession An increase by adding something
accessory, accessary Supplementary item
accidence Basic elements of a subject
accident A mishap
accidie Indifference
accipiter A species of hawk
acclaim To show approval
acclimate To adapt
acclivity An upward slope
accolade Praise
accord To grant
accordion Musical instrument
accost To approach and speak to
account Record of events
accouter, accoutre To equip
accredit To attribute to
accrete To grow together
accrue To accumulate
accumbent Reclining
accurate Correct
accursed, accurst Under a curse
accuse To charge someone with an error
accustom To familiarize
ace A single spot on playing cards, dice and dominoes
acedea Variant of accidie
acellular Containing no cells
acentric Not centered
acequia Irrigation canal

acerate Needle-shaped
acerb Bitter
acerbate To annoy
acerbity Sharpness
acerose Sharp-pointed and slender
acervate Growing in small clusters
acervulus, *pl* **-li** A fruiting mass in certain fungi
acetal A liquid used in cosmetics
acetamide, acetamid A chemical used in explosives
acetate Products derived from cellulose acetate
acetic Containing vinegar
acetify To convert to vinegar
acetin Liquid used in making dynamite
acetone A cleaning chemical
acetous, acetose Sour-tasting
acetum A drug solution
acetyl A chemical compound
acetylate To combine an acetyl group with an organic compound
acetylene A gas
ache To suffer a pain
achene A species of fruit
achieve To accomplish
achiote Seeds of the annatto
achondrite A meteorite
achoo Variant of ahchoo
achromic Colorless
achy Aching
acicula, *pl* **-lae** A needlelike object
acid A chemical compound
acidosis High acidity of the blood
acinar Pertaining to an acinus
aciniform Having the shape of a cluster
acinous Consisting of small lobules
acinus, *pl* **-ni** A grape
aclinic Having no inclination
acme Utmost attainment
acne A disease
acnode A needle
acock In a cocked position
acolyte A follower
aconite A species of plant
acorn Fruit of the oak tree
acoustic Pertaining to sound
acquaint To make familiar
acquiesce Comply passively

acquire To gain possession
acquit To free from a charge
acquittal The judgment of not guilty
acre A unit of area
acred Possessing many acres
acrid Caustic
acridine A coal tar derivative
acrimony Ill-natured animosity
acrobat One skilled in balance
acrodont Having teeth without roots
acrodrome Having veins terminate at the tip, like leaves
acrogen A species of plant
acrolein A chemical liquid
acromion, *pl* **-mia** Part of the shoulder blade
acronym A word formed by combining letters
acropetal In botany, developing upward
acropolis Fortified citadel of ancient Greek cities
acrospire A sprout from a germinating seed
across To cross
acrostic A word square
acrylic A chemical liquid
act Something that is performed
acta Recorded proceedings
actable That which can be acted
actin A muscle protein
actinal Designating part of an animal from which tentacles radiate
actinia, *pl* **-iae** A sea animal
actinide A chemical element
actinism Property in radiation
actinium Radioactive element
actinoid Having a radial form
actinon An isotope of radon
action Process of acting
activism Militant action
actor Theatrical performer
actress Female theatrical performer
actual Real
actuary A person who calculates insurance risks
actuate To put into action

47

acuate Sharpened

acuity Sharpness

aculeate Having a sting

acumen Acuteness

acuminate To sharpen

acute Shrewd

acyclic Not having whorls

acyl A chemical radical

acyloin A chemical compound

ad An advertisement

adage A short proverb

adagio Slowly

adamant A very hard substance

adamsite A chemical compound

adapt To adjust

add To find a sum total

addax An antelope

addend Set of numbers to be added

addendum, *pl* **-da** A supplement to a book

adder A species of snake

addict One who is addicted

addle Confuse

address To speak to

adduce To cite as proof

adducent Drawing together

adduct To pull toward the main axis

ademption Disposal of property in a will

adenine A chemical compound

adenitis Inflammation of a gland

adenoid Glandlike

adenoma A glandular-type tumor

adenosine An organic compound

adept Highly skilled

adequate Suitable

adhere To stick together

adherent Holding fast

adhesion Act of adhering

adhibit To let in

adiabatic Involving expansion without change in heat

adieu Good-by

adios Good-by

adipose Fatty

adit An entrance

adjacent Close to

adjective Words used to limit or qualify a noun or other substantive

adjoin To attach

adjourn To suspend proceedings

adjudge To rule

adjunct Something independent attached to another thing

adjure Appeal to earnestly

adjust To harmonize

adjutant An assistant

adman A man in advertising business

admiral Head of a navy

admire To regard with approval

admission Act of admitting

admit To allow to enter

admix To mix

admixture The act of mixing

admonish To counsel against

adnate Joined to another part

adnoun An adjective when used as a noun

ado Bother

adobe Brick of clay and straw

adopt To take a child into one's family

adore To love very much

adorn To decorate

adown Down

adrenal Pertaining to the adrenal glands

adrenalin Secretion of the adrenal glands

adrift Without direction

adroit Skillful

adscript Written after

adsorb To collect by adsorption

adsorbate An adsorbed substance

adularia A variety of orthoclase

adulate To praise

adult Grown up

adulterer One who commits adultery

adultly Acting as an adult

adumbral In shadow

adumbrate To give a sketchy outline

adunc Curving inward

adust Melancholy

advance To move forward

advantage A favorable position

advection A change of heat

advent Arrival of something important

adventive Not native to

adventure An unusual happening

adverb A part of speech

adversary Enemy

adverse Opposed

adversity Misfortune

advert To call attention to

advertise To call attention to something

advice Counsel

advise To counsel

advisedly Deliberately

adviser, advisor Person who offers advice

advocacy Active support

advocate Supporter of a cause

advowson The right to present a vacant church benefice

adytum, *pl* **-ta** The shrine in ancient temples

adz, adze An axlike tool

ae One

aecium, *pl* **-cia** A structure in rust fungi

aedes A species of mosquito

aedile A Roman magistrate

aegis The shield of Zeus

aeneous, aeneus Having a brassy color

aeolian Variant of eolian

aeolipile An ancient steam engine

aeon Variant of eon

aeonian Variant of eonian

aerate To supply with oxygen

aerial In the air

aerie The nest of a bird

aerobe An organism that requires air to live

aerobic Exercises

aerodyne Any aircraft heavier than air

aerofoil Variant of airfoil

aerogel A colloidal substance

aerogram A radiogram

aerolite, aerolith A silicious meteorite

aerology Total atmospheric meteorology

aerometer A device for determining weight and density of air

aeronaut A pilot of a balloon

aeronomy Study of the upper atmosphere

aeropause The atmosphere that airplanes cannot fly above

aerophore A device to supply air to the lungs

aerophyte An epiphyte

aeroplane Variant of airplane

aerosat Satellites used in air traffic control

aerosol A substance packaged under pressure

aerospace Pertaining to the technology of flight

aerosphere The lower portion of the atmosphere

aerostat A balloon or dirigible

aerugo Copper rust

aerv Ethereal

aery Variant of aerie

aesthete, esthete One who appreciates beauty

aesthetic, esthetic Having a love of beauty

aestival Appearing in summer

aestivate To pass the summer

aetheling Variant of atheling

aether Variant of ether

aethereal Variant of ethereal

aetiology Variant of etiology

afar At a distance

afeard Afraid

afebrile Without fever

affable Amiable

affair, affaire Matters of concern

affect To have an influence

afferent Directed to a central part

affiance Betroth

affiant One who makes an affidavit

affidavit A written statement made under oath

affiliate To adopt

affine A mathematical transformation

affinity Relationship by marriage

affirm To declare firmly

affix To secure

afflatus An inspiration
afflict To inflict suffering
affluent Rich
afflux A flow to a particular area
afford To be able to pay
afforest To change into land
affray A noisy quarrel
affricate A phonetic sound
affright Terrify
affront Confront
affusion A pouring on
afghani Monetary unit of Afghanistan
afield Off the usual track
afire On fire
aflame On fire
afloat Floating
aflutter In a flutter
afoot On foot
afore Before
aforesaid Spoken of earlier
aforetime Previously
afoul In trouble with
afraid Filled with fear
afreet, afrit A monstrous demon
afresh Anew
aft Close to the stern
after Behind in place
aftercare Treatment after surgery
afterclap Unexpected sequel to a matter thought closed
afterdamp An asphyxiating mixture of gases
afterdeck Part of a ship's deck
afterglow The glow after sunset
afterlife A life believed to follow death
aftermath A result of a misfortune
aftermost, aftmost Nearest the stern
afternoon From noon until sunset
aftertime Future
afterward Subsequently
aga Official of the Ottoman Empire
again Once more
against In an opposite direction
agal A cord that holds the head cloth of Arabs
agalloch A wood, aloes
agama A species of lizard

agamete A cell in certain protozoa
agamic, agamous Asexual
agape, *pl* **-pae** Christian love
agar A material prepared from marine algae
agaric Gill fungus
agate A marble
agave A species of plant
age A lifetime
ageism Discrimination of older people
agency Active force
agenda List of things to be done
agendum, *pl* **-da** or **-das** Thing or things to be done
agenesis, agenesia Failure of an organ to develop
agent One that acts
agential Acting as an agent
ageratum A species of plant
aggie A marble
aggrade To build up with landfill
aggravate To make worse
aggregate Total
aggress To start a quarrel
aggressor One who starts a hostile action
aggrieve To distress unjustly
agha Variant of aga
aghast Terrified
agile Active
agin Against
aginner Person against a change
agio A premium paid for changing currencies
agiotage The brokerage business
agist To feed animals for pay
agitate To disturb
agitato Fast and stirring
agleam Shining
aglet A metal piece on the end of a shoe lace
agley, aglee Awry
aglimmer Glimmering
aglitter Glittering
aglow Glowing
agminate Gathered in clusters
agnail A hangnail
agnate Akin
agnomen, *pl* **-nomina** A nickname

agnostic A person who disclaims any knowledge of God
ago Past
agog Astir
agon, *pl* **agons** or **agones** Ancient Greek games
agone Gone
agonic Having no angle
agonist A contracting muscle
agonistic Combative
agony Suffering
agora, *pl* **-rot** or **-roth** An Israel coin
agouti A species of rodent
agraffe, agrafe An iron for holding stones
agrapha The words of Jesus not in the Bible
agraphia A mental affliction marked by inability to write
agrarian Pertaining to rural matters
agree To be in accord
agrestal, agrestial Growing wild
agrestic Rural
agrimony A species of plant
agriology Study of primitive cultures
agrology Science of soils in relation to crops
agronomy Scientific agriculture
aground Stranded
ague An attack of fever
agueweed A species of plant
ah Surprise
aha Surprise
ahchoo Like the sound of a sneeze
ahead In advance
ahem Used to attract attention
ahimsa An Indian doctrine of nonviolence
ahoy Used to hail a ship
ahuehuete An evergreen tree
ai A sloth
aid To assist
aide An assistant
aiglet Variant of aglet
aigrette, aigret Tail feathers of an egret
aiguille A pointed mountain peak
aikido Japanese self-defense

ail To be sick
ailanthus A species of tree
aileron A part of an airplane wing
aim To propose
ain Own
air An invisible mixture of gases
The following words are listed without definition (see Introduction):

airboat	airier	airproof
airborne	airiest	airscrew
airbound	airily	airship
airbrush	airiness	airsick
airburst	airing	airspace
airbus	airless	airspeed
aircoach	airlift	airstream
aircraft	airlike	airstrip
airdrome	airline	airtight
airdrop	airliner	airward
airfield	airmail	airwave
airflow	airman	airway
airfoil	airpark	airworthy
airframe	airplane	airwise
airglow	airport	airwoman
airhead	airpost	airy

aisle A passageway between seats
aitch The letter *h*
aitchbone The rump in cattle
ajar Partly opened
akee A tropical tree
akimbo Elbows bowed outward with the hands on the hips
akin Related
ala, *pl* **-alae** Side petal of certain flowers
alabaster A white gypsum
alack Used to express regret
alacrity Eagerness
alameda A shaded walk
alamo A poplar tree
alamode Served with ice cream
alan A hunting dog
alanine An amino acid
alar Shaped like a wing
alarm Fright
alarum An alarm
alary Wing-shaped
alas Exclamation expressing sorrow
alaska Overshoe

alastor An avenging deity in Greek tragedy
alate Winged
alb Robe worn by a priest
albacore A species of fish
albatross A species of bird
albedo Reflecting power of a planet
albeit Even though
albescent Whitish
albinism State of being an albino
albino An organism that lacks normal pigmentation
albite White feldspar
album A book for photographs
albumen Albumin
albumin Water-soluble proteins found in egg white and various substances
albumose Chemical compounds derived from albumins
alburnum Sapwood
alcaide, alcayde Commander of a fortress
alcalde Chief official in a Spanish town
alcazar A Spanish palace
alchemist A practitioner of alchemy
alchemy A chemical philosophy
alcidine Belonging to a species of bird
alcohol Intoxicating liquor
alcove An extension of a room
aldehyde A chemical compound
alder A species of tree
alderman A member of a municipal body
aldol A liquid used in perfumes
aldose Aldose sugar
aldrin An insecticide
ale An alcoholic beverage
aleatory Pertaining to gambling
alec A herring
alee To the leeward side
alegar Vinegar from ale
alehouse A place where ale is sold
alembic Used for distilling
aleph, alef First letter of the Hebrew alphabet
alert Watchful

aleurone, aleuron A protein
alewife, pl **-wives** A species of fish
alexander A cocktail
alexia Word blindness
alexin, alexine A blood component
alfalfa A plant
alfilaria, alfileria A plant
alfresco Outdoors
algae Aquatic plants
algarroba, algaroba A species of tree
algebra A mathematical system
algebraic Pertaining to algebra
algid Chilly
algin A substance from algae
algoid Resembling algae
algology The study of algae
algometer An apparatus to determine pain caused by pressure
algorism The decimal system
algorithm Any special method of solving a problem
alias, pl **aliases** An assumed name
alibi An excuse
alible Nourishing
alicyclic A chemical compound
alidade, alidad Used in angular measurement
alien Foreign
alienage The state of being an alien
alienee A person to whom ownership of property is transferred
alienism State of being an alien
alienist A physician, an expert on mental competence of witnesses in court
alienor A person who transfers property
alif First letter of the Arabic alphabet
aliform Shaped like a wing
alight To fly down and settle
align To arrange in a line
alike Similar
aliment Food
alimony An allowance for support
aliped A winglike membrane connecting the toes
aliphatic Chemical compounds in which carbon atoms are linked

aliquot Containing an exact number of times

alit Past tense of alight

aliunde From elsewhere

alive Having life

alizarin, alizarine A compound used in dyes

alkahest Hypothetical solvent once sought by alchemists

alkali An alkali metal

alkalify Alkalize

alkaline Containing an alkali

alkalize To make alkaline

alkaloid Organic substances containing alkaline properties

alkalosis Alkali content in the blood and tissues

alkanet A species of plants

alkene Olefin

alkyd A synthetic resin

alkyl A monovalent chemical radical

alkyne, alkine Hydrocarbons

all The total number

allamanda A species of vine

allantoid Having an allantois

allantois A membranous pouch in the embryos of most vertebrates

allay To calm

allege Declare

allegory A symbolic representation

allegro In rapid tempo

allele Mutational forms of a gene

alleluia Praise to God

allergen Causes allergies

allergic Having an allergy

allergist A physician who specializes in allergies

allergy Reaction to various substances that do not affect most people

alleviate Reduce

alley A narrow passageway

alleyway A narrow passage between buildings

alliance A union or relationship

allied United

alligator Large amphibious reptile

allium A species of plant

allocate To designate

allodium, alodium, *pl* **-dia** Land held in absolute ownership

allogamy Cross-fertilization

allograph Writing by one person for another

allometry A study of the growth of an organism

allomorph A crystalline form of a substance

allonym The name of one person assumed by another

allopath A person who practices allopathy

allopathy Therapy that produces effects differing from those of the disease treated

allophane A hydrous aluminum silicate mineral

allophone A variant form of a phoneme

allot To allocate

allotrope An allotropic form

allotropy The existence of chemical elements in different forms

allottee One to whom something is allotted

allow Permit

alloy Relative purity of gold or silver

allseed A species of plant

allspice A tropical American tree

allude To refer in a casual way

allure To tempt with something desirable

allusion The act of alluding

alluvial Composed of alluvium

alluvion The flow of water against a shore

alluvium Waterborne detritus

ally To unite

allyl A chemical compound

alma An Egyptian dancing girl

almanac An annual publication of useful information

almandine A purplish-red garnet

almemar A bema

almighty All-powerful

almond A small tree

almoner One who distributes alms

almost Not quite

alms Money given to the poor
almshouse A poorhouse
almsman A person supported by alms
almuce A garment with a fur-lined hood
alnico Various alloys of iron
aloe A species of plants
aloft Solitary
aloha Love
aloin A laxative
alone Single
along Together
aloof Distant
alopecia Baldness
aloud Loudly
alp A high mountain
alpaca A South American mammal
alpenglow A rosy glow on mountain tops at sunrise or dusk
alpenhorn A horn used by herdsmen in the Alps
alpha First letter of the Greek alphabet
alphabet The letters of a language
alphorn Variant of alpenhorn
alphosis Absence of skin pigment
alpine Pertaining to high mountains
alpinist A mountain climber
already Before
alright All right
alsike A clover
also Likewise
alt High in pitch
altar A raised platform where religious services are held
alter To make different
altercate To quarrel
alternate To occur in turns
althea, althaea A species of plant
althorn A musical instrument
although Even though
altimeter An instrument for measuring elevation
altitude Height above sea level
alto A low female singing voice
altricial Of birds whose newly hatched young are helpless
altruism Unselfish concern for the welfare of others

alula, *pl* **-lae** Feathers on a part of a bird's wing
alum A chemical compound
alumina A form of aluminum oxide
aluminum A ductile metallic element
alumna, *pl* **-nae** A female graduate
alumnus, *pl* **-ni** A male graduate
alumroot A species of plant
alunite A mineral used in alum and fertilizer
alveolar Describing the sound produced with the tongue just behind the front teeth
alveolate Honeycombed
alveolus, *pl* **-li** A small pit
alvine Of the intestines
always At every time
alyssum A species of plant
am Present first person singular of be
amadou Material for lighting fires
amah, ama An Oriental nurse
amain With speed
amalgam An alloy of Mercury and other metals
amandine Garnished with almonds
amanita A species of mushroom
amaranth A species of plant
amarelle A sour cherry
amaryllis A species of plant
amass To accumulate
amateur A nonprofessional who engages in activities for pleasure
amative Amorous
amatol A highly explosive mixture
amatory Pertaining to sexual love
amaurosis Blindness
amaze Astonish
ambage A winding pathway
amber A fossil resin
ambergris A substance formed in the intestines of sperm whales
amberjack A species of fish
ambiance, ambience The atmosphere surrounding a place
ambient Surrounding
ambiguous Uncertain
ambit The scope of something
ambition A strong will to succeed
amble To walk slowly

ambo Pulpit in early Christian churches

amboyna, amboina Wood used for fancy cabinetwork

ambrosia Anything with an especially delicious flavor

ambry A pantry

ambsace Double aces throw of the dice

ambulance Vehicle to carry the sick

ambulant Moving from place to place

ambulate To move about

ambuscade To ambush

ambush A surprise attack

ameba Variant of amoeba

amebean Variant of amoeba

amebiasis Variant of amoebiasis

amebocyte Variant of amoebocyte

ameer Variant of emir

ameerate Amirate

amen Used after a prayer

amenable Willing to follow suggestions

amend To improve

amenity Agreeableness

ament A catkin

amentia Feeblemindedness

amerce To punish by imposing an arbitrary penalty

americium A chemical element

amesace Variant of ambsace

amethyst A form of transparent quartz

ametropia Any eye abnormality

ami A friend

amiable Good-natured

amianthus, amiantus An asbestos

amicable Friendly

amice A liturgical vestment

amid, amidst Surrounded by

amide An organic compound

amidol A compound used as a photographic developer

amidships Midway between the bow and stern

amigo A friend

amine An organic compound

amino Pertaining to an amine

amir Variant of emir

amiss Out of proper order

amitosis A cell division

amity Friendship

ammeter An instrument for measuring electric current

ammine A chemical compound

ammo Ammunition

ammocete Wormlike larvae of the lamprey

ammonia A colorless gas

ammoniac Containing ammonia

ammonic Of ammonia

ammonify To subject to ammonification

ammonite The shell of a mollusk

amnesia Loss of memory

amnesty To pardon

amnion The sac enclosing an embryo

amoeba, *pl* **-bas** or **-bae** Microscopic animals found in soil and water

amoebaean Responding to each other

amoebic Like amoeba

amoeboid Resembling an amoeba

amok Variant of amuck

amole A species of plant

among, amongst In the midst of

amoral Neither moral or immoral

amoretto, *pl* **-retti** A cupid

amorist A lover

amorous Attracted to love

amorphism Being amorphous

amorphous Without definite form

amortize Pay off a debt gradually

amount The sum

amour A love affair

amperage Strength of an electric current expressed in amperes

ampere A unit of electric current

ampersand The sign (&) representing *and*

amphibian Any class of vertebrates that usually begin life in water

amphibole A type of rock-forming minerals

amphioxus Variant of lancelet

amphipod Small crustaceans

amphora, *pl* **-rae** or **-ras** A jar used by ancient Greeks and Romans

ample Abundant

amplidyne Direct current amplifier

amplify To add to

amplitude Abundance

amply Sufficiently

ampoule, ampule, ampul A glass vial to hold hypodermic solution

ampulla, pl **-pullae** A container used in church for wine or water

amputate To cut off a part of the body

amputee A person who has had one or more limbs amputated

amrita Ambrosia prepared by the gods that bestows immortality

amtrac, amtrack Amphibious vehicle used in World War II

amu Atomic mass unit

amuck In a violent rage

amulet An object worn to ward off evil

amuse To cause to laugh

amusia Unmusical

amusive Providing amusement

amygdale An amygdule

amygdule A small gas bubble in lava

amyl A univalent radical

amylase Enzymes that convert starch to sugar

amylene Type of hydrocarbons

amyloid A starchlike substance

amylopsin The enzyme of pancreatic juice

amylose The soluble portion of starch

amylum Starch

an Used before words beginning with a vowel sound

ana A collection of various information

anabaena Various freshwater algae

anabantid A species of tropical fish

anabas A species of freshwater fish

anabasis, pl **-ses** A military advance

anabatic Of rising wind currents

anabiosis Resuscitation

anabiotic Capable of resuscitation

anabolism Constructive metabolism

anabolite A product of anabolism

anaclisis Psychological dependence on others

anaconda A large snake

anacrusis Unaccented syllables at the beginning of a line of verse

anadem A head wreath

anaemia Variant of anemia

anaerobe An organism able to live without oxygen

anaglyph An ornament carved in low relief

anagoge, anagogy A mystical interpretation of words

anagram To transpose letters to form a new word

anal Pertaining to the anus

analcime, analcite A zeolite occurring in traprock

analects, analecta Selection of a literary work

analemma A graduated scale

analeptic Stimulating

analgesia A state of not feeling pain while conscious

analgesic A medication to reduce pain

analogous Comparable in certain respects

analogue Something that bears an analogy to something else

analogy Resemblance in some respects between things otherwise dissimilar

analysand A person who is being psychoanalyzed

analysis, pl **-ses** The separation of a substantial whole into its parts for study

analyst One who analyzes

analytic Pertaining to analysis

analyze To examine carefully

anamnesis, pl **-ses** Recalling to memory

anandrous Having no stamens

ananthous Lacking flowers

anapest, anapaest A type of metrical foot

anaphase A stage of mitosis
anaphora Repetition of words at the beginning of sentences
anaplasia Reversion of cells to a different form
anaplasty Plastic surgery
anarch A leader of anarchy
anarchic Promoting anarchy
anarchism The theory of anarchy
anarchist One who advocates anarchy
anarchy Absence of any form of government
anarthria Loss of the ability to speak
anasarca A form of dropsy
anatase A mineral
anathema A formal ecclesiastical ban
anatomy The science of organisms and their parts
anatto Variant of annatto
ancestor A person from whom one is descended
anchor A heavy object to keep a boat in place
anchoress A female anchoret
anchorite, anchoret A recluse
anchovy A species of fish
anchusa A species of plant
anchylose Variant of ankylose
ancient Very old
ancillary Helping
ancipital Flattened and two-edged, as certain plant stems
ancon, pl **ancones** The elbow
and In addition
andante Moderate in tempo
andantino Slightly faster than andante
andesite Volcanic rock
andiron One of a pair of supports for holding logs
andradite A calcium-iron garnet
androgen A male sex hormone
android Possessing human features
andromeda A species of shrub
anear Near
anecdotal Full of anecdotes

anecdote A brief interesting story
anechoic Neither having nor producing echoes
anele To annoint
anemia A blood deficiency
anemic Relating to anemia
anemology Study of winds
anemone A species of plant
anent Regarding
anergy Lack of energy
aneroid Not using fluid
anestrus An interval of sexual dormancy
aneurysm, aneurism A pathological blood-filled dilation of a blood vessel
anew Again
angary, angaria The right of a belligerent to seize neutral property
angel A winged spiritual being
angelica A species of plants
anger To make angry
angina A disease in which painful spasms occur
angiology The study of blood and lymph vessels
angioma, pl **-mas** or **-mata** A tumor composed of blood or lymph vessels
angle To fish with a hook and line
anglepod A species of plant
anglesite A mineral
angleworm A worm used in fishing
angling The process of fishing with a hook and line
angry Feeling hostility
angst A feeling of anxiety
angstrom A unit of length
anguine Snakelike
anguish To suffer pain
angular Consisting of an angle
angulate Having angles
anhinga The water turkey
anhydride A chemical
anhydrous Without water
ani A species of bird
anil The indigo plant
anile Like an old woman
aniline, anilin A chemical compound

anima The soul
animal Living organism of the Animalia family
animality The nature of an animal
animalize Brutalize
animate To fill with life
animato In a lively manner
animism Primitive belief where the soul exists apart from the body
animus A feeling of hostility
anion A negatively charged ion
anise Aniseed
aniseed Seed of the anise plant
anisette Anise-flavored liqueur
anisogamy A union between different gametes
ankerite A mineral
ankh An ansate cross
ankle Section of leg above the foot
anklet A sock
ankus, *pl* **-es** A hooked pole for leading elephants
ankylose To join by ankylosis
ankylosis Consolidation of bones
anlace Medieval dagger
anlage, *pl* **-gen** or **-ges** Initial cell structure from which an embryonic part develops
anna A former coin of India
annal A record of a single year
annalist A chronicler
annatto, anatto A tropical tree
anneal To temper
annelid Belonging to the phylum of segmented worms
annex To add to
annotate To furnish with critical notes
announce To declare publicly
annoy To irritate
annual Yearly
annuitant A person who receives an annuity
annuity An allowance received regularly
annul To declare void
annular Shaped like a ring
annulate Consisting of rings
annulet Ringlike molding around the capital of a pillar

annulus, *pl* **-luses** or **-li** A ringlike part
anoa A small buffalo
anode Any positively charged electrode
anodyne Relaxing
anoint To apply oil
anole A species of lizard
anomaly An irregularity
anomie, anomy A collapse of the social structure governing a society
anon Again
anonym An anonymous person
anonymous Having no known name
anopheles A species of mosquitoes
anorak A parka
anorexia Loss of appetite
anorthite A rare feldspar
anosmia Loss of the sense of smell
another One more
anoxemia Decline of the oxygen in blood
anoxia Absence of oxygen
ansate Having a handle
anserine, anserous Gooselike
answer A spoken or written reply
ant A species of insect
anta, *pl* **-tae** A part of a Greek temple
antacid Neutralizing acids
ante To put into the pool
anteater A mammal that feeds on ants
antecede Precede
antedate Precede in time
antefix, *pl* **-fixes** or **-fixa** An ornament along the eaves of a roof
antelope A species of animal
antenna, *pl* **-ae** A sensory appendage on the head of an insect
antennule A small antenna
anterior Located forward
anteroom A waiting room
anthelion, *pl* **-lia** or **-ons** Halolike area in the sky
anthem A hymn of praise
anthemion, *pl* **-mia** A pattern of leaves used in Greek art

anther Pollen-bearing part of a stamen

anthesis The blooming of a flower

anthill A mound formed by ants

anthodium, *pl* **-dia** The flower head of composite plants

anthology A collection of literary pieces

anthotaxy The arrangement of the parts of a flower

anthozoan Various marine organisms

anthrax, *pl* **-thraces** A disease of animals

anthropic Pertaining to man

anthurium A species of plant

anti Against

antiar A tree of Java

antibody A body protein that produces immunity

antic A caper

antichlor A neutralizing substance

antichrist An enemy of Christ

anticline A fold with strata sloping downward

antidote A remedy to counteract poison

antigen, antigene A substance that stimulates the production of an antibody

antiknock A substance added to gasoline

antimere A part corresponding to an opposite part in an organism

antimony A metallic element

antinode The point of maximum amplitude between adjacent nodes

antinomy Contradiction

antipasto, *pl* **-ti** An appetizer

antipathy A feeling of opposition

antiphon A hymn sung responsively

antipode A diametrical opposite

antipope A person claiming to be pope

antiquary A dealer of antiques

antiquate To make old-fashioned

antique Belonging to an earlier period

antiquer Collector of antiques

antiquity Ancient times

antiserum Serum containing antibodies

antisocial Unsociable

antitank Used for combat against tanks

antitoxic Counteracting a poison

antitoxin Serum containing antibodies that neutralize poison

antitrust Concerned with the regulation of trusts

antitype An opposite type

antivenin An antitoxin active against venom

antler The horn of an animal

antonym A word opposite in meaning to another word

antre A cave

antrorse Directed forward and upward

antrum, *pl* **-tra** A cavity in a bone

antsy Fidgety

anuran Pertaining to frogs and toads

anuresis Inability to urinate

anuria Absence of urine

anurous Tailless

anus, *pl* **anuses** The excretory opening of the alimentary canal

anvil A heavy iron block for shaping metals

anxiety Worry

anxious Worried

any One, no matter which; some, regardless of quantity

The following words are listed without definition (see Introduction):

anybody anyplace anyways
anyhow anything anywhere
anymore anytime anywise
anyone anyway

aorist A verb tense used in classical Greek

aorta, *pl* **-tas** or **-tae** A main artery

aoudad A wild sheep

apace Swiftly

apache A Parisian gangster

apanage Variant of appanage

aparejo A packsaddle

apart In pieces
apartheid Official policy of racial segregation
apartment A room or rooms in a building designed for living
apatetic Having coloration serving as camouflage
apathetic Uninterested
apathy Lack of interest
apatite A mineral
ape A species of primate
apeak In a vertical position
apercu A summary
aperient A mild laxative
aperiodic Irregular
aperitif A drink before a meal
aperture An opening
apetalous Having no petals
apex, *pl* **apexes** or **apices** The highest point
aphagia Inability to swallow
aphanite Rocks that cannot be seen by the naked eye
aphasia Loss of the ability to articulate ideas
aphelion, *pl* **-lia** Point on a planet farthest from the sun
aphesis The loss of an unstressed vowel from the beginning of a word
aphid A species of insect
aphis, *pl* **aphides** An aphid
aphonia Loss of speech
aphonic Affected by aphonia
aphorism A statement of a principle
aphotic Without light
aphrodite A brightly colored butterfly
aphtha, *pl* **-thae** A small blister
aphyllous Having no leaves
apian Pertaining to bees
apiarian An apiarist
apiarist A beekeeper
apiary Beehives
apical Located at the apex
apiculate Ending with a sharp tip
apiece Each
apish Imitative
apivorous Feeding on bees

aplacental Having no placenta
aplanatic Pertaining to optical systems
aplasia Defective development of an organ
aplastic Lacking form
aplite A granite rock
aplomb Poise
apnea, apnoea Temporary suspension of respiration
apocarp An apocarpous fruit
apocope Omitting the last sound of a word
apocrine Pertaining to a certain type of a gland
apodal Having no limbs
apodictic Incontestable
apodosis, *pl* **-ses** A clause stating the conclusion of a conditional sentence
apoenzyme A protein
apogamy The production of a new plant without sexual reproduction
apogee The farthest point
apollo A young man of great beauty
apologia A formal defense
apologist A person who argues in defense of another
apologue A moral fable
apology A statement asking pardon
apomict An organism that is the result of apomixis
apomixis A kind of reproductive process
apophyge The curvature at the bottom and top of the shaft of a column
apophysis, *pl* **-ses** An outgrowth of an organ
apoplexy Loss of muscular control
aport Toward the port side
apostasy Abandonment of one's religious faith
apostate One who forsakes his faith
apostle One of the twelve witnesses chosen by Christ
apostolic Pertaining to the Apostles

apothegm A proverb

apothem In a regular polygon

appall, appal To fill with dismay

appanage Land given by a king

apparatus A machine

apparel Clothing

apparent Readily seen

apparitor An official to carry out the orders of the court

appeal Urgent request

appear To become visible

appease To placate

appel In fencing, a quick stamp of the foot

appellant One who appeals a court decision

appellate Having the power to hear appeals

appellee One against whom an appeal is directed

append To attach

appendage Something appended

appendant Accompanying

appendix An appendage

appertain To belong as a part

appetence A strong desire

appetite A desire for food or drink

appetizer A food served before the meal

applaud Clapping the hands

applause Expressed approval

apple A tree with edible fruit

applejack Brandy made from hard cider

appliance An electric device used in a household

applicant One who applies for a job

applique To decorate with applique work

apply To put to a special use

appoint To set by mutual agreement

apportion To divide

appose To place side by side

apposite Appropriate

appraise To judge

apprehend To take into custody

appressed Pressed closely against something

apprise To inform

approach To come near

approbate To authorize

approve To regard favorably

apraxia The inability to perform coordinated movements

apricot A tree with edible fruit

apriori Not supported by factual study

apron A garment to protect one's clothes

apropos Appropriate

apse The altar of a church

apsis, *pl* **-sides** An apse

apt Suitable

apteral Having no columns on the side

apterous Having no wings

apteryx The kiwi bird

aptitude A natural ability

aqua, *pl* **aquae** Water

aquacade An entertainment with swimmers

aquanaut A person trained for underwater research

aquaplane A board on which one rides on water

aquarelle A drawing in transparent water colors

aquarist One who keeps an aquarium

aquarium, *pl* **-ums** or **-ia** A tank in which fish are kept

aquatic Living in the water

aquatint A process of etching

aquavit A Scandinavian liquor

aqueduct A channel to transport water

aqueous Watery

aquifer A water-bearing rock

aquilegia A columbine

aquiline Curved like an eagle's beak

ar The letter *r*

arabesque A ballet position

arable Fit for cultivation

arachnid A species of arthropod

arachnoid Resembling a spider's web

aragonite A mineral

arapaima A South American fish

araroba A Brazilian tree

araucaria A species of tree

arbalest, arbelist A medieval missile launcher

arbiter One who decides a disputed issue

arbitrage Buying stock in one market to sell in another at a profit

arbitrate To decide

arbor, arbour A shady shelter in a garden

arboreal Living in trees

arboreous Wooded

arboretum, *pl* **-tums** or **-ta** A place for the display of trees and plants

arborize To have many branches

arbutus A species of tree

arc Anything shaped like an arch

arcade An arched part of a building

arcane Esoteric

arcanum, *pl* **-na** Mystery

arch Anything curved like an arch

archaic Belonging to an ancient time

archaism An archaic expression

archaize To make archaic

archangel A celestial being

archducal Pertaining to an archduke

archduchy The land over which an archduke has authority

archduke A nobleman in royal families

archenemy A principal enemy

archer One who shoots with a bow and arrow

archery The sport of shooting with bows and arrows

archetype A prototype

archfiend The devil

archil Variant of orchil

archimage A great magician

archine A Russian unit of measure

architect A planner

archival Kept in archives

archives A place in which organized records are stored

archivist One who is in charge of archives

archivolt Decorative molding

archon Official of the Byzantine Empire

archway A passageway under an arch

arciform Formed like an arc

arctic Characteristic of the polar regions

arcuate Arched

ardeb A unit of measure

ardency Ardor

ardent Burning

ardor, ardour Strong enthusiasm

arduous Strenuous

are A metric unit of measure

area A piece of ground

areaway A space between two buildings

areca A species of palm

arena A place for contests

areola, *pl* **-lae** or **-las** A small space bounded by veins in an insect's wings

arete Narrow mountain ridge

arethusa A species of orchid

argal Variant of argol

argala A type of stork

argali A wild sheep

argent Silver

argentine Silvery metals

argentite A silver ore

argil Clay used by potters

argillite A metamorphic rock

arginine An amino acid

argol A byproduct of wine making

argon A gaseous element

argonaut A mollusk

argosy A merchant ship

argot A specialized vocabulary

argue To debate

argufy To argue over

argument A debate

argyle, argyll A knitting pattern

aria A song

arid Dry

ariel A gazelle

arietta, ariette A short aria

aright Correctly

aril Outer covering of some seeds

arillode A covering that resembles an aril

ariose Melodic
arioso In the style of an aria
arise To get up
arista, *pl* **-tae** A bristlelike part of an insect's appendage
aristate Having a bristlelike appendage
ark The chest containing the Ten Commandments
arm Upper limb of the body
armada Fleet of warships
armadillo A species of mammal
armament Military weapons
armature Rotating part of a dynamo
armband A brassard
armchair A chair with side structures for the arms
armet A medieval helmet
armhole An opening in a garment for the arm
armiger A squire
armistice A truce
armlet A band worn on the arm
armoire A wardrobe
armor, armour A covering worn for protection
armorer One who makes armor
armorial Pertaining to a heraldry
armory An arsenal
armpit The hollow under the arm
armrest A support for the arm
arms Weapons
armure A fabric
army A large body of men trained for warfare
armyworm A species of insect larvae
arnatto Variant of annatto
arnica A species of plant
aroint Begone
aroma A distinctive odor
aromatize To make fragrant
arose Past tense of arise
around In a circle
arouse To awaken
arpeggio The playing of the tones in a chord rapidly
arpent, arpen An old French unit of measure

arquebus Variant of harquebus
arrack A strong drink of the Middle East
arraign To bring before a court
arrange To put into order
arrant Thoroughgoing
arras A tapestry
array To adorn
arrayal The act of arraying
arrear An unpaid debt
arrest To stop
arris, *pl* **-rises** The sharp edge in a molding
arrive To come to a place
arriviste An upstart
arroba A unit of weight
arrogant Overbearingly proud
arrogate To take without right
arrow A thin shaft shot from a bow
arrowhead The pointed tip of an arrow
arrowroot A tropical American plant
arroyo A dry gulch
arsenal A stock of weapons
arsenate A salt of arsenic acid
arsenic A highly poisonous element
arsenide An arsenic compound
arsenious Containing arsenic
arshin Variant of archine
arsine A poisonous gas
arsis, *pl* **-ses** The upbeat of a musical measure
arson The crime of burning another's property
art Works of beauty
artel An enterprise of workers in Russia
artemisia A species of plant
arterial Like arteries
arteriole A terminal branch of an artery
arteritis Inflammation of an artery
artesian A type of well
arthralgia Neuralgic pain in a joint
arthritis Inflammation of a joint
arthropod A species of invertebrate organism
arthrosis, *pl* **-ses** A joint between

bones
artichoke A type of edible plant
article A small thing
articular Pertaining to joints
artifact An object of historical
interest
artifice Trickery
artillery Large-caliber weapons
artisan A craftsman
artist One who creates works of art
artiste A public performer
arty Appearing artistic
arum A species of plants
aruspex Variant of haruspex
arytenoid Pertaining to muscles of
the larynx
as To the same degree
asafetida A substance formerly
used in medicine
asarum Roots of the wild ginger
asbestos, asbestus A substance
used for insulation
ascarid A species of worm
ascend To rise
ascender One that ascends
ascent The act of ascending
ascertain To find out
ascetic Self-denying
ascidian A species of marine
animal
ascidium, *pl* **-ia** A bottle-shaped
part of an organ
ascites Accumulation of serous
fluid in the abdomen
ascocarp Structure containing
spore sacs of fungi
ascospore A sexual spore
ascot A type of scarf
ascribe To attribute to a specified
cause
ascus, *pl* **asci** A spore sac in certain
fungi
asdic A sonar device
asea At sea
asepsis Being free of pathogenic
organisms
aseptic Lacking emotion
asexual Sexless
ash The residue of something that
has been burned
ashamed Feeling guilt

ashen Consisting of ashes
ashlar, ashler A square stone used
in building
ashore Toward the shore
ashplant A walking stick made
from an ash sapling
ashtray A holder for ashes
ashy Covered with ashes
aside To one side
asinine Stupid
ask To seek information
askance, askant Sidewise
askew Awry
aslant Slanting
asleep Sleeping
aslope At a slant
asocial Avoiding society
asp A species of snake
asparagus A species of plant
aspect The appearance of
something
aspen A species of tree
asper A Turkish monetary unit
asperate Roughen
asperges A Roman Catholic rite
aspergill An instrument for sprink-
ling holy water
asperity Ill temper
asperse To slander
asphalt A mixture used for paving
aspheric Varying slightly from
sphericity
asphodel A species of plant
asphyxia Loss of consciousness
from lack of oxygen
aspic A jellied garnish of meat or
fish
aspirant One who aims for a high
place
aspirate A speech sound followed
by a puff of breath
aspirator A device that removes
liquids or gases
aspire To strive for an ultimate
goal
aspirin A chemical compound
asquint With a sidelong glance
ass A species of hoofed animal
assagai, assegai A tree of southern
Africa
assai A species of palm tree

assail   To assault
assassin   A murderer
assault   A vicious attack
assay   An examination
assemble   To bring together
assent   To concur
assert   To affirm
assess   To charge with a tax or fine
asset   A valuable property
assiduity   Diligence
assiduous   Persistent
assign   To designate
assignat   Former paper currency of France
assist   To help
assize   A session of a court
associate   To join together
assoil   To pardon
assonance   Approximate agreement
assort   To classify
assuage   To satisfy
assuasive   Soothing
assume   To take for granted
assumpsit   A contract
assure   To convince
assurgent   Ascending
astasia   Inability to stand
astatic   Unstable
astatine   A radioactive element
aster   A species of plant
asterisk   A star-shaped figure used to denote a reference
asterism   A cluster of stars
astern   To the rear
asternal   Lacking a sternum
asteroid   Celestial bodies
asthenia, astheny   Weakness
asthenic   Having a slender physique
asthma   A respiratory disease
astir   Moving about
astonied   Bewildered
astonish   To confound
astound   To strike with wonder
astraddle   Astride
astragal   A narrow molding having the form of beading
astrakhan   A fabric with a curly, looped pile
astral   Resembling the stars
astray   Away from the right direction

astrict   To bind
astride   With the legs apart
astringe   To constrict
astrocyte   A star-shaped cell
astrodome   An enclosed stadium
astrogate   To navigate in space
astrolabe   A medieval instrument
astrology   The pseudo-study of the heavenly bodies
astronaut   A navigator of a spacecraft
astronomy   The scientific study of the universe
astute   Keen in judgment
astylar   Not having columns
asunder   Into separate pieces
asyllabic   Not syllabic
asylum, *pl* **-lums** or **-la**   An institution for the mentally ill
asymmetry   Lack of balance
asymptote   A mathematical measure
asyndeton   The omission of conjunctions between coordinate sentence elements
at   In the location of
atabal   A type of drum used by the Moors
ataghan   Variant of yataghan
ataman   A Cossack chief
atap   A thatch of leaves
ataractic   Conducive to peace of mind
ataraxia   Peace of mind
atavic   Pertaining to a remote ancestor
atavism   The reappearance of a characteristic in an organism
ataxia, ataxy   Loss of muscular coordination
ate   Past tense of eat
atelier   An artist's studio
atemporal   Timeless
atheist   One who denies the existence of God
atheling   An Anglo-Saxon prince
atheneum, athenaeum   A library
atheroma   A disease of the arteries
athirst   Thirsty
athlete   One who takes part in

sports

athodyd A ramjet

athwart Crosswise

atilt In a tilted position

atlas, *pl* **-lases** or **atlantes** A collection of maps

atman The principal of life

atmolysis, *pl* **-ses** Separation of gases by diffusion

atmometer An instrument for measuring the rate of water evaporation

atoll A coral island and reef that encloses a lagoon

atom Smallest unit of an element

atomicity The state of being composed of atoms

atomy A tiny particle

atonal Lacking a tonal center

atonality A composition in which tonal key is disregarded

atone To make amends

atonic Not accented

atony Lack of accent

atop On the top

atrip Just clear of the bottom

atrium, *pl* **atria** or **-ums** A bodily cavity

atrocious Monstrous

atrocity An atrocious action

atrophy Any wasting away

atropine, atropin A poisonous alkaloid

attach To connect

attache A person on the staff of a diplomatic mission

attack An assault

attain To accomplish

attainder Dishonor

attaint To disgrace

attar Oil from the petals of flowers

attempt To try

attend To be present at

attenuate To make small

attest Corroborate

attic The room directly below the roof of a house

attire To dress

attitude A state of mind with regard to some matter

attorn To acknowledge a new owner as one's landlord

attorney A person who practices law

attract To draw near

attribute A quality belonging to a person

attrited, attrite Worn down by attrition

attrition Any gradual weakening

attune To tune

atwain In two

atwitter In a state of nervous excitement

atypical, atypic Not typical

aubade A musical composition played in early morning

auberge A tavern

aubergine The eggplant

auburn Reddish brown to brown

auction A sale in which items are sold to the highest bidder

audacious Bold

audacity Boldness

audible Being heard

audience A gathering of people, as at a concert

audient Listening

audile Able to learn, chiefly from auditory stimuli

audio Pertaining to audible sound

audit An examination of records

auditive Auditory

auditory The experience of hearing

augend A quantity to which another quantity is added

auger A tool for boring wood

aught Anything at all

augite A mineral

augment To increase

augur A prophet

augury The rite performed by an augur

august Majestic

auk A species of bird

auklet A species of small auk

auld Old

aulic Courtly

aunt Sister of one's father or mother

auntie, aunty Familiar form of aunt

auntlike Acting like an aunt

aura, *pl* **-ras** or **aurae** A soft breeze

aural Perceived by the ear

aurar Plural of eyrir

aureate Of a golden color

aureole, aureola A halo

auric Containing gold

auricle The external part of the ear

auricula A species of primrose

auricular Pertaining to hearing

auriform Ear-shaped

aurochs An extinct mammal

aurora The light of dawn

auroral Resembling the dawn

aurous Pertaining to gold

aurum Gold

auspex, *pl* **auspices** An ancient Roman augur

auspicate To begin with a ceremony designed to bring good luck

auspice Patronage

austenite An element in iron

austere Somber

austral Coming from the south

autacoid, autocoid A hormone

autarchy Absolute power

authentic Genuine

author Writer of a literary work

authoress A female author

autism Acceptance of fantasy rather than the real thing

auto An automobile

autobahn A German superhighway

autobus, *pl* **-buses** A bus

autoclave Pressurized vessel for sterilization

autocrat A ruler with absolute power

autogamy Self-fertilization

autogiro, autogyro A type of aircraft

autograph A person's signature

autoharp Musical instrument

autolysin A substance that causes autolysis

autolysis The destruction of tissues or cells by enzymes

automat A restaurant where customers put in coins to obtain food

automate To change to automation

automaton, *pl* **-tons** or **-ta** A robot

autonomic Autonomous

autonomy Self-government

autophyte An autotrophic plant

autopilot An automatic pilot

autopsy The examination of a dead body

autosome Any chromosome that is not a sex chromosome

autotomy Casting off of a body part

autotoxin A poison that is produced in the body

autotroph An autotrophic organism

autotruck A motor truck

autumn The season between summer and winter

autunite A mineral

auxesis An increase in the size of a cell without cell division

auxiliary Helping

auxin A species of plant hormones

ava At all

avail To assist

avalanche A slide of a large mass of snow

avarice Greed

avast Used as a nautical command to stop

avatar Incarnation

avaunt Used as a command to be gone

ave Farewell

avenge To take revenge

avens A species of plant

avenue A street

aver To affirm

average Typical

averse Opposed

aversion Intense dislike

avert To turn away

avian Pertaining to birds

aviary A large enclosure for birds

aviation The development of aircraft

aviator One who operates an aircraft

aviatrix A female aviator

avid Eager
avidin A protein in egg white
avidity Eagerness
avifauna All the birds of a specific region
avigation Navigation of aircraft
avionics Science of electronics applied to aeronautics
avirulent Not virulent
avo Monetary unit of Macao
avocado A tropical American tree
avocation An activity for enjoyment
avocet A species of bird
avodire A tree of western Africa
avoid To keep away from
avouch To guarantee
avow To declare openly
avowal An admission of acknowledgment
avulse To rip away
avuncular Resembling an uncle
aw Expression of disbelief
awa Away
await To wait for
awake To waken
award To grant as merited
aware Conscious
awash Flooded
away From a certain place
awe An emotion of wonder
aweary Weary
aweather To windward
aweigh Just clear of the bottom
awesome Inspiring awe
awful Terrible
awhile For a short time
awkward Ungainly
awl A pointed tool for making holes
awlwort A small aquatic plant
awn A bristlelike appendage of certain grasses
awning A canvas used as a shelter from weather
awoke Past tense of awake
awry Twisted toward one side

ax, axe, *pl* **axes** A tool used for cutting wood
axenic Uncontaminated
axial Forming an axis
axil The angle between the upper surface of a leaf and its stem
axilla, *pl* **axillae** The armpit
axillar Axillary
axillary Near the axilla
axiom A self-evident truth
axis, *pl* **axes** A straight line about which an object rotates
axite A fiber of an axon
axle The shaft upon which a wheel revolves
axletree A rod supporting a vehicle
axman A man who cuts trees
axolotl A species of salamander
axon, axone A part of a nerve cell
axseed The crown vetch plant
ayah A nurse in India
aye, ay An affirmative vote
ayin The 16th letter of the Hebrew alphabet
azalea A species of evergreen shrub
azan A Muslim call to prayer
azedarach The chinaberry tree
azimuth An angle of horizontal deviation
azine A chemical compound
azo Containing nitrogen
azoic Pertaining to geological periods
azole A chemical compound
azonic Not local
azote Nitrogen
azotemia Uremia
azoth Mercury
azotic Pertaining to azote
azotise, azotize To nitrogenate
azure Of the color blue
azurite A mineral
azygos An azygous anatomical part
azygous Unpaired

ba The soul in Egyptian mythology
baa The bleat of a sheep
baal, *pl* **-im** A false idol
baba A leavened rum cake
babassu A Brazilian palm tree
babbitt To line with Babbitt metal
babble To utter words idly
babe A baby
babel A confusion of voices
babirusa A wild pig
babka A Polish coffee cake
baboon A species of African
  monkey
baboonery Behavior characteristic
  of baboons
babu, baboo A form of Hindu
  address
babul A tree
babushka A woman's head scarf
baby An infant
babyish Acting like a baby
bacca A berry
baccarat, baccara A card game
baccate Resembling a berry
bacchanal A riotous celebration
bacchant A reveler
bacchante A female participant in a
  riotous celebration
bacciform Having the shape of a
  berry
bach *Slang* To live alone
bachelor An unmarried man
bacillary, bacillar Rod-shaped
bacillus, *pl* **-cilli** Any of various
  rod-shaped bacteria
back To the rear
  The following words are listed
without definition (see Introduction):

backache   backbone   backdoor
backbend   backcourt   backdrop

backfield   backmost   backspin
backfill   backout   backstage
backfire   backpack   backstay
backhand   backrest   backstop
backhoe   backsaw   backswept
backhouse   backseat   backsword
backlash   backset   backtrack
backless   backside   backward
backlist   backslap   backwash
backlit   backslide   backwood
backlog   backspace   backyard

backbite To slander
backboard A board placed under
  the mattress
backcross To cross or breed
backer One who gives to an
  enterprise
bacon Meat from a pig
bacteria Microscopic organisms
bacterin Vaccine prepared from
  dead bacteria
bacterize To change by means of
  bacteria
backteroid Resembling bacteria
bad Wicked
bade Past tense of bid
badge An emblem worn as an identification of office or rank
badger A species of animals
badinage Playful banter
badlands An area of barren land
badman A criminal
baff To strike under a golf ball
baffle To frustrate
bag A woman's purse
bagasse Sugar cane pulp
bagatelle A trifle
bagel A ring-shaped roll
bagful Amount held by a bag
baggage Luggage
bagging Material for making bags

baggy Hanging loosely
bagman *Slang* A person who collects money for crooks
bagnio A brothel
bagpipe A musical instrument
baguette, baguet A gem cut into a rectangular shape
bagwig An 18th century wig
bagworm The larva of certain moths
bah An exclamation of contempt
bahadur A Hindu title
baht Monetary unit of Thailand
bail Money given for the release of an arrested person
bailable Eligible for bail
bailee One to whom property is bailed
bailey Outer wall of a castle
bailie A Scottish municipal officer
bailiff A court attendant
bailiwick A person's area of interest
bailment Process of providing bail
bailor A person who bails property
bailsman One who provides bail
bainmarie A set of cooking pans
bairn A child
bait To lure
baiza An Oman unit of money
baize A woolen fabric
bake To cook in an oven
bakehouse A bakery
baklava A dessert
baksheesh, bakshish A gift of alms
bal A balmoral
balalaika A Russian musical instrument
balance A weighing device
balas A semiprecious gem
balata A tropical American tree
balboa Monetary unit of Panama
balcony A projecting platform of a building, surrounded by a railing
bald Lacking hair
baldachin A fabric of silk and gold brocade
baldpate A baldheaded person
baldric A belt worn to support a sword or bugle

bale To wrap in bales
baleen Variant of whalebone
balk, baulk To refuse
ball A rounded object used in games
ballad A folk poem, intended to be sung
ballade A musical composition
balladry Art of singing ballads
ballast Material placed in a ship for stability
ballerina A female ballet dancer
ballet An artistic dance form
ballista, *pl* **-tae** A medieval military engine
ballistic Pertaining to ballistics
ballonet A gasbag placed inside a balloon
balloon To expand
ballot A secret vote
ballyhoo Sensational advertising
ballyrag Variant of bullyrag
balm A species of tree or shrub
balmacaan A Scottish garment
balmoral A Scottish cap
balmy Having the fragrance of balm
balneal Pertaining to bathing
baloney, boloney Variant of bologna
balsa A tree of tropical America
balsam A substance from balsa
balsamic Pertaining to balsam
baluster Post or support of a handrail
bambino, *pl* **-nos** or **-ni** A baby
bamboo A species of tropical grass
bamboozle To trick
ban To prohibit
banal Ordinary
banana A species of tropical plant
banco A gambling bet
band A neckband or collar
bandage A covering for a wound
bandanna, bandana A large handkerchief
bandbox A box for holding small articles
bandeau, *pl* **-deaux** or **-deaus** A band for the hair

banderole, banderol, bannerol A flag flown from a masthead
bandicoot A species of rat
bandit, *pl* **-dits** or **banditti** A robber
bandog A watchdog
bandoleer, bandolier A belt for carrying cartridges
bandore, bandora An ancient musical instrument
bandsman A musician
bandstand A platform for an orchestra
bandwagon A wagon for musicians in a parade
bandy To toss back and forth
bane A deadly poison
baneberry A species of plant
bang A loud noise
bangkok A hat made of fine straw
bangle A bracelet or anklet
bangtail *Slang* A racehorse
banian A jacket worn in India
banish To exile
banister, bannister A baluster
banjo A musical instrument
bank To pile up
bankbook A depositor's book
bankroll A roll of paper money
bankrupt A person unable to pay his creditors in full
banner The flag of a country
banneret A small banner
bannock Variant of bonnock
banns, bans An announcement in church of an intended marriage
banquet An elaborate feast
banquette A sidewalk
banshee, banshie A female spirit in folklore
bantam A species of fowl
banter To tease mildly
bantling A young child
banyan A species of tree
banzai A Japanese battle cry
baobab A large tree of Africa
baptism A Christian ceremony
baptize To purify
bar A sandbar
barathea A fabric
barb A biting remark

barbarian A cruel person
barbaric Marked by crudeness
barbarous Coarse
barbasco A species of tropical American tree
barbate Having a beard
barbecue An outdoor fireplace
barbel A species of fish
barbell A bar for exercising
barber One who cuts hair
barberry A species of shrubs
barbet A species of bird
barbette A platform
barbican A tower
barbicel A part of a feather
barbital A compound used as a sedative
barbule A small barb
barbwire Barbed wire
barcarole A Venetian gondolier's song
bard A poet
bare Naked
bareback On a horse with no saddle
barefaced Having no beard
barefoot Wearing nothing on the feet
barege A fabric
barf *Slang* To vomit
barfly *Slang* One who frequents bars
bargain An agreement
barge A flat-bottomed boat
bargee A bargeman
barghest, barguest A goblin
barilla A species of Old World plants
barite A mineral
baritone, barytone A male singer
barium A metal
bark Sound uttered by a dog
barkeeper A person who runs a bar
barky Resembling bark
barley A cereal grass
barm The foam of malt liquors
barmaid A woman who serves drinks in a bar
barman A bartender
barmy Full of barm
barn A large farm building

barnacle A species of marine crustaceans

barnstorm To travel about presenting plays

barogram A graphic record produced by a barograph

barograph A recording barometer

barometer An indicator

baron A nobleman

baronage The rank of a baron

baroness The wife of a baron

baronet A title ranking below a baron

baronetcy The rank of a baronet

barong A knife

baronial Pertaining to a baron

barony The domain of a baron

baroque An ornate object

barouche A carriage

barque Variant of bark

barrack To house in barracks

barracoon A barrack for slaves and convicts

barracuda A species of fish

barrage A dam

barranca A deep gorge

barrator, barrater One who commits barratry

barratry The offense of inciting quarrels

barrel A large wooden container

barren Childless

barret A flat cap

barrette A clasp to hold hair in place

barricade A barrier

barrier A wall built to bar passage

barrio A Spanish-speaking community in a U.S. City

barrister A British lawyer

barrow A wheelbarrow

barter To trade goods without money

bartizan, bartisan A small turret on a wall

baryon An atomic particle

barytes A mineral

basal Basic

basalt A volcanic rock

bascule A seesaw

base The foundation

baseball A game

baseboard A board that serves as a base

baseborn Illegitimate

baseman A player assigned to a base

basement The story below ground level

basenji A small dog

bash A heavy blow

bashful Self-conscious

bashlyk A Russian cloth hood

basic Fundamental

basicity The degree of being a chemical base

basidium, *pl* **-ia** A structure on a fungus

basify To make basic

basil An herb

basilar, basilary Pertaining to the base of the skull

basilic Kingly

basilica An ancient Roman building

basilisk A legendary dragon

basin A washbowl

basinet A medieval helmet

basipetal Growing from the top

basis, *pl* **-ses** A foundation upon which something rests

bask To lie in the sun

basket A container

basketry The craft of making baskets

basophil A white blood cell

basque A woman's bodice

bass A low-pitched tone

basset A dog

bassinet A basket for an infant

basso, *pl* **-sos** or **-si** A bass singer

bassoon A musical instrument

basswood A species of tree

bast The outer layer of certain plants

bastard An illegitimate child

bastardy Illegitimacy

baste To pour sauce over meat while cooking

bastille, bastile A prison

bastinado, bastinade A stick

bastion A well-fortified position

bat A species of nocturnal flying mammal

batch Material needed for one baking

bate To take away

bateau, *pl* **-teaux** A light, flat-bottomed boat

batfish A species of fish

batfowl To catch birds at night

bath The act of washing the body

bathe To take a bath

bathetic Anticlimactic

batholith, batholite Igneous rock

bathos Extreme dullness

bathrobe A robe for lounging

bathroom A room for taking a bath

bathtub A tub for bathing

batik, battik A method of dyeing prints

batiste A fabric

batman Soldier servant of a British army officer

baton The rod twirled by a drum major or majorette

batt A mass of cotton fibers

battalion A military unit

batten To become fat

batter The player at bat

battery An emplacement for artillery

battle An armed combat

battue Driving of wild game from cover by beaters

batty *Slang* Crazy

bauble A small ornament

baulk Variant of balk

bauxite Principal ore of aluminum

bawd A prostitute

bawdry Vulgar

bawl To howl

bay A body of water partly enclosed by land

bayadere A fabric

bayberry A species of plant

bayonet A rifle with a knife attached

bayou A body of water

baywood Wood of the mahogany tree

bazaar, bazar An oriental market

bazooka A portable weapon

bdellium A gum resin

be To have reality

be- Indicates a thorough degree; an action that causes a condition to exist. The following compounds are listed without definition (see Introduction):

beblood	bedotted	begroan
becalm	bedraggle	begrudge
became	bedrape	beguile
becap	bedrench	beguiler
becarpet	bedrivel	begulf
because	bedumb	begun
bechalk	bedunce	behalf
bechance	bedwarf	behave
becharm	befall	behaver
beclamor	befinger	behavior
beclasp	befit	behead
becloak	befitting	beheld
beclog	beflag	behest
beclothe	beflea	behind
becloud	befleck	behold
beclown	beflower	beholden
become	befog	beholder
becoming	befool	behoof
becoward	before	behoove
becrawl	befoul	behove
becrime	befret	behowl
becrowd	befriend	being
becrust	befringe	bejewel
becudgel	befuddle	bejumble
becurse	begall	bekiss
bedabble	began	beknight
bedamn	begaze	beknot
bedarken	beget	belabor
bedaub	begetter	belabour
bedazzle	begin	belaced
bedeafen	beginner	belady
bedeck	beginning	belated
bedevil	begird	belaud
bedew	begirdle	belay
bediaper	beglad	beleaguer
bedight	begloom	beleap
bedim	begone	belie
bedimple	begot	belief
bedirty	begotten	belier
bedizen	begrime	believe

73

believer
belike
beliquor
belittle
belive
belong
beloved
below
belying
bemadam
bemadden
bemean
bemingle
bemire
bemist
bemix
bemoan
bemock
bemuddle
bemurmer
bemuse
bemuzzle
bename
beneath
benighted
benign
benignant
benignity
benumb
bepaint
bepimple
bequeath
bequest
berake
berascal
berate
bereave
bereaver
berhyme
berime
beringed

berobed
berouged
bescorch
bescour
bescreen
beseech
beseem
beset
besetter
beshadow
beshame
beshiver
beshout
beshrew
beshroud
beside
besiege
besieger
beslaved
beslime
besmear
besmile
besmirch
besmoke
besmooth
besmudge
besmut
besnow
besoothe
besot
besought
bespangle
bespatter
bespeak
bespoke
bespouse
bespread
besprent
bestir
bestow
bestowal

bestrew
bestride
bestrow
bestud
beswarm
betake
betatter
betaxed
bethank
bethink
bethorn
bethump
betide
betimes
betoken
betook
betray
betrayal
betrayer
betroth
betrothal
between
betwixt
beuncle
bevomit
bewail
bewailer
beware
beweary
beweep
bewig
bewilder
bewinged
bewitch
beworm
beworry
bewrap
bewray
bewrayer
beyond

beacon A lighthouse

bead A rosary

beadle An English university official

beadledom Petty bureaucratic officiousness

beadwork Beaded molding

beady Decorated with beads

beagle One of a breed of small hounds

beak A bird's bill

beaker A drinking cup

beam To transmit

beamish Smiling

beamy Radiant

bean A species of plants

beanbag A bag filled with beans

beanie A small brimless cap

beano A form of bingo

beanpole A pole to support bean vines

beanstalk The stem of a bean plant

bear To hold up

bearberry A trailing shrub

bearcat *Slang* A vigorous person

beard Hair on the face

beardless Having no beard

bearish Like a bear

bearskin A rug made from the skin of a bear

beast A brutal person

beat To hit repeatedly

beatific Showing exalted joy

beatify To make blessedly happy

beatitude Supreme happiness

beatnik A member of the beat generation

beau, *pl* **beaus** or **beaux** Sweetheart

beaut *Slang* Something outstanding

beauteous Beautiful

beautiful Having beauty

beauty Loveliness

beaver A species of rodent

bebop A type of music

beccafico A species of bird

beck A gesture of beckoning

becket A device for holding ropes, spars or oars in position

beckon To signal by waving or nodding

bed A piece of furniture used for sleeping

The following words are listed without definition (see Introduction):

bedbug	bedding	bedlamp
bedchair	bedfast	bedless
bedcover	bedfellow	bedlike
bedded	bedframe	bedmaker
bedder	begown	bedmate

bedpan   bedroll   bestand
bedplate   bedroom   bedstead
bedpost   bedrug   bedstraw
bedquilt   bedside   bedstick
bedrail   bedsore   bedtime
bedrid   bedspread   bedward
bedridden   bedspring   bedwards

bedesman   An almsman

bedlam   A place of noisy uproar

bedlamite   A madman

bee   The letter *b*

beebread   A substance fed by bees to their larvae

beech   A species of tree

beechnut   Edible nut of the beech tree

beef, *pl* **beeves** or **beefs**   A full-grown steer

beefeater   One who eats beef

beefsteak   A piece of beef

beefwood   A species of tree

beefy   Resembling beef

beehive   A hive for bees

beekeeper   One who keeps bees

beeline   A straight, fast course

beer   An alcoholic beverage

beery   Tasting of beer

beestings   The first milk given by a cow after parturition

beeswax   Wax secreted by the honeybee

beeswing   Tartar scales that form on old wines

beet   A species of plant

beetle   A species of insect

beetroot   The beet

beg   To make an urgent plea

beggar   One who begs

beggarly   Very poor

beggary   Extreme poverty

begonia   A species of plant

beguine   A dance

begum   A Moslem lady of rank

behemoth   Something enormous in size

beige   A light grayish brown

bel   A unit of power

belch   To expel gas through the mouth

beldam, beldame   An old woman

belemnite   A species of cephalopod

belfry   A tower in which bells are hung

bell   Something shaped like a bell

bellbird   A species of bird

bellboy   An employee of a hotel

belle   A most attractive female

bellhop   A bellman

bellicose   Pugnacious

bellman   A hotel employee

bellow   To utter in a deep, loud voice

bellows   The lungs

bellwort   A species of plant

belly   The abdomen

bellyache   An ache in the stomach

bellyband   A band for holding in the navel of a baby

bellyfull   An excessive amount of food

bellywhop *Slang*   To dive striking the belly flat against the water

belt   A band worn around the waist

belting   Material used for making belts

beluga   A white whale

belvedere   A structure situated so as to command a good view

bema, *pl* **-mata**   Enclosed area about the altar

ben   A mountain peak

bench   A seat for two or more persons

bend   To cause to assume a curved shape

bender   One that bends

benedict, benedick   A confirmed bachelor, newly wed

benefic   Beneficent

benefice   A church office endowed with fixed assets

benefit   Advantage

bengaline   A fabric

benison   A benediction

benjamin   Benzoin

benne, benni, bene   A species of plant

benny *Slang*   An amphetamine tablet

bent   Crooked

benthos   The bottom of the sea

bentonite   Aluminum silicate clays

bentwood Wood that has been bent into shape

benzene A chemical

benzidine A chemical

benzine, benzin A chemical

benzoate A salt of benzoic acid

benzoin A resin containing benzoic acid

benzol Benzene

benzoyl A chemical radical

benzyl A chemical radical

berberine An alkaloid

berceuse A lullaby

beret A cap worn by male Basques

beretta Variant of biretta

berg An iceberg

bergamot A species of tree

beriberi A disease

berkelium A synthetic element containing isotopes

berlin A carriage

berline A limousine

berm, berme A shoulder of a road

berretta Variant of biretta

berry A species of edible fruit

berseem A clover

berserk Deranged

berserker A fierce warrior

berth A bunk on a ship

bertha A lace collar

beryl A mineral

beryllium A metallic element

besides In addition

besom A broom

best Most excellent

bestial Pertaining to an animal

bestiary Medieval allegorical fables

bet Amount risked in a wager

beta Second letter of the Greek alphabet

betaine A crystalline alkaloid

betatron An electron accelerator

betel A species of plant

beth Second letter of the Hebrew alphabet

bethel A holy place

betony A species of plant

better More suitable

bettor One who bets

bevel A rule with an adjustable arm

beverage A liquid refreshment

bevy A group

bey A Turkish title of honor

bezant An ornamental disk

bezel, bezil A slanting surface on the edge of various cutting tools

bezique A card game

bezoar A gastric mass

bhang A species of plant

bi A bisexual

bi-Indicates two. The following compounds are listed without definition (see Introduction):

biacetyl	biform	biovular
biannual	bifurcate	bipack
biaxal	bigeminal	biparted
biaxial	bigeming	bipartite
bicameral	bihourly	biparty
bicarb	bijugate	biped
bicentric	bijugous	biphenyl
biceps	bilabial	bipinnate
bichrome	bilabiate	biplane
bicipital	bilateral	bipod
bicolor	bilinear	bipolar
bicolour	bilingual	biracial
biconcave	bilobate	biradial
biconvex	bilobed	biramose
bicorn	bilocular	biramous
bicorne	bimanous	bireme
bicuspid	bimanual	bisect
bicycle	bimensal	bisector
bicycler	bimester	biserrate
bicyclic	bimetal	bisexual
bicycling	bimethal	bistate
bidental	bimodal	bisulcate
bidentate	bimonthly	bisulfate
biennial	bimotored	bisulfide
biennium	binal	bisulfite
bifacial	binary	bivalent
bifid	binate	bivalve
bifidity	binaural	bivariate
bifilar	binocle	bivinyl
biflex	binocular	biweekly
bifocal	binomial	biyearly
bifold	biologist	bizone
bifoliate	biology	
biforate	biolysis	
biforked	bionics	

bialy   A baked roll topped with onion flakes

bias   A diagonal line cut across fabric

bib   The part of an apron worn over the chest

bibb   A bibcock

bibber   A drinker

bibcock   A faucet

bibelot   A trinket

bible   An authoritative publication

bibulous   Marked by convivial drinking

bicker   To squabble

bid   To direct

bidarka   A canoe used by eskimos

biddable   Worth bidding on

bidden   A past participle of bid

bidding   A summons

biddy   A hen

bide   To remain the same

bidet   A low wash basin

bier   A stand for a coffin

biff *Slang*   To strike

big   Large

bigamist   One who commits bigamy

bigamous   Guilty of bigamy

bigamy   The offense of marrying one person while still married to another

bigarreau, bigaroon   A species of sweet cherry

bigeye   A species of fish

biggity, biggety   Conceited

bighead   Conceit

bighorn   A wild sheep

bight   A loop in a rope

bigmouth   A species of fish

bignonia   A species of plant

bigot   A person of strong prejudice

bigotry   Intolerance

bigwig   An important person

bijou, *pl* **-joux**   An exquisite trinket

bike   A bicycle

bikini   A brief two-piece bathing suit

bilberry   A species of plant

bilbo   An iron bar used to shackle prisoners

bile   A fluid secreted by the liver

bilge   The lowest inner part of a ship's hull

biliary   Pertaining to bile

bilious   Pertaining to bile

bilirubin   An organic compound

bilk   To cheat

bill   Entertainment offered by a theater

billabong   A stagnant pool

billboard   An advertisement along highways

billet   Assigned quarters

billfish   A species of fish

billfold   A case for carrying money

billhead   A letterhead used for bills

billhook   An implement

billiard   A shot in billiards

billie   A comrade

billion   A number

billionth   One of a billion equal parts

billon   An alloy

billow   A large wave

billy   A short wooden club

billycock   A man's hat

bilsted   The sweet gum tree

biltong   Meat dried in the sun

bimah   Variant of bema

bin   A container

bind   To bandage

bindery   A shop where books are bound

bindweed   A species of plant

bine   The flexible stem of certain plants

binge *Slang*   A drunken spree

bingo   A game

binnacle   The stand for a ship's compass

bio   A biography

bioassay   Evaluation of a drug

biocide   A substance capable of destroying living organisms

biography   A life history

biome   A community of living organisms

bionomics   Pertaining to ecology

biont   A living organism

bioplasm   Living protoplasm

biopsy   The examination of tissue

bioscope   An early motion-picture projector

bioscopy   A type of medical examination

biosphere   Regions of the earth that support ecological systems

biota   A total ecological entity

biotic   Pertaining to life

biotin   A *B* vitamin

biotite   A form of mica

biotope   A stable habitat

biotype   A group of similar organisms

biparous   Producing two offspring in a single birth

birch   A species of tree

bird   A species of flying feathered vertebrate

birdbrain *Slang*   A silly person

birdcage   A cage for birds

birdcall   The song of a bird

birdfarm *Slang*   An aircraft carrier

birdhouse   An aviary

birdie   A small bird

birdlime   Something that captures

birdman   An ornithologist

birdseed   Bird food

biretta   A cap worn by Roman Catholic clergy

birl   A hum

birr   A whirring sound

birth   Fact of being born

birthday   The day of one's birth

birthmark   A mark on the body from birth

birthrate   The number of births per year

birthroot   A species of plant

birthwort   A species of vine

bis   Twice

bise   Alpine wind

biscuit   A small cake

bishop   A Christian clergyman of high rank

bishopric   The rank of a bishop

bismuth   A metallic element

bisnaga   A species of cactus

bison   Buffalo

bisque   A thick cream soup

bister, bistre   A pigment

bistort   A species of plant

bistoury   A surgical knife

bistro   A small tavern

bit   A small amount

bitch   A female dog

bitchy *Slang*   Spiteful

bite   To eat into

bitstock   A handle for a drilling bit

bitt   A post on a ship used to secure cables

bitten   Alternate past participle of bite

bitter   Difficult to accept

bittern   A species of bird

bitternut   A hickory tree

bitters   An alcoholic liquid

bitty   Small

bitumen   An asphalt

bivouac   An encampment

bizarre   Grotesque

biznaga   Variant of bisnaga

blab   A person who blabs

blabber   To chatter

black   The darkest color

blackball   To ostracize

blackbird   A species of bird

blackbody   An absorber of radiation

blackbuck   An antelope

blackcap   A small European bird

blackcock   The male of the black grouse

blackdamp   A gas found in mines after fires

blackface   An actor in a minstrel show

blackfish   A species of fish

blackhead   A species of bird

blackish   Somewhat black

blackjack   A hand weapon

blackleg   A disease of sheep and cattle

blacklist   A person suspected of disloyalty

blackmail   Extortion

blackout   Temporary loss of consciousness

blackpoll   A North American warbler

blacktop   Asphalt

bladder   A membranous sac
bladdery   Resembling a bladder
blade   A sword
blah Slang   Worthless nonsense
blain   A blister
blamable, blameable   Deserving of
   blame
blame   To accuse
blanch   To bleach
bland   Free of irritation
blandish   To cajole
blank   Vacant
blanket   A large bed covering
blare   To sound loudly
blarney   Flattering talk
blase   Filled with ennui
blaspheme   To revile
blast   A strong gust of wind
blastema   A region of embryonic
   cells
blastie   A dwarf
blastoff   The launching of a rocket
blastula, pl **-las** or **-lae**   An embryonic form
blat   To blab
blatant   Obtrusive
blather, blether   To babble
blaw   To blow
blaze   A flame
blazer   A sports jacket
blazon   A coat of arms
blazonry   A coat of arms
bleach   To make white
bleak   Barren
blear   To blur
bleat   To utter in a whining voice
bleb   A small blister
bleed   To lose blood
blemish   A defect
blench   Variant of blanch
blend   To mix
blende   A species of mineral
blenny   A species of fish
blent   Alternate past participle of
   blend
blesbok, blesbuck   An African
   antelope
bless   To sanctify
blest   Alternate past tense of bless
blet   A decaying fruit

blight   A plant disease
blighty Slang   Home
blimey Slang   A British
   exclamation
blimp   A nonrigid, buoyant air ship
blind   Without the sense of sight
blinder   A person that causes
   blinding
blindfish   A species of fish
blindfold   To cover the eyes
blindworm   A lizard
blini   Buckwheat pancakes served
   with caviar or sour cream
blink   To flash on and off
blinkard   An obtuse person
blintz, blintze   A type of pancake
blip   A spot of light on a radar
   screen
bliss   Serene happiness
blister   A swelling on the skin
blite   An annual herb
blithe   Cheerful
blitz   An intense campaign
blizzard   A violent snowstorm
bloat   To cause to inflate
blob   A shapeless daub of color
bloc   A group united for common
   action
block   A solid piece of wood
blockade   To block
blockage   An obstruction
blockhead   A stupid person
blockish   Dull
blocky   Stocky
bloke Slang   A man
blond, blonde   A blond person
blood   Fluid circulated by the heart
blooded   Thoroughbred
bloodline   Pedigree
bloodroot   A woodland plant
bloodshed   Carnage
bloodshot   Irritated and red
bloodworm   A species of worm
bloodwort   A species of plant
blooey, blooie Slang   Go out of order
bloom   The blossoms of a plant
bloop   To hit a ball
blooper   A fly ball
blossom   A flower
blot   A stain

blotch A splotch
blotter A piece of blotting paper
blotto Slang Drunk
blouse A piece of clothing
blow To storm
blowfish A species of fish
blowfly A species of fly
blowgun A pipe through which darts are blown
blowhard Slang A braggart
blowhole An air vent
blown Inflated
blowoff Something blown off
blowout A ruptured object
blowpipe A blowgun
blowtorch A gas burner that produces a hot flame
blowup An explosion
blowy Breezy
blowzy, blowsy Unkempt
blubber To sob noisily
blucher A high shoe
bludgeon A heavy club
blue A color
bluebeard A killer of women
bluebell A species of plant
bluebill A duck
bluebird A species of bird
bluecoat A policeman
bluecurls A species of plant
bluefish A species of fish
bluegill A sunfish
bluegrass A species of grass
bluehead A marine fish
blueing, bluing A coloring agent
blueish, bluish Slightly blue
bluejack An oak tree
blueline Lines in an ice hockey rink
bluenose A puritanical person
blueprint A carefully designed plan
blues A style of jazz
bluestone Stone used for paving
bluet A meadow flower
blueweed A plant
bluff To mislead
blunder A clumsy act
blunt Not sharp
blur To smear
blurb A brief notice

blurt A sudden statement
blush To become rosy
bluster A violent, gusty wind
bo Slang A fellow
boa A species of snake
boar A wild pig
board A flat slab of lumber
boardwalk A walk of wooden planks
boarfish A species of fish
boarhound A large dog
boarish Coarse
boast To brag
boat A ship
boatbill A wading bird
boatload The number of persons a boat can hold
boatman One who deals with boats
boatswain An officer of a ship
bob A light blow
bobbin A spool that holds thread
bobbinet A machine-made net
bobble To bob up and down
bobby Slang A policeman
bobcat A wild cat
bobolink A migratory songbird
bobsled A long sled
bobstay A steadying rope
bobtail A shortened tail
bobwhite A quail
bocaccio A rockfish
bod Slang Body
bodacious Slang Intrepidly daring
bode To be an omen of
bodega A grocery
bodice A corset
bodiless Having no body
bodkin An ornamental hairpin
body The torso of a human
bog A marsh
bogbean A plant
bogey A one over par golf score
bogeyman Variant of boogieman
boggle To bungle
boggy Swampy
bogie A railroad car
bogle The devil
bogus Fake
bogwood A preserved tree wood
bogy A hobgoblin

bogyman Variant of boogieman
bohea A black Chinese tea
boil To seethe
boiserie Wood paneling
bola A rope weapon
bold Courageous
boldface Printed in boldface
bole The trunk of a tree
bolection A molding
bolero A Spanish dance
boletus, pl **-tuses** or **-ti** A fungus
bolide A meteoric fireball
bolivar Monetary unit of
　Venezuela
bolivia A woolen cloth
boll The seed pod of certain plants
bollard A thick post on a wharf
bollix, bollox Slang To bungle
bollworm The larva of a moth
bolo A machete
bologna, baloney A sausage
bolson A flat arid valley
bolster A pillow
bolt A bar to fasten doors
boltonia A species of plant
boltrope A rope sewn into a sail
bolus, pl **-luses** or **-li** A small round
　mass
bomb An explosive weapon
bombard An early form of cannon
bombardon A musical instrument
bombast Pompous speech
bombe A frozen dessert
bombycid A moth
bonanza A rich mine
bonbon A candy
bond Anything that binds
bondage Servitude
bondmaid A female bondservant
bondsman A male bondservant
bone To debone
boneblack A black pigment
bonefish A marine game fish
bonehead Slang A dense person
boner Slang A blunder
boneset A species of plant
bonfire An outdoor fire
bong The sound of a bell
bongo An antelope
bonhomie Good nature

boniface An innkeeper
bonito, bonita A species of fish
bonne A maid
bonnet A hat with ribbons
bonny, bonnie Pretty
bonsai The art of growing dwarfed
　trees of shrubs
bonspiel, bonspell A curling match
bontebok An antelope
bonus, pl **-nuses** An extra dividend
bony Made of bone
bonze A Mahayana Buddhist monk
bonzer Slang Very good
boo To say "boo"
boob Slang A foolish person
booby A dunce
boodle Slang Money
boogieman A hobgoblin
boohoo To weep noisily
book A printed literary work
　The following words are listed
without definition (see Introduction):
bookcase　　bookmaker　bookshop
bookend　　bookman　　bookstall
bookish　　bookmark　　bookstand
booklet　　bookplate　　bookstore
booklore　　bookrack　　bookworm
booklouse　bookrest
bookie Slang A bookmaker
boom A booming sound
boomerang A flat, curved missile
boon A blessing
boondocks Slang Jungle
boor A bumpkin
boorish Rude
boost To increase
boot A shoe
bootblack A person who polishes
　shoes
bootee, bootie A baby shoe
booth A small enclosure
bootjack A device for holding a
　boot
bootleg To engage in bootlegging
bootlick To be servile toward
booty Stolen goods
booze Alcoholic drink
bop A blow
bora A violent cold wind

borage A plant
boral A compound used in reactor control
borane A chemical compound
borate A salt of boric acid
borax A white crystalline compound
borazon A boron nitride
bordello, bordel A brothel
border To put a border on
bordure A border around a shield
bore To make a hole
boreal Pertaining to the north
borecole A vegetable
boredom Condition of being bored
boreen An Irish lane
borer A tool used for boring
boric Containing boron
boride A boron compound
born Brought into life
borne A past participle of bear
bornite A copper ore
boron A nonmetallic element
borough An incorporated town
borrow To receive something on loan
borscht, borsht, borsch A Russian beet soup
bort An impure diamond
borzoi A Russian hound
boscage, boskage A thicket
bosh Nonsense
bosk, bosket A small thicket
bosky Wooded
bosom The female breasts
boson An atomic particle
boss A foreman
bossism Domination by political bosses
bossy Overbearing
bosun Variant of boatswain
bot, bott The larva of a botfly
botanical, botanic Pertaining to plants
botanist One who studies plants
botanize To secure plants for study
botany Biological science of plants
botch To bungle
botfly A species of insect
both The two

bother To irritate
bottle A receptacle
bottom The underside
bottomry A maritime contract
botulin A nerve poison
botulism A food poisoning
boucle A type of yarn
boudoir A dressing room
bouffant Puffed-out
bouffe Comic opera
bough A branch of a tree
bought Past tense of buy
bougie A wax candle
bouillon A clear broth
boulder A large rounded stone
boule A legislative assembly
boulevard A broad street
boulle Variant of buhl
bounce To rebound
bound To spring
boundary Something that indicates a limit
bounden Obliged
bounteous Plentiful
bountiful Plentiful
bounty A reward
bouquet A cluster of flowers
bourbon A whiskey
bourdon An organ stop
bourg A medieval town
bourgeois The middle class
bourn, bourne A small brook
bourre A French dance
bourse A stock exchange
bouse To pull up with a tackle
bout A contest
boutique A small gift shop
bouvardia A species of shrub
bovid A bovine
bovine A species of animal
bow The front of a boat
bowel An intestine
bower An arbor
bowery An early Dutch farm
bowfin A freshwater fish
bowfront Having an outward-curved front
bowhead A whale
bowknot A knot with decorative loops

bowl A drinking goblet
bowlder Variant of boulder
bowleg A leg having an outward curvature
bowler One that bowls
bowline A type of a knot
bowman An archer
bowse Variant of bouse
bowshot Distance an arrow can be shot
bowsprit A ship spar
bowstring The string of a bow
bowyer An archer
box A container
boxcar A railway car
boxfish A tropical marine fish
boxhaul To turn a ship around
boxthorn A shrub
boxwood A shrub or tree
boxy Like a box
boy A male youth
boyar A former Russian aristocrat
boycott To refrain from buying as a protest
boyish Characteristic of a boy
bozo *Slang* A guy
bra A brassiere
brabble To wrangle
brace A device that holds two parts together
bracelet An ornamental wrist band
bracero A Mexican laborer
brach A bitch hound
brachial A part of the arm
brachiate To swing by the arms
brachium, *pl* **brachia** The upper part of the arm
braciola, *pl* **-le** A meat dish
bracken A fern
bracket To classify
brackish Briny
bract A leaflike plant part
bracteole, bractlet A small bract
brad A small nail
bradawl A small awl
brae A hillside
brag To boast
braggart A bragger
braid To edge with ornamental trim

brail A line for furling sails
brain To smash the skull
brainless Stupid
brainpan The cranium
brainsick Mad
brainstem Part of the brain
brainwash To brainwash
brainy Smart
braise To cook in fat
brake To reduce the speed
brakeman A railroad employee
bramble A species of plant
bran The seed husks of cereals
branch A local unit of a business
branchia, *pl* **-chiae** A breathing organ
brand A trademark
brandish To wave a weapon
brandy An alcoholic beverage
branks A metal bridle
brannigan *Slang* A binge
branny Containing bran
brant A species of goose
brash Impudent
brasier Variant of brazier
brass An alloy of copper and zinc
brassard, brassart A cloth badge worn around the arm
brassie, brassy A golf club
brassiere A woman's undergarment
brat A nasty child
brattice A partition
brattle A clattering sound
bratwurst A sausage
bravado, *pl* **-does** or **-dos** False bravery
brave Valiant
bravo, *pl* **-voes** or **-vos** A killer
bravura A showy display
braw Splendid
brawl A noisy fight
brawn Solid muscles
bray To utter a loud cry
brayer A roller to spread ink
braze To make with brass
brazen Made of brass
brazier One who works in brass
brazilin, brasilin A chemical compound

breach A violation
bread A food
breadnut A tree
breadroot A plant
breadth Wide scope
break To smash
breakfast First meal of the day
breakneck Dangerous
breakup Act of breaking up
bream A species of fish
breast The human mammary gland
breath A momentary pause
breathe To live
breathy Marked by noisy breathing
breccia A type of rock
bred Past tense of breed
brede A braid
bree Broth
breech The buttocks
breeches Trousers
breed To bring about
breeks Breeches
breen Brownish-green color
breeze A gentle wind
breezeway A passageway
breezy Windy
bregma, pl **-mata** A junction point of the skull
brethren Plural of brother
breve A symbol over a vowel to designate a short sound
brevet A commission promoting an officer
brevetcy A rank awarded by brevet
breviary A prayer book
brevier A size of type
brevity Briefness of duration
brew To make a beverage
brewage Process of brewing
brewery A place where malt liquors are made
brewhouse A brewery
brewis A broth
briar A species of shrub or tree
briard A large dog
briarroot Root of the briar
briarwood Wood from briar root
bribe To offer a bribe to
brick A block of clay

brickbat Criticism
brickkiln A kiln in which bricks are baked
brickwork Working with bricks
brickyard A place where bricks are made
bricole A cushion shot in billiards
bridal A wedding
bride A woman to be married
bridge A card game
bridging Wooden braces between beams
bridle To control
bridoon A cavalry bit
brief Short in time
briefcase A portable case
brier Variant of briar
brig A ship's prison
brigade To group together
brigand A robber
bright Shining
brill An edible flatfish
brilliant Full of light
brimful, brimfull Completely full
brimstone Sulfur
brin One of the ribs of a fan
brindle A brindled color
brine Sea water
bring To carry along
brink The verge of something
briny Salty
brio Vigor
brioche A light-textured roll
briolette A pear-shaped gem
briquet, briquette A small block
brisance The shattering effect of an explosion
brisk Invigorating
brisket The chest of an animal
brisling A fish
bristle To react with fear
brit, britt Minute marine organisms
britannia A metal alloy
britches Breeches
brittle Fragile
broach A spit for roasting meat
broad Covering a wide scope
broadax, broadaxe A battle-ax
broadbill A species of bird

84

broadbrim A hat with a broad brim
broadcast To transmit a television or radio program
broadhead A flat arrowhead
broadleaf A tobacco plant
broadloom Designating a type of carpet
broadside An explosive denunciation
broadtail A breed of sheep
brocade A fabric
brocatel A fabric resembling brocade
broccoli A plant
broche Brocaded
brochette A small skewer
brochure A pamphlet
brock A badger
brocket A species of deer
brogan A heavy work shoe
brogue A strong accent
broider To embroider
broil To cook over a grill
broke Bankrupt
bromate To combine with bromine
brome A species of grass
bromide A bore
bromine A volatile liquid element
bromism Poisoning from overuse of bromides
bronchia Bronchial tubes
brochus, pl **-chi** A tracheal branch
broncho, bronco A wild horse
bronze An alloy of copper and tin
brooch A decorative pin
brood The young of certain animals
brooder One that broods
broody Moody
brook A small stream
brookite A mineral
brooklet A small brook
broom To sweep
broomrape A species of plant
broth A thin, clear soup
brothel A house of prostitution
brother A male having the same mother and father as another
brougham A carriage
brought Past tense of bring
brouhaha An uproar

brow A facial expression
browbeat To domineer
brown A color
brownie A cooky
brownout A partial dimming of lights
browse To look over casually
brucine A poisonous alkaloid
brugh A borough
bruin A bear
bruise To mar
bruiser *Slang* A large, husky man
bruit To repeat
brumal Wintry
brume Heavy fog
brunch A combination meal of breakfast and lunch
brunet, brunette Dark or brown in color
brunt The impact of a blow
brush A brief encounter
brushwork Work done with a brush
brusque, brusk Blunt
brut Very dry
brutal Cruel
brute A beast
brutify To brutalize
brutish Crude in manner
bryology The botany of bryophytes
bryony A climbing plant
bryozoan A species of animal
bub Fellow
bubble To form bubbles
bubbler A type of fountain
bubbly Full of bubbles
bubby *Slang* A woman's breast
bubinga A tree
bubo, pl **-boes** An inflamed swelling of a gland
bubonic Pertaining to a bubo
buccal Of the cheeks or mouth cavity
buccaneer A pirate
buck To rear up
buckaroo A cowboy
buckbean A marsh plant
buckboard A carriage
bucket A container
buckeye A species of tree

buckish Dandified
buckle To fasten
buckler A defense
bucko A bully
buckram A cotton fabric
bucksaw A wood-cutting saw
buckshee *Slang* A gratuity
buckshot A large lead shot
buckskin Skin of a male deer
buckthorn A species of shrub
bucktooth, *pl* **-teeth** A projecting upper front tooth
buckwheat A species of plant
bucolic Pastoral
bud To begin to grow
buddle A trough for separating ore
buddleia A shrub
buddy A good friend
budge To move slightly
budget To figure expenditures
budgie A bird
buff A color
buffalo To intimidate
buffet A meal where guests serve themselves
buffo, *pl* **-fi** A male comic opera singer
buffoon A clown
bug A species of insect
bugaboo A bugbear
bugbane A species of plant
bugbear An object of dread
bugger *Slang* A fellow
buggery Sodomy
buggy A small carriage
bughouse *Slang* An insane asylum
bugle A brass wind instrument
bugleweed A species of plant
bugloss A species of plant
bugseed A species of plant
bugsha A monetary unit of Yemen
buhl A style of decorative furniture
build To construct something
bulb Any plant that grows from a bulb
bulbar Characteristic of a bulb
bulbil A small bulb
bulbous Resembling a bulb
bulbul A species of songbird
bulge A protruding part

bulimia Insatiable appetite
bulk Great volume
bulkhead An upright partition in a ship
bull An adult male bovine mammal
bulla, *pl* **bullae** A large blister
bullace A plum
bullate Having a blistered appearance
bullbat A nighthawk
bulldog Stubborn
bulldoze To move with a bulldozer
bullet A projectile
bulletin A printed statement
bullfrog A species of frog
bullhead A species of catfish
bullhorn An electric megaphone
bullion Uncoined silver or gold
bullnose A disease of swine
bullock A steer
bullpen A pen where bulls are confined
bully A cruel person
bullyrag To mistreat by bullying
bulrush A marsh plant
bulwark A breakwater
bum A tramp
bumble To botch
bumboat A small boat
bumf, bumph *Slang* Toilet paper
bump To collide with
bumpkin An awkward person
bumptious Pushy
bun A small bread roll
bunch A group of items
bunco, bunko A confidence game
bund An embankment
bundle A number of objects tied together
bung A bunghole
bungalow A small cottage
bunghole The hole in a barrel
bungle To act ineptly
bunion A painful swelling on the foot
bunk A place for sleeping
bunker A sand trap
bunkmate A person who shares rough sleeping quarters
bunkum Meaningless talk

bunny   A rabbit

bunt   The act of bunting

buntline   A rope used for hauling up a sail

bunya   An evergreen tree

buoy   A device for keeping a person afloat

buoyancy   Cheerfulness

buoyant   Having buoyancy

buprestid   A species of beetles

bur, burr   A plant producing burs

buran, bura   A violent Russian windstorm

burble   A bubbling sound

burbot   A freshwater fish

burden   A responsibility

burdock   A species of plant

bureau, *pl* -**reaus** or **bureaux**   A chest of drawers

burette, buret   A measuring tube

burg   A city

burgee   A flag displayed by a yacht

burgeon   To begin to blossom

burger   A hamburger

burgess   A citizen of an English borough

burgh   A borough in Scotland

burgher   A solid citizen

burglar   A housebreaker

burgle   To burglarize

burgoo   Oatmeal gruel

burgrave   A German governor

burhead   A person with a close-cropped haircut

burial   The interment of a dead person

burin   The technique of an engraver's work

burke   To murder by suffocation

burl   A knot in cloth

burlap   A coarsely woven cloth

burlesque   Vaudeville entertainment

burley   A tobacco

burly   Husky

burn   To destroy with fire

burnet   A species of plant

burnish   To polish by rubbing

burnoose, burnous   A hooded cloak worn by Arabs

burnout   A fire

burnsides   Side whiskers

burnt   Scorched

burp   To belch

burr   A rough edge

burro   A small donkey

burrow   A tunnel dug by a small animal

burry   Prickly

bursa, *pl* -**sae** or -**sas**   A saclike cavity

bursal   Fiscal

bursar   A treasurer

bursary   A treasury

burse   A small pouch

burseed   A plant

bursiform   Shaped like a pouch

bursitis   Inflammation of a bursa

burst   An explosion

burton   A tackle used to tighten rigging

burweed   A species of plant

bury   To place in the ground

bus, *pl* **buses** or **busses**   A motor vehicle for carrying passengers

busby   A tall fur hat

bush   A thicket

bushbuck   An African antelope

bushel   A unit of measure

bushing   A metal lining used to reduce friction

bushtit   A titmouse

bushwhack   To ambush

busily   In a busy manner

business   The trade in which a person is engaged

busk   A corset

buskin   A high shoe

busman   One who operates a bus

buss   To kiss loudly

bust   A woman's bosom

bustard   A species of Old World bird

buster *Slang*   A man

bustle   Commotion

busty   Full-bosomed

busy   Occupied

busybody   A person who meddles into the affairs of others

but   On the contrary

butane   A flammable gas
butanol   A flammable alcohol
butanone   A flammable ketone
butch   Masculine in appearance
butcher   One who sells meats
butchery   A slaughterhouse
buteo   A species of hawk
butle   To serve as a butler
butler   A male servant
butlery   A serving room
butt   To ram
butte   An isolated hill
butter   Flattery
butterbur   A species of plant
buttercup   A species of plant
butterfat   Fat of milk from which butter is made
butterfly   A species of insect
butternut   A tree
buttery   Spread with butter
buttock   Either of the two parts of the rump
button   The tip of a foil
buttress   Serves to support
butyl   A hydrocarbon radical
butylene   A gaseous hydrocarbon
butyrate   A salt of butyric acid

butyric   Derived from butter
butyrin   A chemical compound found in butter
buxom   Ample of figure
buy   To purchase
buzz   To bustle
buzzard   A species of vulture
bwana   Boss
by   Next to
bye   A side issue
bygone   Past
bylaw   A rule
bypast   Bygone
byre   A barn
byrnie   A coat of mail
byroad   A back road
byssus, *pl*-**suses** or **byssi**   A linen used for wrapping mummies
bystander   A person who views an event
bystreet   A side street
bytalk   Small talk
byway   A side road
byword   A proverb
bywork   Work done during one's spare time
byzant   Variant of bezant

cab   A taxicab
cabal   A secret plot
cabala, cabbala   A secret doctrine
cabalism   Adherence to a cabala
caballero   A cavalier
cabana   A bathhouse
cabaret   A restaurant with entertainment
cabbage   An edible plant
cabby   A cab driver

caber   A heavy wooden pole heaved in a Scottish contest
cabezon, cabezone   A large, edible fish
cabin   A small hut
cabinet   A cupboard with shelves and drawers
cable   A heavy steel rope
cablegram   A telegram sent by undersea cable

cablet A small cable
cableway A suspended conveyor system
cabman The driver of a horse-drawn cab
cabochon A style of gem cutting
cabomba Plants of the waterlily family
caboodle The bunch
caboose The last car on a freight train
cabotage Trade in coastal waters
cabretta Leather made from sheepskin
cabrilla A species of sea bass
cabriole A type of furniture leg
cabriolet A two-wheeled carriage
cabstand Place where taxicabs are parked
cacao An evergreen tropical American tree
cachalot The sperm whale
cache A place to hide valuables
cachectic Pertaining to cachexia
cachepot An ornamental container for a flowerpot
cachet A seal on a document
cachexia A wasting of the body during a chronic disease
cachou An astringent
cachucha An Andalusian solo dance
cacique An Indian chief
cackle The sound of cackling
cacodyl A poisonous liquid
cacophony Dissonance
cactus, *pl* **-ti** or **-tuses** A species of plant
cacuminal A phonetical sound
cad An ungentlemanly man
cadaster, cadastre A public record of land ownership
cadaver A dead body
caddie, caddy A boy who does odd jobs
caddis, caddice A coarse woolen fabric
cade A European plant
cadelle A small beetle
cadence, cadency Rhythmic flow

cadent Having rhythm
cadenza An elaborate flourish in music
cadet A student training to be an officer
cadge To get by begging
cadi A Moslem judge
cadmium A metallic element
cadre A framework
caduceus, *pl* **-cei** An ancient staff
caducity Senility
caducous Transitory
caecum Variant of cecum
caesium Variant of cesium
caestus Variant of cestus
caesura, *pl* **-ras** or **-surae** A pause in a line of poetry
cafard Boredom
cafe A bar
cafeteria A type of restaurant
caffeine, caffein An alkaloid
caftan A full-length tunic
cage Anything that confines
cageling A caged bird
cagey, cagy Careful
cahier A notebook
cahoots A questionable partnership
caid A Muslim leader
caiman A species of crocodile
cain Variant of kain
caique A small sailing vessel
caird An itinerant handyman
cairn A memorial made of stones
caisson A watertight structure
caitiff A wretch
cajeput, cajuput An Australian tree
cajole To coax
cake A baked dessert
cakewalk A strutting dance
calabash A tropical American tree
calaboose *Slang* Jail
caladium A species of plant
calamine An oxide used in skin lotions
calamint A species of plant
calamite A species of plant
calamity A disaster
calamus, *pl* **-mi** A species of tropi-

cal palm

calando Gradually diminishing in tempo and volume

calash A woman's folding bonnet

calathus, *pl* **-thi** A Greek vase-shaped basket

calcar, *pl* **calcaria** An anatomical spur

calces Alternate plural of calx

calcic Composed of calcium

calcicole A plant that thrives in soil rich in lime

calcific Containing salts of lime

calcify To make chalky

calcine To undergo calcination

calcite A mineral

calcium A metallic element

calcspar A calcite

calculate To reckon

calculous Pertaining to calculus

calculus, *pl* **-li** A branch of mathematics

caldera A volcanic crater

caldron A large kettle

calendar To schedule

calender A machine that smooths paper or cloth

calends The first day of the month in the ancient Roman calendar

calf, *pl* **calves** A young cow

calfskin The hide of a calf

caliber, calibre Degree of worth

calibrate To determine the caliber of

calices Plural of calix

caliche A mineral

calico Made of calico

calipash An edible part of a turtle

calipee Another edible part of a turtle

caliper An instrument for measuring

caliph, calif A Muslim leader

caliphate The office of a caliph

calisaya The bark from which quinine is obtained

calix, *pl* **calices** A chalice

calk To caulk

call To awaken

calla A species of plant

callboard A backstage bulletin board

callboy One who tells actors when it is time to go on

calliope A musical instrument

calliper Variant of caliper

callosity Hardheartedness

callous Toughened

callow Immature

callus A hard growth

calm Composed

calomel A chemical compound

caloric Relating to calories

calorie A unit of heat

calotte A skullcap

caloyer A monk

calpac, calpack A cap worn in Turkey

calque To adapt a borrowing of a word from one language to another

caltrop, caltrap A species of plant

calumet A ceremonial pipe

calumny Slander

calutron A spectrometer used to separate isotopes

calvary A representation of the Crucifixion

calve To give birth to a calf

calx, *pl* **calxes** or **calces** Lime

calycine Resembling a calyx

calycle An epicalyx

calypso A type of music

calyptra A hood-shaped organ of flowers

calyx, *pl* **-lyxes** or **calyces** A cuplike animal structure

cam A wheel mounted on a rotating shaft

camas, camass A species of plant

camber To give a slight arch to

cambist A dealer in international exchange

cambium A layer of plant tissue

cambogia A gum resin

cambric A fabric

came Past tense of come

camel A humped mammal

camelback Having a shape with a hump

cameleer A person who drives a

camel

camellia, camelia A species of shrub

cameo A brief appearance by an actor

camera An apparatus for taking pictures

cameral Pertaining to a judge's chamber

camion A truck

camisa A shirt

camisado A surprise attack by night

camise A tunic

camisole A short negligee

camlet An Oriental cloth

camomile, chamomile A medicinal herb

camp Army life

campaign A series of military operations

campfire An outdoor camp fire

camphene A chemical compound

camphire Henna

camphor A chemical compound

campion A species of plant

campo A grassy plain

camporee A gathering of Boy Scouts

campsite An area for camping

campstool A folding stool

campus The grounds of a school

camshaft An engine shaft

can Ability

canaille The masses

canal A man-made waterway

canalize To convert into a canal

canape An appetizer

canard A false story

canary A songbird

canasta A card game

cancan A dance

cancel To annul

cancer Malignant growth

cancroid Similar to a cancer

candela A unit of luminous intensity

candent Incandescent

candid Fair

candidate A person who seeks an office

candied Cooked with sugar

candle A wax that is burned for light

candlenut A tree

candlepin A bowling pin

candor, candour Sincerity

candy A sweet confection

cane A walking stick

canebrake A thicket of cane

canescent Hoary

cangue A Chinese punishing device

canine A canine animal

canister A container

canker An animal disease

canna A species of plant

cannabin A material extracted from cannabis

cannabis The dried tops of the hemp plant

cannel A coal

cannelon A roll stuffed with meat

cannery A place where foods are canned

cannibal A person who eats the flesh of another

cannikin, canikin A wooden bucket

canning The act of canning foods

cannon A weapon

cannonade To assault with cannon fire

cannoneer A gunner

cannonry Artillery

cannot The negative form of can

cannula, pl **-las** or **-lae** A tube for draining fluid

canny Shrewd

canoe A light boat

canon A secular law

canoness A member of a religious community

canonical, canonic Authoritative

canonist A person skilled in canon law

canonize To sanctify

canonry The position of a canon

canoodle To caress

canopy A high covering

canorous Tuneful

canst The second person singular

present tense of can

cant A slanted edge

cantabile In a smooth flowing style

cantala A century plant

cantata A musical composition

canteen A flask for drinking water

canter A moderate gait

canthus, *pl* **-thi** A corner of the eye

canticle A song

cantina A saloon

cantle The rear part of a saddle

canto A division of a long poem

canton A division of a flag

cantor The soloist in a synagogue

cantrip A prank

canula Variant of cannula

canulate Variant of cannulate

canvas A heavy fabric

canvass To poll

canyon A narrow chasm

canzone A poetic form

canzonet A lighthearted song

cap A covering for the head

capable Having ability

capacious Roomy

capacity Volume

caparison Horse trappings

cape A promontory

capelin A small fish

caper A skip

capeskin Soft leather made from sheepskin

caph Variant of kaph

capias A writ authorizing an arrest

capillary Fine and slender

capital Material wealth

capitate Enlarged at an end

capitol A building for the state legislature

capitular Belonging to a chapter

capo A bar used in playing certain guitars

capon A castrated rooster

caporal A tobacco

capote A hooded cloak

capper One that makes caps

capriccio, *pl* **-cios** or **-ci** A fanciful whim

caprice An impulsive change of mind

caprifig A variety of fig

capriole A leap

capsicin A liquid used in flavoring

capsicum A species of plant

capsize To overturn

capstan An apparatus for hoisting weights

capstone The final stroke

capsular Pertaining to a capsule

capsulate In a capsule

capsule A gelatinous sheath enclosing medicine

captain One who leads

caption A motion picture subtitle

captious Deceptive

captivate To fascinate

captive One who is confined as a prisoner

captor One who keeps a person captive

capture To take captive

capuche, capouch A hood on a cloak

capuchin A hooded cloak worn by women

capybara A rodent

car An automobile

caraboa The water buffalo

carabin, carabine Variants of carbine

caracal A wild cat

caracara A species of bird

carack Variant of carrack

caracole, caracol A half turn performed by a horseman

caracul Fur of a karakul lamb

carafe A decanter

carageen Variant of carrageen

caramel A candy

carangid A species of fish

carapace A hard outer covering

carat A unit of weight for precious stones

caravan A large covered vehicle

caravel A light sailing ship

caraway A plant

carbide A carbon compound

carbine A rifle

carbinol Wood alcohol

carbon A nonmetallic element

carbonate To carbonize
carbonyl A metal compound
carboxyl A univalent radical
carboy A container for corrosive liquids
carburet To mix with carbon
carcajou The wolverine
carcanet A jeweled necklace
carcass A dead body
card An amusing person
cardamom, cardamum, cardamon A tropical plant
cardia An opening of the esophagus
cardiac Pertaining to the heart
cardigan A sweater
cardinal Dark to deep red color
cardioid A heart-shaped curve
cardoon A plant
cardsharp An expert in cheating at cards
care Caution
careen To move rapidly
career Life work
carefree Free of worry
caress A gentle touch
caret A proofreading symbol
careworn Weary from worry
carfare Fare charged a passenger
cargo Freight carried by a vehicle
carhop A waiter
caribe The piranha
caribou A large deer
caries Decay of a tooth
carillon A set of bells
carina, pl **-nae** A ridge in the petals of flowers
carinate Ridged
carioca A dance
cariole A cart
carious Decayed
carl, carle A rude person
carling, carline A beam supporting the deck of a ship
carmine A crimson pigment
carnage A massacre
carnal Sensual
carnation A plant
carnauba A palm tree
carnelian A variety of chalcedony
carnival A festival

carnivore A flesh-eating mammal
carny *Slang* A person who works for a carnival
carob An evergreen tree
caroche, caroach, caroch A carriage
carol To sing
carom A billiard
carotene, carotin A plant pigment
carotid An artery
carousal A wild drinking party
carouse Drunken merrymaking
carousel A merry-go-round
carp To fuss
carpal Near the carpus
carpel The female organ of a flower
carpenter To work as a carpenter
carpet A covering for the floor
carpetbag A bag made of carpet
carping Complaining
carpology An area of botany
carpus, pl **-pi** The wrist
carrack, carack A merchant ship
carrel, carrell A cubicle for private study
carriage A horse-drawn vehicle
carrion Decaying flesh
carroom Variant of carom
carrot A vegetable
carroty Similar to a carrot
carry To hold something while moving
carryall A large bag
carsick Sickness by vehicular motion
cart A two-wheeled vehicle
cartage The process of transporting by cart
carte A menu
cartel A bloc
cartilage A fibrous tissue
carton A container
cartoon A humorous drawing
cartouch, cartouche An ornamental scroll-like tablet
cartridge A container
cartwheel The wheel of a cart
caruncle A fleshy outgrowth
carve To slice
carvel Variant of caravel
caryatid A column sculptured in

the form of a woman

casaba A variety of winter melon

casava Variant of cassava

cascade A waterfall

cascara The cascara buckthorn

case The situation

caseate To undergo caseation

casefy To become cheeselike

casein A milk protein

casemate An artillery enclosure

casement A covering

caseous Resembling cheese

casern, caserne A military barracks

caseworm An insect larva

cash Currency

cashaw Variant of cushaw

cashbook A book of money records

cashew An evergreen tree

cashier An employee who handles money

cashmere A fine wool

casimere A woolen cloth

casing A case

casino A gambling house

cask A barrel

casket A coffin

casque A helmet

cassation Annulment

cassava A species of plant

casserole A dish in which food is baked and served

cassette A case containing videotape

cassia A species of tree

cassino A card game

cassis A European bush

cassock A garment

cast To throw away

castanets A pair of shells to clap together for rhythmical accompaniment

castaway Thrown away

caste A social class

caster A person that casts

castigate To punish

castle A mansion

castoff Something that has been discarded

castor A beaver hat

castrate To geld

casual Informal

casuist One who solves problems

cat A carnivorous mammal

cataclysm A violent upheaval

catacombs Underground chambers

catalase An enzyme

catalo A hybrid between a cow and a buffalo

catalogue, catalog To list in a catalog

catalpa A species of tree

catalyst A substance that increases chemical reaction

catalyze To modify the chemical reaction

catamaran A boat with two hulls

catamite A boy kept by a pederast

catamount A species of wildcat

catapult A slingshot

cataract A large waterfall

catarrh Inflammation of the mucous membranes

catbird A North American songbird

catboat A sailboat

catbrier A species of vine

catcall A whistle expressing disapproval

catch To overtake

catchall A container for a variety of possessions

catchfly A species of plant

catchpole A sheriff's officer

catchup Variant of ketchup

catchword An often repeated word

catchy Tricky

cate A choice food

catechism A book of the basic principles of a religion

catechist One who catechizes

catechu A resin used in tanning

category A division in a system of classification

catena, *pl* **-nae** or **-nas** A closely linked series

catenary A mathematical curve

catenate To form into a chain

cater To provide food

catface A deformity in fruit

catfall An anchor chain
catfish A species of fish
catgut A strong cord
cathead A beam projecting from the bow of a ship
cathedra, *pl* **-drae** The office of a bishop
cathedral An important church
catheter A tube inserted into a body channel
cathexis The concentration of emotional energy upon some object
cathode A negatively charged electrode
catholic Universal
cathouse *Slang* A brothel
cation A positively charged ion
catkin A drooping flower cluster
catlike Silent
catling, catlin Catgut used for stringing a musical instrument
catmint Catnip
catnip A plant to which cats are attracted
catoptric Of reflected images
catsup Variant of ketchup
cattail A species of marsh plant
cattalo Variant of catalo
cattle Domesticated bovines
catty Catlike
catwalk A narrow pathway
caucus, *pl* **-cuses** or **-cusses** A political meeting
caudad Toward the tail of the body
caudal Taillike
caudate Having a tail
caudex, *pl* **-dices** or **-dexes** A woody, trunklike stem
caudillo A military leader who sets himself up as a dictator
caudle A beverage
caught Past tense of catch
caul A fetal membrane
cauldron Variant of caldron
caulicle A small stem
cauline Growing on a stem
caulk To make cracks airtight
causal Involving a cause
cause A basis for a decision
causerie A chat
causeway A paved road

caustic Able to dissolve by chemical action
cauterize To sear
cautery A caustic agent
caution A warning
cavalcade A display
cavalier A gallant gentleman
cavalla A species of fish
cavalry A mobile army unit
cave An opening beneath the earth's surface
caveat A warning
cavefish A species of fish
cavern A large cave
cavernous Filled with caverns
cavetto, *pl* **-vetti** or **-tos** A molding for cornices
caviar, caviare The roe of sturgeon
cavicorn Having hollow horns
cavil To quibble about
cavity A hole
cavort To frolic
cavy A species of rodent
caw The sound uttered by a crow
cay A key
cayman Variant of caiman
cayuse An Indian pony
cease To discontinue
cecum, *pl* **-ca** A cavity with only one opening
cedar A species of evergreen tree
cede To yield
cedi The monetary unit of Ghana
cedilla A pronunciation mark
cee The letter *c*
ceiba A species of tree
ceil To make a ceiling for
ceiling The maximum limit
celadon A color
celandine A plant
celebrant A person who participates in a religious rite
celebrate To observe an occasion with festivity
celebrity A famous person
celeriac A variety of celery
celerity Speed
celery A plant
celesta, celeste A musical instrument
celestial Pertaining to the heavens

95

celiac Relating to the abdomen

celibacy Condition of being sexually dormant

celibate One who remains sexually inactive

cell A room in a jail

cella, *pl* **cellae** Inner room of an ancient Roman temple

cellar A room under a building

cellarer A member of a monastery

cello A musical instrument

celloidin A cellular material

cellular Containing a cell

cellule A small cell

celt A prehistoric tool

cembalo A harpsichord

cement To bind

cementum A substance covering the root of a tooth

cemetery A graveyard

cenacle A small dining room

cenobite A member of a religious community

cenotaph An empty tomb

cenote A limestone well

cense To perfume with incense

censer A vessel for incense

censor A person who censures

censure To blame

census An official count of the population

cent A monetary unit

cental A hundredweight

centaur A mythological creature

centaury A species of plant

centavo A Spanish monetary unit

centenary Occurring once every 100 years

center An axis

centile Percentile

centime The 100th part of a franc

centimo A small coin

centipede A species of arthropod

centner A unit of weight

cento A literary work

central Being the center

centric Having a center

centrist One who takes a position in the political center

centroid The center of mass of an object

centrum, *pl* **-trums** or **-tra** The major part of a vertebra

centum One hundred

centuple Multiplied by a hundred

centurion A Roman officer

century A period of 100 years

ceorl A freeman of low birth

cephalad Toward the head

cephalic Relating to the head

cephalin A chemical

ceramal An alloy

ceramic An item made by firing clay

cerastes A species of snake

cerate A medicated fat

ceratoid Hornlike

cercaria, *pl* **-iae** or **-as** The larva of a worm

cercis A shrub

cercus, *pl* **-ci** An insect appendage

cere To wrap in a cloth

cereal An edible grain

cerebral Pertaining to the brain

cerebrum, *pl* **-brums** or **-bra** A part of the brain

cerement Cerecloth

ceremony A strict observance

cereus A species of cactus

cerise A color

cerium A metallic element

cermet A ceramal

cernuous Drooping

cero An edible fish

cerotype A process of engraving

cerous Containing cerium

certain Positive

certes Truly

certify To vouch for in writing

certitude Complete assurance

cerulean Azure

cerumen Earwax

ceruse White lead

cerusite Lead carbonate

cervical Pertaining to the neck

cervine Resembling a deer

cervix, *pl* **-vixes** or **-vices** The neck

cesium A metallic element

cess A tax

cession A surrendering

cesspool A sewer

cestode A species of flatworm
cestus, *pl* **-ti** A girdle
cetacean An aquatic mammal
cetane A diesel fuel
cete A company of badgers
cetology The study of aquatic mammals
chacma A baboon
chaconne A dance
chaeta, *pl* **-tae** A bristle of certain worms
chafe To annoy
chafer A species of beetle
chaff Worthless matter
chagrin To humiliate
chain A mountain range
chainman A person who holds the measuring chain in surveying
chair A piece of furniture
chairman One who presides over a meeting
chaise A light carriage
chalah Variant of challah
chalaza, *pl* **-zae** or **-zas** A band of tissue in an egg
chalcid A species of wasp
chaldron A unit of dry measure
chalet An Alpine dwelling
chalice A goblet
chalk Calcium carbonate
challah Jewish bread
challenge An objection
challis, challie A fabric
chalone A hormone
cham A khan
chamber A judge's office
chambray A type of gingham
chameleon A species of lizard
chamfer To bevel
chamfron, chamfrain Armor for a horse's head
chamiso, chamise A shrub
chamois Leather made from animal hide
champ A champion
champagne A white wine
champaign A plain
champak, champac A tree of India
champion One that wins first prize
chance An opportunity

chancel Space around the altar
chancery A court of public record
chancre A hard lesion
chancroid A soft lesion
chancy Uncertain
chandelle A sudden, climbing turn of an aircraft
chandler A person who makes candles
change To alter
channel The bed of a river
chanson A song
chant A song or melody
chantage Blackmail
chanteuse A woman nightclub singer
chantey, chanty A song sung by sailors
chantry An endowment to cover expenses of prayers
chaos Total confusion
chap A fellow
chaparral A dense thicket
chapati Bread of India
chapbook A small book of poems
chape A metal tip of a scabbard
chapeau, *pl* **-peaux** A hat
chapel A place of worship
chaperon A person who supervises a group of young people
chapiter The capital of a column
chaplain A clergyman
chaplet A wreath for the head
chapman A peddler
chaps Leather trousers
chapter A division of a book
char To scorch
characin, characid A species of fish
character Reputation
charades A parlor game
charcoal A black, porous carbon
chard A variety of beet
charge To command
charily Carefully
chariot An ancient vehicle
charisma, charism A rare quality
charity An act of good will
charkha, charka A spinning wheel of India

charlatan   A quack
charlock   A weedy plant
charlotte   A cold dessert
charm   A quality that attracts
charnel   A charnel house
charqui   Jerky
charr   Variant of char
chart   To make a chart of
chartist   A stock market specialist
chary   Careful
chase   To run after
chasm   A deep narrow gorge
chasse   A dance movement
chasseur   A soldier
chassis   The landing gear of an aircraft
chaste   Modest
chasten   To restrain
chastise   To punish
chastity   Virginity
chasuble   A garment worn by a
priest
chat   An informal talk
chateau, pl chateaux   A French
manor house
chatelain   The keeper of a castle
chattel   A slave
chauffeur   One employed as a
driver
chausses   Armor for the legs and
feet
chaw   To chew
chayote   A tropical American vine
chazan, chazzen   A cantor in a
synagogue
cheap   Inexpensive
cheat   To swindle
cheaters Slang   Eyeglasses
chebec   A small bird
check   A ticket of identification
checkmate   To defeat completely
checkoff   The collection of dues
deducted from wages
checkrein   A rein on a horse's bit
checkrow   To plant in checkrows
cheek   Sauciness
cheeky   Saucy
cheep   The sound of a young bird
cheer   Happiness
cheerio   Used in greeting or parting

cheese   A food prepared from the
curd of milk
cheetah   A wild cat
chef   A cook
chela   A pupil of a guru
chelate   Chemically bonded
cheloid   Variant of keloid
chemic   Chemical
chemical   Pertaining to chemistry
chemise   A woman's undergarment
chemist   A scientist specializing in
chemistry
chemurgy   The development of new
chemical products
chenille   A fabric
chenopod   A species of plant
cheque   Variant of check
cherish   To hold dear
cheroot   A cigar with square-cut
ends
cherry   A species of tree
chert   A compact rock
cherub, pl -ubim   A winged celestial
being
chervil   A species of plant
chess   A game
chessman   Piece used in playing
chess
chest   A sturdy container
chestnut   A species of tree
chesty   Conceited
chetah   Variant of cheetah
cheth   Variant of heth
chevalet   The bridge of a musical
instrument
chevron   A V-shaped pattern
chew   To masticate
chewink   The towhee bird
chez   At the home of
chi   The 22nd letter of the Greek
alphabet
chiao   A monetary unit of China
chiasma, chiasm   A crossing of two
tracts
chiasmus, pl -mi   A rhetorical
inversion
chiaus   An official Turkish
emissary
chibouk   A Turkish tobacco pipe
chic   Stylish

chicane To deceive
chicanery A trick
chiccory Variant of chicory
chichi Showy
chick A child
chickadee A species of bird
chickaree A squirrel
chicken Domestic fowl
chickpea A bushy plant
chickweed A species of plant
chicle The juice of the sapodilla
chico A species of greasewood
chicory A plant
chide To reprimand
chief A leader
chieftain The leader of a tribe
chiffchaff A small European
  warbler
chiffon A fabric
chigger A parasitic mite
chignon A knot of hair worn at the
  back of the head
chigoe A small flea
chilblain An inflammation
child A son or daughter
childbed The state of a woman in
  childbirth
childe A child of noble birth
childish Foolish
childlike Like a child
children Plural of child
chili, chile, chilli A hot pepper
chiliad One thousand years
chiliasm A religious doctrine
chill A moderate coldness
chiller A thriller
chilly Cold
chilopod A species of arthropod
chime A bell
chimera A fire-breathing monster
chimney A structure from which
  smoke escapes
chimp A chimpanzee
chin To chatter
china Porcelain ware
chinch A bedbug
chine The spine
chink A narrow opening
chino A fabric
chintz, chints A fabric

chintzy Cheap
chip A small piece broken off
chipmunk A species of rodent
chippy The chipping sparrow
chirk Cheerful
chirp To peep
chirr A trilling sound
chirrup To twitter
chisel A metal tool
chit A check
chital The axis deer
chitchat Small talk
chitin A component of insect shells
chiton A tunic worn in ancient
  Greece
chitter To twitter as a bird
chivalry A group of knights
chivaree A noisy serenade for
  newlyweds
chive A plant
chivvy, chivy To scurry
chlamys A short mantle worn in
  ancient Greece
chloral A chemical compound
chlorate A chemical salt
chloric Pertaining to chlorine
chloride A chlorine compound
chlorine A gaseous element
chlorite A mineral
chock A wedge placed under
  something
chocolate A candy
choice The selection
choir A company of singers
choke To become suffocated
chokebore A shotgun bore
choler Anger
cholera An epidemic disease
choleric Bad-tempered
choline A B vitamin
cholla A species of cactus
chomp Variant of champ
chon The monetary unit of South
  Korea
chondrite A meteoric stone
choose To prefer above others
chop To cut into bits
chopine, chopin A 17th century
  shoe
choragic Pertaining to a choragus

99

choragus, *pl* **-gi** The leader of the chorus in Greek drama
choral Pertaining to a choir
chorale A choir
chord Harmony
chordal Relating to a harmonic chord
chordate A species of animal
chore A minor task
chorea A nervous disorder
choriamb A type of metrical foot
choric In the style of a chorus
chorine *Slang* A chorus girl
chorion The membrane enclosing the embryo in reptiles, birds, and mammals
chorister A choirboy
choroid A membrane of the eye
chortle To chuckle throatily
chorus A body of singers
chose Past tense of choose
chosen Selected from others
chott The bed of a salt marsh
chough A crowlike bird
chow A dog
chowchow A relish
chowder A soup
chresard Water in the soil
chrism A consecrated oil
chrisom A cloth worn by an infant for baptism
christen To baptize
christy, christie A ski turn
chroma The purity of a color
chromate A salt of chromic acid
chromatic Pertaining to colors
chrome Chromium
chromic Pertaining to chromium
chromite A chromium ore
chromium A metallic element
chromous Pertaining to chromium
chronaxy The time necessary to stimulate a muscle electrically
chronic Lingering
chronicle A record of historic events
chthonic Pertaining to the spirits of the underworld
chub A species of fish
chubby Plump

chuck To toss
chuckle To laugh to oneself
chufa A sedge
chug A sound made by a laboring engine
chukar An Old World partridge
chukka A short boot
chukker, chukkar A period of play in a polo match
chum A friend
chummy Friendly
chump A dolt
chunk A substantial amount
church A building for worship
churl A boorish person
churlish Boorish
churn To make butter
churr The trilling sound made by some birds and insects
chute A waterfall
chutney, chutnee A relish
chutzpah, chutzpa *Slang* Gall
chyle A digestive fluid
chyme Partly digested food
chymosin An enzyme
ciborium, *pl* **-boria** A canopy over an altar
cicada, *pl* **-das** or **-dae** A species of insect
cicatrix, *pl* **cicatrices** Scar tissue
cicely Parsley herb
cicero A unit of measurement for type
cicerone, *pl* **-nes** or **-ni** A guide for sightseers
cichlid A species of fish
cider The juice pressed from apples
cigar A roll of tobacco leaves for smoking
cigarette, cigaret A roll of finely cut tobacco for smoking
cigarillo A small, narrow cigar
cilantro Coriander used in Oriental cooking
ciliary Resembling cilium
ciliate Having cilia
cilice A haircloth
cilium, *pl* **cilia** A hairlike projection
cimex, *pl* **cimices** A species of insect

100

cinch A girth for a saddle
cinchona A species of tree
cincture A girdle
cinder A burned substance not reduced to ashes
cinema, cine A motion picture
cineol, cineole Eucalyptol
cinerin Compound used in insecticides
cingulum, pl **-la** A girdlelike band
cinnabar The principal ore of mercury
cinnamon A spice from tree bark
cinquain A five-line stanza
cinque The number five
cion A cutting from a tree
cipher Zero
circa About
circadian Exhibiting an approximate 24-hour period
circle To revolve around
circlet A small circle
circuit A closed curve
circular Of a circle
circulate To distribute
circus An entertainment featuring a variety of acts
cirque A steep hollow
cirrate Cloudy
cirrhosis A disease of the liver
cirriped A species of crustacean
cirrus, pl **cirri** A high-altitude cloud
cisco A species of fish
cislunar Between the earth and the moon
cist A receptacle
cistern A tank for catching water
cisterna, pl **-nae** A fluid-containing sac
citadel A fortress
citation The act of citing
cite To commend
cithara A musical instrument
cither, cithern A musical instrument
citied Having cities
citizen A resident of a city
citral A liquid used in perfume

citrate A salt of citric acid
citric Of citrus fruits
citrine A variety of quartz
citron A variety of watermelon
citrus, citrous A species of tree
cittern A guitar
city An incorporated town
civet A species of catlike mammal
civic Pertaining to a city
civicism Adherence to the rules of civic government
civil Pertaining to a city
civilian A person in civil life
civility Courtesy
civvies, civies Slang Civilian clothes
clabber Curdled milk
clack To cackle as a hen
clad To cover with a medal
clag To clog
claim To maintain
claimant A person making a claim
clam To dig for clams
clamant Loud
clambake A seashore picnic
clamber To scramble
clamor A public outcry
clamp A device used to grip
clamshell The shell of a clam
clamworm A species of marine worm
clan A group of relatives
clang To make a metallic sound
clangor Loud ringing
clank A metallic sound
clannish Pertaining to a clan
clansman One belonging to a clan
clap To strike the palms of the hands together
clapboard A long, narrow board
claptrap Insincere language
claque A group of adulating admirers
clarence A carriage
claret A wine
clarify To make clear
clarinet A musical instrument
clarion A medieval trumpet

clarity Clearness
clarkia A species of plant
claro A mild cigar
clary A species of plant
clash To strike together
clasp A fastening
class A social stratum
classic Having lasting significance
classis A religious governing body
classy *Slang* Elegant
clastic Fragmental
clathrate Having a lattice-like structure
clatter To talk noisily
clause A provision in a document
clavate Club-shaped
clave Past tense of cleave
claver To gossip
clavicle The collarbone
clavier A keyboard
claw To scratch
clay Mud
claymore A large broadsword
clean Unsoiled
cleanse To clean
cleanser A soap
cleanup A large profit
clear Unclouded
clearweed A plant
clearwing A species of moth
cleat A device used to grip a pole
cleave To stick fast
cleek A golf club
clef A symbol on a musical staff
cleft Separated
clematis A species of plant
clemency Mercy
clement Mild
clench To grip tightly
cleome A species of plant
clepe To call by the name of
clergy The body of men ordained for religious service
cleric Pertaining to the clergy
clerihew A humorous quatrain
clerisy The well-educated class
clerk A person who keeps records
clerkly Pertaining to a clerk
clever Bright
clevis A metal piece used for attaching a drawbar to a plow

clew A ball of thread
cliche A trite expression
click A sharp sound
client A customer
clientele A body of patrons
cliff, clift An overhanging face of rock
climate Meteorological conditions
climax Culmination
climb To rise up
clime Climate
clinch To make final
cline A series of changes within members of a species
cling To hold fast
clingfish A species of fish
clinic A medical center
clinician A doctor specializing in clinical studies
clink To jingle
clip To cut off
clipt Past participle of clip
clique An exclusive group
clitoris A female sex organ
cloaca, *pl* **-cae** A sewer
cloak A garment
clobber To maul
cloche A woman's hat
clock An instrument for measuring time
clockwise In the same direction as the hands of a clock
clod A lump of earth
clodpate A foolish person
clog A wooden-soled shoe
cloisonne A type of enamelware
cloister A monastery
cloistral Secluded
clomp To walk noisily
clone, clon To reproduce by asexual means
clonk Variant of clunk
clonus A form of muscular contraction
clop The sound of a horse's hoof
close Compact
closet A small room
closure Something that closes
clot A coagulated mass
cloth A piece of material
clothe To dress

clothier One who makes clothing
cloture A parliamentary procedure
cloud A visible mass in the air
clout An archery target
clove An East Indian evergreen tree
cloven Divided
clover A species of plant
clown A jester
cloy To supply with too much
club A cudgel
clubby Sociable
clubfoot A deformity of the foot
clubman A member of a club
cluck To utter the cry of a hen
clue Anything that guides in the solution
clump A lump
clumsy Awkward
clung Past tense of cling
clunk To thump
clupeid A species of fish
cluster A bunch
clutch To snatch
clutter A litter
clypeate Shaped like a round shield
clypeus, *pl* **-ei** A shieldlike structure
clyster An enema

co- Indicates together with; similar; complement of. The following compounds are listed without definition (see Introduction):

coact	coauthor	coeternal
coaction	coaxal	coeval
coactive	coaxial	coexert
coadjutor	cochair	coexist
coadmire	cocreate	coextend
coadmit	codebtor	cofactor
coadunate	coderive	cohabit
coaeval	coeditor	coheir
coagency	coeffect	coheiress
coagent	coembody	cohere
coalesce	coemploy	coherence
coalition	coenact	coherent
coannex	coenamor	coherer
coappear	coendure	cohering
coapt	coenure	cohesion
coassist	coenzyme	cohort
coassume	coequal	coincide
coattend	coequate	coinhere
coattest	coerect	coinmate
coinsure	copastor	cosign
cointer	copatron	cosigner
colocate	copilot	costar
comaker	coplanar	cotangent
comate	coplot	cotenant
cooperate	corelate	cotidal
coparent	corotate	cowinner
copartner	correlate	coworker

coach A carriage
coachman A person who drives a coach
coal A fossilized plant used as a fuel
coaming A raised rim designed to keep out water
coarse Inferior quality
coast The seashore
coastward Directed toward a coast
coastwise Following the coast
coat A garment
coati A species of mammal
coax To persuade
cob A male swan
cobalt A metallic element
cobber Comrade
cobble To mend
cobbler A person who mends shoes
cobia A game fish
coble A fishing boat
cobnut A tree
cobra A species of snake
cobweb The web spun by a spider
coca A South American tree
cocaine, cocain A narcotic
coccid A species of insect
coccus, *pl* **cocci** A bacterium
coccyx, *pl* **coccyges** A bone at the base of the spinal column
cochlea, *pl* **-leae** A tube in the inner ear
cock A rooster
cockade A rosette worn on the hat
cockatiel, cockateel A parrot
cockatoo A species of parrot
cockboat A small rowboat
cockcrow Dawn
cockerel A young rooster
cockeye A squinting eye
cockle To pucker
cocklebur A species of weed
cockloft A small garret

cockney A British dialect
cockpit Space for a pilot
cockshy A target
cocksure Absolutely sure
cocktail A mixed alcoholic drink
cockup A cap with an upturned front
cocky Conceited
coco The coconut palm
cocoa Powder made from cacao seeds
cocobolo, cocobola A tropical American tree
coconut, cocoanut Fruit of the coconut palm
cocoon A covering spun by the larvae of moths
cocotte A prostitute
cod A species of fish
coda A passage at the end of a musical composition
coddle To baby
code A colection of laws
codeine A narcotic
codex, pl codices A manuscript volume
codfish The cod
codger An old man
codicil A supplement to a will
codify To reduce to a code
codling An unripe apple
codon A sequence of three nucleotides
codpiece A pouch for breeches
coed A female student
coelom A body cavity in certain animals
coenurus, pl -nuri Larval stage of a tapeworm
coerce To force to act
coffee A species of tree
coffer A canal lock
coffin A horse's hoof
coffle To fasten together
cog A cogwheel
cogent Forcibly convincing
cogitate To ponder
cognac A brandy
cognate Related
cognizant Fully informed

cognomen A surname
cognovit An admission of liability
cogon A species of grass
cogwheel A toothed wheel
coho A small salmon
cohosh A species of plant
cohune A tropical palm tree
coif A cap worn by nuns
coiffeur A hairdresser
coiffure Hair style
coil A spiral pipe
coin To make coins
coinage Metal currency
coir Fiber from the husk of a coconut
coitus Sexual intercourse
coke To convert into a fuel
col A pass between two peaks
cola A soft drink
colander A kitchen utensil
colcannon A food dish
colcothar An iron oxide
cold Feeling no warmth
cole A species of plant
coleslaw A salad
coleus A species of plant
colewort A plant
colic Abdominal pain
coliform Resembling the colon bacillus
coliseum A large structure for assemblies
colitis Inflammation of the colon
collage An artistic composition
collagen A protein
collapse To cave in
collar A necklace
collard A variety of kale
collate To assemble
colleague An associate
collect To gather
colleen An Irish girl
college A school of higher learning
collet A metal collar used in watchmaking
collide Direct impact
collie A breed of dog
collier A coal miner
colliery A coal mine
collins An alcoholic drink

collision A crash
collogue To conspire
colloid A secretion of the thyroid gland
collop A small slice of meat
colloquy A written dialogue
collude To act together secretly
colly To make dirty
cologne A scented liquid
colon, *pl* **-lons** or **-la** A part of the intestine
colonel An officer
colonial Pertaining to the colonial period
colonist A founder of a colony
colonnade A series of columns
colony A settled territory
colophon A publisher's trademark
color A dye that imparts color
colorado Of medium color
colorant Anything that colors
colorist A painter
colossal Tremendous
colossus, *pl* **-lossi** A huge statue
colour Variant of color
colpitis Inflammation of the vaginal mucous membrane
colt A young male horse
colter A blade on a plow
coltish Playful
colubrid A species of snake
colugo The flying lemur
columbine A species of plant
column An article in a newspaper
coly A species of bird
colza A cabbage plant
coma A prolonged unconsciousness
comatose Unconscious
comb A currycomb
combat To resist
combine To blend
combings Material removed from a comb
combo A small group of musicians
combust To burn
come To appear
comedian An actor who does comedy
comedic Relating to comedy

comedo A blackhead
comedy A humorous work
comely Graceful
comet A celestial body
comfit A confection
comfort To console
comfrey A species of plant
comfy Comfortable
comic Humorous
comitia An assembly in ancient Rome
comity Courtesy
comma A punctuation mark
command To give orders to
commando A raid made by a small fighting force
commence To start
commend To praise
comment A remark
commerce The buying and selling of goods
commie A Communist
commissar An official of the Communist Party
commit To entrust
committee An official group
commix To mix
commode A toilet
common General
commoner One of the common people
commons A hall for dining
commotion Disorder
commove To excite
communal Public
commune Communion
communion Participation
communism A political doctrine
commute To travel
comp To play a musical accompaniment
compact Dense
compadre A friend
companion A comrade
company A gathering
compare To liken
compart To subdivide
compass To go around
compeer A peer
compel To subdue

105

compete To vie
competent Well qualified
compile To gather
complain To express feelings of resentment
complaint An expression of resentment
complect To interweave
complete Thorough
complex Consisting of interconnected parts
compliant Submissive
complice An accomplice
complin, compline Time of day set aside for prayer
comply To act in accordance with a wish
compo A mixed substance
component A constituent
comport To agree
compose To create
compost Decaying organic matter
compote A long-stemmed dish
compound To mix
compress To compact
comprise To contain
compute To determine an amount
comrade A friend
con Against
conation The aspect of behavior directed toward change
conatus Any directed effort
concave Curved
conceal To hide
concede To admit
conceit Vanity
conceive To imagine
concenter To direct toward the center
concept A general idea
concern To trouble
concert A musical performance
concerto, pl **-tos** or **-ti** A musical composition
conch The shell of a mollusk used for ornament
concha, pl **-chae** A shell-like structure
concierge A janitor
concise Succinct

conclave A secret meeting
conclude To finish
concoct To contrive
concord Accord
concordat A compact
concourse An open space for the passage of crowds
concrete Real
concubine A secondary wife
concur To agree
concuss To injure by concussion
condemn To criticize
condense To compress
condign Merited
condiment A food seasoning
condition State of health
condole To express sympathy
condom A prophylactic
condone To forgive
condor A vulture
conduce To contribute
conduct To manage
conductor A person who leads
conduit A tube enclosing a cable
condyle A prominence on a bone
cone To shape like a cone
conenose A species of bug
coney Variant of cony
confab To talk informally
confect To put together
confer To hold a conference
conferee A person in a conference
conferva, pl **-vae** or **-vas** A species of algae
confess To admit
confessor One who confesses
confetti Candies
confidant One to whom secrets are confided
confide To tell something in confidence
confine To restrict
confirm To verify
conflict A struggle
conflux A crowd
confocal Having the same focus
conform To comply
confound To bewilder
confrere A colleague
confront To come face to face

confuse To befuddle
confute To confound
conga A dance
conge, congee An abrupt dismissal
congeal To jell
congener A member of the same class
congenial Agreeable
conger A species of eel
congest To overcrowd
congius, pl **-gii** A gallon
congou A variety of Chinese black tea
congress A formal assembly
congruent Corresponding
conic Shaped like a cone
conidium, pl **-ia** An asexual fungus spore
conifer A species of evergreen tree
coniine, conin, conine A poisonous alkaloid
conium A species of plant
conjoin To unite
conjoint Joined together
conjugal Of marriage
conjunct United
conjure To effect as by magic
conjurer, conjuror One who practices magic
conk *Slang* To hit on the head
connate Inborn
connect To join together
connive To conspire
connote To imply in addition to the literal meaning
conquer To defeat
conquest Person whose love has been captivated
conquian A card game
conscious Awake
conscript A draftee
consensus General agreement
consent To agree
conserve To preserve
consider To study
consign To entrust
consist To be made up
console To comfort
consols Bank securities
consomme A clear soup

consonant Harmonious in sound
consort A partner
conspire To act together
constable A policeman
constant Unchanging
constrain To oblige
constrict To compress
construct To erect
construe To translate
consul An official serving abroad
consulate The premises occupied by a consul
consult To ask advice
consume To waste
contact A connection
contain To enclose
conte A short novel
contemn To despise
contempt Bitter scorn
contend To fight
content Satisfied
contest A competition
context A situation
continent A land mass of the earth
continue To carry forward
continuo An instrumental part
conto A money of account in Portugal
contort To twist out of shape
contour An outline
contract An agreement
contrail A vapor trail
contralto, pl **-tos** or **-ti** A female singer
contrary Completely different
contrast A dissimilarity
contrite Penitent
contrive To scheme
control To regulate
contuse To bruise
conundrum A riddle
convene To assemble
convent A nunnery
converge To come together
converse To talk
convert To transform
convex Curving outward
convey To transport
conveyer, conveyor One who conveys

convict A prisoner
convince To persuade
convivial Jovial
convoke To convene
convolve To coil up
convoy A fleet of ships
convulse To laugh uproariously
cony A rabbit
coo To talk fondly
cooch *Slang* A sinuous dance
coocoo Variant of cuckoo
cooee, cooey A shrill cry
cook To prepare food
cookery A place for cooking
cookout An outdoor meal
cooky, cookie A small cake
cool Calm
coolant A cooling agent
coolie, cooly An Oriental laborer
coolly In a cool manner
coon A raccoon
cooncan A card game
coonhound A hound used in hunting raccoons
coonskin The pelt of a raccoon
coontie An evergreen plant
coop A cage for poultry
cooper One who makes tubs and casks
coot A species of bird
cootie *Slang* A body louse
cop A policeman
copacetic, copasetic, copesetic *Slang* Great
copaiba A resin
copal A resin
cope An ecclesiastical vestment
copeck Variant of kopeck
copepod A species of crustacean
copious Abundant
copper A metallic element
copperas A compound
coppice A thicket
copra Dried coconut meat
copremia Blood poisoning
coprolite Fossilized excrement
copse A thicket
copter A helicopter
copula, *pl* **-las** or **-lae** Something that links

copulate To engage in coitus
copy A reproduction
copybook A book of penmanship
copycat An imitator
copyist One who makes copies
copyright The exclusive right granted for an original work
coquet To flirt
coquetry Flirtation
coquette A woman who flirts
coquille A cooking dish
coquina A small marine clam
coquito A palm tree
cor A British exclamation
coracle A small boat
coracoid A bone projecting from the scapula
coral A species of marine coelenterates
coralline Producing coral
corban An offering to God
corbeil A sculptured basket of flowers
corbel A bracket used to support a cornice
corbie A raven
corbina A species of fish
cord A rope of twisted fibers
cordage An amount of wood
cordate Having a heart-shaped outline
cordial Sincere
cordite An explosive powder
cordoba Monetary unit of Nicaragua
cordon An ornamental band of stone
cordovan A fine leather
corduroy A fabric
cordwood Wood piled in cords
core The center
corf, *pl* **corves** A truck used in a mine
corgi A short-legged dog
corium, *pl* **coria** The skin beneath the epithelium
cork A bottle stopper
corkage A charge for liquor not bought on the premises
corkwood A species of tree

corky Like cork
corm A stem of certain plants
cormel A young corm
corn A species of cereal plant
cornball *Slang* A boob
corncake Bread made with white cornmeal
corncob The core of an ear of corn
corncrib A container for storing corn
cornea A part of the eye
cornel A species of plant
corneous A hornlike substance
corner The place where two surfaces meet
cornet A musical instrument
cornetcy A rank of a cornet cavalry officer
cornfed Fed on corn
cornhusk The husk surrounding an ear of corn
cornice The molding between the walls and the ceiling
cornmeal Meal made from corn
cornu, *pl* **-nua** A hornlike bone protuberance
cornute Horn-shaped
cornuto, *pl* **-nuti** A cuckold
corny *Slang* Trite
corolla The outer envelope of flowers
corona, *pl* **-nas** or **-nae** A luminous ring around a celestial body
coronal A wreath
coronary Pertaining to the heart
coroner A public officer who investigates questionable deaths
coronet A small crown
corporal Bodily
corporate Incorporated
corps A military unit
corpse A dead body
corpsman An enlisted man trained as a hospital assistant
corpus, *pl* **-pora** A body
corpuscle A minute globular particle
corrade To erode
corral A place for confining livestock

correct Accurate
corrida A bullfight
corridor A narrow hallway
corrie A cirque
corrival An opponent
corrode To deteriorate
corrosion The process of wearing away
corrupt Dishonest
corsac An Asian fox
corsage A small bouquet of flowers
corsair A pirate ship
corse Corpse
corselet, corslet A light corset
corset A supporting undergarment
cortege A retinue
cortex, *pl* **-tices** or **-texes** The outer layer of an organ
cortical Pertaining to the cortex
corticate Having a cortex
cortin A hormone
cortisol A hormone
cortisone A corticoid used to treat various diseases
corundum A hard mineral
corvee Labor with no pay
corvette, corvet A small warship
corvine Belonging to the crow family
corymb A flower cluster
coryphee A ballet dancer
coryza A head cold
cos A type of lettuce
cosh *Slang* A blackjack
cosher To pamper
cosine A trigonometric function of an angle
cosmetic A product for beautifying the body
cosmic Pertaining to the universe
cosmonaut An astronaut
cosmos A species of plant
cosset To fondle
cost The amount paid for a purchase
costa, *pl* **-tae** A rib
costard A variety of apple
costate Having ribs
coster A hawker of vegetables
costive Sluggish

costmary An herb used as seasoning
costrel A drinking vessel
costume Clothes worn in a play
cosy Variant of cozy
cot A narrow bed
cote To pass by
coteau, pl **-teaux** The higher ground
coterie A clique
cotillion A dance
cotquean A hussy
cotta, pl **cottae** or **-tas** A short surplice
cottage A small house
cotter A cotter pin
cottier A peasant who rents land directly from its owner
cotton A species of plant
cottony Fluffy
cotyloid Shaped like a cup
couch A sofa
couchant Lying down
cougar A mountain lion
cough To expel air from the lungs
coulee A stream of molten lava
coulisse A side scene of a stage
couloir A deep gully
coulomb An electrical measure
coumarin An organic compound
council A group of appointed persons
counsel Guidance
count The act of counting
countess The wife of a count
country The territory of a nation
county A subdivision of a state
coup A masterstroke
coupe A dessert dish
couple A pair
coupler A device for joining two cars
couplet A pair
coupon A small certificate
courage Confidence
courante A dance
courier A messenger
courlan A wading bird
course Movement in time
courser A swift horse
court A royal palace

courteous Considerate
courtesan A prostitute
courtesy Gracious manner
courtier An attendant at a royal court
courtship The act of wooing a woman
couscous A food dish
cousin A relative
couth Suave
couture The business of a fashion designer
couturier One who designs clothes
couvade A primitive birth rite
cove A cavern
coven An assembly of 13 witches
covenant A contract
cover To clothe
coveralls A one-piece garment
coverlet, coverlid A bedspread
covert Secret
covet To wish for
covey A flock of birds
coving A molding
cow A domesticated animal

The following words are listed without definition (see Introduction):

cowbell	cowier	cowpox
cowboy	cowiest	cowshed
cowgirl	cowland	cowskin
cowhand	cowman	cowy
cowherd	cowpat	
cowhide	cowpoke	

cowage A tropical vine
coward One who lacks courage
cowardice Lack of courage
cowbane A species of plant
cowberry An evergreen shrub
cowbird A species of blackbird
cower To cringe
cowfish A species of whale
cowherb A European plant
cowl A garment worn by monks
cowlick A tuft of unruly hair
cowpea A tropical vine
cowry A species of marine mollusk
cowslip A flowering plant
cox A coxswain
coxa, pl **coxae** The hip joint

coxalgia Pain in the hip
coxcomb A cap worn by a jester
coxcombry Foolishness
coxswain A person in charge of a racing crew
coy Shy
coyote A wolf
coypu A rodent
coz Cousin
cozen To deceive
cozenage Fraud
cozy Snug and warm
crab A species of marine crustacean
crabby Grouchy
crabgrass A species of grass
crack To break down
crackle To make a succession of snapping sounds
cracknel A hard biscuit
crackpot An eccentric person
cracky Used to express surprise
cradle A bed for an infant
craft To make by hand
crag A projected rock on a cliff
crake A species of bird
cram To stuff
crambo A rhyming word game
cramp A sudden muscular pain
crampon An iron spike attached to a shoe
cranberry A species of plant
crane A species of wading bird
cranial Pertaining to the skull
cranium, pl -**ums** or -**nia** The skull
crank A grouch
crankpin A bar in the arm of a crank
cranky Ill-tempered
cranny A crevice
crap A losing throw of the dice
crape Variant of crepe
crappie A species of fish
crash To smash
crasis, pl -**ses** A vowel contraction
crass Coarse
crate A container
cravat A scarf
crave To desire intensely
craven A coward

craw An animal's stomach
crawl To advance slowly
crawly Creepy
crayfish A species of freshwater crustacean
crayon A stick of colored wax
craze To make insane
crazy Insane
creak To make a creaking sound
cream A color
creamery A place where dairy products are sold
crease To make a fold
create To originate
creatine, creatin An organic acid
creator One that creates something
creature An animal
creche A Nativity scene
credence Belief
credenza A buffet
credible Believable
credit Trust
creditor A person to whom money is owed
credo Creed
creed A confession of faith
creek A small brook
creel A wicker basket
creep To move slowly
cremate To incinerate a body
crenate Having an edge with rounded projections
creodont A species of mammal
creosol A chemical compound
creosote A wood preservative
crepe A fabric
crept Past tense of creep
crescendo A sound gradually increasing in volume
crescent Crescent-shaped
cresive Growing
cresol A chemical
cress A species of plant
cresset A torch
crest The top of a peak
cresylic Pertaining to cresol
cretic A metrical foot
cretin A person afflicted with cretinism
cretinism A thyroid deficiency

cretonne A fabric
crevalle A game fish
crevasse A chasm
crevice A fissure
crew A gang
crewel A yarn
crib A child's bed
cribbage A card game
cribbing A supporting framework
cribwork A framework made of logs
crick A creek
cricket A species of insect
cricoid Ring-shaped
crime A serious offense
criminal One who is guilty of a crime
criminate To charge with a crime
crimp To form into waves
crimson A color
cringe To cower
cringle A small ring of rope
crinite Hairy
crinkle To form into ripples
crinoid A marine animal
crinoline A fabric
crinum A species of plant
cripes An exclamation
cripple To damage
crisis A turning point
crisp Fresh
crispate Crimped
crispy Crisp
crisscross To mark with crossing lines
crissum, pl **crissa** An area of feathers on a bird
crista A crest
cristate Forming a crest
criteria Standards of judgment
critic A judge
critique A critical review
critter, crittur An animal
croak To utter the sound of a frog
croc A crocodile
crocein A dye
crochet A type of needlework
crock An earthenware jar
crockery Earthenware
crocket An architectural ornament

crocodile A species of reptile
crocoite A mineral
crocus, pl **-cuses** or **-ci** A species of plant
croft A small farm
croissant A pastry
cromlech A prehistoric monument
crone A withered old woman
crony A close friend
crook Something curved
crookneck A variety of squash
croon To sing softly
crop Cultivated plants
cropt Past participle of crop
croquet An outdoor game
croquette A small cake fried in deep fat
croquis A fashion sketch
crore Monetary unit of India
crosier A bishop's staff
cross A crucifix
crossbar A horizontal bar
crossbill A species of bird
crossbow A weapon
crosscut To cut across
crosse A lacrosse stick
crossfire Lines of fire crossing one another
crossjack A sail
crosslet A small heraldic symbol
crosstie A supporting beam
crossway A crossroad
crotch The fork of a limb
croton A species of plant
crouch To stoop
croup A throat disease
croupier A gambling attendant
crouton A small piece of toasted bread
crow A species of black bird
crowbar A lever
crowd A large number of people together
crowfoot A species of plant
crown Upper part of a hat
croze A cooper's tool
cruces Alternate plural of crux
crucial Critical
cruciate Cross-shaped
crucible A trial

crucifer A species of plant
crucifix An image of Christ on the cross
cruciform Cross-shaped
crucify To torment
crud *Slang* Refuse
crude Lacking taste
cruel Mean
cruet A glass bottle
cruise An ocean voyage
cruller A small sweet cake
crumb A piece of broken bread
crummie A cow having crooked horns
crummy *Slang* Cheap
crump To crunch with the teeth
crumpet A light, soft muffin
crumple To rumple
crunch To chew noisily
crunode A point where two curves intersect
cruor Clotted blood
crupper The rump of a horse
crural Pertaining to the thigh
crus, *pl* **crura** A part of the leg
crusade A holy war
crusado A Portuguese coin
cruse A small pot
crush To squeeze
crust A pastry shell
crustal Pertaining to a crust
crusty Curt
crutch To support
crux, *pl* **cruxes** or **cruces** The basic thing
cruzeiro Monetary unit of Brazil
crwth Ancient stringed instrument
cry To weep
crybaby A person who cries with little reason
cryogen A refrigerant
cryolite A mineral
cryonics The practice of freezing dead bodies
cryostat A device to maintain low temperature
crypt An underground chamber
cryptic Concealed
crystal Clear glass
ctenoid Comblike

cub A novice
cubage Cubature
cubature Cubic contents
cubby A small room
cubbyhole A small room
cube The third power of a number
cubeb A woody vine
cubic Having the shape of a cube
cubiform Having the shape of a cube
cubism A style of art
cubit A unit of measure
cubital Pertaining to the forearm
cuboid, cuboidal Having the shape of a cube
cuckold To make a cuckold of
cuckoo A species of bird
cucullate Having the shape of a hood
cucumber A garden vegetable
cucurbit A species of vine
cud Regurgitated food
cudbear A dye
cuddle To hug
cuddy A small cupboard
cudgel A heavy club
cudweed A species of plant
cue The letter q
cuesta A land elevation
cuff Part of a sleeve
cuirass A piece of armor
cuisine A style of cooking
cuisse Plate armor
culch An oyster bed
culet A piece of armor
culex, *pl* **-lices** A species of mosquito
culinary Pertaining to cooking
cull To gather
cullet Broken glass for remelting
cullion A wretched fellow
cullis, *pl* **-lises** A gutter in a roof
cully To cheat
culm Waste from coal mines
culminate To climax
culottes, culotte A divided skirt
culpa Misconduct
culpable Blameworthy
culprit One guilty of a crime
cult A religious society

cultigen A cultivated plant
cultivar A horticulturally derived plant
cultivate To till
cultrate Knifelike
culture A style of artistic expression
cultus, pl **-tuses** or **-ti** A religious cult
culver A dove
culverin A cannon
culvert A drain
cum Plus
cumber To burden
cumbrous Cumbersome
cumin, cummin An Old World plant
cumquat Variant of kumquat
cumshaw A present
cumulate To accumulate
cumulus, pl **-li** A cloud
cundum Variant of condom
cuneal Wedge-shaped
cuneate Wedge-shaped
cuniform, cuneiform Wedge-shaped
cunner A marine fish
cunning Crafty
cup A container
cupboard A closet
cupcake A small cake
cupel A small vessel
cupid Roman God of love representation
cupidity Greed
cupola A domed ceiling
cuppa A cup of tea
cupping A medical process
cupreous Coppery
cupric Containing copper
cuprite Copper ore
cuprous Containing copper
cupula, pl **-lae** A domed cap over a structure
cupule A cup-shaped structure
cur A mongrel
curable Capable of being cured
curacao, curacoa A liqueur
curacy The office of a curate
curare, curari A muscle relaxant

curarine A poisonous alkaloid
curassow A species of bird
curate A clergyman in charge of a parish
curator Director of a museum
curb To restrain
curculio A species of weevil
curcuma A species of plant
curd To curdle
cure To restore to health
curette, curet A surgical instrument
curfew A regulation to retire at a prescribed hour
curia, pl **curiae** A Roman senate
curie A unit of radioactivity
curio An unusual object of art
curiosa Pornographic books
curiosity A desire to learn
curious Eager for knowledge
curium A radioactive element
curl To form ringlets
curlew A species of bird
curlicue, curlycue A fancy curl
curly Having curls
currach A boat
currant A species of shrub
currency Money
current A steady flow
curricle A carriage
currier One who curries
currish Bad-tempered
curry To groom an animal
curse A profane oath
cursive Flowing
cursory Not thorough
curst Past tense of curse
curt Abrupt
curtail To abbreviate
curtain A window covering
curtal Anything cut short
curtate Abbreviated
curtesy A legal tenure
curtsy To bow
curule Of the highest rank
curvature Act of curving
curve A smooth bend
curvet To prance
curvy Curvacious
cuscus A species of marsupial

cusec A unit of volumetric flow of liquids
cushaw A squash
cushion A pillow
cushy *Slang* Comfortable
cusk A food fish
cusp A pointed end
cuspate Having a cusp
cuspid A canine tooth
cuspidor A spittoon
cuss To curse
custard A dessert
custody Guardianship
custom A tradition
customer A person who purchases goods
custos, *pl* custodes A custodian
custumal Customs of a monastery
cut To harvest
cutaway A formal coat
cutch Catechu
cute Pretty
cutgrass A species of swamp grass
cuticle The epidermis
cutie *Slang* A cute girl
cutin A waxy substance on plants
cutis The corium
cutlass A sword
cutler A person who makes knives
cutlery Tableware
cutlet A slice of meat
cutoff A short cut
cutout Something cut out
cutover Cleared of trees
cutpurse A pickpocket
cutthroat A murderer
cuttle A fish
cutup A prankster
cutwork A type of embroidery
cutworm A caterpillar
cwm Variant of cirque
cyan A color
cyanate A salt of cyanic acid
cyanic Pertaining to cyanogen
cyanide, cyanid A poisonous compound
cyanine A dye
cyanite A mineral
cyanogen A poisonous gas
cyanosis Discoloration of the skin

cycad A seed-bearing plant
cycas A tropical plant
cycle A period of time
cyclic, cyclical Relating to cycles
cyclist, cycler One who rides a bicycle
cycloid Resembling a circle
cyclone A violent windstorm
cyclopean Suggestive of the Cyclops
cyclorama A large mural
cyclosis, *pl* -ses Circulation of protoplasm
cyclotron A circular accelerator
cyesis, *pl* -ses Pregnancy
cygnet A young swan
cylinder A cylindrical container
cyma, *pl* -mae or -mas A curved molding
cymatium, *pl* -tia A cyma
cymbal A percussion instrument
cyme A flower cluster
cymene A hydrocarbon
cymling, cymlin A squash
cymogene A flammable compound
cymoid Resembling a cyma
cymose, cymous Resembling a cyme
cynic A cynical person
cynosure A center of admiration
cypher Variant of cipher
cypress A species of evergreen tree
cyprinid A species of freshwater fish
cyprinoid Resembling a carp
cypsela, *pl* -lae An achene in plants
cyst A sac
cysteine An amino acid
cystine An amino acid
cystitis Inflammation of the urinary bladder
cystocele Hernia of the bladder
cystoid Resembling a cyst
cytology The study of cells
cytoplasm The protoplasm outside a cell nucleus
cytosine A substance in the genetic code
czar An emperor

czardas A dance
czarevna The daughter of a czar
czarina, czaritza The wife of a czar

czarism Absolute monarchy
czarist A supporter of czarism

da Yes
dab To poke
dabchick A species of grebe
dabster A bungler
dace A species of fish
dacha A villa
dachshund A breed of dog
dacoit, dakoit A robber in India
dactyl, dactylus, *pl* **-li** A metrical foot
dada An artistic and literary movement
daddle Variant of diddle
daddy Dad
dado A section of a pedestal between the base and crown
daff To act a fool
daffodil A bulbous plant
daffy Foolish
daft Crazy
dag A lock of wool
dagga Marijuana
dagger A weapon
daggle To make muddy
daglock Dirty wool
dah A dash in Morse code
dahlia A species of plant
dahoon An evergreen shrub
daily Pertaining to every day
daimio, daimyo A Japanese nobleman
daimon Variant of demon
dainty Exquisite

daiquiri A cocktail
dairy A place that sells milk
dais, *pl* **-ises** A speaker's platform
daisy A species of plant
dak Transportation by relays
dale A valley
dalesman One who lives in a dale
daleth The fourth letter of the Hebrew alphabet
dalles The sides of a gorge
dally To flirt
dalmatic A garment worn by a bishop
daltonic Pertaining to color blindness
dam To confine
damage To harm
daman The hyrax
damask A fabric
dame A married woman
dammar, damar, dammer A hard resin
damn To condemn
damnable Hateful
damnify To cause damage to
damosel, damozel A damsel
damp Moist
damsel A maiden
damselfly A species of insect
damson A plum tree
dance To frolic
dandelion A species of plant
dander To become aroused

dandify To dress up as a dandy
dandiprat An obnoxious fellow
dandle To bounce a small child
dandruff A scaly scurf formed on the scalp
dandy A man who is extremely conscious about his clothes and manners
danger Peril
dangle The act of dangling
danio A species of fish
dank Damp
danseur A male ballet dancer
danseuse A female ballet dancer
dap To dip lightly into water
daphne A species of shrub
daphnia A species of crustacean
dapple Spotted marking
darb *Slang* Outstanding
dare To have courage
daric A Persian coin
dariole A cream tart
dark With no light
darkle To grow dark
darkling In the dark
darling A loved person
darn To mend
darnel A species of grass
darshan A Hindu blessing
dart A pointed missile
dartle To dart repeatedly
dash To bespatter
dasheen The taro plant
dashy Dashing
dassie A hyrax
dastard A sneaking coward
dasyure A species of mammal
data Plural of datum
datary A cardinal
date The day of the month
dative A grammatical case
datto The head of a Malay tribe
datum, *pl* **data** or **-tums** A fact used to make a decision
datura A species of plant
daub To apply
daube A method of cooking
daughter One's female child
daunt To discourage
dauphin The eldest son of the king of France
daut To caress
daven To recite a Jewish prayer
davenport A large sofa
davit A small crane
daw The jackdaw
dawdle To linger
dawk Variant of dak
dawn When daylight starts to appear
day Time between dawn and nightfall
The following words are listed without definition (see Introduction):

daybook	daylong	daystar
daybreak	daymare	daytime
daydream	dayroom	daywork
dayglow	dayside	
daylight	dayspring	

dayfly The mayfly
daysman A mediator
daze To shock
dazzle To amaze
de Used in personal names
de- Indicates reversal or undoing; removal, reduction, disparagement. The following compounds are listed without definition (see Introduction):

deaerate	declass	deduction
deair	declasse	deductive
deaminate	decline	deface
deamonize	decliner	defacer
deash	decoct	defame
debar	decode	defamer
debark	decoder	defat
debase	decolor	default
debaser	decolour	defeat
debate	decontrol	defeature
debater	decoy	defence
debone	decoyer	defile
deboner	decrease	defiler
debrief	decried	deflate
debug	decrier	deflator
debunk	decrown	deflea
debunker	decry	deflect
decalcify	decrypt	deflexed
decamp	decurve	deflower
decipher	deduct	defoam

defog
defogger
defoliant
defoliate
deforce
deforest
deform
defraud
defray
defrayal
defrayer
defrock
defrost
defuse
defuze
degas
degasser
degauss
degerm
deglaze
degrade
degrease
degum
dehorn
dehydrate
deice
deionize
delay
delead

delime
delist
delouse
deluster
demark
demask
demean
demerit
demob
demote
demount
denature
denazify
denote
denude
deodorant
deodorize
deoxidize
depaint
depart
deperm
deplane
deploy
deplume
depolish
deport
deportee
depose
deprave

depress
deraign
derail
derange
derat
desalt
desand
desex
desilver
desorb
despite
despoil
destain
desugar
desulphur
dethrone
detick
detour
detoxify
detract
detrain
devalue
devein
devoice
dewater
dewax
dewool
deworm
dezinc

dearth Famine

death The act of dying

deathbed The bed on which a person lies

deathblow A fatal event

deave To deafen

deb Debutante

debacle A sudden collapse

debauch To seduce

debility Feebleness

debit An entry in an account

debonair Suave

debouch To issue

debouche An outlet

debris Rubble

debt An obligation

debtor One who owes

debut A first appearance

debutante A young lady making her debut into society

decade Ten years

decadence Decay

decadent In a state of decay

decagon A polygon

decagram Ten grams

decal A design to be transferred

decanal Pertaining to a dean

decane A hydrocarbon

decant To pour from one bottle to another

decanter A bottle

decapod A species of crustacean

decare A unit of measure

decathlon An athletic contest

decay To rot

decease To die

decedent The deceased

deceit Deception

deceive To mislead

decemvir, *pl* **-virs** or **-viri** A Roman magistrate

decenary A tithing

decency The state of being decent

decennary Pertaining to a ten-year period

decennial Lasting for ten years

decent Generous

deception An imposture

decibel A unit to express the difference in power

deacon A clergyman

deaconess A female church assistant

deaconry Office of a deacon

dead Lifeless

deadbeat *Slang* A loafer

deadeye An expert marksman

deadfall An animal trap

deadhead A dull person

deadline A time limit

deadpan *Slang* An expressionless face

deadwood Dead wood

deaf Incapable of hearing

deal To pass cards

dealate Having lost its wings

dealfish A marine fish

dealt Past tense of deal

dean The head of a college

deanery The dean's office

dear Expensive

decide To settle

decidua A mucous membrane of the uterus

decigram One-tenth of a gram

decile A statistical interval

decimal A fraction

decimate To destroy

decipher To decode

decision The act of reaching a conclusion

decisive Conclusive

deck A pack of cards

deckle, deckel A rough edge on cut paper

declaim To speak loudly

declare To make a declaration

decor Interior scenery

decorate To embellish

decorous Proper

decorum Conformity to social conventions

decoupage A style of art

decree The judgment of a court

decrepit Broken-down

decretal A decree

decuple Tenfold

decurion A company of ten men

decussate To cross each other

dedans A gallery

dedicate To unveil a monument

deduce To reason

dee The letter d

deed An exploit

deejay *Slang* A disc jockey

deem To think

deep Profound

deer A species of mammal

deerskin Leather from the hide of the deer

deerweed A species of plant

defecate To clarify

defect An imperfection

defend To guard

defendant One against whom an action is brought

defense The act of defending

defer To postpone

deferent Deferential

deferment Postponement

defiance Resistance

defiant Marked by defiance

deficient Incomplete

deficit A shortage

defilade To protect from enemy fire

define To clarify

definite Positively

deft Skillful

defunct Dead

defy To challenge

degage Casual

degame Lemonwood

degree An academic title

degust To taste with pleasure

dehisce To split open

dei Used in personal names

deicide One who kills a god

deictic Proving by argument

deific Godlike

deify To worship

deign To grant

deil The devil

deism A religious philosophy

deity Divinity

deject To cast down

deke To feint in hockey

del An operator in calculus

delaine A fabric

delate To accuse

dele A typesetter's mark

delegate An agent

delete To leave out

delft A style of earthenware

deli, delly A delicatessen

delicacy The quality of being delicate

delicate Exquisite

delicious Very pleasant to the taste

delict An offense

delight Joy

delimit To establish the boundaries

delineate To sketch out

delirious Pertaining to delirium

delirium, *pl* **-ums** or **-ia** Mental confusion

deliver To hand over

dell A secluded wooded valley

delta The fourth letter of the Greek alphabet

deltoid Triangular

delude To elude

119

deluge A downpour
delusion A false belief
deluxe Of special luxury
delve To search
demagogue, demagog A leader
demand To lay legal claim to
demarcate To delimit
demarche A maneuver
deme A township in ancient Attica
dement To make insane
dementia Mental illness
demesne Grounds belonging to a mansion
demigod A minor god
demijohn A bottle
demilune A half-moon
demirep A harlot
demise To transfer by will
demit To relinquish
demitasse A small cup
demiurge A magistrate of ancient Greece
democracy Government by the people
democrat A member of the Democratic party
demode Outmoded
demolish To wreck
demon A devil
demoniac A fiend
demonic Fiendish
demos The common people
demotic Popular
demur To object
demure Reserved
demurrer A person who demurs
demy A size of paper
den A lair
denarius, pl **-narii** An ancient Roman coin
denary Tenfold
dendrite A mineral
dendroid Shaped like a tree
dene A valley
dengue A tropical disease
deniable Questionable
denial A rejection
denigrate To defame
denim A fabric
denizen A resident

denounce To accuse
dense Thick
density Dullness
dent To make a dent in
dental Pertaining to the teeth
dentate Toothed
denticle A toothlike projection
dentil A small rectangular block
dentine Part of a tooth
dentist One who practices dentistry
dentistry The treatment of teeth
dentoid Toothlike
denture Artificial teeth
denudate To denude
deny To contradict
deodar A tall cedar
departee One who has departed
departure A going away
depend To rely for support
dependent Subordinate
depict To describe
depilate To remove hair
deplete To exhaust
deplore To lament
depone To testify under oath
deponent One that depones
deposit To place
depot A railroad station
deprecate To protest
depredate To plunder
deprive To deny
depth Deepness
depurate To purify
depute To delegate
deputize To appoint as a deputy
deputy A law officer
derby A hat
dere Dire
derelict A vagrant
deride To ridicule
derision A laughingstock
derisive Mocking
derive To deduce
derma, derm A layer of skin
dermal, dermic Pertaining to the skin
dermis Derma
dermoid Skinlike
derogate To take away

120

derrick A large crane
derriere The rear
derringer A pistol
derris A species of vine
derry A meaningless song lyric
dervish A member of a Moslem order
des Used in names
descant The highest part sung in music
descend To come or go down
descent The act of descending
describe To tell about
descry To discern
desecrate To profane
desert Desolate
deserve To be worthy of
desiccate To dry out
design To conceive
designate To point out
designee One who has been designated
desinence Finishing
desire To crave
desist To cease doing something
desk A table for writing
deskman One who works at a desk
desman A species of mammal
desmid A species of algae
desmoid A tumor
desolate Deserted
despair Lack of hope
despatch Variant of dispatch
desperado A criminal
desperate Showing despair
despise To regard with contempt
despond To give up
despot An autocratic ruler
dessert A sweet served after dinner
destine To preordain
destiny Preordained course of events
destitute Impoverished
destrier A war horse
destroy To get rid of
destruct Intentional destruction
desuetude The state of disuse
desultory Rambling
detach To disconnect
detail A particular

detain To confine
detect To discover
detent A device that stops or releases a movement
detente A relaxing
deter To prevent
deterge To cleanse
detergent A cleaning substance
determine To decide
detest To loathe
detinue An act to recover something
detonate To explode
detriment Something that causes harm
detrition The act of wearing away
detritus Debris
deuce A playing card bearing two spots
deuteron An atomic particle
deutzia A species of shrub
devastate To lay waste
develop, develope To elaborate
devest To take away from
deviant Deviating
deviate To move away from
device A scheme
devil An evil spirit
devilfish A manta
devilish Fiendish
devilkin A little devil
devilry Wickedness
deviltry Evil magic
devious Erring
devisal The act of devising
devise To invent
devisee One to whom a devise is made
devisor One who makes the devise
devitrify To cause the loss of a glassy quality
devoid Without
devoir Compliments
devolve To delegate
devon A breed of cattle
devote To consecrate
devotee One devoted to something
devotion Ardent affection
devour To destroy
devout Pious

dew Moisture
dewan An official in India
dewclaw A claw on certain mammals
dewdrop A drop of dew
dewfall The formation of dew
dewlap A fold of loose skin
dewy Wet with dew
dexter Located on the right side
dexterity Cleverness
dextral Right
dextran A plasma substitute
dextrin, dextrine A thickening agent
dextro Turning to the right
dextrorse Growing upward in a turning spiral
dextrose A form of glucose
dey A former ruler of North Africa
dhak A tree of tropical Asia
dharma A Hindu law
dharna A form of protest in India
dhole A wild dog
dhoti, dhooti A loincloth worn by Hindu men
dhow An Arabian vessel
diabase An igneous rock
diabetes A metabolic disorder
diabetic Having diabetes
diabolic Satanic
diacid A form of acid
diaconal Of a deacon
diaconate The rank of a deacon
diacritic Diagnostic
diadem A crown of royalty
diagnose To identify by diagnosis
diagonal Having a slanted direction
diagram A sketch
dial The face of a clock
dialect A variety of speech
dialogic Written in dialogue
dialogist One who writes dialogue
dialogue, dialog Lines spoken by an actor
dialysis, pl **-ses** The separation of smaller molecules from larger molecules
dialyze To undergo dialysis
diameter The width of anything

diamine A chemical compound
diamond A precious gemstone
diandrous Having two stamens
dianthus A species of plant
diapason A stop on a pipe organ
diapause A period in which growth is suspended
diaper An infant's garment
diaphony Organum
diaphragm A membranous part that divides
diarchy A government with two rulers
diarist One who keeps a diary
diarrhea An intestinal disorder
diary A daily record
diaspore An aluminum oxide
diastase An enzyme
diastema A bodily fissure
diaster A stage in mitosis
diastole The lengthening of a short syllable
diatom A species of algae
diatomic Composed of two atoms
diatonic Using eight tones without chromatic variations
diatribe A bitter criticism
diazine, diazin A chemical compound
diazo Relating to an organic compound
diazole A chemical compound
dibasic Containing replaceable hydrogen atoms
dibble, dibbler A gardening tool
dibs Slang A claim on something
dicast A citizen in ancient Athens
dice A game
dicentra A species of plant
dicer One who plays dice
dicey Risky
dichroic Dichromatic
dichroite A mineral
dick Slang A detective
dickens Devil
dicker To bargain
dickey A woman's garment
dictate To say something to be recorded
dictator One who dictates

diction Distinctive speech

dictum, *pl* **dicta** or **-tums** A dogmatic pronouncement

did Past tense of do

didact A didactic person

didactic Orally instructive

didapper A dabchick

diddle To dawdle

dido A caper

didst Past tense of do

didy A diaper

didymous Occurring in pairs

die To expire

dieback Gradual dying of plant shoots

dieresis, *pl* **-ses** The separation of two adjacent vowels into separate syllables

diesel A type of engine

diesis, *pl* **-ses** A reference mark in printing

diestock A device for holding dies

diet Daily sustenance

dietetic Pertaining to diet

differ To disagree

difficult Hard to do

diffident Timid

diffract To break up into rays of light

diffuse To disseminate

dig To make a hole

digamma An early Greek letter

digamy Remarriage after death or divorce

digastric Having two fleshy ends connected

digest To summarize

dight To adorn

digit A finger or toe

digital Having digits

digitalin A poisonous powder

digitalis A species of plant

digitate Having digits

dignity A high office

digraph A pair of letters that represents a single speech sound

digress To turn aside

dihedral Two-sided

dihybrid A child of parents differing in two pairs of genes

dihydric Containing two hydroxyl radicals

dike A levee

diktat A settlement that deals harshly with a defeated nation

dilatant Dilating

dilate To cause to expand

dilatory Intended to delay

dilemma A predicament

diligent Industrious

dill An aromatic herb

dilly *Slang* Something remarkable

diluent Capable of diluting

dilute To thin

diluvial Pertaining to a flood

dim Faint

dime A coin

dimension Size

dimer A molecule composed of two simpler molecules

dimeter A verse

dimethyl Ethane

diminish To make smaller

dimity A fabric

dimorph A dimorphic form

dimple A small indentation in the flesh

dimwit *Slang* A stupid person

din To make a loud noise

dinar A monetary unit of various Middle East countries

dine To eat dinner

dinero Money

dinette An alcove for eating

ding To clang

dingbat A gadget

dinghy A small boat

dingle A dell

dingo A wild dog

dingus *Slang* A gadget whose name is not known

dingy Dirty

dinkey, dinky A small locomotive

dinner An evening meal

dinosaur An extinct reptile

dint A dent

diocesan Pertaining to a diocese

diocese A bishopric

diode An electron tube

dioicous Unisexual

diopside A mineral
diopter A measure of refractive power
dioptric Refractive
diorama A three-dimensional scene
diorite A species of crystalline rocks
dioxane A flammable liquid
dioxide A type of oxide
dip To scoop
diphase, diphasic Having two phases
diphenyl Biphenyl
diphthong A speech sound
diplegia Paralysis of same parts on both sides of the body
diplex Capable of reception of two messages over the same channel
diploe Bony tissue of the cranium
diploid Twofold
diploma An official document
diplomat A government representative
diplomate A physician
diplont An organism having somatic cells with diploid chromosomes
diplopia A disorder of vision
diplopod A species of arthropod
diplosis A method of chromosome formation
dipnoan A species of fish
dipody A prosodic unit
dipolar Having a dipole
dipole Two equal and opposite electric charges
dippy *Slang* Foolish
dipsas A fabled serpent
dipstick A rod for measuring liquid
dipt Past tense of dip
dipteran, dipteron A dipterous insect
dipterous A species of insect
diptych An ancient writing tablet
dire Disastrous
direct To regulate
director One who supervises
directrix The median line in the trajectory of fire

dirge A funeral lament
dirham Monetary unit of Morocco
dirigible A lighter-than-air craft
diriment Nullifying
dirk A weapon
dirl To tremble
dirndl A ful-skirted dress
dirt Earth

dis- Indicates removal; reverse; invalidation; completion of negative action. The following compounds are listed without definition (see Introduction):

disable	disenable	disobey
disabuse	disendow	disoblige
disaccord	disengage	disorder
disaffect	disentail	disorient
disaffirm	disentomb	disown
disagree	disesteem	dispart
disallow	disfavor	dispatch
disannul	disfigure	dispend
disappear	disforest	displace
disarm	disfrock	displant
disarray	disgorge	display
disavow	disgrace	displease
disband	disguise	displume
disbar	disgust	disposal
disbelief	dishallow	dispose
disbosom	dishelm	dispraise
disbound	disherit	disprize
disbowel	dishonest	disproof
disbranch	dishonor	disprove
disbud	disinfect	dispute
disburden	disinfest	disquiet
disburse	disinter	disrate
discard	disject	disregard
discase	disjoin	disrelish
discharge	disjoint	disrepair
disclaim	disjunct	disrepute
disclimax	dislike	disrobe
disclose	dislimn	disroot
discolor	dislocate	dissave
discord	dislodge	disseat
discount	disloyal	disseise
discourse	dismantle	disseize
discredit	dismast	disserve
discrown	dismay	dissever
disdain	dismember	dissolve
disembark	dismiss	distaste
disembody	dismount	distemper

distend   distrain   disunity

distill   distrust   disuse

distort   disunion   disvalue

distract   disunite   disyoke

disaster A total failure

disc A phonograph record

discalced Barefooted

discern To discriminate

disciple A companion of Christ

discoid, discoidal Having the shape of a disk

discomfit To vanquish

discover To be the first

discovert Having no husband

discreet Modest

discrete Distinct

discus, *pl* **-cuses** or **-disci** A disk used in athletic events

discuss To speak about

disease To make sick

dish An open container

dishevel To let fall in disarray

disk A flat, circular plate

dismal Feeling gloomy

disparage To belittel

disparate Completely dissimilar

dispel To dispense with

dispense To give out

disperse To distribute widely

dispirit To dishearten

displode To explode

disport To play

disrupt To throw into confusion

dissect To cut apart

disseizee A person who is robbed of property

dissemble To make a false show of

dissent To differ

dissident A person who disagrees

dissipate To scatter

dissolute Debauched

dissonant Sounding harsh

dissuade To persuade one not to do something

distaff A type of staff used by a woman

distain To discolor

distal Located away from the originating point

distance The space between two

objects

distant Remote

distich A couplet

distinct Different

distingue Distinguished

distraint A distress

distress To worry

district To divide into districts

disturb To upset

disulfide A chemical compound

dit A dot in Morse code

ditch A narrow trench

dither A state of nervousness

dittany A species of plant

ditto To repeat

ditty A simple song

diuresis Excessive discharge of urine

diuretic A drug that tends to increase urine discharge

diurnal Daily

diva, *pl* **-vas** or **-ve** An operatic prima donna

divagate To ramble

divalent Bivalent

divan A couch

dive To submerge

diverge To differ

divers Several

diverse Different

divert To distract

divest To strip

divide To separate

dividend A share of profits

divine Holy

divinity The state of being devine

divinize To deify

divisible Capable of being divided

division The process of dividing

divisive Creating dissension

divorce Dissolution of a marriage

divorcee A divorced woman

divot A piece of turf

divulge To reveal

divvy *Slang* A share

diwan Variant of dewan

dixit A statement

dizen To dress in fine clothes

dizzy Feeling giddy

djin Jinni

125

djinni, djinny Variant of jinni
do To complete
doable Capable of being done
doat Variant of dote
dobbin A workhorse
dobie, doby Adobe
dobra A monetary unit of Sao Tome and Principe
dobson The larva of the dobsonfly
doc *Slang* Doctor
docent A lecturer
docile Easily trained
dock A wharf
dockage Docking of ships
docket An agenda
dockyard An area where ships are repaired
doctor A physician
doctorate A degree
doctrinal Concerning doctrine
doctrine Something that is taught
document To support with evidence
dodder To tremble
dodge To avoid
dodgem *Slang* An amusement park ride
dodo A flightless extinct bird
doe Female deer
doeskin The skin of a doe
doest Second person singular, present tense of do
doeth Third person singular, present tense of do
doff To remove one's hat
dog A domesticated mammal
dogbane A species of plant
dogberry A wild gooseberry
dogcart A small cart
doge The chief magistrate of the former republics of Venice and Genoa
dogface *Slang* A soldier
dogfish A species of shark
dogged Stubborn
doggerel, doggrel Trivial verse
doggery Meanness
doggone To damn
doggy, doggie A little dog
dogie, dogy A stray calf

dogleg An abruptly angled fairway
dogma, *pl* **-mas** or **-mata** A system of principles
dogmatic Pertaining to dogma
dogtooth, *pl* **-teeth** A canine tooth
dogtrot A steady trot
dogwatch A period of watch duty
dogwood A species of tree
doily A small napkin
doit A former Dutch coin
dojo A judo or karate school
dol A unit to measure pain
dolce Sweetly
doldrums A period of depression
dole Distribution of money
doleful Mournful
dolerite A variety of basalt
doll A child's toy
dollar Monetary unit of the United States
dollop A portion
dolly A doll
dolman A turkish outer robe
dolmen A prehistoric megalithic structure
dolomite A mineral
dolor, dolour Sorrow
doloroso Plaintive
dolphin A species of marine mammal
dolt A blockhead
dom A title given to certain monks
domain Realm
dome A hemispherical vault
domestic Pertaining to the family
domical, domic Shaped like a dome
domicile, domicil A home
dominant The fifth tone of the diatonic scale
dominate To control
domineer To tyrannize
dominical Associated with the Lord
dominie A minister
dominion Rule
dominium Control of property
domino A cape worn by clergymen
don To put on
dona A Spanish gentlewoman
donate To give

donative A bounty
done Finished
donee Recipient of a gift
dong Monetary unit of North Vietnam
donga A South African gully
donjon Fortified tower of a castle
donkey The domesticated ass
donna An Italian gentlewoman
donnee Events used in the development of a story
donnish Bookish
donor One who gives blood
donut Doughnut
doodad A gadget
doodle To scribble
doodlebug An insect
doohickey A doodad
doom A tragedy
doomsday The day of the Last Judgment
door Entrance to a room
doorbell A bell outside a door
doorknob A door handle
doormat A mat for wiping shoes
doornail A nail
doorsill The threshold
doorstep A step leading to a door
doorstop A wedge used to keep a door open
doorway Entranceway
dooryard A yard in front of the door
doozy Slang Anything outstanding
dopant A small quantity
dope A lubricant
dopey, dopy Slang Silly
dor A species of insect
dorm A dormitory
dormant Asleep
dormer A type of window
dormitory Sleeping quarters
dormouse, pl **-mice** A species of rodent
dormy, dormie Ahead of an opponent by as many holes in golf as remain to be played
dornick A cloth
dorsad In the direction of the back
dorsal Near the back

dorsum, pl **-sa** The back
dory A fishing boat
dosage An amount
dose An amount
doss Slang A flophouse
dossal, dossel An ornamental covering
dosser A basket
dossier A collection of papers on a single subject
dost Second person singular, present tense of do
dot A point
dotage Senility
dotard A senile person
dote To lavish excessive affection
doth Third person singular, present tense of do
dotterel, dottrel A species of bird
dottle, dottel Tobacco ash left in the pipe bowl
dotty Shaky
double Twice as much
doublet A jacket
doubloon An obsolete Spanish coin
doublure The lining of a book cover
doubly Twice
doubt Distrust
douceur A bribe
douche To cleanse with a stream of water
dough A flour mixture
doughboy A soldier
doughnut A ring-shaped cake
doughty Courageous
dour Forbidding
dourine A disease of horses
douse To put out
dove A species of bird
dovecote, dovecot A roost for pigeons
dovekie, dovekey A sea bird
dovetail To cut into
dowager A dignified elderly lady
dowdy Shabby
dowel To fasten with wooden rods
dower A dowry
down Toward the bottom
downbeat The conductor's stroke to indicate the first beat

downcast Sad
downfall An unexpected rain
downhaul Ropes for hauling down a sail
downright Candid
downstage Front part of the stage
downtime Period of time when a factory is inactive
downy Soft
dowry A gift
dowse To douse
doxology A liturgical formula
doxy *Slang* A paramour
doyen, doyenne The eldest member of a group
doyley, doyly Variants of doily
doze To nap
dozen Twelve
dozy Drowsy
drab Dull
drabble To bedraggle
dracaena A species of plant
drachm A dram
drachma, *pl* **-mas** or **-mae** Monetary unit of Greece
draconic Pertaining to a dragon
draff Dregs
draft A current of air
draftee One drafted
draftsman One who draws plans
drag To pull
dragee A candy
draggle To follow slowly
dragline A line used for dragging
dragnet A trawl
dragoman An interpreter in Near Eastern countries
dragon A monster
dragonet A species of fish
dragonfly A species of insects
dragoon To harass
drain To empty
drake A male duck
dram A unit of weight
drama A play
dramatic Pertaining to drama
dramatist A playwright
drank Past tense of drink
drape To hang
drapery Curtains

drastic Extreme
drat Darn!
drave Past tense of drive
draw To attract
drawback An inconvenience
drawbar A railroad coupler
drawbore A hole for joining a tenon and mortise
drawee The person on whom a payment is drawn
drawl To speak slowly
drawn Haggard
dray A heavy cart
drayage To transport by dray
dread To be in fear
dream An ambition
dreary Dismal
dreck *Slang* Trash
dredge To deepen
dree To suffer
dreggy Full of dregs
dregs Residue
drench To saturate
dress To clothe
dressage The training of a horse
drest Past tense of dress
drew Past tense of draw
drib To drip
dribble To trickle
driblet A drop of liquid
drier One that dries
drift To stray
driftage The act of drifting
drill A tool for boring holes
drink To swallow liquids
drip To fall in drops
drippy wet
dripstone Stalactites or stalagmites
dript Past tense of drip
drive To urge forward
drivel To drool
drizzle A gentle rain
drogue A sea anchor
droit A legal right
droll Comical
dromedary A camel
drommond, dromon A medieval galley
drone To make a humming sound

drongo A species of Old World bird
drool To drivel
droop To sag
drop To fall in drops
dropforge To forge a metal between dies
droplet A tiny drop
dropout A nongraduating student
dropsy Edema
dropt Past tense of drop
dropwort A plant
droshky, drosky A carriage
dross Waste matter
drought, drouth A long period with no rain
drove Past tense of drive
drown To suffocate in water
drowse To doze
drub To whip severely
drudge To do menial work
drug A narcotic
drugget A fabric
druggist A pharmacist
druid A member of an ancient Celtic order of priests
drum A musical instrument
drumfire Heavy gunfire
drumlin A ridge of glacial drift
drunk Intoxicated
drunkard One who is habitually drunk
drupe A fleshy fruit
drupelet A small drupe
druse A crust of small crystals lining a rock cavity
dry Not wet
dryad A wood nymph
dryasdust A dull speaker
duad A pair
dual Double
dualism Duality
dub To nickname
dubbin A material for dressing leather
dubiety An uncertainty
dubious Undecided
ducal Pertaining to a duke
ducat A gold coin
duce, *pl* **duci** A chief
duchess The wife of a duke

duchy Territory ruled by a duke
duck A species of aquatic bird
duckbill The platypus
duckpin A bowling pin
duckweed A species of plant
ducky *Slang* Very good
duct A tubular passage
ductile Plastic
dud A bomb that fails to explode
dude A dandy
dudeen A clay pipe
dudgeon Resentment
duds Clothes
due Owing
duel A combat between two persons
duello The art of the duel
duenna A chaperon
duet A song for two
duff Coal dust
duffel, duffle A blanket fabric
duffer A dull-witted person
dug Past tense of dig
dugong A marine mammal
dugout A canoe
duiker A species of antelope
duke A nobleman
dukedom A duchy
dulcet An organ stop
dulciana An organ stop
dulcify To sweeten
dulcimer A musical instrument
dulia Homage paid to angels
dull Blunt
dullard A dolt
dulse A seaweed
duly Rightfully
dumb Mute
dumbbell A weight for exercising
dumdum A type of bullet
dumfound To stun
dummy An imitation
dump To empty out
dumpling A dessert
dun A color
dunce A stupid person
dune A hill of windblown sand
dung To fertilize with manure
dungaree A fabric
dungeon A dark chamber used to

confine prisoners
dunghill A heap of manure
dunk To immerse
dunlin A sandpiper
dunnage Baggage
dunt A heavy blow
duo, pl -os or -dui A duet
duodenum, pl -odena The first part of the small intestine
duopsony A stock market condition of two buyers only
duotone A printing process
dupe To deceive
dupery State of being duped
duple Double
duplex Having two identical units
duplicate Double
durable Lasting
dural Of the spinal membrane
duramen Heartwood
durance Imprisonment
duration A period of time
durbar A reception hall
duress Coercion
durian A tree
during Throughout the duration of
durmast An oak tree
durn Variant of darn
duro A Spanish silver dollar
duroc A hog
durra A cereal grain
durst Past tense of dare
durum A hardy wheat
dusk The darker stage of twilight
dust To remove dust
dustbin A container for trash
dustup An argument
dutchman One of Dutch descent
duteous Dutiful
dutiful Obedient
duty An obligation

duumvir, pl -virs or -viri A member of a two-man office
duvetyn, duvetine, duvetyne A fabric
dwarf, pl dwarfs or dwarves A very small person
dwarfism A condition of stunted growth
dwell To reside
dwindle To diminish
dyad A pair of units
dyadic Twofold
dye A substance used to color fabrics
dyestuff Material used as a dye
dyewood Wood used as a dyestuff
dyke Dike
dynamic Vigorous
dynamism The state of being dynamic
dynamite An explosive
dynamo A generator
dynast A ruler
dynasty A royal family that maintains power for generations
dynatron An electron tube
dyne A unit of force
dynode An electrode
dysentery An infection of the intestinal tract
dysgenic Causing the deterioration of hereditary qualities
dyslexia Impairment of the ability to read
dyspepsia Disturbed digestion
dysphagia Difficulty in swallowing
dysphonia Difficulty in speaking
dyspnea Difficulty in breathing
dystrophy Defective nutrition
dysuria Difficult urination

each One of two
eager Anxious
eagle A species of bird of prey
eaglet A young eagle
eagre A tidal flood
ear The organ of hearing
earache Pain in the ear
eardrop An earring
eardrum The tympanic membrane
eared Having ears
earflap A part of a cap designed to cover the ears
earing A line on a ship
earl A British peer
earlap The lobe of the external ear
earldom The title of an earl
early Near the beginning of a period of time
earmark An identifying mark
earmuff One of a pair of warm ear coverings
earn To gain salary for one's services
earnest Eager
earphone A listening device
earring An ornament for the ear lobe
earshot Hearing distance
earth Land surface of the world
earthborn Mortal
earthen Made of earth
earthly Of the earth
earthnut A species of plant
earthstar Any of a genus of puffball fungi
earwax Cerumen
earwig A species of insect
earworm Corn earworm
ease Poise
easeful Restful
easel A frame for an artist's canvas

east A cardinal point on the compass
eastern Facing the east
easting Distance sailed by a ship going east
easy Not difficult
eat To consume food
eatery A diner
eats *Slang* Food
eau, *pl* **eaux** Water
eave, eaves Projecting overhang of a roof
ebb To recede
ebon Black
ebonite A hard black rubber
ebony A species of tree
eccentric Erratic
ecclesia, *pl* **-siae** A church
eccrine Secreting externally
ecdysis, *pl* **-ses** The shedding of an outer layer of skin
ecesis The establishment of an organism in a new environment
echard Water in the soil not available to plants
echelon A level of authority
echidna A species of mammal
echinate Spiny
echinoid An echinodern
echinus, *pl* **-ni** A curved molding on a Doric capital
echo An imitation of something
echoic Imitative of sounds
echoism The formation of words in imitation of sounds
eclair A pastry
eclat Brilliance
eclectic One whose beliefs are drawn from several sources
eclipse Cutting off of light
eclipsis An ellipsis

ecliptic The path of the sun among the stars

eclogue A bucolic poem

eclosion The emergence of an insect larva from the egg

ecology The science of the environments

economic Pertaining to material wealth

economy A saving

ecotone An ecological community

ecotype A subdivision of an ecospecies

ecru A color

ecstasy A state of exalted delight

ecstatic Relating to ecstasy

ectoblast Ectoderm

ectoderm Outermost layers of an embryo

ectomere A cell that develops into ectoderm

ectopia Congenital displacement of an organ

ectoplasm The outer layer of the cytoplasm of a cell

ectosarc The outermost layer of protoplasm of certain protozoans

ectype An imitation

ecu, pl **ecus** Various French coins

eczema An inflammation of the skin

edacious Voracious

edaphic Pertaining to soil

eddo The taro plant

eddy A byway

edelweiss An Alpine plant

edema, pl **-mas** or **-mata** An excessive accumulation of serous fluid

edentate Lacking teeth

edge A rim

edgewise, edgeways Toward the edge

edging A border

edgy Nervous

edh A letter of the old English alphabet

edible Fit to eat

edict A formal decree

edifice An imposing building

edify To enlighten

edit To delete

edition A copy of a newspaper

editor A person who edits

educable Capable of being educated

educate To train

educe To evolve

educt Something educed

eel A species of snakelike fish

eelgrass A species of aquatic plant

eelpout A species of fish

eelworm A species of worm

eerie, eery Weird

eff, ef The letter f

effable Capable of being expressed

efface To erase

effect An outcome

effector An organ at the end of a nerve

effendi A Turkish title of respect

efferent Carrying away from a central part

effete Barren

efficacy Capacity to produce the desired effect

efficient Effective

effigy A likeness

effluent Flowing out

efflux An emanation

effort Exertion

effuse To disseminate

eft A newt

eftsoons, eftsoon Presently

egad A mild oath

egest To discharge from the body

egesta Egested matter

egg An ovum

egger A species of moth

egghead Slang An intellectual

eggnog A drink

eggplant Blackish purple

egis Variant of aegis

ego Conceit

egomania Extreme egotism

egregious Outrageous

egress The exit

egret A species of bird

eh Used to express surprise

eider A species of sea duck

eidetic Of mental images

eidolon, *pl* **-lons** or **-la** An apparition

eight The cardinal number 8

eighth The ordinal number eight in a series

eightieth The ordinal number 80 in a series

eightvo Octavo

einkorn A one-seeded wheat

either One or the other

ejaculate To exclaim

eject To expel

ejecta Ejected matter

ejector A thing that ejects

ejido Mexican farmland

eke To supplement with great effort

el, ell The letter *l*

elaborate To develop completely

elan Style

eland An antelope

elapid A species of snake

elapse To slip by

elastic Quick to recover

elastin A bodily protein

elate To encourage

elaterid A species of beetle

elbow A joint

elder An older person

eldritch Weird

elect To choose

elector One who elects

electret A nonconductor

electric Thrilling

electrode A solid state electric conductor

electron An atomic particle

electrum An alloy of silver and gold

elegant Characterized by grace

elegiac Mournful

elegist The composer of an elegy

elegit A writ of execution

elegy A poem

element A component part

elemi An oily resin

elenchus, *pl* **-chi** A syllogistic refutation

elenctic Logic

elephant A large mammal

elevate To raise

eleven The cardinal number 11

eleventh The ordinal number 11 in a series

elevon An airplane control surface

elf, *pl* **elves** A dwarf

elfin Elfish

elflock A tangled lock of hair

elhi Elementary and high-school

elicit To evoke

elide To suppress

eligible Qualified

eliminate To remove

elision Act of eliding

elite The best

elitism Government rule by an elite

elixir A sweet medicinal liquid

elk A North American deer

elkhound A hunting dog

ell An extension at right angles

ellipse A plane curve

ellipsis A mark used in writing

ellipsoid A geometric surface

elliptic Having the shape of an ellipse

elm A species of tree

elocution The art of public speaking

eloign To carry away

elongate To extend

elope To run away with

eloquent Vividly expressive

else Other

elucidate To clarify

elude To avoid

elusive Tending to elude

eluvium Residual deposits

elver A young eel

elvish Variant of elfish

elytron, *pl* **-tra** Leathery forewing of certain insects

em The letter *m*

emaciate To make thin

emanate To issue

embalm To preserve

embank To protect with banks

embar To imprison

embargo A prohibiton

embark To start

embarrass To complicate

embassage Embassy

embassy A mission to a foreign government

embattle To prepare for battle

embay To enclose in a bay

embed To fix firmly

embellish To adorn

ember A live coal

embezzle To steal

embitter To make bitter

emblaze To set on fire

emblazon To ornament

emblem A symbol

embody To incarnate

embolden To encourage

embolic Relating to embolism

embolism Intercalation

embolus, *pl* **-li** An air bubble

emboly Embryonic growth

emborder To edge

embosom To embrace

emboss To carve in relief

embow To curve

embowel To disembowel

embrace To surround

embroider To embellish

embroil To entangle

embrown To darken

embryo An organism in its early stage

emcee A master of ceremonies

eme An uncle

emeer Variant of emir

emend To correct

emendate To amend

emerald A gemstone

emerge To come into view

emeritus One who is emeritus

emersed Rising out of water

emery A granular corundum

emesis Vomiting

emetic An agent that induces vomiting

emetine An alkaloid

emeu Variant of emu

emeute A riot

emigrant Emigrating

emigrate To leave

emigre An emigrant

eminent Prominent

emir An Arabian prince

emirate The office of an emir

emissary An agent representing another

emission The act of emitting

emit To release

emmer A kind of wheat

emmet An ant

emollient An agent that softens

emote To express emotion

emotion A strong feeling

empathy Ability to share in another's feelings

emperor A ruler

empery An empire

emphasis Force of feeling

emphatic Positive

empire Imperial dominion

empiric A charlatan

emplace To put into place

employ To put to work

employee One who works

employer One who employs

empoison To embitter

emporium A marketplace

empower To authorize

empress A female sovereign

emprise, emprize An undertaking

empty Vacant

empurple To color with purple

empyema, *pl* **-mata** Pus in a body cavity

empyreal Celestial

empyrean The sky

emu An Australian bird

emulate To strive to excel

emulous Eager to surpass

emulsion A light-sensitive coating

en The letter n

en- Indicates to put into or on; to go into or on; to cover; to provide with; to resemble. The following compounds are listed without definition (see Introduction):

enable	encage	encircle
enact	encamp	enclasp
enactive	encase	enclose
enactor	encash	enclosure
enactory	enchain	encode
enamor	enchant	encompass
enamour	encipher	encourage

134

encroach
encrust
encumber
encyst
endamage
endanger
endear
endow
endowment
endure
endurable
endurance
enface
enfeeble
enfetter
enfever
enflame
enfold
enforce
enframe
engage
engarland
engender
engild
engird
engirdle
englut
engorge
engraft
engrain
engrave
engross
engulf
enhalo
enhance
enisle
enjoin

enjoy
enjoyment
enkindle
enlace
enlarge
enlighten
enlist
enlistee
enlister
enliven
enmesh
ennoble
ennobler
enplane
enquire
enquiry
enrage
enrapt
enrapture
enravish
enrich
enrobe
enrol
enroll
enrollee
enroller
enroot
ensample
enscroll
enserf
ensheathe
enshrine
enshroud
ensilage
ensky
enslave
ensnare

ensoul
ensphere
ensure
ensurer
enswathe
entangle
enter
enterer
enthral
enthrall
enthrone
enthuse
entice
entitle
entomb
entrain
entrance
entrap
entreat
entreaty
entrench
entrust
entwine
entwist
envelop
envelope
envenom
envisage
envision
enwheel
enwind
enwomb
enwrap
enwreathe

enamel A vitreous coating
enate Growing outward
encaustic Pertaining to a painting
  process
enceinte Pregnant
enchase To set with gems
enchilada A Mexican food
encina An evergreen oak
enclave A territorial unit
enclitic A word pronounced as part
  of the preceding word
encomiast An eulogist
encomium, *pl* **-ums** or **-mia** An

eulogy
encore To demand an encore
encounter A meeting
end The outcome
endarch Maturing from the center
  outward
endbrain A part of the brain
endeavor An earnest effort
endemic, endemial Native to a certain region
endermic Acting by absorption
endive A plant used in salads
endlong Lengthwise
endmost Last
endocarp The inner layer of the
  pericarp
endocrine Secreting internally
endoderm The innermost germ
  layer of an embryo
endogamy Marriage within a particular group
endorse To sign a document
endorsee One to whom a document
  is transferred
endoscope A medical instrument
endosome A cellular particle
endosteum, *pl* **-tea** Bone membrane
endotoxin A toxic substance
endpaper Paper used in
  bookbinding
endplate A nerve terminal
endrin An insecticide
endue To clothe
endwise End to end
enema A douche
enemy A foe
energid A nucleus surrounded by
  cytoplasm that does not constitute
  a cell
energy Vigor
enervate To weaken
enfeoff To surrender
enfilade To direct gunfire the
  length of the target
eng A phonetic symbol
engine A locomotive
engineer One who operates an
  engine
enginery Machinery
engrail To decorate the edge

engram, engramme An effect produced in the psyche by stimulation
enigma Something hard to explain
enmity Hostility
ennead A group of nine
ennui Boredom
enol A chemical compound
enormity Excessive wickedness
enormous Great in size
enough Adequate
enounce To announce
enow Enough
ens An entity
ensconce To settle securely
ensemble A group
ensiform Sword-shaped
ensign A naval officer
ensile To store in a silo
ensorcel, ensorcell To enchant
ensue To result
entail To impose
entente An agreement
enteral Enteric
enteric Of the intestine
enteritis Inflammation of the intestinal tract
enteron The intestine
entertain To amuse
enthalpy A thermodynamic function
entia Plural of ens
entire Total
entity Being
entoil To entrap
entourage A group of followers
entozoa A species of animal
entrails Internal organs
entrant One who enters
entrechat A ballet leap
entree Admittance
entrepot A warehouse
entresol A mezzanine
entropy A thermodynamic measure
entry The act of entering
enucleate To explain
enumerate To count
enunciate To speak clearly
enuresis Involuntary urination
environ To encircle

envoi Concluding stanza of a poem
envoy A representative
envy A resentment
enzootic A disease in animals
enzyme A protein
eohippus An extinct mammal
eolian Pertaining to the wind
eolith A prehistoric stone tool
eon An age
eonian Ageless
eosin A red dye
epact The difference of time between the solar year and the lunar year
eparch A bishop
eparchy A greek diocese
epaulet A shoulder ornament
epee A fencing sword
epergne A serving dish
ephah, epha A Hebrew unit of measure
ephebe A youth of ancient Greece
ephemera, *pl* **-as** or **-erae** Something short-lived
ephemerid A species of insect
ephod An ancient Hebrew vestment
ephor, *pl* **-ors** or **-ori** A magistrate of ancient Sparta
epiboly Gastrulation
epic A long narrative poem
epicarp An exocarp
epicedium, *pl* **-dia** A funeral dirge
epicene Womanish
epicrisis, *pl* **-ses** A critique of a literary work
epicure A gourmet
epicycle A circle that rolls on the circumference of another circle
epidemic A widespread disease
epidote A mineral
epigeal Living near the surface
epigene Formed below the surface
epigone A second-rate imitator
epigram A short poem
epigraph An inscription
epilepsy A nervous disorder
epilogue, epilog A concluding speech
epinasty A downward bending

epiphany A spiritual event
epiphyte A species of plant
episcopal Pertaining to a bishop
episode A portion of a narrative
epistle A letter
epistler One who writes epistles
epistyle An architrave
epitaph An inscription on a tombstone
epitasis, *pl* **-ses** Main part of a classical drama
epithet A term used to characterize a person
epitome An abstract
epizoic Living on the exterior of an animal
epoch A period of time
epode A type of poem
eponym One for whom something is named
eponymy The derivation of a name
epopee Epic poetry
epos An epic poem
epoxy A glue
epsilon The fifth letter of the Greek alphabet
equable Steady
equal The same
equate To balance
equator A circle around the earth's surface
equerry An officer in charge of horses
equine Pertaining to a horse
equinox A point on the celestial sphere
equip To provide with necessities
equipage Accouterments
equipment Furnishings
equitable Characterized by fairness
equitant Overlapping
equity Something that is fair
equivocal Evasive
equivogue A pun
er Used to express hesitation
era A period of time
eradiate To radiate
eradicate To erase

erase To rub out
erasion Act of erasing
erbium A metallic element
ere Before
erect Standing upright
erectile Able to be erected
erelong Soon
eremite A religious recluse
erenow Before now
erepsin A mixture of enzymes
erethism Abnormal irritability
erewhile Formerly
erg A unit of energy
ergo Hence
ergot A fungus
ergotism Poisoning by ergot-infected grain
erica A shrub
eristic An expert in debate
erlking A mythological evil spirit
ermine A weasel
erne, ern A species of sea eagle
erode To corrode
erose Jagged
erosion The state of being eroded
erotic Concerning sexual love
erotica Art dealing with sexual love
err To go astray
errancy State of going astray
errand A short trip to perform a task
errant Erring
errantry Condition of being errant
erratic Wandering
erratum, *pl* **-ta** An error
errhine Promoting nasal discharge
error A mistake
ersatz Artificial
erst At first
erstwhile Former
eruct To belch
erudite Scholarly
erupt To explode
eryngo A species of plant
erythema A redness of the skin
escalade To climb over a wall
escalate To intensify
escapade A caper
escape To break free

escapee One who escapes
escargot En edible snail
escarole A variety of endive
escarp A steep cliff
eschalot A shallot
eschar A dry scab
escheat To confiscate
eschew To shun
escolar A species of fish
escort A companion
escrow Placed in custody of a third party
escudo Monetary unit of Portugal
esculent Edible
eserine A toxic alkaloid
eskar, esker A ridge of gravel
esophagus, *pl* **-gi** A tube for the passage of food
esoteric Abstruse
espalier A trellis
esparto A grass of Africa
especial Exceptional
esperance Hope
espial The act of spying
espionage The craft of spying
esplanade A promenade
espousal A wedding ceremony
espouse To marry
espresso A strong coffee
esprit Spirit
espy To spy
esquire A squire
ess, es The letter s
essay To try out
essence A fundamental quality
essential Absolute
essonite A garnet
establish To make secure
estancia A cattle ranch
estate All of one's property
esteem To think of with respect
ester A chemical compound
esterase An enzyme
esthesia The ability to feel sensations
esthetic Appreciative of the beautiful
estimate To approximate
estop To plug up
estoppel A legal restraint

estovers Necessities granted by law
estragon Tarragon
estrange To make hostile
estray A stray animal
estriol An estrogen
estrogen A female hormone
estrone An estrogen
estrous In heat
estrus Period of heat in female animals
estuary The part of the river where its current is influenced by tides
esu Electrostatic unit
et Past tense of eat
eta The seventh letter of the Greek alphabet
etagere A piece of furniture
etch To imprint clearly
eternal Timeless
eterne Eternal
eternity Infinite time
etesian Recurring annually
eth Variant of edh
ethane An odorless gas
ethanol An alcohol
ethene Ethylene
ether A volatile liquid
ethereal Exquisite
etherify To convert into ether
ethic Moral principles
ethicize To make ethical
ethmoid A bone of the nasal cavity
ethnarch A ruler
ethnic Pertaining to a racial group
ethology Study of animal behavior
ethos Character peculiar to a culture
ethyl A univalent chemical radical
ethylene A flammable gas
etiolate To become blanched
etiquette Prescribed social manners
etude A practice piece of music
etui, etwee A case for holding small articles
etymology The origin of a word
etymon, *pl* **-mons** or **-ma** The earliest known form of a word
eucaine An anesthetic

euchre A card game
euclase A mineral
eudemon A good spirit
eugenics The science of hereditary improvement
eugenol An aromatic oil
euglena A species of freshwater organism
eulachon The candlefish
eulogy Great praise
eunuch A castrated man
euonymus A species of tree
eupatrid A member of the aristocracy of ancient Athens
eupepsia Good digestion
euphemism The substitution of a word that is considered less offensive
euphonic Relating to euphony
euphony Agreeable sound
euphoria Bliss
euphotic Pertaining to the uppermost layer of a body of water
euphrasy An annual herb
euphroe A batten through which ropes are tightened to support an awning
euphuism An affected elegant style of writing
euplastic Healing readily
eupnea Normal breathing
eureka Used to express triumph
euripus, *pl* **-pi** A turbulent sea channel
euro A kangaroo
europium A metallic element
eurythmy Graceful movement
eustacy A change in sea level
eustele A part of a plant
eutaxy Good arrangement
eutectic Pertaining to the lowest possible melting point
euxenite A mineral
evacuate To withdraw
evacuee A person withdrawn
evade To elude
evaluate To appraise
evanesce To fade away
evangel An evangelist
evaporate To change into a vapor

evasion Dodging
evasive Intentionally vague
eve Evening
evection Irregularity in the lunar orbit
even Flat
evenfall Twilight
evening Period between the end of a work day and bedtime
evensong A vesper service
event An experience
eventide Evening
ever Always
everglade Marsh land
evergreen Having foliage throughout the year
evermore Forever
eversion The act of everting
evert To turn outward or inside out
every Each thing
everyday Ordinary
everyone Every person
evict To dispossess
evidence Data on which proof may be established
evident Obvious
evil Wicked
evildoer One who does evil
evince To exhibit
evitable Avoidable
evoke To call forth
evolute A geometric curve
evolution A thing evolved
evolve To develop
evulsion The act of pulling out
evzone A Greek soldier
ewe A female sheep
ewer A large jug
ex, *pl* **exes** The letter x
exact Precise
exalt To elevate
exam An examination
examen A critical study
examine To inspect
example A sample
exarch A ruler of a province in the Byzantine Empire
exarchy The domain of an exarch
excaudate Tailless
excavate To dig out

exceed To surpass
excel To outdo
excellent Superb
excelsior Wood shavings
except Other than
excerpt A passage selected from a book
excess An overabundance
exchange Interchange
exchequer A treasury
excise An indirect tax
excite To arouse emotions
exciton An energy level of a crystal
excitor A stimulant
exclaim To speak out suddenly
exclave A portion of a country isolated in alien territory
exclude To expel
exclusive Not shared with others
excoriate To chafe
excrement Waste material
excreta Waste matter
excrete To eliminate
excurrent Having an outward flow
excursion A pleasure tour
excusive Rambling
excursus A digression
excuse Forgive
exec An executive
execrate To denounce
executant One who performs
execute To perform
executor One that executes
executrix A female executor
exedra A curved outdoor bench
exegesis, *pl* **-ses** Critical explanation
exegete One skilled in exegesis
exegetic Analytic
exemplar A model
exempt To excuse
exequies Funeral rites
exercise Physical exertion
exergue A space on a coin
exert To put forth
exes Plural of ex
exeunt They go out
exhalant Something that exhales
exhale To breathe out
exhaust To drain

exhibit To display
exhort To incite
exhume To uncover
exigent Urgent
exigible Requisite
exiguity Meagerness
exile Banishment
exist To be
exit The act of going away
exocarp Outermost layer of fruit skin
exocrine Secreting through a duct
exoderm The ectoderm
exodus A departure
exogamy Custom of marrying outside the tribe
exonerate To declare blameless
exorable Persuadable
exorcise To free from evil spirits
exordium, *pl* **-ums** or **-dia** A beginning
exospore The outer layer of a spore
exoteric Popular
exotic Strikingly beautiful
exotica Things excitingly different
expand To spread out
expanse A wide area
expatiate To speak at length
expect To look forward to
expedient Useful for effecting a desired result
expedite To help alone
expel To drive out
expellant Tending to expel
expend To spend
expense A price
expert A person with a special skill
expertise Expert advice
expiable Capable of being expiated
expiate To atone for
expire To terminate
expiry An expiration
explain To define
explant To take from the natural site of growth and place in a culture
expletive An oath
explicate To explain
explicit Specific
explode To fly into a sudden rage

exploit　A deed
explore　To examine
explosion　A sudden violent release of energy
exponent　One who expounds
export　To ship abroad
expose　To make known
expound　To set forth
express　To state
expresso　Espresso
expulsion　The act of expelling
expunge　To erase
exquisite　Beautifully made
exscind, exsect　To cut out
exsert　To thrust out
extant　Still in existence
extend　To stretch out
extensile　Capable of being stretched out
extension　The act of extending
extensity　The quality of having extension
extensor　A muscle that stretches a limb
extent　Scope
exterior　External
extern, externe　A nonresident of an institution
external　Exterior
extinct　Having died out
extirpate　To root up
extol　To eulogize
extort　To exact
extra　Additional
extract　To pull out
extradite　To obtain the extradition of
extrados　The upper curve of an arch
extreme　Drastic
extricate　To disengage
extrinsic　Extraneous

extrorse　Facing outward
extrovert　A person whose interest is more in other people than in himself
extrude　To push out
exuberant　Full of high spirits
exudate　An exuded substance
exude　To ooze forth
exult　To be jubilant
exuberia, exurb　A residential area lying beyond the suburbs of the city
exuvium, *pl* **-viae** or **-via**　Larvae and nymphs of insects
eyas　A falcon or young hawk
eye　An organ of vision
The following words are listed without definition (see Introduction):

eyeball	eyeless	eyesore
eyebeam	eyelet	eyespot
eyebrow	eyelid	eyestalk
eyecup	eyelike	eyestone
eyed	eyeliner	eyestrain
eyedness	eyepiece	eyewash
eyeful	eyeshade	eyewater
eyeglass	eyeshot	eyewink
eyehole	eyesight	
eyelash	eyesome	

eyebolt　A bolt designed to receive a rope
eyebright　A species of plant
eyehook　A hook attached to a ring
eyeleteer　An instrument for piercing eyelets in cloth
eyetooth, *pl* **-teeth**　A cuspid
eyra　A wild cat
eyre　A journey
eyrie　Variant of aerie
eyrir, *pl* **aurar**　Monetary unit of Iceland
eyry　Variant of aerie

fa The fourth tone of the diatonic scale
fable A story
fabliau, pl -liaux Medieval verse
fabric Cloth
fabricate To fashion
fabulist A composer of fables
fabulous Astonishing
facade The face of a building
face A grimace
faceplate An attachment for a lathe
facet An aspect
facete Witty
facetiae Witty sayings
facetious Trying to be jocular
facies Outward appearance
facile Easy
facility Aptitude
facsimile A reproduction
fact Something real
factor An agent
factorage Duties of a factor
factorial Relating to a factor
factory A plant
factotum An employee with many duties
facture That which is made
facula, pl -lae Spots on the sun's photosphere
faculty Skill
fad A fashion that enjoys brief popularity
faddish Having the nature of a fad
fade To dim
fado A Portuguese folk song
faena The final passes of the matador before the killing
faerie, faery A fairy
fag Drudgery
fagot, faggot A bundle of twigs
faience A variety of glazed pottery
fail To be unsuccessful

faille A fabric
fain Preferably
faineant Idle
faint Feeble
fair Lovely
fairing A gift
fairish Of moderate quality
fairway Part of a golf course
fairy A supernatural being
faith A belief in something
faitour An imposter
fake Fraudulent
fakir, fakeer A Hindu religious mendicant
falafel A sandwich stuffing
falbala A ruffle
falcate Sickle-shaped
falchion A broad sword
falciform Falcate
falcon A species of bird of prey
falconer One who breeds falcons
falconet A young falcon
falconry The sport of hunting with falcons
falderal, falderol Variants of folderol
faldstool A stool used for praying
fall To be cast down
fallacy A false notion
fallal A piece of finery
fallfish A freshwater fish
fallible Capable of erring
fallout Radioactive debris
fallow Not pregnant
false Incorrect
falsehood An untruth
falsetto An artificially high singing voice
falsie A pad worn under a brassiere
falsify To misrepresent
falsity An untruth

faltboat A small boat
falter To hesitate
fame To make famous
familial Pertaining to a family
familiar Common
family A group of related persons
famine Starvation
famish To suffer from hunger
famous Well-known
famulus, *pl* **-li** A servant
fan To cool
fanatic A zealot
fancy Decorative
fandango A dance
fandom Celebrity followers
fane A temple
fanfare A loud flourish
fanfaron A braggart
fang A long, pointed tooth
fanlight A type of window
fanny *Slang* The buttocks
fanon, fano A cape worn by the
   pope
fantail A species of pigeon
fantasia A free-form musical
   composition
fantast A dreamer
fantastic Wondrous
fantasy An illusion
fantod A nervous condition
fanwise Opened like a fan
fanwort A species of aquatic plant
fanzine A magazine for fans
faqir, faquir Variants of fakir
far To a great distance
farad A unit of capacitance
faraday A unit of electricity
faradic Pertaining to a type of
   electric current
faradism Faradization
faradize To treat with faradic
   currents
farandole A dance
faraway Very distant
farce Something ludicrous
farceur, farcer An actor in a farce
farcical Pertaining to a farce
farcy A disease
fard To apply cosmetics to
fardel A load

fare A charge
farewell Goodby
farina Meal from cereal grain
farinose Similar to farina
farm To cultivate as a farm
farnesol An alcohol used in
   perfumes
faro A card game
farouche Shy
farrago A mixture
farrier One who shoes horses
farriery A farrier's shop
farrow A litter of pigs
fart *Slang* An old fool
farther To a more distant point
farthing A British coin
fasces A symbol of power in
   ancient Rome
fascia, *pl* **-ciae** Fibrous tissue
   beneath the skin
fasciate Abnormally flattened
fascicle A small bundle
fascinate To bewitch
fascine A bundle of sticks
fascism An oppressive political
   system
fascist One who practices fascism
fashion The current style in dress
fast Swift
fasten To connect
fastness Condition of being fast
fat Obesity
fatal Mortal
fatality A death
fatback A strip of fat
fate Supposed force that deter-
   mines events
fathead *Slang* A dolt
father A male parent
fathom To understand
fatidic Prophetic
fatigue To weary
fatling An animal fattened for
   slaughter
fattish Chubby
fatuity Vanity
fatuous Inane
faubourg A suburb
faucal, faucial Relating to the
   fauces

fauces The passage from the mouth to the pharynx

faucet A device for controlling the flow of water

faugh Used to express disgust

fault A flaw

faun A deity of mythology

fauna, *pl* **-nas** or **-nae** Animals of a particular region

fauteuil An armchair

fauve A fauvist

fauvism A movement in painting

fauvist An advocate of fauvism

favela A slum area

favonian Mild

favor A kind attitude

favus A skin disease

fawn To seek favor

fax To reproduce by electronic means

fay To join

fayalite A mineral

faze To bother

fazenda A plantation

feal Loyal

fealty Allegiance

fear A state of alarm

feasance The performance of a duty

fease To faze

feasible Possible

feast An elaborate meal

feat An act of courage

feather To cover with feathers

feathery Covered with feathers

feature A prominent quality

febricity Condition of having a fever

febrific Having fever

febrile Feverish

fecal Pertaining to feces

feces Excrement

feckless Feeble

feculent Foul

fecund Fertile

fed *Slang* A federal agent

federacy An alliance

federal A supporter of federal government

federate To join

fedora A soft felt hat

fee A fixed charge

feeble Weak

feed To give food to

feedback Information about the result

feedbag A nosebag

feel To touch

feeze To faze

feh Variant of peh

feign To pretend

feint A misleading movement

feis A cultural festival

feist A mongrel

feisty Frisky

feldspar A mineral

felicity Bliss

feline An animal of the cat family

fell To cut down

fellah A peasant

fellatio Oral stimulation

feller One that fells

fellow A man

felly, felloe The rim of a wheel

felon An evil person

felonious Wicked

felonry Felons collectively

felony A crime

felsite An igneous rock

felspar Variant of feldspar

felt A fabric

felucca A sailing vessel

felwort A species of plant

female Feminine

feme A woman

feminie Womankind

feminine Belonging to the female sex

femme A wife

femoral Pertaining to the femur

femur, *pl* **-murs** or **femora** The thigh

fen A marsh

fenagle Variant of finagle

fence To surround

fend To defend

fenestra, *pl* **-trae** A small opening

fennec A small fox

fennel A species of plant

fenny Marshy

feoff To invest with a fee

feral Savage
fere A spouse
feretory A shrine
feria, *pl* **-as** or **feriae** A holiday
ferine Untamed
ferity Ferocity
fermata The sustaining of a musical note
ferment Fermentation
fermion A type of atomic particle
fermium A radioactive element
fern A species of plant
fernery A bed of ferns
ferny Relating to ferns
ferocious Fierce
ferocity The condition of being ferocious
ferrate A ferrite
ferret A piece of tape used to edge fabric
ferriage Transportation by ferry
ferric Containing iron
ferrite A magnetic substance
ferrous Pertaining to iron
ferrule A bushing
ferry To transport by ferry
ferryboat A boat used to ferry passengers
ferryman A man who owns or operates a ferry
fertile Able to mature
ferula, *pl* **-lae** A small whip
ferule To punish
fervent Passionate
fervid Burning
fervor Ardor
fescue A species of grass
fess, fesse To confess
festa A festival
festal Festive
fester To decay
festival A time of celebration
festive Merry
festoon A wreath of flowers hanging in a loop
fet To fetch
feta A Greek cheese
fetal Pertaining to a fetus
fetch To get
fete A feast

feterita A variety of sorghum
feticide Destruction of a human fetus
fetid Stinking
fetish, fetich An object believed to have magical powers
fetlock A joint of a horse's leg
fetor A strong odor
fetter A shackle
fettle Good spirits
fetus, *pl* **-tuses** Unborn organism from the end of the eighth week to the moment of birth
feud A quarrel
feudal Pertaining to feudalism
feudatory A vassal
fever High temperature
feverfew An aromatic plant
few A small number
fey Enchanted
fez, *pl* **fezzes** A cap worn in the Near East
fiacre A coach
fiance A man engaged to be married
fiancee A woman engaged to be married
fiasco A complete failure
fiat Sanction
fib A lie
fiber A threadlike object
fibril, fibrilla A small fiber
fibrin A protein
fibroid Resembling fibrous tissue
fibroin A protein
fibroma, *pl* **-mas** or **-mata** A benign tumor
fibrosis The formation of fibrous tissue
fibrous Having fibers
fibula, *pl* **-lae** or **-las** A bone of the leg
fice A feist
fichu A scarf
fickle Capricious
fico A worthless thing
fictile Moldable
fiction A literary work not based on fact
fictive Fictitious
fid A support for the topmast

fiddle   A musical instrument
fidelity   Loyalty
fidget   To fuss
fiducial   Fiduciary
fie   Used to express distaste
fief   A fee
field   A meadow
fieldfare   An Old World thrush
fiend   A demon
fierce   Ferocious
fiery   Resembling a fire
fiesta   A festival
fife   A musical instrument
fifteen   The cardinal number 15
fifth   The ordinal number five in a series
fiftieth   The ordinal number 50 in a series
fifty   The cardinal number 50
fig   The fruit of the fig tree
fight   To argue
figment   A fabrication of the imagination
figural   Consisting of human forms
figurant   A walk-on
figure   A number
figurine   A statuette
figwort   A species of plant
fil   A coin
filament   A thin thread
filar   Pertaining to a thread
filaree   A European weed
filaria, pl -**iae**   A species of worm
filature   The process of spinning
filbert   An edible nut
filch   To pilfer
file   To catalogue
filefish   A species of fish
filet   A net
filial   Pertaining to a son or daughter
filiate   To affiliate
filibeg   A kilt
filicide   One who kills his child
filiform   Threadlike
filigree, filagree, fillagree   Intricate ornamentation
fill   To make full
fillet   A strip of boneless meat
fillip   A stimulus

filly   A young colt
film   A mist
filmdom   The movie industry
filmgoer   One who goes to movies
filmstrip   A length of film
filmy   Transparent
filose   Threadlike
fils   Son
filter   A device for removing suspended matter
filth   Foulness
filtrate   To put through a filter
filum, pl -**la**   A filament
fimbria, pl -**briae**   A fringe
fin   An external paddlelike structure
finable, fineable   Liable to a fine
finagle   To wangle
final   Concluding
finale   The concluding part
finance   To supply the capital for
finback   A whale
finch   A species of bird
find   To arrive at
fine   Admirable
finespun   Delicate
finesse   Craftiness
finger   One of the five digits of the hand
finial   A crowning ornament
finical   Finicky
finicky   Fussy
finis   The end
finish   To terminate
finite   Limited
finitude   The state of being finite
fink Slang   To inform
finnicky   Variant of finicky
finny   Having fins
finochio   A variety of fennel
fiord   Variant of fjord
fipple   A plug of wood in an organ pipe
fir   A species of evergreen tree
fire   To become ignited
fireball   A burning sphere
firebird   Any of various birds having bright scarlet or orange plumage
fireboat   A boat equipped to fight

fires
firebox A chamber in which fuel is burned
firebrand A piece of burning wood
firebrat An insect
firebreak A strip of cleared land used to stop a fire
firebug A person who sets fires
firedog An andiron
firedrake A fiery dragon
firefly A species of beetle
firelock A flintlock
fireman A fire fighter
firepan A brazier
fireplace A hearth
fireplug A hydrant
firer One that fires
fireroom A room containing the ship's boilers
firestone A fire-resistant stone
firetrap A building that is likely to catch fire
firkin A small keg
firm Solid
firn Granular snow that accumulates at the top of a glacier
firry Abounding in firs
first Earliest
firsthand Directly
firstling The first-born offspring
firstly To begin with
firth A fjord
fisc A royal treasury
fiscal Pertaining to finances
fish To catch fish
fishbowl A bowl in which fish are kept
fisheye A suspicious stare
fishgig An instrument for spearing fish
fishhook A metal hook used for catching fish
fishmeal A fertilizer produced from fish parts
fishnet A net for catching fish
fishplate A plate used to bolt rails together
fishpond A small body of water abounding in edible fish
fishtail Suggestive of a fishtail in movement
fishwife, *pl* **-wives** A woman who sells fish
fissile Capable of being split
fission To split into parts
fissiped A mammal that has separated toes
fissure To split
fist A grasping hand
fistic Pugilistic
fisticuff A punch
fistula, *pl* **-las** or **-lae** An abnormal duct
fit Healthy
fitch A polecat
fitchew, fitchet A fitch
fitter One who alters garments
five The cardinal number 5
fivefold Five times greater
fiver *Slang* A five-dollar bill
fix To repair
fixate To make fixed
fixings Trimmings
fixity Stability
fixt Past tense of fix
fixture A permanent part of a house
fizgig A giddy woman
fizz To make a hissing sound
fjeld A high, barren plateau
fjord A narrow inlet from the sea
flab A flabby body tissue
flaccid Flabby
flacon A small stoppered bottle
flag A species of plant
flageolet A musical instrument
flagging Languid
flaggy Drooping
flagman One who carries a flag
flagon A large vessel
flagrant Shocking
flagship The ship bearing the flag of the fleet
flagstaff A flagpole
flagstone Stone used in paving
flail To beat
flair A natural aptitude
flak Antiaircraft artillery
flake A chip
flam A deception
flambeau, *pl* **-beaux** A lighted torch

flambee, flambe Flaming
flame A sweetheart
flamen, pl **-mens** or **flamines** A priest of ancient Rome
flamenco A dance
flamingo A species of wading bird
flammable Highly combustible
flamy Flaming
flan A tart
flanerie Idling
flaneur A loafer
flange A protruding edge
flank The side
flannel A fabric
flap To beat
flapjack A pancake
flare To erupt
flash To sparkle
flashover An unintended electric arc
flask A small container
flasket A basket
flat Having no curves
flatboat A boat with a flat bottom
flatcar A railroad car
flatfish A species of fish
flatfoot, pl **-feet** A foot condition
flatiron A pressing iron
flatling Flat
flattish Flat
flattop A type of haircut
flatus Intestinal gas
flaunt To show off
flautist A flutist
flavin A yellow pigment
flavine Flavin
flavone A chemical compound
flavor A seasoning
flaw A blemish
flax A species of plant
flaxseed The seed of flax
flaxy Resembling flax
flay To plunder
flea A species of insect
fleabane A species of plant
fleabite The bite of a flea
fleche A church spire
flechette A missile
fleck A tiny spot
fledge To cover with feathers

flee To run away
fleece The wool of a sheep
fleecy Like fleece
fleer To scoff
fleet A group of warships
flense, flench To strip the blubber
flesh The soft tissue of the body
fleshly Pertaining to the flesh
fleshpot A pot for cooking meat
fletch To feather
flew Past tense of fly
flex To bend
flexible, flexile Pliable
flexion The act of bending
flexor A muscle that acts to flex
fley To frighten
flick A snap
flight The act of flying
flighty Fickle
flimflam A swindle
flimsy Unconvincing
flinch To retreat
flinders Fragments
fling To hurl
flint A spark-producing rock
flintlock A firearm
flip To toss
flippant Talkative
flirt To behave amorously
flit To dart
flitch A cured side of bacon
flivver Slang An old automobile
float To drift
floc A flocculent mass
floccose Having woolly tufts
floccule A tuft-like mass
flock A group of animals
floe A large mass of ice
flog To beat with a whip
flood A deluge
flooey Slang Phooey
floor A base
floorage Floor space
floosy, floozie floozy Slang A prostitute
flop To plop
flophouse A cheap hotel
flora, pl **-ras** or **florae** Plants
floral Pertaining to flowers
florence A gold coin

floret A small flower
florid Ruddy
florin A British coin
florist One who sells flowers
floruit Flourished
floss A soft silky fiber
flossy Slang Stylish
flotage Flotation
flotilla A fleet of small ships
flotsam Discarded wreckage
flounce A strip of pleated material
flounder A species of fish
flour To cover with flour
flourish To succeed
flout To scorn
flow To circulate
flowage The act of flowing
flower A blossom
floweret A small flower
flown Steeped
flu Influenza
flubdub Slang Nonsense
fluctuate To vary
flue A channel through which hot air may pass
fluent Flowing
fluff Light down
fluid Flowing easily
fluidics The technology of fluids
fluke A species of fish
fluky Uncertain
flume A narrow gorge with a stream flowing through it
flummery A sweet dessert
flummox Slang To confuse
flump To drop noisily
flung Past tense of fling
flunk To fail
flunky A lackey
fluor Fluorite
fluoresce To show fluorescence
fluoride A compound of fluorine
fluorine A gaseous element
fluorite A mineral
flurry A sudden gust of wind
flush To flood
fluster To make nervous
flute A musical instrument
flutter To flap the wings
fluvial Pertaining to a river

flux A flowing
fly To travel by air
flyaway Flighty
flyblow The larva of a blowfly
flyblown Contaminated
flyboy Slang A pilot
flyby A flight close to a specified place
flyleaf, pl **-leaves** A blank page at the beginning or the end of a book
flypaper Paper used to catch flies
flyspeck A minute spot
flytrap A plant that traps insects
flywheel A rotating wheel
foal To give birth to
foam To form foam
fob A watch chain ornament
focal Pertaining to a focus
focus, pl **-cuses** or **-ci** A focal point
fodder Feed for livestock
foe An enemy
foehn, fohn A warm wind
fog Condensed water vapor
fogbound Clouded by fog
fogbow An arc-shaped light seen in a fog
fogdog A clear spot in a fog bank
foggy Surrounded by fog
foghorn A warning horn
fogy, fogey An old-fashioned person
foible A failing of character
foil To thwart
foilsman A fencer
foin To thrust with a pointed weapon
foison A good crop
foist To palm off
fold To bend over parts
foldboat A faltboat
folderol Nonsense
foliage The leaves of plants
foliar Pertaining to leaves
foliate To coat with metal foil
folio A large book
foliose Bearing numerous leaves
folium, pl **-lia** A thin layer
folk A people
folklore The study of folk culture
folkmote, folkmoot A general

assembly of people

folknik A devotee of folk songs

folksy Unsophisticated

folkway A traditional custom of a people

follicle A small body cavity

follies An elaborate theatrical revue

follow To come or go after

folly A lack of understanding

foment To stir up

fond Affectionate

fondant A candy

fondue, fondu A food dish

font A stoup

fontanel The soft area in the skull of a baby

food Nourishment

foofaraw A fuss

fool A stupid person

foolery A jest

foolhardy Rash

foolproof Completely dependable

foolscap A fool's cap

foot The lower extremity of the leg on which the body stands and moves

The following words are listed without definition (see Introduction):

footage	footless	footslog
football	footlike	footsore
footbath	footmark	footstep
footboard	footpace	footstone
footed	footpath	footstool
footer	footprint	footway
footfall	footrace	footwear
footgear	footrest	footwork
foothold	footrope	footworn
footing	footsie	

footboy A serving boy

footcloth A carpet

foothill A hill near the base of a mountain

footle To trifle

footling Foolish

footloose Free

footman A servant

footnote To furnish with explana-tory notes

footpad A street robber

foots Dregs

footstall The pedestal of a pillar

fop A dandy

foppery The manner of a fop

foppish Dandified

for Directed toward

forage Fodder

foramen, *pl* **-ramina** or **-mens** An aperture in a bone

foray A military advance

forb A species of plant

forbear To cease

forbid To prohibit

force Power

forcemeat Ground meat used for stuffing

forceps An instrument for holding

ford A shallow place in water

fordo To kill

fore Located at or toward the front

fore- Indicates before in time; the front or first part. The following compounds are listed without definition (see Introduction):

forearm	forehead	foresaid
forebear	forehoof	foresail
forbode	forejudge	foresee
forebody	foreknow	foresheet
foreboom	foreland	foreshow
forebrain	foreleg	foreside
forecast	forelimb	forespeak
forecourt	forelock	forestay
foredate	foremast	foretaste
foredeck	foremilk	foretell
foredoom	foremost	foretime
foreface	forename	foretoken
forefeel	forenoon	forewarn
forefoot	forepart	forewent
forefront	forepast	forewing
forego	forepaw	foreword
foregone	forepeak	foreyard
foregut	forerank	
forehand	forerun	

foreclose To shut out

foreign Away from one's native country

forelady A woman who acts as a foreman

foreman One who has charge of a group of workers

forensic Rhetorical

foreshore The shore covered at high tide

foresight The act of looking forward

forest A dense growth of trees and plants

forestall To prevent

foretop A forelock

forever Eternally

forefeit A forefeiture

forfend To avert

forficate Deeply notched

forge A smithy

forgery Something counterfeit

forget To pass over

forgetive Capable of inventing

forging A forgery

forgive To pardon

forgo To forsake

forint Monetary unit of Hungary

forjudge Variant of forejudge

fork A utensil for eating

forlorn Desperate

form To produce

formant A sound wave special to a particular vowel sound

format The layout for a publication

formate A chemical salt

formic Pertaining to ants

formula, pl **-las** or **-lae** A method for doing something

formyl A univalent radical

fornicate Vaulted

fornix, pl **-nices** A vaulted space

forsake To renounce

forsooth Indeed

forspent Exhausted

forswear To perjure

forsythia A species of shrub

fort A fortification

fortalice A small fort

forte Forcefully

forth Onward

fortieth The ordinal number 40 in a series

fortis Pronounced with strong articulation

fortitude Strength of mind

fortnight Two weeks

fortress A fortified place

fortune Success

forty The cardinal number 40

forum, pl **-rums** or **fora** A public square in ancient Rome

forward Near the front

forwent Past tense of forgo

forwhy For what reason

forworn Worn-out

fossa, pl **fossae** A depression

fosse, foss A ditch

fossick To search for gold

fossil Remains from a past geological age

foster To rear

fou Drunk

fought Past tense of fight

foul Disgusting

foulard A fabric

found To establish

foundry A place where metal is cast

fount A fountain

fountain A spring

four The cardinal number 4

fourfold Quadruple

fourgon A wagon for carrying baggage

fourscore Eighty

foursome A group of four persons

fourteen The cardinal number 14

fourth The ordinal number four in a series

fovea, pl **-veae** A shallow depression in a bone

fowl A species of bird

fox A species of mammal

foxfire A glow produced by fungi

foxglove A species of plant

foxhole A pit dug by a soldier

foxhound A hunting dog

foxing A piece of material used on a shoe

foxtail A species of grass

foxy Sly

foy A farewell feast

foyer A lobby

fozy Too ripe

fracas A quarrel
fracted Broken
fraction A scrap
fragile Frail
fragment An odd piece
fragrant Sweet-smelling
frail Fragile
frailty Weakness
fraise A barrier of pointed stakes
fraktur A style of letter
frambesia Yaws
framboise A brandy
frame To build
franc Monetary unit of France
franchise A grant of certain rights to a company
francium A radioactive element
francolin A species of Old World bird
frangible Breakable
frank Straightforward
franklin A country gentleman
frantic Desperate
frap To tighten
frappe A dessert
frat A college fraternity
frater A brother in a fraternity
fraternal Brotherly
fraud A swindle
fraught Laden
fraulein A German governess
fray A brawl
frazil Ice crystals
frazzle To fray
freak A streak of color
freckle To dot with freckles
free At liberty
freeboot To plunder
freeborn Born as a free person
freedman An emancipated slave
freedom The condition of being free
freeform Having a free flowing shape
freehand Drawn by hand
freehold An estate held for life
freeload *Slang* To sponge
freeman A person not in slavery
freesia A species of plant
freest Superlative of free
freeze To solidify

freight A charge
fremitus A palpable vibration
french The Romance language
frenetic Frantic
frenum, *pl* **-nums** or **-na** A connecting fold of membrane
frenzy Mania
frequent Occurring often
frere A brother
fresco A type of painting
fresh Different
freshet A stream of fresh water
freshman A beginner
fret To distress
fretwork Ornamental work
friable Brittle
friar A member of a religious order
friarbird A species of bird
friary A monastery
fribble To waste time
fricasse Meat served with a thick gravy
friction The rubbing of one object against another
fridge A refrigerator
friend A favored companion
frieze A fabric
frigate A warship
fright Alarm
frigid Extremely cold
frijol, *pl* **frijoles** A Spanish food
frill A ruffled border
frilly Decorated with frills
fringe A decorative edging
frippery Trivia
frise A fabric
friseur A hairdresser
frisk To search
frisket A frame used on a printing press
frit Material used in making glass
frith An estuary
fritter To squander little by little
frivol To behave frivolously
friz A tight curl
frizette, frisette A curled fringe of hair
frizz To form into tight curls
fro Away
frock An outer garment

froe A cleaving tool
frog A species of aquatic amphibians
frogeye A plant disease
frogfish A species of anglerfish
froggy Full of frogs
frogman A person equipped for underwater swimming
frolic Merriment
from Out of
fromage Cheese
frond A type of leaf
frondose Bearing fronds
frons Part of an insect
front Forefront
frontal The facade of a building
frontier The region beyond a settled area
frontlet The forehead of an animal or bird
frore Frosty
frosh A freshman
frost The process of freezing
froth Foam
froufrou A rustling sound
frow Froe
froward Obstinate
frown To wrinkle the brow
frowsty Musty
frowzy, frouzy, frowsy Shabby
froze Past tense of freeze
fructify To make fruitful
fructose A very sweet sugar
frug A dance
frugal Thrifty
fruit To bear fruit
fruitage The time of bearing fruit
fruiter A tree that bears fruit
fruition Pleasure
frumenty A dish of wheat boiled in milk
frump A colorless person
frustrate To thwart
frustule The shell of a diatom
frustum, pl -**tums** or -**ta** A part of a conical solid
fry To cook in fat
fub To fob
fubsy Chubby
fuchsia A species of shrub

fuchsin, fuchsine A red dye
fucoid A seaweed
fucus, pl -**fuci** Any of a genus of brown algae
fud Slang An old-fashioned person
fuddle To drink
fudge A candy
fuel Anything consumed to produce energy
fug Stuffy air
fugal In the style of a fugue
fugio A copper coin
fugitive Fleeting
fugle To make signals
fugleman A leader
fugue A musical style
fuhrer, fuehrer A leader
fuji A fabric
fulcrum, pl -**crums** or -**cra** The point on which a lever turns
fulfill To effect
fulgent Shining brightly
fulgurous Emitting flashes of lightning
full Filled
fulmar A gull-like bird
fulminate To explode
fulmine To fulminate
fulsome Disgusting
fumarole A hole in a volcanic area
fumble To blunder
fume A state of anger
fumigate To destroy pests
fumy Producing fumes
fun Amusing diversion
function Assigned activity
fund A sum of money
fundus, pl -**di** The inner basal surface of a body organ
funeral Ceremonies held for the dead
funest Portending death
funfair An amusement park
fungal A fungus
fungible Something that may be exchanged for another equivalent unit
fungo A practice fly ball
fungoid Fungus-like

153

fungus, *pl* **-fungi** or **-guses** A species of plant
funicular A cable railway
funk Panic
funky A term used in music
funnel A cone-shaped utensil
funny Mirthful
fur The hair covering the body of various animals
furan, furfuran A flammable liquid
furbelow A ruffle on a garment
furbish To burnish
furcate To fork
furcula, *pl* **-lae** A forked process
furfur Dandruff
furfural A chemical compound
furioso With great force
furious Angry
furl To roll up and secure
furlong A unit of distance
furlough A leave of absence
furnace A hot, enclosed place
furnish To provide furniture for
furniture The things in a room which equip it for living
furor Anger
furrier One who deals in furs
furriery The business of a furrier
furring A trimming made of fur
furrow A narrow trench
furry Covered with fur
further Additional
furtive Stealthy

furuncle A boil
fury Rage
furze A spiny shrub
fusain Charcoal used in drawing
fuse To blend
fusee A colored flare
fuselage The central part of an airplane
fusible Capable of being fused
fusile Formed by melting
fusilier, fusileer A soldier armed with a fusil
fusion A union resulting from fusing
fuss Commotion
fustian A fabric
fustic A tropical American tree
fusty Moldy
futhark, futharc, futhorc, futhork The runic alphabet
futile Useless
futility Uselessness
futtock A curved timber in the frame of a wooden ship
future Time that is yet to come
futurity The future
fuze To fuse
fuzz To become fuzzy
fyce Feist
fyke A fishnet
fylfot A swastika
fytte A division of a poem

gab, gabby To talk excessively or thoughtlessly
gabardine Cotton, rayon or wool twill

gabbard, gabbart Flat-bottomed barge
gabble To speak rapidly
gabbro Coarse-grained rock

gabelle Salt tax
gaberdine A cloak or frock
gabfest *Slang* A gathering for gossip
gabion Wicker basket of stones and earth
gabionade Wall built with gabions
gable Triangular section of a wall
gaboon A spittoon
gad To roam about
gadabout Person who gads
gaddi, gadi A hassock
gadfly A species of fly
gadget A small specialized device
gadgeteer One who designs gadgets
gadgetry Gadgets collectively
gadoid, gadid A species of fish
gadroon Ornamental molding
gadwall A species of duck
gadzooks Used as a mild oath
gae To go
gaff A hook
gaffe Awkward social error
gaffer An old man
gag A practical joke
gaga *Slang* Crazy
gage To pledge as security
gager Variant of gauger
gagger Person that gags
gaggle A flock of geese
gagman, gagster Person who writes jokes
gahnite A mineral
gaiety Merriment
gaily Merrily
gain To acquire
gainly Graceful
gainsay To contradict
gait Manner of walking, running
gaiter A legging, spat
gal A girl
gala A celebration
galactic Pertaining to a galaxy
galactose Sugar
galago African primates
galah A cockatoo
galangal A plant of Asia
galantine Meat or fish served cold
galatea Cotton fabric

galax A plant of southeastern U.S.
galaxy A large number of celestial bodies
galbanum Gum resin
gale A strong wind
galea, *pl* **-leae** Part of an insect or plant
galeate Possessing a galea
galeiform Helmet-shaped
galena Lead ore
galilee A small chapel in medieval churches
galingale Root of East Indian plant
galiot, galliot Galley ship
gall Bitterness
gallant Chivalrous
galleass, galliass Three-masted galley
galleon Large three-masted ship
gallery A roofed promenade
gallet A chip of stone
galleta Grass
galley An ancient ship propelled by oars
gallfly A species of insect
galliard A French dance
gallic An acid
gallinule A species of wading bird
gallipot Earthenware jar
gallium A metallic element
gallivant, galivant To roam aimlessly
galliwasp A species of lizard
gallnut Rounded plant gall
gallon A liquid measure
gallonage Amount measured in gallons
galloon Trimming braid
galloot, galoot *Slang* Clumsy person
gallop Gait of a horse
gallows Structure for execution by hanging
galluses Suspenders
galop, galopade, gallopade A 19th century dance
galore In abundance
galosh, galoshe Waterproof overshoe
galvanic Pertaining to direct-

current electricity

galvanism Direct-current electricity

galyak, galyac Fur from a stillborn lamb

gam A herd of whales

gamba, gambe An animal's leg

gambado A leaping movement

gambeson Leather garment under armor

gambir, gambier Extract from a vine of southcentral Asia

gambit An opening remark

gamble To speculate

gamboge A strong yellow

gambol To frolic

gambrel Hock of an animal

game A pastime

gamecock A fighting rooster

gamelan Southeast Asian orchestra

gameness Courage

gamesome Playful

gamester A game player

gamete A germ cell

gamic Fertilization in reproduction

gamily Gamely

gamin A male street urchin

gamine A female street urchin

gaming Practice of gambling

gamma The third letter of the Greek alphabet

gammadion A cross of four Greek gammas

gammer An elderly woman

gammon Backgammon victory

gamp Baggy umbrella

gamut Entire range of anything

gamy Odor or flavor of game

gan Past tense of gin

gander A male goose

ganef, ganof A scoundrel

gang A goup of laborers

ganger A gang foreman

gangling, gangly Ungraceful

ganglion, *pl* **-glia** Nerve cells

gangplow Multi-bladed plow

gangrel A vagabond

gangrene Decay of body tissue

gangue Useless rock in which valuable minerals are found

ganister, gannister Material for lining furnaces

gannet A species of sea bird

ganoid Pertaining to a species of fish

gantlet To overlap

gantline Rope used for hoisting

gantry A support

gaol Variant of jail

gap An opening

gape To yawn

gapeworm A species of worm

gapy Afflicted with gapes

gar A species of fish

garage An inside space for a car

garb Clothing

garbage Food waste

garbanzo A chickpea

garble To distort

garboard Planks next to ship's keel

garboil Confusion

garcon A waiter

gardant Variant of guardant

garden A yard with flowers

gardenia A flower

garderobe A wardrobe

garfish A species of fish

garganey A species of duck

garget Disease of cattle

gargle To utter a gargling sound

gargoyle Grotesque ornament

garibaldi 19th century blouse

garish Gaudy

garland Wreath of flowers

garlic A plant

garlicky Tasting of garlic

garment An article of clothing

garner To acquire

garnet A silicate mineral

garnish To embellish

garnishee To attach a debtor's assets

garniture Embellishment

garpike A species of fish

garret A room on the top floor

garreteer One who lives in a garret

garrison A military post

garrote, garrotte Strangulation

garrulity Chattiness

garrulous Wordy
garter An elastic band
garth Garden
gas A gaseous fuel
The following words are listed without definition (see Introduction):

gasbag	gasify	gasses
gaseous	gasless	gassing
gasholder	gaslight	gassy
gashouse	gaslit	gastight
gasified	gasman	gasworks
gasifier	gassed	
gasiform	gasser	

gascon A boastful person
gasconade Boastfulness
gaselier, gasolier Chandelier with gas jets
gash A deep cut
gasket A seal used in machinery
gaskin Part of the hind leg of a horse
gasoline A fuel
gasometer Device for measuring gas
gasp To breathe hard
gasper *Slang* A cigarette
gasser Natural gas well
gast To scare
gastric Pertaining to the stomach
gastrin Secretion that stimulates gastric juices
gastritis Stomach inflammation
gastropod A species of mollusk
gastrula, *pl* **-las** or **-lae** An embryo
gat A channel
gate An opening in a wall
gatefold Folded insert in a publication
gather To convene
gauche Clumsy
gaucherie Tactlessness
gaud Something gaudy
gaudery Things that are showy
gauffer Variant of goffer
gauge A measurement
gauger One that gauges
gaum To smear
gaun Present participle of gae
gaunt Angular

gauntlet A protective glove
gauntry Variant of gantry
gaur Mammal of southeastern Asia
gauss Measuring unit in electricity
gauze A material
gavage Method of forcing liquids into the stomach
gavel A mallet
gavelkind An English system of land tenure
gavial A species of reptile
gavotte, gavot A French peasant dance
gawk An awkward person
gay Lively
gayal A mammal of India and Burma
gayety Variant of gaiety
gayly Variant of gaily
gaywings A plant
gazabo *Slang* A fellow
gaze A steady look
gazebo A pavilion
gazehound A dog that stalks its prey by sight
gazelle A species of hoofed mammal
gazette A newspaper
gazetteer A geographical index
gazogene An apparatus for carbonating liquids
gazpacho A spicy, cold soup
gear A toothed machine part
geck To mock
gecko A species of lizard
gee The letter g
geek *Slang* Carnival freak
geepound A unit of weight
geese Plural of goose
geezer *Slang* An eccentric old man
geisha A Japanese hostess
gel A jelly
gelable Gelling
gelada A baboon
gelatin, gelatine A jelly made with gelatin
gelation Formation of a gel
geld To castrate
gelid Icy
gelt *Slang* Money

gem A precious or semiprecious stone

geminate Forming a pair or double

gemma, pl **gemmae** An outgrowth which develops into a new organism

gemmate Reproducing by gemmae

gemmule A small gemma

gemmy Set with gems

gemology Study of gems

gemot Medieval English assembly

gemsbok An antelope

gemstone A stone used as a jewel when cut and polished

gendarme French policeman

gender To engender

gene A hereditary unit

genealogy A record of a family

generable Capable of being generated

general Widespread

generate To produce

generic Referring to an entire group

generous Unselfish

genesis, pl **-ses** Creation

genet A species of Old World mammal

genetic Of genetics

genetics Science of heredity

genial Kindly

genic Genetic

genie A supernatural being

genip A tropical tree

genipap An evergreen tree

genital Pertaining to the genitals

genitalia The reproductive organs

genitival Of the genitive case

genitive A grammatical case

genitor One who creates

genius, pl **-iuses, genii** Exceptional intellectual power

genocide Planned annihilation of a people

genome, genom Chromosomes

genotype A class of organisms

genre A kind or type

genro Japanese elder statesmen

gens, gentes A type of clan

gent A man

genteel Well-bred

gentian A species of plant

gentile Non-Jewish

gentle Kindly

gentry The upper middle class

genu The knee

genuflect To kneel

genuine Authentic

genus, pl **genera** A group with common attributes

geode A rock with crystals on the inside wall

geodesic Three-dimensional Euclidean space

geodesy Geological sciences of the shape and size of the earth

geodetic Pertaining to geodesy

geoduck A large edible clam

geognosy Study of the earth and its materials

geoid Earthlike

geologize To study geology

geology Scientific study of the earth

geomancy Devination by random figures

geometric Pertaining to geometry

geometrid A species of moth

geometry A system of mathematics

geophagy The eating of earth or clay

geophyte A plant

geoponic Relating to farming

georgette A fabric

georgic A poem concerning rural life

geotaxis The movement of an organism in response to gravity

gerah Hebrew coin

geranial A flavoring

geraniol A chemical

geranium A species of flowering plant

gerbil A species of rodent

gerent An overseer

gerenuk African gazelle

geriatric Pertaining to old age

germ A small organic structure that causes disease

german A cotillion

germander A species of aromatic

plant
germane Pertinent
germanium A metallic element
germicide An agent that kills germs
germinal Pertaining to a germ cell
germinant Germinating
germinate To sprout
gerund A verbal noun
gesso A preparation of plaster
gest, geste A notable deed
gestalt A configuration
gestate To carry unborn young
gestic Pertaining to movement in
 dancing
gesture A motion to express
get To obtain
geta Japanese clog
getaway An escape
gewgaw A bauble
gey Very
geyser A natural hot spring
geyserite A deposit formed around
 natural hot springs
ghastly Dreadful
ghat, ghaut Mountain pass
ghazi Moslem warrior
ghee, ghi Butter made from butterfat of buffalo or other milk
gherao Coercive tactic
gherkin A small cucumber
ghetto A slum section of a city
ghibli Hot desert wind
ghillie A shoe used in Scottish
 dances
ghost Spirit of a deceased person
ghoul A demon
giant A person of great size
giantess A female giant
giantism Condition of being a giant
giaour A non-Moslem infidel
gib A wedge-shaped piece of wood
 or metal
gibber To chat
gibberish Nonsensical talk
gibbet A gallows
gibbon A species of ape
gibbosity A swelling
gibbous Rounded
gibe To heckle
giblet Part of a fowl

gid Disease of sheep
giddy Dizzy feeling
giddyap Go faster
gie Give
gift A present
gig Two-wheeled carriage
gigantic Very large
gigantism State of being very large
giggle To laugh spasmodically
giggly Inclined to giggle
gigolo A man kept by a woman
gigot Leg of mutton, lamb or veal
gigue A dance
gilbert A unit of magnetomotive
 force
gild To cover with gold
gill Organ of fishes
gillie, gilly A guide for sportsmen
gilt A young sow
gimbals A device holding a ship's
 compass or lantern
gimcrack A cheap, showy object
gimel The third letter of the
 Hebrew alphabet
gimlet A small hand tool
gimmal A ring of two interlocking
 rings
gimme *Slang* Give me
gimmick A novel gadget
gimp To limp
gin To begin
ginger To flavor with ginger
gingerly Cautiously
gingham Cotton fabric
gingiva The gum
gink *Slang* An odd man or boy
ginkgo, gingko A tree native to
 China
ginseng A species of plant
gip Variant of gyp
giraffe A long-necked mammal
girandole A branched candleholder
girasol, girosol An opal
gird To encircle
girl A female child
girlish Pertaining to girls
girt To gird
girth To encircle
gisarme A medieval weapon
gismo, gizmo A mechanical device

159

gist Essence
git Go
give To present
gizzard A digestive organ
glabella Smooth area between the eyebrows
glabrous Smooth
glace Candied
glacial Pertaining to glaciers
glaciate Subject to glacial action
glacier A large mass of moving ice
glacis An incline
glad Pleased
glade Open space in a forest
gladiate Sword-shaped
gladiator A professional fighter
gladiolus, pl **-li** A species of plant
gladsome Joyful
glair, glaire Size of egg white
glaive A broadsword
glamorous Characterized by glamour
glamour, glamor Charm
glance To look quickly
gland An excretory organ
glanders Disease of animals
glans, glandes The glans penis
glare To stare
glass A transparent material
glassine Glazed paper
glassman Glassmaker
glasswort A species of plant
glassy Lifeless
glaucoma Disease of the eyes
glaucous Green with a grayish cast
glaze A shiny coating
glazier One who works with window glass
glaziery A glasswork
gleam To shine
glean To gather
gleba, pl **-bae** Inner mass of a puffball
glebe A clergyman's land during office
glede A species of bird
glee Merriment
gleed A glowing ember
gleeman A minstrel
gleesome Gleeful

gleet A disease
gleg Quick to respond
glen A valley
gley A layer of moist soil
gliadin A protein
glib Insincere
glide To move smoothly
glim A source of light
glimpse A brief look
glint A sparkle
glissade A ballet step
glissando A blending of one musical tone into the next
glisten To shine by reflection
glister To glisten
glitzy *Slang* Glittery
gloaming Twilight
glob A drop
global Spherical
globate Globular
globe A body with a spherical shape
globefish A species of fish
globin A protein
globoid Globelike shape
globose, globous Globular
globular The shape of a globe
globule A small drop of liquid
globulin A protein
glogg A hot punch
glomerate Tightly clustered
glomerule A cluster of flowers
gloom Atmosphere of sorrow
gloria A halo
gloriole A halo
glory To rejoice
gloss To give a bright luster
glossal Pertaining to the tongue
glossary A collection of glosses
glost A lead glaze
glottal Relating to the glottis
glottis, pl **-tises** or **glottides** Vocal structure of the larynx
glout To scowl
glove A covering for the hand
glover Person who makes gloves
glow To shine steadily
glower To frown
gloxinia A species of South American plant

gloze To gloss
glucose Sugar
glucoside Glucose
glue An adhesive substance
glug To drink
glum Gloomy
glume A growth on grasses
glut To satiate
glutamic An acid
glutamine An acid
gluten Mixture of plant proteins
gluteus Muscles of the buttocks
glutinous Sticky
glutton A big eater
glyceride Fatty acids
glycerol A syrup from fats and oils
glyceryl The trivalent radical of glycerin
glycine A very sweet acid
glycogen Liver starch
glycol Dihydric alcohols
glycolic A crystalline compound
glyconic Verses having a particular rhythmic structure
glycoside A species of organic compounds in plant
glyph A vertical groove
glyptic Relating to engraving on precious stones
gnarr, gnarl, gnar To growl
gnash To grind the teeth together
gnat A species of insect
gnathic Relating to the jaw
gnathite Jaw of an insect
gnaw To chew
gneiss Foliated metamorphic rock
gnocchi Dumplings
gnome In fables, a dwarflike creature
gnomic Pertaining to the nature of gnomes
gnomon Part of a sundial
gnosis Knowledge in spiritual truths
gnostic Possessing spiritual knowledge
gnu African antelope
go To proceed
goa A gazelle
goad A long stick for prodding animals
goal An objective
goat A species of horned mammal
goatee A chin beard
goatfish A species of fish
gob A small lump
gobang A Japanese game
gobbet A piece of raw meat
gobble To eat greedily
gobbler A male turkey
goblet A drinking glass
goblin An elf-like creature
gobo A black screen
goby A species of fish
god A being with supernatural powers
godchild One whom a person sponsors at baptism
goddess A female god
godhead Divinity
godhood State of being a god
godlike Of the nature of a god
godling A minor god
godroon Variant of gadroon
godsend A windfall
godson A male godchild
godwit A species of bird
goethite A mineral
goffer To flute
goggle To stare with wide eyes
goiter, goitre Enlargement of the thyroid gland
gold A precious metal
goldarn *Slang* Expression of anger
goldbrick *Slang* A shirker
goldeneye A species of duck
goldstone An aventurine
golem Artificially created human in Jewish folklore
golf An outdoor game
golgotha A place of burial
goliard Medieval wandering student
goliardic Of satirical verse
golliwog, golliwogg Grotesque person
golly Surprise
golosh Variant of galosh
gombo Variant of gumbo
gombroon Persian pottery

gomphosis Rigid socket and peg articulation
gonad A sex gland
gondola A narrow boat
gondolier Boatman of a gondola
gone Past
goner *Slang* One who is doomed
gonfalon A banner in an ecclesiastical procession
gong A percussion instrument
gonidium, *pl* **-ia** A reproductive cell that is reproduced asexually
gonion Part of the lower jaw
gonophore A reproductive cell
gonopore A reproductive pore
gonorrhea A disease
gonzo *Slang* Bizarre
goo A sticky substance
goober Peanut
good Having desirable qualities
goodish Goodly
goodman A husband
goodwife, *pl* **-wives** A wife
gooey Sticky
goof *Slang* A silly mistake
goofy *Slang* Silly
googol A very large number
gook *Slang* Goo
goon A thug
gooney An albatross
goop *Slang* Ill-mannered person
goosander A species of bird
goose A species of water bird
goosefish A species of fish
goosefoot A species of plant
gooseherd Person who tends a flock of geese
gooseneck Curved object
goosy, goosey Foolish
gopher A burrowing mammal
goral A species of antelope
gore Blood
gorge To eat greedily
gorgeous Beautiful
gorgerin The necking of a column
gorget An ornamental collar
gorgonian A species of coral
gorgonize To petrify with fear
gorilla A large ape
gormand Variant of gourmand

gorse A species of shrub
gosh Used to express surprise
goshawk A large hawk
gosling A young goose
gospel The teachings of Jesus
gospeler One who reads the gospel
gospodin Soviet form of male address
gossamer A sheer fabric
gossip, gossiper Idle talk
gossipry Gossiping
gossipy Inclined to gossip
gossoon A servant boy
gouache Method of painting
gouge A chisel
goulash A stew
gourami A species of fish
gourd A species of vine
gourde Monetary unit of Haiti
gourmand Person who eats well
gourmet An epicure
gout A metabolic disease
gouty Suffering from gout
govern To rule
governess Female governor
governor A person who governs
gowan A species of flower
gowk A cuckoo
gown A garment
gownsman Person who wears a gown in his profession
gox Gaseous oxygen
goy, *pl* **goyim** or **goys** A Gentile
grab To seize
grabble To grope
graben Depression of the earth's crust
grace Beauty
gracile Graceful
gracioso A Spanish clown
gracious Marked by kindness
grackle A species of bird
grad A graduate
gradate To arrange in grades
grade A gradual slope
gradient A slope
gradin Series of steps
gradual Occurring in moderate stages
graduate To receive an academic degree

gradus, *pl* **-duses** A dictionary for writing poetry
graffito, *pl* **-ti** A crude drawing
graft To unite
graftage Process of creating a graft
graham Made from whole-wheat flour
grail Medieval chalice
grain Cereal grasses
gram A unit of mass and weight
grama A species of grass
gramarye Magic
gramatom The mass of an element
gramercy Used to express surprise
grammar The study of language
grampus A marine mammal
granary A building for storing grain
grand Splendid
grandam, grandame A grandmother
grandee Person of high rank
grandeur Splendor
grandiose Grand
grandioso In a grand manner
grandma Grandmother
grandpa Grandfather
grandsire A grandfather
grange An association of farmers
granger A member of a grange
graniform Resembling grain
granite A kind of rock
granny, grannie A grandmother
granolith A paving stone
grant To bestow
grantee Person to whom a grant is made
grantor Person who makes a grant
granular Composed of granules
granulate To form into granules
granule A small grain
granulite A species of rock
granuloma Nodules of infected tissue
granulose A surface covered with granules
grape A berry
grapery Area where grapes are grown
grapeshot Iron balls shot from a cannon
grapestone Seed of a grape
graph A drawing
grapheme A letter of an alphabet
graphic Described in clear detail
graphite A carbon
grapnel An anchor
grappa Italian brandy
grapple Iron shaft with claws
grapy Like grapes
grasp To take hold
grass A species of plant
grate To reduce to fragments by rubbing
gratify To please
gratin A crust of crumbs, butter and cheese
gratis Free
gratitude An appreciation
gratuity A gift
gratulant Congratulatory
gratulate To congratulate
graupel Soft hail
gravamen Prominent part of an accusation
grave A burial place
gravel Mixture of rock
graven As a graven image
graver A person who engraves
gravid Pregnant
gravitate To move
graviton A hypothetical particle
gravity The force of gravitation
gravure Method of printing
gravy Juices from cooked meat
gray Dull
graybeard An elderly man
grayish Quality of grayness
grayling A species of fish
graywacke A species of sandstone
graze To feed on grass
grazier Person who grazes cattle
grazioso Graceful
grease Melted animal fat
great Large
greaten To enlarge
greave Leg armor
grebe A species of bird
gree To agree
greed Avarice

greegree   Variant of grigri
green   A color
greenbelt   A belt of land surrounding a community
greenfly   A species of insect
greengage   A variety of plum
greenhead   A male mallard duck
greenhorn   Immature person
greening   A variety of apple
greenlet   A species of bird
greenling   A species of fish
greenroom   A theatre lounge for performers
greensand   A sand of dark greenish color
greenwood   A forest when the foliage is green
greet   To welcome
gregarine   Pertaining to parasitic protozoans that live in insects
grego   A hooded cloak
greige   A gray-beige color
greisen   A granitic rock
gremlin   Imaginary gnomelike creature
grenade   A hand-thrown missile
grenadier   A member of the British Grenadier Guards
grenadine   A fabric
grew   Past tense of grow
grey   Variant of gray
greyhen   Female of the black grouse
gribble   A species of marine crustacean
grid   A football field
griddle   A flat cooking utensil
gridiron   A football field
grief   Deep remorse
grieve   To distress
grievous   Causing pain
griffe   A clawlike ornament
griffin, griffon   A mythological beast
grift *Slang*   A swindle
grig   A lively person
grigri   An African Negro charm
grill   To broil
grillage   Frame of crossed timbers
grille   A metal grating
grilse   A young salmon

grim   Forbidding
grimace   Facial contortion to show pain
grimalkin   A cat
grime   To cover with dirt
grimy   Dirty
grin   To smile broadly
grind   To sharpen by friction
gringo   A foreigner in Latin America and Mexico
grip   A firm grasp
gripe   To annoy
grippe   A severe cold
gripsack   Small suitcase
gript   Past tense of grip
grisaille   A style of painting
griseous   Grayish
grisette   French working girl
griskin   Lean pork
grisly   Gruesome
grison   A species of carnivorous mammal
grist   Ground grain
gristle   Cartilage in meat
gristly   Containing gristle
gristmill   A mill where grain is ground
grit   Indomitable spirit
grith   Sanctuary or protection in Old English law
grivit   African monkey
grizzle   To make gray
grizzly   Grayish
groan   To utter a painful sound
groat   Old English coin
grocer   A storekeeper who sells food
grog   An alcoholic liquor
grogram   A coarse fabric
groin   The hollow where the abdomen joins either thigh
grommet   A reinforced eyelet
gromwell   A species of plant
groom   A bridegroom
groove   A long, narrow channel
groovy   Smooth
grope   To feel one's way
grosbeak   A species of finch
groschen   An Austrian coin
grosgrain   A heavy rayon or silk

fabric
gross Exclusive of deductions
grosz, groszy A Polish coin
grot A grotto
grotesque Bizarre
grotto A small cave
grouch To grumble
ground Surface of the earth
groundnut A species of plant
groundsel A species of plant
group A number of people
grouper A species of fish
groupoid A mathematical formula
grouse A species of bird
grout Mortar used to fill cracks
grove A small stand of trees
grovel To humble oneself
grow To cultivate
growl Sound made by an animal
grown Mature
growth Full development
grub To dig
grubber A person who grubs
grubby Dirty
grubstake Money advanced for starting a business
grudge A feeling of resentment
grue A shiver of fear
gruel A porridge
gruesome Frightful
gruff Harsh
grugru A palm tree
grum Sullen
grumble To mumble
grume A clot of blood
grummet Variant of grommet
grumous, grumose Formed of clustered roots
grump A cranky person
grungy *Slang* Dirty and messy
grunion A species of fish
grunt To utter a deep, guttural sound
gryphon Variant of griffin
guacamole A salad with avocado
guacharo A nocturnal bird
guaco A species of plant
guaiacol A chemical compound
guaiacum, guaiac A species of tree
guan A species of bird

guanaco A South American mammal
guanidine A crystalline base found in plant and animal tissues
guanine, guanin A chemical compound
guano Dung of sea birds and bats
guarani Monetary unit of Paraguay
guarantee To vouch for
guarantor One that makes a guarantee
guaranty An agreement of responsibility
guard To watch over
guardant In heraldry, an animal shown full face
guardian One who guards
guava A species of shrub and tree
guayule A woody plant
guberniya Administrative subdivision of a Soviet
guck *Slang* A messy substance
gudgeon A species of fish
guenon A species of monkey
guerdon A reward
guernsey A knitted wool shirt
guerrilla, guerilla A revolutionary soldier
guess To assume
guest A visitor
guff *Slang* Nonsense talk
guffaw Hearty laughter
guidance Act of guiding
guide To show the way
guideword A catchword
guidon A small flag
guild An association of persons of the same trade
guilder Monetary unit of the Netherlands
guildehall Town hall
guildsman A member of a guild
guile Craft
guillemot A species of bird
guilloche An ornamental border
guilt Awareness of having done wrong
guimpe Short-sleeved blouse
guinea A former British coin
guipure A trimming
guise Outward appearance

guitar A musical instrument

gul A motif found in Oriental carpets

gulag A Russian prison

gular Pertaining to the throat

gulch A small ravine

gulden Variant of guilder

gules In heraldry, the color red on a blazon

gulf To swallow up

gulfweed A species of seaweed

gull A species of bird

gullet The throat

gullible Easily deceived

gully A deep ditch made by running water

gulp To swallow rapidly

gum A sticky viscous substance

gumbo A soup thickened with okra

gumboil A small abscess on the gum

gumdrop A candy

gumma, *pl* **-mas** or **gummata** A tumor found in an advanced stage of syphilis

gummosis Patches of disease-causing gum on plants

gummous, gummose Gumlike

gummy Sticky

gumption Boldness

gumshoe An overshoe

gumwood The wood of a gum tree

gun A weapon

The following words are listed without definition (see Introduction):

gunboat	gunman	gunpowder
gunfight	gunmetal	gunroom
gunfire	gunner	gunrunner
gunflint	gunnery	gunshot
gunless	gunplay	gunsmith
gunlock	gunpoint	gunstock

guncotton An explosive

gunk Slimy substance

gunnel A species of fish

gunny Burlap fabric

gunwale Upper edge of a ship's side

guppy A species of fish

gurge A whirlpool

gurgle The act of gurgling

gurnard A species of fish

gurry Fish offal

guru A spiritual teacher

gush To flow forth

gusset A triangular insert in a garment

gust An abrupt rush of wind

gustation Taste

gustative Gustatory

gusto Vigorous enjoyment

gut The alimentary canal

gutless Lacking courage

gutta, *pl* **guttae** Ornament on a Doric entablature

guttate Resembling a drop

gutter A trough for draining off water

guttural Produced in the throat

gutty Vivid

guy A man

guyot A flat-topped seamount

guzzle To drink greedily

gweduc Variant of geoduck

gybe Variant of jibe

gym A gymnasium

gymkhana Display of equestrian contests

gymnasium A room for gynmastics

gymnast One skilled in gymnastics

gynaeceum, *pl* **-cea** Women's quarters in ancient households

gynandry Hermaphroditism

gynarchy Government by women

gynoecium, *pl* **-cia** Female reproductive organs of a flower

gynophore The stalk of a pistil

gyp To cheat

gypsum A mineral

gypsy A nomadic people

gyral Moving in a circular motion

gyrate To circle

gyre A circular motion

gyrene *Slang* A marine

gyrfalcon A large falcon

gyroplane A helicopter

gyroscope Any spinning mass

gyrostat A gyrostabilizer

gyrus, *pl* **-ri** A ridge in the brain

gyve A shackle

ha Sound of surprise
haaf Deep-sea fishing ground
haar A fog
habanera A Cuban dance
habdalah A Jewish religious ceremony
habergeon A coat of mail
habile Handy
habit Customary practice
habitant An inhabitant
habitat Natural environment of an organism
habitude A customary manner
habitue A frequent customer
habitus Physical characteristics
habu A poisonous snake
hachure Lines on a map
hacienda A large ranch
hack To chop
hackamore A halter
hackberry A species of tree
hackbut A gun
hackie *Slang* A taxi
hackle To hack
hackly Jagged
hackman Driver of a carriage
hackney A coach
hacksaw A saw for cutting metal
haddock A food fish
hade To incline
hades Hell
hadj A pilgrimage to Mecca
hadji One who has made a hadj
hadst Past tense of have
hae To have
haet Whit
hafiz A Moslem who has memorized the Koran
hafnium A metallic element
haft A handle
hag A witch

hagborn Born of a witch
hagbut Variant of hackbut
hagfish A species of eel-shaped fish
haggadic Pertaining to the story of Exodus
haggard Exhausted
haggis A Scottish dish
haggle To dicker
hagride To harass
hah Variant of ha
haik Garment worn by Arabs
haiku A Japanese poem
hail Hailstones
hair Threadlike filaments growing from the skin
The following words are listed without definition (see Introduction):

hairball	haired	hairlock
hairband	hairier	hairnet
hairbrush	hairiest	hairpin
haircloth	hairless	hairwork
haircut	hairlike	hairy
hairdo	hairline	

hairworm A species of worm
haj, hajj Variants of hadj
haji, hajji Variants of hadji
hake A species of fish
hakim, hakeem A Moslem physician
halakist A Hebrew judge
halation A ring of light
halberd, halbert A weapon
halcyon A fabled bird
hale Robust
haler Czech monetary unit
half, *pl* **halves** One of two equal parts
halfback A football player
halfbeak A species of fish
halftone A tone between light and

dark

halfway   In the middle

halibut   A species of flatfish

halide   A chemical compound

halidom   Holiness

halite   Rock salt

halitosis   Bad breath

hall   A corridor

hallah   Challah

hallel   A chant of praise

halliard   Variant of halyard

hallmark   An official mark

hallo, halloo, halloa   To shout

hallow   To make holy

hallux, *pl* **halluces**   The big toe

halo   The ring of light surrounding
sacred figures

halogen   A nonmetallic element

halt   To stop

halvah   A Turkish confection

halve   To divide

halyard   A rope used for sails

ham   To overact

hamal, hamaul, hammal   A porter in
Moslem countries

hamate   A wrist bone

hamburger   A sandwich

hame   Part of a harness

hamlet   A small town

hammer   A tool

hammock   A hanging lounge

hamper   To impede

hamster   A species of rodent

hamulus, *pl* **-li**   A small projection
at the end of a bone

hamza, hamzah   An Arabic
apostrophe

hanaper   A hamper

hance   A half arch

hand   The terminal part of the arm
below the wrist

The following words are listed
without definition (see Introduction):

handbag	handclasp	handhold
handball	handcuff	handier
handbill	handfast	handiest
handbook	handful	handily
handcar	handgrip	handiwork
handcart	handgun	handle

handler	handoff	handshake
handless	handout	handspike
handlike	handpick	handstand
handling	handrail	handwork
handlist	handsaw	handwrit
handloom	handset	
handmade	handsewn	

handicap   To hinder

handiness   Quality of being handy

handmaid   A personal maid

handsel   A gift

handsome   Pleasing in appearance

handy   Easy to use

hang   To suspend

hangar   A garage for aircraft

hangbird   A bird that builds a hanging nest

hangdog   Guilty

hangman   One who executes by
hanging

hangnail   A piece of dead skin

hangout   A place often visited

hangover   A letdown

hank   A coil

hanker   To have a craving

hanse   A medieval guild of
merchants

hansel   Variant of handsel

hansom   A carriage

hant   To haunt

hanuman   A monkey

hap   Chance

hapax   A word that occurs only
once

haphazard   Mere chance

hapless   Luckless

haploid   A cell with only one set of
chromosomes

haplosis   Reduction of chromosomes by one half

haply   Perhaps

happen   To take place

happy   Gratified

hapten, haptene   An incomplete
antigen

haptic   Having to do with the sense
of touch

harangue   A tirade

harass   To irritate

harbinger   A forerunner

harbor A shelter
hard Rigid
hardback A hardcover book
hardball A baseball
hardboot A horseman
hardcase Tough
hardcore Unyielding
hardhack A woody plant
hardhat A construction worker
hardhead A stubborn person
hardpan Bedrock
hards Refuse of flax
hardset Fixed
hardship Adversity
hardtack A hard biscuit
hardtop A type of auto
hardware Metal goods
hardwood Wood of various trees
hare A species of mammal
harebell The bluebell plant
harelip A deformity of the upper lip
harem, hareem Section of a Moslem household reserved for women
haricot A highly seasoned stew
hark To listen
harl Fibers
harlequin A clown
harlot A prostitute
harm Wrong
harmony Sympathy
harness To put gear on a draft animal
harp A musical instrument
harpoon A spearlike weapon
harpy A shrewish person
harridan A vixen
harrow To break up soil
harry To pillage
harsh Stern
hart A male deer
hartal A stoppage of work
haruspex An ancient Roman soothsayer
harvest To gather a crop
has Present third person singular of have
hash A food dish
hashish, hasheesh A narcotic
haslet Edible viscera of animals
hasp A metal fastener

hassle A fight
hassock A footstool
hast Second person singular present indicative of have
hastate Triangular
haste Swiftness
hat A covering for the head
The following words are listed without definition (see Introduction):

hatband	hatlike	hatted
hatbox	hatmaker	hatter
hatcheck	hatpin	hatting
hatful	hatrack	
hatless	hatsful	

hatch A hatchway
hatchet A short-handled ax
hatchway An opening in the deck of a ship
hate To detest
hath Third person singular present indicative of have
hatred Dislike
hauberk A tunic made of chain mail
haugh A low-lying meadow
haughty Vain
haul To pull
haulage A charge made for hauling
haulm A plant stem
haunch The hindquarter
haunt To visit often
hausen A Russian sturgeon
hausfrau A housewife
hautboy An oboe
hauteur Arrogance
have To own
havelock A covering for a cap
haven A port
haversack A bag
havoc Devastation
haw To turn left
hawfinch A species of bird
hawk A species of bird of prey
hawkweed A species of plant
hawse A part of a ship's bow
hawser A cable used in mooring a ship
hawthorn A species of thorny shrub
hay Grass used for fodder

haycock A mound of hay
hayfork A tool for pitching hay
hayloft A loft where hay is stored
haymaker One who makes hay
haymow The hay stored in a hayloft
hayrack A rack used in hauling hay
hayride A wagon ride
hayseed Grass seed
haystack A stack of hay
haywire Wire used for baling hay
hazard A peril
haze Atmospheric moisture
hazel A species of shrub and tree
hazelnut The nut of a hazel
hazen A cantor
he A male person
head To be the leader
headache Pain in the head
headband A band worn on the head
headdress A hairdo
headgear A covering for the head
headlamp A light on the front of an auto
headland A cliff
headline The title of a newspaper article
headlock A wrestling hold
headlong Headfirst
headmost Foremost
headnote A prefixed note
headpin A bowling pin
headrace A watercourse
headrest A support for the head
headsail A type of sail
headset Headphones
headship The position of a leader
headsman An executioner
headstall Part of a bridle
headway Progress
headwork Mental work
heal To cure
health Well being
heap A pile
hear To listen to
hearken To give heed
hearsay Secondhand information
hearse A vehicle for carrying a dead body
heart Capacity for generosity

heartache Deep sorrow
heartbeat Pulsation of the heart
heartburn A burning sensation
hearten To encourage
heartfelt Earnest
hearth The fireside
heartland A central region
heartsick Sick at heart
heat A form of energy
heath A species of shrub
heathen An uncivilized person
heather A species of plant
heathery Like heather
heathy Healthy
heaume A medieval helmet
heave To hoist
heaven Firmament
heavy Having great weight
heavyset Stocky
hebdomad A week
hebetate To make dull
hebetic Pertaining to puberty
hebetude Mental dullness
hecatomb A large-scale sacrifice
heck Hell
heckle To harass
hectare A unit of area
hectic Confusion
hectogram A unit of mass
hector To intimidate
heddle A part of a loom
heder A Jewish school
hedge A species of shrub
hedgehog A species of Old World mammal
hedgehop To fly near the ground
hedgerow A row of hedges
hedonic Marked by pleasure
hedonism Pursuit of pleasure
hedonist One who believes that pleasure is foremost
heed To consider
heehaw The sound made by a donkey
heel The raised part of a shoe
heelball Used for polishing
heelpost A post to which a gate is attached
heeltap A lift
heeze To hoist

heft Bulk
hegemony Predominance
hegumen The head of a religious community
heifer A young cow
heigh Used to attract attention
height The highest point
heil To salute
heinie *Slang* The buttocks
heinous Vile
heir A person who inherits property
heirdom An inheritance
heiress A female heir
heirloom An inherited possession
heirship The right to inherit
heist *Slang* A robbery
held Past tense of hold
heliac Heliacal
heliacal Pertaining to the sun
helical Shaped like a helix
helicoid A type of geometrical surface
helicon A musical instrument
helicopt To travel by helicopter
helio A signaling mirror
helipad A heliport
heliport An airport for helicopters
helium A gaseous element
helix, *pl* **-lixes** or **helices** A spiral form
hell The underworld where condemned souls dwell
hellbent Determined
hellbox A printer's receptacle
hellcat A vixin
helldiver A New World grebe
hellfire The fires of hell
hellhole A hellish place
hellhound A fiend
hellion A mischievous person
hellish Devilish
hello To greet
helluva Disagreeable
helm Steering gear of a ship
helmet A head covering
helminth A worm
helmsman One who steers a ship
helot A serf
helotism Serfdom

helotry Helotism
help To aid
helpmate A helper
helpmeet A helpmate
helve A handle
hem An edge of cloth
hemagog An agent that promotes blood flow
hemal Pertaining to the blood
hematein A chemical compound
hematic Acting on blood
hematin Heme
hematite An iron ore
hematoid Bloody
hematoma A swelling filled with blood
heme A component of hemoglobin
hemic Of blood
hemin A chloride of heme
hemline A hem
hemlock A species of evergreen tree
hemocyte A cell in the blood
hemostat An agent that stops bleeding
hemp A species of plant
hempen Made of hemp
hempweed Climbing hempweed
hen A female bird
henbane A poisonous plant
henbit A plant
hence As a result
henchman One of a criminal gang
hencoop A cage for poultry
henequen, henequin A tropical American plant
henna A color
hennery A poultry farm
henpeck To harass
henry A unit of inductance
hent To grasp
hep Hip
heparin A biochemical
hepatic Of the liver
hepatica A species of plant
hepatitis Inflammation of the liver
hepcat *Slang* A swing devotee
heptad A group of seven
heptagon A seven-sided polygon
heptane A hydrocarbon

her The possessive form of she
herald A messenger
heraldic Pertaining to heraldry
heraldry Pomp and ceremony
herb A plant with a nonwoody stem
herby Abounding in herbs
hercules One of great strength
herd A group of animals
herdic A horse-drawn cab
here At this time
hereafter After this
hereat At this time
hereby By this means
heredity The genetic transmission of characteristics
herein In
hereinto Into this
hereof Concerning this
hereon Hereupon
heres, pl **heredes** An heir
heresy An opinion contrary to church doctrine
heretic One that upholds heresy
hereto To this
hereunto Hereto
hereupon At this
herewith Hereby
heriot A feudal tribute
heritage Inheritance
heritor An inheritor
heritress A female inheritor
herl A fishing fly
herma, pl **-mae** or **-mai** A type of statue
hermetic Sealed
hermit A recluse
hermitage An abbey
hern A heron
hernia, pl **-as** or **-niae** A rupture
hero One who displays great courage
heroin A narcotic
heroine A brave woman
heron A species of wading birds
herpes A viral disease
herring A species of fish
herself A form of the third person singular feminine pronoun
hertz A unit of frequency

hesitant Tending to hesitate
hessian A cloth
hessite A mineral
hest Command
het Past tense of heat
hetaera, pl **-ras** or **-taerae** A concubine
hetero A heterosexual
heth The eighth letter of the Hebrew alphabet
hetman A cossack leader
hew To fell
hex A curse
hexad A group of six
hexagon A polygon having six sides
hexagram A six-pointed star
hexane A volatile liquid
hexapod A species of insect
hexosan A carbohydrate
hexose A simple sugar
hexyl A hydrocarbon radical
hey Used to attract attention
heyday Prime
hi Used as a greeting
hiatus, pl **hiatuses** A missing section
hibachi A portable brazier
hibernal Pertaining to winter
hibernate To pass winter in sleep
hibiscus A species of plant
hic Slang Hiccups
hiccup A spasm of the diaphragm
hick A yokel
hickey A gadget
hickory A species of tree
hidalgo A minor Spanish nobleman
hide To conceal
hideous Ugly
hideout A place of concealment
hidrosis Perspiration
hie To hurry
hiemal Pertaining to winter
hierarch A religious leader
hieratic Associated with sacred offices
hifalutin Pompous
higgle To haggle
high Tall
highball A railroad signal

highborn Of noble birth
highboy A chest of drawers
highbred Highborn
highbrow One who has superior tastes
highbush Forming a tall bush
highchair A baby's chair
highjack Variant of hijack
highland Elevated land
highroad A main road
hight Named
hightail *Slang* To hurry
hijack To seize a vehicle while in motion
hike To walk an extended distance
hila, hilar Of hilum
hilarity Boisterous merriment
hill A mound
hillbilly A person from a rural mountain area
hillock A small hill
hilt The handle of a weapon
hilum, pl -la The nucleus of a starch grain
him The objective case of the third person pronoun he
himation, pl -ia A garment of ancient Greece
himself A form of the third person singular masuline pronoun
hin A Hebrew unit of liquid measure
hind Posterior
hinder To hamper
hindgut The posterior portion of the embryonic alimentary canal
hindmost Last
hindrance Act of hindering
hinge A jointed device
hinny Offspring of a male horse and a female ass
hint A clue
hip Used as a cheer
hipbone A pelvic bone
hipparch A cavalry commander
hippie A nonconformist
hippo A hippopotamus
hippy Having broad hips
hipshot Awkward
hipster *Slang* One who is hip

hiragana A Japanese cursive script
hircine Of a goat
hire To employ
hirsute Hairy
hirudin An anticoagulant
his The possessive form of the pronoun he
hisn His
hispid Bristly
hiss To make a hiss
histone A simple protein
history A chronicle
hit To strike
hitch To tie
hither To this place
hitherto Up to now
hive A colony of bees
ho Used to express joy
hoagie *Slang* A hero sandwich
hoar Hoary
hoard A treasure
hoarfrost White frost
hoarse Husky
hoatzin, hoactzin A tropical bird
hoax To cheat
hob A sprite
hobbit A small, imaginary being
hobby A pastime
hobgoblin A bugbear
hobnail A short nail with a thick head
hobnob To associate
hobo A vagrant
hock To pawn
hockey A game
hockshop A pawnshop
hocus To cheat
hod A coal scuttle
hoe A garden tool
hoecake A cake made of cornmeal
hoedown A square dance
hog, hogg A domesticated pig
hogan A Navaho dwelling
hogback A sharp ridge
hogfish A species of fish
hoggish Filthy
hogtie To tie the legs together
hogwash Worthless talk
hogweed A species of plant
hoist To raise

173

hokum Fakery
hold To support
holdall A carryall
holdfast A device to fasten something
holdout One who withholds
holdup A robbery
hole A cavity in a solid
holey Having holes
holiday A vacation
holiness The state of being holy
holism A theory
holland A fabric
holler To shout
hollo To hallo
hollow Empty
holly A species of tree
holm An island in a river
holmic Pertaining to holmium
holmium A metallic element
holocaust Total destruction
hologram A three-dimensional photograph
holotype A plant specimen
holozoic Eating solid foods
holp Past tense of help
holpen Past participle of help
holstein A breed of cattle
holster A case for a gun
holt A copse
holy Sacred
holyday A religious holiday
holytide A time for religious observance
homage To pay tribute to
hombre *Slang* A man
homburg A felt hat
home A residence
homebody A domestic person
homebred Domestic
homeland One's native land
homer A home run
homespun Homemade
homeward Toward home
homey, homy Homelike
homicide Murder
homily A sermon
homing Returning home
hominid The family of two-legged primates, including all forms of man

hominoid Manlike
hominy Boiled kernels of corn
homo The extinct and extant species of man
homogeny Correspondence between parts related by common descent
homonym A namesake
homy Variant of homey
honan A fine silk
honcho A chief
honda A part of a lariat
hone To sharpen
honest Truthful
honewort A species of plant
honey Sweetness
honeybee A species of social bee
honeycomb A structure constructed from beeswax by honeybees
honeydew A melon
honeyed Sweetened with honey
hong A Chinese factory
honk Sound uttered by a wild goose
honor, honour Respect
honorific Showing honor
hooch *Slang* Liquor
hood A loose covering for the head
hoodlum A thug
hoodoo Bad luck
hoodwink To trick
hooey *Slang* Nonsense
hoof, *pl* **hoofs** or **hooves** The hard covering of the feet of various animals
hoofer *Slang* A tap dancer
hook A fishhook
hookah, hooka A water pipe
hooknose An aquiline nose
hookup A connection
hookworm A species of worm
hooligan A hoodlum
hoop A circular band
hoopla *Slang* Confusing talk
hoopoe An Old World bird
hooray Variant of hurrah
hoosegow *Slang* A jail
hoot The cry of an owl
hootch Variant of hooch

hop To move, using one foot
hope To trust
hophead *Slang* A habitual user of drugs
hoplite A soldier of ancient Greece
hopscotch A game
hora, horah A dance
horal Hourly
horary Lasting one hour
horde A swarm
horehound A species of plant
horizon The intersection of the earth and sky
hormone A substance formed by one organ and conveyed to another
horn A musical instrument
hornbeam A species of tree
hornbill A species of Old World bird
hornbook A rudimentary text
hornet A species of wasp
hornito A mound of volcanic matter
hornpipe A dance
hornpout A freshwater catfish
horntail A species of sawfly
hornworm The larva of the hawk moth
hornwort A species of aquatic plant
horologe A timepiece
horologic Relating to horology
horology The science of measuring time
horoscope A forecast of one's future
horrent Bristling
horrible Dreadful
horrid Offensive
horrify To shock
horror Terror
horse A large domesticated mammal
horsecar A streetcar drawn by horses
horseman A cavalryman
horsemint A species of plant
horseplay Prankish play
horseshoe A game
horseweed Butterweed

horsewhip To flog
horst A part of the earth's crust
horsy Coarse
hosanna A shout of praise
hose Stockings
hosier A maker of hose
hosiery Hose
hospice A shelter
hospital An institution for the sick
host One who entertains guests
hostage A person held as security
hostel A lodge for youths
hosteler An innkeeper
hostelry An inn
hostess A woman who acts as a host
hostile Antagonistic
hostler A stableman
hot Highly spiced
hotbed A bed of rich soil
hotbox An overheated axle
hotch To fidget
hotchpot A pooling of property of different persons for equal distribution
hotdog A sandwich
hotel A house that provides lodging
hotfoot To hurry
hothead One who is intemperate
hothouse A heated greenhouse
hotrod A car modified for increased speed
hots *Slang* Strong sexual desire
hotshot *Slang* A showily skillful person
hotspur A hothead
hound A breed of dog
hour A period of sixty minutes
houri, *pl* **-ris** A beautiful woman
house A residence
housecarl A member of a household troop
housefly A common fly
housel The Eucharist
houseleek A species of plant
housemaid A woman employed for housework
housetop The roof of a house
housewife, *pl* **-wives** A married woman

hove Past tense of heave
hovel A miserable dwelling
hover To waver
how In what way
howbeit Nevertheless
howdah A seat on the back of an elephant
howdy Used to express greeting
howe A valley
however Nevertheless
howf, howff A place frequently visited
howitzer A cannon
howk To dig
howl To cry like a wolf
howlet An owl
howsoever By whatever means
hoy A barge
hoyden A high-spirited girl
hoyle A rule book
huarache, huaracho A flat-heeled sandal
hub A focal point
hubbly Bumpy
hubbub Uproar
hubby A husband
hubcap A cap for the hub of a wheel
hubris Arrogance
huck A fabric
huckaback A fabric
huckle The hip
huckster A peddler
huddle To gather in a huddle
hue Color
huff To blow
huffish Sensitive
hug To hold closely
huge Of great size
hugeous Huge
huh Used to express surprise
hula A dance
hulk The hull of an old ship
hull The husk
hum To sing without saying the words
human A person
humane Compassionate
humanist One who studies the humanities
humanoid An android

humble Modest
humblebee A bumblebee
humbug A hoax
humdinger *Slang* A marvel
humdrum Ordinary
humectant A moistening agent
humeral Of a bone of the shoulder
humerus, pl -meri The long bone of the upper arm
humic Pertaining to humus
humid Containing a high amount of water vapor
humidor A case for tobacco products
humility Modesty
hummock A knoll
humor Funniness
humoral Pertaining to bodily fluids
hump Hummock
humpback A hunchback
humph Used to express contempt
humus Decomposed organic matter
hun A destructive person
hunch A premonition
hundred The cardinal number 100
hundredth The ordinal number 100 in a series
hung Past tense of hang
hunger A strong desire for food
hungry Desiring food
hunk A chunk
hunky *Slang* A bohunk
hunnish Resembling a hun
hunt To search for
huntress A female hunter
huntsman A hunter
hup Used to mark a marching cadence
hurdle An obstacle
hurl To pitch
hurrah To cheer
hurricane A severe storm
hurry To move quickly
hurt To wound
hurtle To crash
husband A woman's spouse
husbandry Farming
hush To quiet
hushaby Go to sleep
hushpuppy A cornmeal fritter

husk   To remove the husk
hussar   A cavalry soldier
hussy   A saucy girl
hustings   An English court
hustle   To jostle
hut   A shack
hutch   A cupboard for storage
huzza, huzzah   A cheer
hwan   Monetary unit of South Korea
hyacinth   A species of plant
hyaena   Variant of hyena
hyalin, hyaline   A transparent substance
hyalite   A clear opal
hyaloid   Hyaline
hybrid   Something of mixed origin
hydatid   A cyst caused by a tapeworm
hydra, *pl* **-dras** or **-drae**   A species of polyp
hydrant   A fire hydrant
hydranth   The oral opening of a polyp
hydrate   To combine with water
hydraulic   Operated by a fluid
hydric   Containing hydrogen
hydride   A chemical compound
hydrocele   An accumulation of serous fluid in a bodily cavity
hydrofoil   A hydroplane
hydrogen   A gaseous element
hydroid   A polyp
hydromel   A mixture of honey and water
hydrosol   An aqueous colloidal solution
hydrous   Containing water
hydroxide   A chemical compound
hydroxy   A hydroxy acid
hydroxyl   The radical containing oxygen and hydrogen
hyena   A species of carnivorous mammal
hyetal   Relating to rain
hygiene   The science of health

hymen   A vaginal membrane
hymeneal   A wedding song
hymenium, *pl* **-nia** or **-ums**   A layer in certain fungi
hymn   A song of praise
hymnal   A book of church hymns
hymnbook   A hymnal
hymnist   A composer of hymns
hymnody   The singing of hymns
hymnology   Hymnody
hyoid   A bone at the base of the tongue
hyoscine   A sedative
hyp   Hypochondria
hype   A deception
hyperon   An atomic particle
hyperope   A farsighted person
hypha, *pl* **-phae**   A threadlike filament of a fungus
hyphen   A mark of punctuation
hypnoid   Of sleep
hypnosis   An artificially induced sleep
hypnotic   Inducing hypnosis
hypo   An injection
hypobaric   Below normal pressure
hypocrite   A person given to hypocrisy
hypogeal   Underground
hypogene   Formed below the earth's surface
hypogeum, *pl* **-gea**   An ancient catacomb
hypopnea   Abnormally shallow breathing
hypothec   A type of mortgage
hypoxia   Deficiency in oxygen
hyrax, *pl* **-raxes** or **-races**   A species of mammal
hyson   Chinese green tea
hyssop   A woody plant
hysteria   Excessive emotionalism
hysteric   A person suffering from hysteria
hyte   Insane

iamb   A metrical foot
iambus, *pl* -buses or -bi   An iamb
iatric   Medical
ibex   A wild goat
ibidem   In the same place
ibis   A species of long-billed wading bird
ice   Frozen water
iceberg   A floating body of ice
iceblink   A glare over an ice field
iceboat   A vehicle that sails on ice
icebound   Locked in by ice
icebox   A refrigerator
icecap   A covering of ice
icefall   An avalanche of ice
icelike   Resembling ice
iceman   A man who delivers ice
ich   A disease of fish
ichnite   A fossilized footprint
ichor   A watery discharge from a wound
ichthyic   Pertaining to fish
icicle   A hanging spike of ice
icily   In an icy manner
iciness   The state of being icy
icky *Slang*   Disgusting
icon   An image
icteric   Having jaundice
icterus   Jaundice
ictus, *pl* -tuses   A stroke
id   A part of the psyche
idea   A thought
ideal   A goal
ideality   The state of being ideal
ideally   Perfectly
ideate   To imagine
idem   The same
identic   Identical
identical   Being the same
identity   The character of a person
ideogram   A graphic symbol

ideology   A body of ideas
ides   A day in the Roman calendar
idiocy   Stupidity
idiolect   A person's speech pattern
idiom   A speech form
idiot   An imbecile
idle   Inactive
idocrase   A mineral
idol   One that is worshipped
idolater   One who worships
idyll, idyl   A poem describing rural life
idyllic   Having a natural charm
idyllist   A writer of idylls
if   A possibility
iffy   Characterized by uncertainty
igloo, iglu   An eskimo house
igneous   Relating to fire
ignite   To set fire to
ignitron   A rectifier tube
ignoble   Common
ignominy   Dishonor
ignorant   Without education
ignore   To disregard
iguana   A species of lizard
ihram   Sacred dress of Moslem pilgrams
ikon   Variant of icon
ilea   Of ileum
ileac   Ileal
ileitis   Inflammation of the ileum
ileum, *pl* -ea   A part of the small intestine
ileus   Intestinal obstruction
ilex   A species of tree
ilium, *pl* -ia   A bone of the pelvis
ilk, ilka   Every
ill   Sick
illation   A deduction
illegal   Prohibited by law
illegible   Not legible

illicit Unlawful
illite Clay minerals
illume To illuminate
illumine To illuminate
illusion A false perception
illusory Illusive
illy Badly
ilmenite A titanium ore
image A likeness
imagine To create in the mind
imagism A literary movement
imago An adult insect
imam, imaum A Moslem scholar
imamate Office of an imam
imaret A Turkish inn
imbalance A lack of balance
imbecile One who is feeble-minded
imbed Variant of embed
imbibe To drink
imbricate Ornamented with overlapping edges
imbroglio A predicament
imbrue To stain
imbrute To become brutal
imbue To saturate
imid Imide
imide A chemical compound
imine A chemical compound
imitate To copy the mannerisms of
immanent Inherent
immature Unripe
immediate Near
immense Large
immerge To immerse
immerse To submerge
immie An agate
immigrant One who comes into a
  foreign place
imminent Ready to occur
immingle To blend
immix To blend
immobile Not moving
immodest Lacking modesty
immolate To kill as a sacrifice
immoral Contrary to established
  morality
immortal Not subject to death
immune Exempt
immure To imprison
imp A small child

impact A collision
impair To diminish
impala An antelope
impale To pierce with a stake
impanel To enroll
imparity Inequality
impark To confine
impart To bestow
impasse Dead end
impassion To arouse the passions
  of
impaste To make into a paste
impasto A painting technique
impavid Brave
impeach To degrade
impearl To adorn
impede To block
impel To compel
impend To threaten
imperfect Not perfect
imperial Pertaining to an empire
imperil To endanger
impetigo A skin disease
impetrate To beseech
impetuous Impulsive
impetus An impulse
impi A body of warriors
impiety The lack of piety
impinge To strike
impious Not pious
impish Mischievous
implant To infix
implead To sue
implement A tool
implicate To imply
implicit Implied
implode To collapse inward
implore To beseech
imply To hint
impolite Not polite
impone To wager
import To bring in
important Noteworthy
importune To beseech with
  repeated requests
impose To levy
impost Something levied
imposter A tax assessor
impostor One who deceives under
  an assumed identity

impotent Powerless
impound To seize
impresa An emblem
impress To affect deeply
imprest A loan
imprimis In the first place
imprint To stamp a mark on
imprison To put in prison
impromptu Not rehearsed
improper Incorrect
improve To make better
improvise To invent
imprudent Rash
impudent Rude
impugn To criticize
impulse A sudden urge
impunity Exemption from penalty
impure Not pure
impute To ascribe to another
in Inside

in- Indicates not; without. The following compounds are listed without definition (see Introduction):

inaction	indispose	insane
inactive	indocile	insanity
inanimate	indolent	insatiate
inapt	inedible	insecure
inarable	inedited	insensate
inaudible	inelastic	insincere
incapable	inelegant	insipid
incivil	inequity	insoluble
incog	inerrant	insolvent
incognita	inexact	insomnia
incognito	inexpert	insomniac
incorrect	infecund	instable
incorrupt	infertile	intestate
increate	infinite	intrepid
incult	infinity	inurbane
incurable	infirm	invalid
incurious	informal	invariant
indecent	infrugal	inverity
indecorum	ingrate	inviable
indelible	inhuman	inviolate
indevout	inhumane	invirile
indignant	innocuous	inviscid
indignity	inodorous	invisible
indirect	inquiet	invital

inamorata A woman with whom one is in love
inamorato A male lover

inane Empty
inanity Quality of being inane
inarch To graft
inboard Within the hull of a ship
inborn Inherited
inbound Incoming
inbreathe To breathe into
inbred Innate
inbreed To engender
inburst That which bursts in
incage Variant of encage
incarnate To personify
incase Variant of encase
incense To enrage
inception The beginning of something
incessant Unceasing
incest Sexual union between closely related persons
inch A unit of length
inchmeal Gradually
inchoate Just beginning
inchworm A measuring worm
incident An occurrence
incipient In an early stage
incipit Here begins
incise To cut into
incisor A cutting tooth
incite To stir up
inclasp Variant of enclasp
inclement Stormy
incline To slant
inclose Variant of enclose
include To contain
income Money earned regularly
incony Pretty
increase To become greater
increment A growth
incrust Variant of encrust
incubate To brood
incubus, *pl* **-buses** or **-bi** A nightmare
inculcate To instill
inculpate To incriminate
incumbent Leaning upon something
incur To run into
incurve To curve inward
incus, *pl* **incudes** A bone in the middle ear

180

incuse Stamped in
indaba A gathering of tribes
indamine A chemical compound
indebted Beholden
indeed Truly
indemnify To insure
indemnity Compensation for damages
indene A hydrocarbon
indent To make a dent in
index, pl **-dexes** or **-dices** A reference guide
indican A chemical compound
indicant Something that indicates
indicate To demonstrate
indicia Signs
indict To charge
indictee One that is indicted
indicter One that indicts
indictor Indicter
indigen, indigene A native
indigent Needy
indign Unworthy
indigo A species of plant
indigoid A blue dye
indigotin A chemical compound
indite To compose
indium A metallic element
indole A chemical compound
indoor Pertaining to the interior
indorse Variant of endorse
indraft An inward flow
indrawn Drawn in
indri, pl **-dris** A large lemur
induce To influence
induct To install
indue Variant of endue
indulge To yield to the desires of
indult A privilege granted by the pope
indurate To harden
industry Commercial production of goods
indwell To live within
inebriate To intoxicate
ineffable Taboo
inept Not fitting
inert Unable to act
inertia The tendency to resist acceleration

infamous Notorious
infamy Infamous
infancy Period of being an infant
infant A baby
infanta A daughter of a Spanish or Portuguese king
infante A son of a Spanish or Portuguese king not heir to the throne
infantile Lacking maturity
infantry Footsoldiers
infarct An area of dying tissue
infatuate To behave foolishly
infect To contaminate
infer To deduce
inference Something inferred
inferior Lower in quality
infernal Relating to hell
inferno Hell
infest To overrun
infidel Having no religious beliefs
infield A part of a baseball field
infirmary A small hospital
infirmity Disability
infix To instill
inflame To kindle
inflate To fill with gas
inflect To bend
inflexed Curved inward
inflict To impose
inflow Something that flows in
influence Power to sway
influent Flowing into
influenza A viral disease
influx A flowing in
infold To fold inward
inform To disclose information
infract To infringe
infrared A part of the invisible spectrum
infringe To violate
infuriate To anger
infuse To fill
ingate A channel through which molten metal flows
ingenious Displaying ingenuity
ingenue An actress playing an innocent young girl
ingenuity Cleverness
ingenuous Innocent
ingest To take into the body

ingesta Ingested matter
ingoing Entering
ingot A casting mold for metal
ingraft Variant of engraft
ingrain To fix
ingress A place of entering
ingroup A group united by common interests
ingrown Grown within
ingrowth The act of growing inward
inguinal Located in the groin
ingulf Variant of engulf
inhabit To dwell
inhalant Used for inhaling
inhale To breathe in
inhaul A rope used to draw in a ship's sail
inhere To be innate
inherent Intrinsic
inherit To receive property
inhibit To forbid
inhume To bury
inimical Not harmful
iniquity Wickedness
initial The first letter of a word
initiate To originate
inject To force into
injure To hurt
inkberry A shrub
inkblot A pattern of spilled ink
inkhorn A container to hold ink
inkpot An inkwell
inkstand An inkwell
inkwell A container for ink
inkwood A tropical tree
inlace Variant of enlace
inlaid Past tense of inlay
inland The interior of a country
inlay To set into a surface
inlet An estuary
inlier A type of rock formation
inly Inwardly
inmate One confined to an institution
inmost Innermost
inn A hotel
innards Inner parts
innate Inborn
inner Occurring within

innervate To stimulate
innerve To stimulate
innocent Sinless
innovate To be creative
innuendo A subtle implication
inoculate To inject a serum in order to create immunity
inoculum Material used in an inoculation
inorganic Artificial
inositol An isomeric alcohol
inphase Having the same phase
input To enter data
inquest A judicial inquiry
inquire To request information
inroad An intrusion
inrush An influx
inscribe To engrave
insect Any of numerous small invertebrate animals
insert To put into
inset To insert
inshore Close to the shore
inshrine Variant of enshrine
inside The inner part
insidious Treacherous
insight Penetration
insignia An emblem
insinuate To hint
insist To demand
insnare Variant of ensnare
insofar To such an extent
insolate To expose to sunlight
insole The inner sole of a shoe
insolent Arrogant
insoul Variant of ensoul
inspect To examine
insphere Variant of ensphere
inspire To elicit
inspirit To enliven
install To establish
instance To cite as an example
instant A moment
instar To adorn with stars
instate To install
instead In the place of
instep Part of a shoe
instigate To stir up
instill, instil To implant
instinct An innate behavioral

pattern

institute To initiate

instroke An inward stroke

instruct To educate

insular Of an island

insulate To isolate

insulin A hormone

insult To treat offensively

insure To guarantee

insurgent One who revolts

intact Whole

intaglio, pl **-glios** or **-tagli** A type of printing

intake The act of taking in

intarsia A mosaic

integer A whole number

integral Whole

integrate To unify

integrity Unity

intellect Capacity of knowledge

intend To plan

intense Profound

intent Aim

inter To bury

inter- Indicates between or among; mutually or together. The following compounds are listed without definition (see Introduction):

interact	interline	interpose
intercede	interlock	intersect
intercrop	intermix	intersex
interlace	internode	intervale
interleaf	interplay	

intercept To stop

intercom An intercommunication system

interdict To destroy

interest A feeling of curiosity

interface An area forming a common boundary

interfere To impede

interim An interval

interior The inside

interject An interruption

interlard To intersperse

interlope To intrude

interlude A musical piece

intermit To interrupt

intern, interne An advanced student

internal Inherent

internist One who practices internal medicine

interpret To translate

interrex, pl **-reges** A type of sovereign

interrupt To break in upon

interval A space between two points

intervene To come in between

interview A meeting

intestate Having made no will

intestine A part of the alimentary canal

inthrall Variant of enthrall

inthrone Variant of enthrone

intima, pl **-mae** or **-mas** The innermost layer of an organ

intimate Private

intitule To entitle

into To the inside of

intonate To intone

intone To speak in a singing voice

intort To twist inward

intown Located in the center of town

intrados The inner curve of an arch

intreat Variant of entreat

intrench Variant of entrench

intrigue Mystery

intrinsic Inherent

intro An introduction

introduce To present

introit A hymn sung at the opening of a service

intromit To admit

introrse Facing inward

introvert To turn inward

intrude To force oneself in

intrust Variant of entrust

intubate To insert a tube into

intuit To know

intuition Sharp insight

inturn A turning inward

intwine Variant of entwine

intwist Variant of entwist

inulin A carbohydrate

inundate To swamp

inure To make used to something undesirable

inurn To inter
inutile Useless
invade To enter by force
invasion The act of invading
inveigh To protest
inveigle To induce by flattery
invent To originate
invert To turn upside down
invest To endow with authority
invite To welcome
invocate To invoke
invoice A bill
invoke To appeal to
involute Complex
involve To complicate
inward Located inside
inweave To weave into a fabric
inwind Variant of enwind
inwrap Variant of enwrap
iodate To iodize
iodide A compound of iodine
iodine A nonmetallic element
ion An atom
ionic Containing ions
ionone A chemical compound
iota The ninth letter of the Greek alphabet
ipecac A medicinal shrub
irate Angry
ire Anger
ireful Angry
irenic Promoting peace
iridic Pertaining to the eye
iridium A metallic element
iris, *pl* **irises** or **irides** A species of plant
iritis Inflammation of the eye
irk To irritate
irksome Tedious
iron A metallic element
ironbark A species of tree
ironclad Rigid
ironic Pertaining to irony
ironware Hardware
ironweed A species of plant
ironwood A species of tree
ironwork Work in iron
irony The use of words to convey opposite of what is literally said
irradiate To expose to radiation

irregular Not symmetrical
irrigate To make fertile
irritant Irritating
irritate To provoke
irrupt To break
is The third person singular present indicative of be
isba A Russian hut
ischium, *pl* **-chia** A pelvic bone
island Land surrounded by water
isle An island
islet A small island
ism A distinctive doctrine
isobar A line on a map
isocline A type of rock strata
isodose Points representing equal doses of radiation
isogamy The fusion of similar gametes
isogloss A line on a map
isogon An equiangular polygon
isogram A line on a map
isohel A line on a map
isohyet A line on a map
isolate To set apart
isomer A chemical compound
isometry Equality of measure
isomorph An object similar to something else
isopod A species of crustacean
isoprene A volatile liquid
isospin A quantum number
isostasy Balance in the earth's crust
isotherm A line on a weather map
isotonic Of equal tension
isotone A type of atom
isotope A form of an element
issei A Japanese immigrant to the United States
issuant Emerging
issue An outflow
isthmian Forming an isthmus
isthmus, *pl* **-muses** or **-mi** A strip of land connecting two larger masses of land
istle The pita plant
it The thing previously mentioned
italic A style of print
itch A desire for something

item A single article
iterate To repeat
iterum Once again
ither Other
itinerant Traveling from place to place
itinerary A record of a journey
itinerate To travel
its The possessive form of it

itself A reflexive form of it
ivory Part of the elephant tusk
ivy A species of plant
iwis Certainly
ixia A flowering plant
izar A woman's garment worn in Moslem countries
izzard Variant of zee

jab To poke
jabiru A tropical bird
jabot Frills on a shirt
jacal, pl **-als** or **jacales** A hut
jacamar A species of bird
jacana A species of bird
jacaranda A species of tree
jacinth A variety of zircon
jack A man
jackal A species of mammal
jackass A male donkey
jackboot A heavy boot
jackdaw A crow-like bird
jackeroo An inexperienced ranch hand
jacket A short coat
jackknife, pl **-knives** A pocketknife
jackleg Not properly trained
jackpot The top prize
jackscrew A lifting jack
jackstay A ship rope
jacobin A pigeon
jacobus A gold coin
jaconet A cotton cloth
jacquard An intricately woven fabric
jactation Boasting
jade A gemstone
jadeite A mineral

jaeger A species of sea bird
jag A barb
jaggery Unrefined sugar
jaguar A large feline animal
jail A prison
jailbird A prisoner
jake *Slang* All right
jakes A privy
jalap A Mexican plant
jalopy An old dilapidated auto
jalousie A shutter
jam A preserve
jamb Part of a door frame
jambeau, pl **-beaux** A piece of armor
jamboree A celebration with entertainment
jane *Slang* A girl
jangle A metallic sound
janitor A maintenance man
japan A black lacquer
japanize To make Japanese
jape To joke
japonica The camellia shrub
jar A container
jargon Gibberish
jarl A medieval chieftain
jasmine A species of vine
jasper A variety of quartz

jato A takeoff aided by jet propulsion
jaundice A disease
jaunt A short trip
java Coffee
javelin A light spear
jaw The bony framework of the mouth
jawbone Bone of the jaw
jay The letter *j*
jayvee A junior varsity
jaywalk To cross a street illegally
jazz A type of American native music
jealous Envious
jean A fabric
jebel A hill
jee To gee
jeep A motor vehicle
jeepers Used as a mild oath
jeer To mock
jejune Dull
jejunum, *pl* **-na** A part of the small intestine
jell To congeal
jellybean A candy
jemadar An official of the Indian government
jemmy Variant of jimmy
jennet A small horse
jenny A female donkey
jeopardy Peril
jerboa A species of rodent
jeremiad A tale of woe
jerk To move abruptly
jerkin A vest
jerkwater Remote
jeroboam A wine bottle
jerry *Slang* A German soldier
jersey A fabric
jess A strap put on a hawk
jest A frivolous mood
jesuit A scheming person
jet An outlet
jete A ballet step
jetliner An airplane
jetport An airport
jetsam Discarded cargo
jettison To cast overboard
jetty A wharf

jeu, *pl* **jeux** A game
jewel A gem
jewfish A species of fish
jezebel A scheming woman
jib To draw back
jibe To harmonize
jiffy, jiff A moment
jig A dance
jigsaw A saw
jihad A crusade
jill Variant of gill
jillion A very large number
jilt To reject a lover
jiminy Used to express surprise
jimmy A crowbar
jingle A catchy rhyme
jingo A blatant patriot
jink A sudden turn
jinni, jinn, jinnee In Moslem legend, a supernatural being
jinriksha An oriental carriage
jinx Bad luck
jipijapa A palmlike plant
jitney A small bus
jitter To fidget
jitterbug A dance
jive Swing music
jo A sweetheart
job A profession
jobbery Corruption in public office
jock *Slang* A disc jockey
jockette A female jockey
jockey One who rides a horse in a race
jocko A monkey
jocose Joking
jocular Meant in jest
jocund Merry
jodhpur A type of boot
joe *Slang* A fellow
joey A young kangaroo
jog To run
joggle To shake
john *Slang* A toilet
johnny A sleeveless hospital gown
join To bring together
joint A point where two things are joined
jointure Property set aside
joist A supporting beam

joke An amusing remark
jokester A practical joker
jole Variant of jowl
jollify To cheer up
jolly Fun-loving
jollyboat A small boat
jolt To jostle
jongleur A wandering minstrel
jonquil A plant
jordan A container
jorum A drinking bowl
jospeh A riding coat
josh To tease
joss A Chinese idol
jostle To push together
jot To write down
jota A dance
joule A unit of energy
jounce A jolting bounce
journal A diary
journey A trip
joust A combat
jovial Good-natured
jowl The jaw
joy Happiness
joyance Delight
joypop *Slang* To use drugs
joyride A pleasure ride
joystick *Slang* The control stick of an airplane
juba A dance
jube A platform in a church
jubilate To rejoice
jubilee A special anniversary
judas A peephole
judge To pass judgment
judgment Wisdom
judicial Pertaining to the courts
judo A form of jujitsu
jug A container
jugate Joined in pairs
juggle To balance
jughead *Slang* A dull person
jugular Pertaining to the throat
jugum, *pl* **-ga** or **-gums** A process of hooking forewings and hind wings of an insect together
juice Liquid part of a fruit
jujitsu, jujutsu Japanese art of self-defense
juju An amulet
jujube A species of tree
juke To take out of position
jukebox A coin-operated phonograph
julep A mint julep
julienne Broth
jumble To mix
jumbo Larger than average
jumbuck A sheep
jump To spring off the ground
jun A coin of North Korea
junco A species of bird
junction The condition of being joined
juncture The point where two things are joined
jungle Land overgrown with tropical vegetation
junior Younger
juniper A species of tree
junk Discarded items
junket An outing
junkie *Slang* A narcotics addict
junkman One who buys and sells junk
junta A political council
junto A clique
jural Pertaining to law
jurant One who takes an oath
jurat An affidavit
juratory Of an oath
jurist A lawyer
juror One serving on a jury
jury A committee to judge
jus, *pl* **jura** Law
jussive A word used to express command
just Fair
justice Fairness
jut To project
jute A fiber
jutty To jut
juvenal A young bird's plumage
juvenile Youthful
juxtapose To place together

ka   The soul in ancient Egyptian religion
kabob   Shish kebab
kabuki   Japanese drama
kaddish   A Jewish prayer
kadi   Variant of qadi
kaf   The eleventh letter of the Hebrew alphabet
kaffir, kafir   A variety of sorghum
kaftan   Variant of caftan
kago   A Japanese palanquin
kaimakam   A deputy in the service of the Ottoman Empire
kain   Rent payments
kainite   A mineral salt
kaiser   An emperor
kaka   A parrot
kakapo   A parrot
kakemono   A Japanese scroll
kaki   Japanese persimmon
kale   A variety of cabbage
kamala   An Asian tree
kame   A mound formed during the melting of glacial ice
kami   A divine power
kamikaze   Agent of a suicidal attack
kana   Japanese syllabic script
kangaroo   A species of marsupial
kanji   A Japanese system of writing
kantar   A unit of weight
kaolin, kaoline   A white clay
kaon   Either of two mesons
kaph   Variant of kaf
kapok   A fiber
kappa   The tenth letter of the Greek alphabet
kaput, kaputt   Wrecked
karakul   A breed of sheep
karat   A unit of quality for gold
karate   Japanese art of self-defense

karma   Fate
kaross   Rug of an animal skin
karroo   An arid plateau
kasbah   Variant of casbah
kasha   Buckwheat groats
kashmir   Variant of cashmere
kat   Variant of khat
katakana   A phonetic Japanese syllabary
katydid   A species of insect
kauri   A species of tree
kava   A shrub
kay   The letter k
kayak   An Eskimo canoe
kayo   A knockout
kazak   A member of the Kirghiz people
kazoo   A toy musical instrument
kea   A parrot
keck   To retch
keckle   To wind with rope
kedge   A light anchor
kedgeree   An Indian food dish
keek   To spy
keel   The principal structural member of a ship
keelboat   A flat-bottomed boat
keelhaul   To castigate
keelson, kelson   A beam in a ship
keen   Vivid
keep   To retain
keepsake   A memento
keeshond   A breed of dog
keet   A young guinea fowl
keg   A small cask
kegler   A bowler
keister, keester *Slang*   The buttocks
keloid   A scar
kelp   A species of seaweed
kelpie   A water sprite
kelvin   A unit of temperature

kemp A champion
kempt Well-groomed
ken To know
kennel A shelter for dogs
kenning A metaphorical expression
keno A game of chance
kenosis The incarnation of Christ
kepi A type of cap
kept Past tense of keep
keratin A fibrous protein
kerchief A woman's scarf
kere An annotation in the margin of a Hebrew Bible
kerf A groove made by a saw
kermes A red dye
kermis An outdoor fair
kern A loutish person
kernel A grain or seed
kernite A mineral
kerosene A fuel oil
kerry A breed of cattle
kersey A fabric
kestrel An Old World falcon
ketch A sailing vessel
ketchup A spicy tomato sauce
ketene A toxic gas
ketone A chemical compound
ketose A simple sugar
ketosis An accumulation of ketones
kettle A metal pot
kevel A belaying pin
kex A dry, hollow stalk
key A device designed to open a lock
keyboard A row of keys on a piano
keyhole The hole in a lock
keynote The main speech
keystone The central stone of an arch
keyway A slot for a key
khadi Cloth made in India
khaki A fabric
khalif Variant of caliph
khamsin A hot wind from the Sahara
khan An Asian ruler
khanate The realm of a khan
khat A shrub

khedive A Turkish viceroy
khi Variant of chi
kiang A wild ass
kiaugh Trouble
kibbe A Near Eastern dish
kibble Prepared dog food
kibbutz A farm in Israel
kibe An ulcerated chilblain
kibei A native American citizen of Japanese immigrant parents
kibitz To meddle
kiblah The direction toward which Moslems face when praying
kibosh A check
kick To strike with the foot
kickback A repercussion
kickoff A beginning
kickshaw A delicacy
kickup An argument
kicky *Slang* Stylish
kid A young goat
kiddy, kiddie *Slang* A small child
kidnap To abduct
kidney A bodily organ
kidskin Leather made from the skin of a young goat
kier A vat for dyeing fabrics
kif Indian hemp
kilim An oriental textile
kill To slay
killdeer A bird
killick A small anchor
killjoy One who spoils the fun of others
kiln A brick-lined oven
kilo A kilometer
kilogram A unit of mass
kiloton One thousand tons
kilowatt One thousand watts
kilt A skirt worn by men
kilter Proper form
kimono A Japanese robe
kin One's family
kinase An enzyme
kind Good
kindle To set fire
kindred A family
kine A television tube
kinescope A film
kinetic Produced by motion

kinfolk, kinfolks Variant of kinsfolk
king A male monarch
kingbird A species of New World bird
kingbolt A bolt serving as a pivot
kingdom A government ruled by a king
kingfish A species of fish
kinglet A king who rules over a small country
kingpin An important person
kingship A kingdom
kingwood A South American tree
kink A crick
kinkajou Honey bear
kino A gum resin
kinsfolk Kindred
kinship Related
kinsman A male relative
kiosk A pavilion
kip The untanned hide of a calf
kipper To cure fish
kirigami Japanese art of folding paper
kirk A church
kirsch A brandy
kirtle A woman's skirt
kishke, kishka A sausage
kismet Fate
kiss To touch with the lips
kist A locker
kit An outfit
kitchen A room where food is prepared
kite A flying toy
kith Friends and neighbors
kitten A young cat
kittenish Flirtatious
kittle Touchy
kitty A pool of money
kiva A ceremonial room in a Pueblo Indian village
kiwi A species of flightless bird
klatch, klatsch A social gathering
klavern A local branch of the Ku Klux Klan
klieg, kleig A carbon-arc lamp
kloof A deep ravine
klutz *Slang* A clumsy person

klystron An electron tube
knack A specific talent
knap A summit
knapsack A bag
knapweed A species of plant
knar A knot on a tree
knave The jack
knawel A weedy plant
knead To make by kneading
knee A joint of the leg
kneecap The patella
kneehole A space for the knees
kneel To rest on bent knees
kneepad A covering for the knee
knell To toll
knew Past tense of know
knickers Long bloomers
knife, *pl* **knives** A cutting tool
knight A medieval soldier
knish Dough stuffed with filling
knit To make into a garment
knob A rounded dial
knock To hit
knoll To toll
knop A boss
knot A closed loop
knotgrass A weedy plant
knothole A hole in lumber
knotweed A species of plant
knout A leather whip
know To be certain of
knowledge Learning
knuckle A joint of a finger
knur, knurl A knot
koa A timber tree
koala An Australian mammal
koan A Buddhist paradox
kob An antelope
kobold A gnome
koel A species of cuckoo
kohl An eye makeup
kohlrabi Turnip cabbage
koine A type of dialect
kola An African tree
kolacky A pastry
kolinsky A species of mink
kolkhoz A Soviet colective farm
kolo A dance
koodoo Variant of kudu
kook *Slang* A zany person

kop A hill
kopeck A Russian coin
koph Nineteenth letter of the Hebrew alphabet
koppa A letter in the early Greek alphabet
kor A Hebrew unit of measure
koruna, *pl* **-ny** or **-nas** Monetary unit of Czechoslovakia
kosher Prepared in accordance with Jewish dietary laws
koto A Japanese musical instrument
kowtow, kotow An obsequious act
kraal An enclosure for livestock
kraft A wrapping paper
krait A species of snake
kraken A legendary sea monster
kraut Sauerkraut
kremlin A Russian citadel
kreuzer A small coin
krill Small marine crustaceans
krimmer Fur from the pelts of lambs
kris A sword
krona, *pl* **-nur** Monetary unit of Iceland

krone, *pl* **-ner** Monetary unit of Denmark
kroon, *pl* **kroons** or **krooni** Former monetary unit of Estonia
krypton A gaseous element
kuchen A coffee cake
kudos Acclaim
kudu A large antelope
kudzu An Asian vine
kue The letter *q*
kulak A rich peasant
kumiss A beverage
kummel A type of liqueur
kumquat A species of tree
kunzite A mineral
kuru A disease
kvass, kvas A Russian beverage
kvetch To complain
kwacha Monetary unit of Zambia
kyack A packsack
kyanite A mineral
kyat Monetary unit of Burma
kylix, *pl* **kylikes** A drinking cup
kyphosis Abnormal curvature of the spine
kyte The stomach

la The tone A
laager An encampment encircled by wagons
lab A laboratory
labarum, *pl* **-ara** An ecclesiastical banner
labdanum A species of plant
labellum, *pl* **-bella** Enlarged lip of an orchid

labial Pertaining to the lips
labiate Having lips
labium, *pl* **-bia** A liplike structure
labor Physical exertion
labret An ornament worn in a perforation of the lip
labrum, *pl* **-bra** A lip
laburnum A species of tree
labyrinth A structure of intercon-

necting passages
lac A resinous secretion
lace A fabric
lacerate To tear
lacewing A species of insect
laches Culpable negligence
lack Want
lackaday Used to express regret
lackey A footman
laconic Concise
lacquer A glossy substance
lacrosse A game
lactary Of milk
lactase An enzyme
lactate To produce milk
lacteal Milky
lactic Derived from milk
lactone A cyclic ester
lactose A lactic sugar
lacuna, *pl* **-nae** or **-nas** A gap
lacunar, *pl* **-nars** or **-naria** A ceiling
   of recessed panels
lacy Resembling lace
lad A young man
ladder A means of ascent and
   descent
laddie A young lad
lade To burden
ladino A clover
ladle A spoon
lady A woman of gentle manners
ladybug A species of beetle
ladylike Refined
ladylove A sweetheart
ladyship A form of address
lag To loiter
lagan Cargo thrown into the sea
lager A type of beer
laggard A straggler
lagoon A body of water
laic, laical Secular
laicize Secularize
laid Past tense of lay
lain Past tense of lie
lair The den of a wild animal
laird The owner of a landed estate
laity Nonprofessionals
lake An inland body of water
laker A ship used on lakes
laky Bloodred

lam *Slang* To flee
lama A Buddhist monk
lamasery A Lamaist monastery
lamb A young sheep
lambaste *Slang* To whip
lambda The eleventh letter of the
   Greek alphabet
lambent Luminous
lambert A unit of brightness
lambkill A shrub
lambkin A small lamb
lambskin The skin of a lamb
lame Crippled
lamed, lamedh The twelfth letter of
   the Hebrew alphabet
lamella, *pl* **-mellae** or **-las** A thin
   scale forming a gill of a mushroom
lament To grieve
lamia, *pl* **-as** or **-ae** A vampire
lamina, *pl* **-nae** or **-nas** A thin plate,
   sheet, or layer
laminate To cover with thin sheets
lamp A device that gives off light
lampion An oil-burning lamp
lamplight Light shed by a lamp
lampoon A satire
lamprey A species of fish
lanai A veranda
lanate Consisting of hairs
lance A weapon
lancelet A species of marine
   organism
lancer A cavalryman armed with a
   lance
lancet A surgical knife
land Solid ground of the earth
landau A carriage
landaulet A small landau
landfall An approach to land
landfill A system of waste disposal
landlady A female landlord
landler A dance
landlord An innkeeper
landmark A fixed marker
landside A part of a plow
landslide A great victory
landsman One who works on land
lane A narrow country road
lang Long
langlauf A cross-country ski run

langley A unit of illumination
langouste The spiny lobster
langrage A type of case shot
langsyne Long ago
language A method of communicating ideas
languet A tonguelike part
languid Weak
languish To fade
languor Sluggishness
langur A species of monkey
lank Gaunt
lanner A falcon
lanneret A male lanner
lanolin, lanoline A fatty substance obtained from wool
lanose Woolly
lantana A species of shrub
lantern A lighthouse
lanugo Fine, soft hair
lanyard A fastening rope
lap To fold around something
lapboard A substitute for a desk
lapel The flap of a garment
lapidary Relating to precious stones
lapillus, *pl* **-pilli** A fragment of lava
lapin A rabbit
lappet A decorative flap
lapse To decline
lapstreak Clinker-built
lapsus A lapse
lapwing A species of Old World bird
lar, *pl* **lares** or **lars** A spirit of an ancient Roman household
larboard The port side
larceny Theft
larch A species of tree
lard The rendered fat of a hog
lardon, lardoon A strip of fat
lardy Resembling lard
large Big
largess A bounty
larghetto Moderately slow in tempo
largish Fairly large
largo In a slow, solemn manner
lariat A lasso
lark A species of Old World bird

larkspur A species of plant
larrigan A type of moccasin
larrup To flog
larum An alarm
larva, *pl* **-vae** The form of various insects when newly hatched
larynx, *pl* **larynges** or **-ynxes** The upper part of the respiratory tract
lasagna, lasagne An Italian dish of noodles
lascar An East Indian sailor
lase To function as a laser
laser A device that amplifies light waves
lash An eyelash
lass, lassie A girl
lassitude A state of exhaustion
lasso A lariat
last Coming after all others
lat Former monetary unit of Latvia
latakia Turkish tobacco
latch To close
latchet A thong to fasten a sandal
latchkey A key for opening a latch
late Delayed
lateen A sailing vessel
latency The state of being latent
latent Present but inactive
lateral Sideways
laterite A rich soil
latex, *pl* **latices** or **-texes** Milky sap of certain trees
lath A building material
lathe A potter's wheel
lather Foam formed by soap
latish Fairly late
latitude Breadth
latrine A communal toilet
latten A brass-like alloy
latter More recent
lattice A framework of interwoven strips
laud Praise
laudanum A tincture of opium
laudatory Eulogistic
laugh To express mirth by a series of inarticulate sounds
launce A marine fish
launch To propel
launder To wash clothes

laundress A woman employed to wash

laundry Where washing is done

laura A type of monastery

laureate Pre-eminent

laurel A species of shrub and tree

lava Molten rock

lavabo, *pl* **-es** A ceremonial washing

lavage A washing

lavaliere A pendant

lavatory A bathroom

lave To bathe

lavender A species of aromatic plant

laver A large basin

laverock A skylark

lavish Extravagant

law A rule established by authority and society

lawgiver A lawmaker

lawn A fabric

lawsuit A legal action

lawyer One who practices law

lax Not strict

laxative A drug that stimulates evacuation of the bowels

laxity The state of being lax

lay To put down

layette Clothing for a newborn child

layman One who does not have special training

layoff The suspension of employees

layout The laying out of something

layover A stopover

laywoman A female member of the laity

lazar A leper

laze To loaf

lazuli A mineral

lazurite A mineral

lazy Slothful

lazybones *Slang* A lazy person

lea A meadow

leach To be dissolved and washed out

lead To escort

leaden Sluggish

leadoff Opening

leadplant A shrub

leadwort A species of plant

leaf, *pl* **leaves** Foliage

leafage Leaves

leaflet A printed flier

league An alliance

leaguer A siege

leak Something escaping

lean To incline

leap To vault

leapfrog A game

learn To gain knowledge

leary Variant of leery

lease A contract granting use of

leash To control

least Lowest in rank

leather The tanned hide of an animal

leathern Resembling leather

leave To go out

leaven An ingredient in dough that produces fermentation

leavings Leftovers

lech *Slang* To behave like a lecher

lecher One given to promiscuous sexual indulgence

lecithin A phosphatide

lectern A speaker's stand

lection A reading from Scripture

lector A public lecturer

lecture A discourse

led Past tense of lead

ledge A shelf

lee A shelter

leeboard A board attached to a side of a sailing vessel

leech A species of worm

leek A plant

leer To look suggestively

leet A manorial court in England

leeward The lee side

leeway Latitude

left The left side

leftism The ideology of the Left

leftover An unused remnant

lefty *Slang* A left-handed person

leg A lower limb

legacy Property bequeathed to someone

legal Authorized by law

legalism Strict adherence to law
legate An official emissary
legatee The inheritor of a legacy
legato In an even, smooth style
legator One who makes a will
legend A story handed down
leger Variant of ledger
leges Plural of lex
leggy Having attractively long legs
leghorn A fabric
legible Capable of being read
legion A multitude
legist A specialist in law
legit *Slang* Legitimate drama
legume A species of plant
lehua A tropical tree
lei A garland of flowers
leister A fishing spear
leisure Unhurried
lek Monetary unit of Albania
leman A lover
lemma, *pl* **-mas** or **lemmata** A theme indicated in a title
lemming A species of rodent
lemniscus, *pl* **-nisci** Nerve fibers located in the brain
lemon A fruit
lemonade A beverage made of lemon juice
lemony Having the odor or flavor of lemons
lempira Monetary unit of Honduras
lemur A species of arboreal primate
lemures The spirit of the dead in ancient Rome
lend To give
length The fact of being long
lenient Liberal
lenis Weak
lenitive Capable of easing pain
lenity Leniency
leno A fabric
lens A device used to form an image for viewing
lent Past tense of lend
lentic Living in water
lenticel A pore on stems of woody plants

lentigo A freckle
lentil A plant with edible seeds
lentisk The mastic tree
lento Slowly
leone Monetary unit of Sierra Leone
leonine Characteristic of a lion
leopard A large feline mammal
leotard A garment worn by dancers
leper One afflicted with leprosy
lepidote Covered with scurfy scales
leporine Characteristic of rabbits
leprose Leprous
leprosy A chronic disease
leprous Having leprosy
leprous Having leprosy
lepton, *pl* **-ta** A small coin of ancient Greece
lesbian Female homosexual
lesion A wound
less A smaller amount
lessee One holding a lease
lesson Something to be learned
lessor A landlord
lest For fear that
let To allow
letch A strong craving
letdown A disappointment
lethal Causing death
lethargy Sluggish indifference
letter A written message
lettuce A species of plant
letup A slowdown
leu Monetary unit of Rumania
leucine An amino acid
leucite A mineral
leukemia A disease of the blood
leukoma A dense, white opacity of the cornea
lev, *pl* **leva** Monetary unit of Bulgaria
levant A type of leather
levator A surgical instrument
levee A pier
level A flat surface
leveler One that levels
lever A handle
leveret A young hare
levigate To make smooth
levin Lightning

levirate The practice of marrying the widow of one's brother

levitate To rise and float in the air

levity Lightness

levo Counterclockwise

levulose A sugar

levy To impose a tax

lewd Lustful

lewis A device for listing heavy stones

lewisite A chemical compound

lex, *pl* **leges** Law

lexical Relating to the vocabulary

lexicon A dictionary

ley Variant of lea

li A Chinese unit of measure

liable Likely

liaison A close relationship

liana, liane A species of vine

liang A former Chinese unit of weight

liar One who lies

lib Liberation

libation The pouring of a liquid

libeccio A southwest wind in Italy

libel A statement that damages a person

libelant The plaintiff

libelee The defendant

liberal Generous

liberate To set free

libertine A dissolute person

liberty Privilege

libido Sexual desire

libra, *pl* **-brae** An ancient Roman unit of weight

library A repository for books and reference materials

librate To oscillate

libretto The text of an opera

lice Plural of louse

license Permission granted

lichen A species of plant

lichenin A gelatinous compound

licit Legal

lick To pass the tongue over

lickerish Eager

licorice A species of plant

lictor An ancient Roman magistrate's attendant

lid A cover

lidded Covered with a lid

lido A beach resort

lie An untruth

lief Beloved

liege A lord in feudal law

liegeman A feudal subject

lien A claim on the property of another

lienal Relating to the spleen

lierne A rib used in Gothic vaulting

lieu In place of

life A living being

lifeblood The vital part

lifeboat A small boat

lifer *Slang* One serving a life sentence

lifesaver One who saves a life

lifetime The time one lives

lifework Work to which one devotes his life

lift To pick up

liftoff The instant in which a craft commences flight

ligament A connecting bond

ligate To bind with a ligature

ligature A bond

liger An offspring of a lion and tiger

light A source of illumination

lightning Natural electric discharge in the atmosphere

ligneous Woody

lignify To turn into wood

lignin A part of woody tissue

lignite Brownish coal

ligroin A flammable liquid

ligula, *pl* **-lae** or **-las** A mouth part in certain insects

ligure A precious stone

like To find pleasant

liking Fondness

likuta, *pl* **makuta** Monetary unit of Zaire

lilac A species of shrub

lilt A light, graceful movement

lily A species of plant

lima A species of plant

limacine Resembling a slug

limb A branch of a tree

limbate Having an edge of a different color
limber Pliable
limbo A region of neglect
limbus, pl **-bi** A distinctive border
lime A calcium compound
limeade A beverage made from lime juice
limekiln A type of furnace
limelight A stage light
limen, pl **-mens** or **limina** A sensory threshold
limerick A nonsensical verse
limes, pl **limites** A fortified boundary
limey *Slang* A British seaman
limit To restrict
limnetic Living in the open waters
limo A limousine
limonene A chemical compound
limonite An ore of iron
limousine A large passenger vehicle
limp To walk lamely
limpet A species of mollusk
limpid Clear
limpkin A brownish wading bird
limy Resembling lime
linage The number of lines of printed matter
linalool, linalol A fragrant alcohol
linchpin A locking pin
linden A species of tree
lindy A dance
line A thin, continuous mark
lineage Ancestry
lineal Linear
linear Straight
lineate Marked with lines
linecut A type of printing plate
lineman One who inspects railroad tracks
linen A fabric
linesman An official in court games
ling A species of fish
lingam, linga A Hindu phallic symbol
lingcod A food fish
linger To tarry
lingerie Women's underwear

lingo Strange language
lingua, pl **-guae** A tongue
lingual Resembling the tongue
linguini Pasta
linguist One who speaks several languages
liniment A medicinal fluid
linin Substance in the nucleous of cells
link A cufflink
linkboy One hired to carry a torch to light dark streets
linkwork Joined links
linn A waterfall
linnet A small Old World songbird
linoleum A floor covering
linsang A species of mammal
linseed The seed of flax
linstock A forked stick for holding a match
lint Fuzz
lintel Part of a door frame
linter A machine that removes lint
liny Narrow
lion A large feline mammal
lioness A female lion
lionize To treat as a celebrity
lip Fleshy protuberance that surrounds the opening of the mouth
lipase An enzyme
lipid, lipide Any of numerous fats
lipoid Fatty
lipoma, pl **-mata** or **-mas** A tumor of fatty cells
lipstick A cosmetic used in coloring the lips
liquate To separate by melting
liquefy To melt
liquer An alcoholic beverage
liquid A substance that flows easily
liquor An alcoholic beverage
lira, pl **-lire** or **-ras** Monetary unit of Italy
liripipe A scarf hanging from a hood
lisle A cotton thread
lisp A speech defect
lissome, lissom Lithe
list To itemize

listel A molding
listen To give heed
lister A type of plow
listless Languid
lit Monetary unit of Lithuania
litany A liturgical prayer
litchi A Chinese tree
liter, litre A unit of capacity
literacy Ability to read and write
literal Word for word
literary Dealing with literature
literate Able to read and write
literati Scholars
literatim Literally
litharge A monoxide of lead
lithe Supple
lithia Lithium oxide
lithic Pertaining to stone
lithium A metallic element
litho Lithograph
litigant Engaged in a lawsuit
litigate To subject to legal proceedings
litmus A blue, amorphous powder
litotes An understatement for effect
litter A stretcher
litterbug One who litters
little Small
littoral A coastal region
liturgics The study of liturgies
liturgist A scholar in liturgics
liturgy The rite of the Eucharist
live To reside
livelong Long in passing
liven To become lively
liver A secreting organ
liverish Having a liver disorder
livery The uniform worn by servants
livestock Domestic animals
livid Furious
livre Former monetary unit of France
lizard A species of reptile
llama A ruminant mammal
llano A large, grassy plain
lo Used to attract attention
loach A species of fish
load Material transported by a vehicle
loaf To waste time
loam A type of soil
loan To lend
loath Reluctant
loathe To detest
loathly Loathsome
lob A ball hit in a high arc
lobar Relating to a lobe
lobate Having lobes
lobby A waiting room
lobe A rounded projection
lobefin A species of bony fish
lobelia A species of plant
loblolly A mire
lobo The timber wolf
lobotomy Surgical incision into a lobe
lobster A species of marine crustacean
lobule A small lobe
lobworm A lugworm
local Not express
locale The setting
locate To find by looking
locative A type of grammatical case
loch A lake
lochia Discharge of blood after childbirth
lock A device for fastening a door
lockjaw Tetanus
locknut A type of nut
lockout A closing of a business
lockup A jail
loco Locoweed
locoism Loco disease
locular Having small cells
locule A small cavity
locus, _pl_ -ci A place
locust A species of grasshopper
locution Style of speaking
lode A vein of mineral ore
lodestar A star used as a point of reference
lodge A cottage
lodgment The act of lodging
lodicule A small scale at the base of a flower in grasses
loess A soil deposit

loft An attic
log The trunk of a felled tree
logan A balanced stone
logbook Official record book of a ship
loge A box in a theater
loggia An open balcony
logic A system of reasoning
logician A practitioner of logic
logion, *pl* **-gia** Sayings attributed to Jesus
logistic Of logistics
logjam A tangled mass of floating logs
logo An identifying symbol
logogram A symbol used to represent an entire word
logotype A piece of type
logroll To work toward the passage of
logwood A tropical American tree
logy Sluggish
loin A cut of meat
loiter To loaf
loll To lounge
lollipop, lollypop Candy
lolly A lollipop
lollygag To waste time
loment A type of plant pod
lone Isolated
long Having great length
longboat The largest boat carried by a ship
longbow A wooden bow
longeron Part of an aircraft's fuselage
longhair One dedicated to classical music
longhead A person having a long skull
longish Fairly long
longitude Length
longsome Tiresome
longspur A species of bird
longwise Lengthwise
loo A card game
looby A lubber
loofa, loofah A species of vine
looie *Slang* A lieutenant

look To turn one's attention
lookdown A marine fish
lookout One who keeps watch
lookup Process of looking something up
loom A device from which cloth is produced
loon A species of diving bird
loony *Slang* A crazy person
loop To form into a loop
loophole A means of escape
loose Unbound
loot Stolen goods
lop To trim
lope A steady gait
loppy Hanging limp
lopsided Leaning to one side
loquat A small tree
loquitur Begins to speak
loral Having to do with the eyespace of a bird
loran A type of navigational system
lord A man of high rank
lordling A young lord
lordosis A curvature of the spine
lore Knowledge
lorgnette Opera glasses
lorica, *pl* **-cae** A protective shell
lorikeet A species of parrot
loris A species of primate
lorn Forlorn
lorry A wagon
lory A small parrot
lose To mislay
losel One who is worthless
loss Something that is lost
lossy Dampening undesirable oscillations
lost Missing
lot A number of things
lotah, lota A container
lotion A cosmetic liquid
lottery A chance drawing
lotto A game of chance
lotus, lotos An aquatic plant
loud Clamorous
louden To make louder
lough A lake

louis A former gold coin of France
lounge To recline in a relaxed manner
loup To leap
loupe A small magnifying glass
louse, *pl* **lice** or **louses** A species of insect
lousy Infested with lice
lout A boor
louver, louvre A slatted ventilation opening
lovage A plant
love A beloved person
lovebird A species of parrot
lovelock A lock of hair
lovelorn Not loved
lovesick Languishing with love
low Not tall
lowborn Of humble birth
lowboy A chest of drawers
lowbred Lowborn
lowbrow An uncultivated person
lowdown *Slang* The whole truth
lowery Overcast
lowland Low lying land
lowlife *Slang* A disgusting person
lox Smoked salmon
loyal Faithful
lozenge A cough drop
luau A Hawaiian feast
lubber A clumsy person
lube A lubricant
lucarne A dormer window
lucent Luminous
lucerne Alfalfa
luces Plural of lux
lucid Clear
lucifer A match
luck Fortune
lucre Money
luculent Clear
lues Syphilis
luff To steer into the wind
lug To drag
luggage Baggage
lugsail A type of sail
lugworm A species of worm
lukewarm Tepid
lull To soothe
lullaby A soothing song

lulu *Slang* A beautiful girl
lumbago Rheumatism
lumbar Near the loins
lumber Prepared timber
lumen, *pl* **-mens** or **-mina** The inner space of a tubular organ
luminary An object that gives light
luminous Emitting light
lummox A lout
lump A cube of sugar
lumper A stevedore
lumpfish A fish
lumpish Dull
luna An alchemical designation for silver
lunatic Insane
lunch The midday meal
lune A crescent-shaped figure
lunette, lunet A circular opening in a vaulted roof
lung A respiratory organ
lunge A sudden movement
lungfish A species of fish
lungi, lungee A loincloth in India
lungwort A species of plant
lunisolar Caused by both the sun and the moon
lunk, lunkhead A stupid person
lunker A large game fish
lunt A torch
lunula, *pl* **-lae** A small crescent-shaped structure
lupine A species of plant
lupulin A powder obtained from the strobiles of the hop plant
lupus A disease of the skin
lurch To stagger
lure An appeal
lurid Causing shock
lurk To ambush
luscious Delicious
lush Luxurious
lust Sexual craving
lustral Pertaining to a lustrum
lustrate To purify
lustrum A ceremonial purification
lutanist A lute player
lute A musical instrument
luteal Pertaining to the luteum
lutein A yellow pigment

lutetium A metallic element
luteum, *pl* **lutea** A hormone-secreting body
lutist One who makes lutes
lux, *pl* **luxes** or **luces** A unit of illumination
luxate To put out of joint
luxe Elegance
luxury Enjoyment of the best
lyceum A concert hall
lychnis A species of plant
lyddite An explosive
lye A solution used in making soap
lymph A clear fluid resembling blood plasma
lyncean Sharp-sighted
lynch To hang
lynx A species of wild cat
lyrate Having the form of a lyre

lyre A musical instrument
lyrebird An Australian bird
lyric A lyric poem
lyricism The quality of being lyrical
lyricist One who writes lyrics
lyrism Lyricism
lyrist A lyricist
lyse To cause to undergo lysis
lysin An antibody that destroys blood cells
lysine An amino acid
lysis The destruction of cells
lysozyme An enzyme
lytic Causing lysis
lytta, *pl* **lyttae** A band of cartilage lying along the underside of the tongue of certain animals

ma Mother
maar A volcanic crater
mac, mack A raincoat
macabre Ghastly
macadam A type of pavement
macaque A species of monkey
macaroni A pasta
macaroon A cooky
macaw A species of parrot
maccabaw, maccaboy A perfumed snuff
mace A medieval club
macerate To soften
mach A number representing the ratio of speed of an object to the speed of sound
machete A large knife

machinate To plot
machine A mechanical device
macho Masculine
machree My dear
mackerel A species of marine fish
mackinaw A coat
mackle To blur
macle A crystalline form
macrame A coarse fringe
macro Computer instruction
macrocosm The universe
macron A symbol placed above a vowel
macula, *pl* **-lae** A blemish
macule To blur
mad Insane
madam, madame A title of respect

madcap   An impulsive person
madding   Frenzied
maddish   Somewhat mad
made   Past tense of make
madeira   A wine
madeleine   A rich cake
madhouse   An asylum
madman   A maniac
madonna   An Italian female title
madras   A fabric
madre   Mother
madrepore   A species of coral
madrigal   A polyphonic song
madrona, madrono   An evergreen tree
maduro   A cigar
madwoman   An insane woman
madwort   A species of plant
madzoon   Variant of matzoon
mae   More
maelstrom   A whirlpool
maenad, pl -nads or maenades   A frenzied woman
maestoso   Majestic
maestro, pl -tros or -tri   A musical conductor
maffia, mafia   A secret society of criminals
maffick   To rejoice
mafic   Pertaining to minerals
magazine   A periodical
magdalen, magdalene   A reformed prostitute
mage   A magician
magenta   A color
maggot   Larva of various insects
magic   The art of sleight of hand
magistery   The philosopher's stone
magistral   Principal
magma, pl magmata or -mas   Pomace,
magnate   An influential man
magnesia   Magnesium oxide
magnesite   A mineral
magnet   A body that attracts
magneto   A type of generator
magneton   A unit of magnetic moment
magnific   Magnificent
magnifico   A nobleman

magnify   To enlarge
magnitude   Great in size
magnolia   A species of evergreen tree
magnum   A large bottle
magot   An Oriental figurine
magpie   A species of bird
maguey   A species of plant
maharajah, maharaja   A prince in India
maharani, maharanee   The wife of a maharajah
mahatma   A person venerated for great knowledge
mahjong, mahjongg   A game of Chinese origin
mahogany   A species of tree
mahone   A joyful hideaway
mahout   The keeper of an elephant
mahuang   A species of plant
mahzor, pl mahzorim   A Hebrew prayer book
maid   A female servant
maidhood   The stage of being a maiden
maieutic   The Socratic method of a person becoming aware of memories
maigre   Not containing flesh or its juices
mail   Postal material
mailbag   A canvas sack for mail
mailbox   A box for depositing mail
maile   A vine of the Pacific islands
maillot   A fabric
maim   To impair
main   Principal
mainland   A principal land mass
mainline Slang   To inject narcotics directly into a major vein
mainmast   The main mast of the ship
mainsail   The main sail of the ship
mainsheet   A rope on a ship
mainstay   A principal support
maintain   To carry on
maintop   A platform on a ship
mair   More
maize   Corn
majesty   A royal personage

202

majolica A type of pottery
major Serious
majority The greater part of something
majuscule Writing that uses large letters
make To construct
makeshift Something made as a temporary substitute
makeup Cosmetics
mako A shark
makuta Plural of likuta
malachite A mineral
maladroit Clumsy
malady An ailment
malaise A feeling of depression
malamute, malemute, malemuti A breed of dog
malapert Bold
malar Of the cheekbone
malaria An infectious disease
malarkey, malarky *Slang* Nonsense
malate A chemical salt
male Virile
maledict To curse
malefic Causing evil
malic Pertaining to apples
malice Ill will
malign To slander
malignant Harmful
malihini A newcomer
malines A veiling material
malinger To pretend to be ill
malison A curse
mall A shopping center
mallard A wild duck
malleable Capable of being formed
mallee A species of evergreen tree
mallemuck A species of sea bird
mallet A hammer
malleus, *pl* **mallei** A bone in the middle ear
mallow A species of plant
malm Limestone
malmsey A white wine
malt A drink
maltase An enzyme
maltha A tar
maltose Malt sugar

maltreat To treat badly
malvasia A grape from which wine is made
malvoisie Malmsey wine
mama, mamma Mother
mamba A species of snake
mambo A dance
mamie A tropica tree
mammal Warm-blooded vertebrate
mammilla, *pl* **-millae** A teat
mammoth An extinct elephant
mammy, mammie Mother
man An adult male
mana A supernatural force
manacle To handcuff
manage To control
manakin A species of bird
manana Tomorrow
manatee A species of aquatic mammal
mandala Oriental symbolic designs
mandamus A legal writ
mandarin A high public official in imperial China
mandate An authoritative order
mandible A mouth part in insects
mandola An ancient lute
mandolin A musical instrument
mandrake A species of plant
mandrel, mandril A shaft on which a tool is mounted
mandrill A baboon
mane Long, thick human hair
manege A riding academy
manes Deified souls of the dead
maneuver A planned movement
manful Manly
mangabey A species of monkey
manganese A metallic element
manganic Containing manganese
mange A skin disease
manger A feed box for livestock
mangle To disfigure
mango A tropical tree
mangonel A medieval military machine
mangrove A species of evergreen tree
mangy Wretched

manhole A hole for entry
manhood The state of being a man
manhunt An organized search
mania Exaggerated enthusiasm
maniac A lunatic
manicotti An Italian pasta dish
manicure Polishing of the nails
manifest Obvious
manifold Varied
manikin, mannikin A model of the human body
manila, manilla A fiber
manioc, manioca A tropical plant
maniple A silk band hanging on an Eucharistic vestment
manitou, manitu, manito A spirit believed in by the Algonquian Indians
mankind The human race
manlike Resembling a man
manna Spiritual nourishment
mannequin A dummy
manner One's behavior
mannish Resembling a man
mannitol An alcohol
mano A stone used for grinding various foods
manor Any landed estate
manque Frustrated
manrope A rope rigged as a handrail
mansard A type of roof
manse A clergyman's house
mansion A manor house
manta A fabric
manteau, pl **-teaus** or **-teaux** A cloak
mantel The facing around a fireplace
mantelet A short cape
mantic Prophetic
manticore A monster
mantilla A lace scarf
mantis, pl **-tises** or **-tes** A species of insect
mantissa The decimal part of a logarithm
mantle A type of coat
mantra A sacred formula in Hinduism

mantua A woman's gown
manual Done by the hands
manumit To emancipate
manure To fertilize
manus The end of the forelimb in vertebrates
manward Toward man
manwise In a manly manner
many Numerous
map To survey a region
maple A species of tree
maqui A wine
maquis A dense growth
mar To damage
marabou, marabout A species of bird
maraca A musical instrument
maranta A species of plant
marasca A European cherry tree
marasmus A wasting away of the body
marathon A long-distance race
maraud To pillage
marble A small ball used in children's games
marbling The process of giving something the appearance of marble
marc The residue left after juice has been pressed from fruits
marcel A hair style
march To walk in a military manner
marchesa, pl **-se** The wife or widow of a marchese
marchese, pl **-si** An Italian nobleman
mare A female horse
margaric Pearly
margarine, margarin A butter substitute
margarita A cocktail
margarite A pearl
margay A spotted wildcat
margin Blank space bordering a printed page
margrave A medieval military governor
maria Plural of mare
mariachi Mexican musical group

marigold A species of plant
marijuana, marihuana The hemp plant
marimba A musical instrument
marina A boat basin
marinade To marinate
marinate To pickle in brine
marine Pertaining to the sea
mariner A seaman
mariposa A species of plant
marital Pertaining to marriage
maritime Concerned with navigation
marjoram An aromatic plant
mark A sign
market A building where goods are sold
markka, pl -**kaa** Monetary unit of Finland
marksman One skilled at shooting
markup A raise in price
marl A mixture of clays
marlin A species of game fish
marline A rope used on a ship
marlite, marlstone A type of marl
marmalade A preserve
marmite A soup kettle
marmoset A species of monkey
marmot A species of rodent
maroon To abandon a person
marplot One who spoils a plan
marque An emblem used to identify an auto
marquee A rooflike structure over the entrance to a theater
marquis The title of a nobleman
marquise The wife or widow of a marquis
marram A beach grass
marriage Wedlock
marron The Spanish chestnut tree
marrow Vitality
marry To become united in matrimony
marseille A fabric
marsh A swamp
marshal A Federal officer
marsupia Abdominal pouches of certain animals
mart A trading center

martagon A lily
marten A species of mammal
martial Suggesting war
martian A supposed inhabitant of Mars
martin A species of bird
martinet One who demands strict adherence to rules
martini A cocktail
martlet The martin
martyr One who sacrifices
martyrdom Extreme suffering
martyrize To martyr
marvel A sense of astonishment
marvelous Splendid
marzipan A candy
mascara A cosmetic
mascot Something supposed to bring good luck
masculine Male
maser A device for amplifying electrical impulses
mash To crush
mashie A golf club
masjid A mosque
mask A facial covering
masochism The deriving of pleasure from being dominated
mason One who works with stone
masonry The trade of a mason
masque A dramatic entertainment
mass A grouping of elements
massacre Savage killing
massage A rubbing of the body
masse A shot in billiards
masseur A man who massages
masseuse A woman who massages
massicot A yellow pigment
massif A mountain pass
massive Bulky
mast A vertical pole
mastaba, mastabah An ancient Egyptian tomb
master The captain of a merchant ship
mastery Superior skill
masthead The top of a ship's mast
mastic A pastelike cement
masticate To chew
mastiff A breed of dog

mastitis Inflammation of the breast
mastodon An extinct mammal
mastodont Pertaining to mastodons
mastoid Shaped like a breast
mat A floor pad
matador A bullfighter
match Counterpart
mate A spouse
matelote A fish stew
mater Mother
material Yard goods
materiel The equipment of a military force
maternal Motherly
maternity The state of being a mother
matey Friendly
math Mathematics
matilda A hobo's bundle
matin, matinal A morning song
matinee A daytime performance
matriarch A woman who rules
matricide One who kills his mother
matrix, *pl* **matrices** A die
matron A married woman
matt To matte
matte To produce a dull finish
matter What a thing is made of
mattock A digging tool
mattress A soft pad used as part of a bed
maturate To mature
mature Ripe
matutinal Early
matza, matzah Variants of matzo
matzo, *pl* **-zoth** or **-zos** or **-zot** Unleavened bread
matzoon Similar to yogurt
maud A gray, striped plaid
maudlin Emotional
maul A hammer
maulstick Stick used by painters
maun Must
maund A unit of weight
mausoleum A tomb
mauve A color
maverick An unbranded range animal
mavis, mavie The song thrush

maw Mother
mawkish Overly sentimental
maxi A very long skirt
maxilla, *pl* **-lae** or **-las** The jawbone
maxim A statement of a general truth
maximal The greatest possible
maximum, *pl* **-mums** or **-ma** The greatest possible number
maxixe A dance
maxwell A unit of magnetic flux
may Possibility
maya In Hinduism, the origin of the world
maybe Perhaps
mayday A distress call
mayflower A variety of plants that bloom in May
mayfly A species of winged insect
mayhap Perhaps
mayhem Havoc
mayo Mayonnaise
mayor The chief magistrate of a city
mayoress A woman mayor
maypop A flowering vine
mayst Used with thou
mayweed A weed
mazard The face
maze A labyrinth
mazer A goblet
mazuma *Slang* Money
mazurka A dance
mazzard A wild cherry
me Objective case of I
mead A meadow
meadow An area of grassland
meager, meagre Scanty
meal Food served and eaten
mealie An ear of corn
mealtime The usual time for a meal
mealy Resembling meal
mealybug A species of insect
mean To intend
meander To wander
meanly In a mean manner
meantime Interval
measles A virus disease
measly Measled
measure A system of measurement

meat The edible flesh of animals
meatball A small ball of ground meat
meathead *Slang* A blockhead
meatus, *pl* **meatuses** A body passage
mecca A place visited by many people
mechanic A worker skilled with tools
mechanist A mechanician
meconium Fetal excrement discharged at birth
medaka A species of Japanese fish
medal A commemorative piece of metal
medallion A large medal
meddle To interfere
media Plural of medium
medial Median
median Located toward the middle
mediant The third tone in the diatonic scale
mediate To resolve a settlement
mediator One that mediates
medic, medick A species of plant
medical Pertaining to the practice of medicine
medicate To treat medicinally
medicine A drug used to treat disease
medico A doctor
medieval Belonging to the Middle Ages
mediocre Average
meditate To ponder
medium, *pl* **-dia** or **-ums** Mass communication
medlar A tree
medley A group of melodies
medulla, *pl* **-las** or **-lae** The inner core of various vertebrate body structures
medusa, *pl* **-sas** or **-sae** A jellyfish
meed A reward
meek Submissive
meet To make acquaintance of
megabit Computer information
megabuck *Slang* One million dollars

megadeath One million dead persons
megahertz One million cycles per second
megalith A large prehistoric stone
megapode A species of bird
megaton A unit of explosive force
megavolt A unit of electromotive force
megawatt A unit of power
megillah An involved story
megrim A severe headache
meinie, meiny A crowd
meiosis, *pl* **-ses** A type of cell division
mel Honey
melange A mixture
melanian Pertaining to black pigmentation
melanic Afflicted with melanosis
melanin A dark pigment
melanite A variety of garnet
melanoid A dark pigment
melanoma A dark-pigmented tumor
melanous Having dark complexion and dark hair
meld To blend
melee A free-for-all
melilot A species of plant
melinite An explosive
meliorate To improve
melisma, *pl* **-mata** or **-mas** A succession of different notes sung upon a single syllable
mell To mix
mellow Soft
melodeon A small organ
melodic Pertaining to melody
melodize To write a melody
melodrama A dramatic play
melody Pleasing sounds
meloid A blister beetle
melon A species of gourd
melt To dissolve
meltage The process of melting
melton A fabric
mem The thirteenth letter of the Hebrew alphabet
member One who belongs to a

group

membrane A layer of animal or vegetable tissue
memento A souvenir
memo A memorandum
memoir An autobiography
memorial A monument
memory The mental faculty of remembering
memsahib A title of respect in colonial India
menace A threat
menage A household
menagerie A collection of animals
menarche The first occurrence of menstruation
mend To repair
mendicant A beggar
mene Numbered
menhaden An inedible fish
menhir A prehistoric monument
menial A servant
meninx, pl **meninges** Any of the membranes enclosing the brain and spinal cord
meniscus, pl **menisci** A crescent-shaped body
menology An ecclesiastical calendar
menopause Cessation of menstruation
menorah A candleholder used in Jewish services
mensal Monthly
mensch An admirable person
menses Dead cell debris
menstrual Monthly
mensural Pertaining to measure
mental Intellectual
menthol An alcohol
mention An incidental reference
mentor A wise teacher
menu Food dishes
meow The sound of a cat
mephitis A stench
mercenary Greedy
mercer A dealer in textiles
mercery A mercer's store
merchant A shopkeeper
mercurial A medicine containing mercury

mercuric Containing bivalent mercury
mercury A metallic element
mercy Kind treatment
merde An exclamation of irritation
mere A pond
merely Only
merganser A fish-eating duck
merge To blend together
meridian A circle around the earth
meringue A topping for pies
merino A breed of sheep
meristem Formative plant tissue
meristic Made up of segments
merit Excellence
merle, merl Blackbird
merlin Pigeon hawk
merlon The solid part of a wall
mermaid A fabled creature of the seas
merman A fabled creature of the seas
meropia Partial blindness
merriment Hilarity
merry Jolly
mesa A flat-topped elevation
mescal A cactus
mesh A net
meshwork Network
mesial Toward the middle
mesmerize To hypnotize
mesne Intervening
mesocarp The middle of a pericarp
mesoderm An embryonic germ layer
meson An atomic particle
mesopause The atmospheric zone
mesquite, mesquit A species of shrub
mess A muddle
message A communication
messaline A fabric
messenger A bearer of news
messmate One with whom one eats regularly
messuage A dwelling house
mestiza A female mestizo
mestizo A person of mixed ancestry

meta Pertaining to positions in a benzene ring

metage A measurement of weight

metal Any of a class of chemical elements

metallic Pertaining to metal

metalline Containing metal ions

metalloid A nonmetallic element

metamere A somite

metaphor A figure of speech

metate A stone used for grinding grains

metazoan A member of one of the two bodies of the animal kingdom

mete To allot

meteor A meteoroid

meter A specific musical rhythm

methane A flammable gas

methanol Methyl alcohol

metheglin A type of spiced mead

methinks It seems to me

method Orderliness

methought Past tense of methinks

methyl A univalent radical

methylal A flammable liquid

metier A profession

metis One of mixed ancestry

metisse A female metis

metonym A word used in metonymy

metonymy A figure of speech

metope Space between triglyphs

metopic Of the forehead

metre Variant of meter

metric A standard of measurement

metritis Inflammation of the uterus

metronome A device that marks time

mettle Spirit

mew A hideaway

mewl A weak cry

mezereon, mezereum A shrub

mezuzah, *pl* **mezuzoth** A Judaic scroll

mezzanine The lowest balcony

mezzo A mezzosoprano

mezzotint A method of engraving

mho A unit of conductance

mi The third tone of the diatonic scale

miaou, miaow Variants of meow

miasma, *pl* **-mas** or **-mata** A poisonous vapor

mib A marble

mica A mineral silicate

micawber One who remains optimistic despite hardships

mice Plural of mouse

micelle, micella, *pl* **-lae** A hypothetical, submicroscopic structural unit

mickey *Slang* A drugged drink

mickle Great

microbe A minute life form

microfilm A film upon which contents are greatly reduced

microform An arrangement of images reduced in size

micron A unit of length

mid The middle

mid- Indicates a middle part, time, or location. The following compounds are listed without definition (see Introduction):

midair	midmonth	midstream
midbrain	midmost	midsummer
midcourse	midnight	midterm
midday	midnoon	midtown
midfield	midpoint	midway
midgut	midrange	midweek
midland	midship	midwinter
midleg	midspace	midyear
midline	midstory	

midcult A pseudo-intellectual culture

midden A refuse heap

middle Central

middleman A go-between

middling Ordinary

middy A blouse

midge A species of fly

midget A small person

midiron A golf club

midrash A Jewish commentary

midrib Vein of a leaf

midriff A part of the body

midst Center

midwife A woman who assists in childbirth

mien One's manner

miff   A petty quarrel
might   Power
migraine   A headache
migrant   An itinerant worker
migrate   To move
mikado   The emperor of Japan
mike   A microphone
mil   A unit of length
milady, miladi   My lady
milch   Giving milk
mild   Light
mildew   A coating produced by fungi
mile   A unit of length
mileage   Total length
milepost   A post indicating distance
milestone   A turning point
milfoil   The yarrow plant
miliaria   A skin disease
miliary   Like a millet seed
milieu   Environment
militant   Fighting
military   Armed forces
militate   To have force
militia   A citizen army
milium   A small nodule of the skin
milk   To draw out
milkfish   A large fish
milkmaid   A girl who milks cows
milkman   A man who delivers milk
milksop   A weakling
milkweed   A species of plant
milkwort   A species of plant
mill   A place where grain is ground
millage   Taxation
millboard   A paperboard used in book binding
milldam   A dam
mille   A thousand
millet   A species of grass
milliard   Billion
milliary   A Roman mile
millieme   A coin
millime   Monetary unit of Tunisia
milline   A unit of measurement
milliner   One who sells women's hats
million   The cardinal number 1,000,000
millpond   A pond

millrace   Water that drives a mill wheel
millrun   The output of a sawmill
millstone   A stone used in grinding grain
milo   A grain soghum
milord   My lord
milreis   A coin
milt   Fish sperm
mime   The art of pantomime
mimesis   Imitation
mimetic   Imitative
mimic   To imitate
mimicry   The art of mimicking
mimosa   A species of plant
mina, pl -**nas** or -**nae**   An ancient unit of weight
minaret   A slender tower on a mosque
minatory   Threatening
mince   To cut into small pieces
mincemeat   Finely chopped meat
mind   What one thinks
mine   Belonging to me
minefield   A field of explosive mines
mineral   Any substance that is neither animal nor vegetable
mingle   To combine
mini   Smaller
miniature   A copy on a very small scale
minibike   A small motorcycle
minibus   A small bus
minicab   A small taxicab
minicar   A small auto
minify   To make smaller
minikin   Diminutive
minim   A unit of fluid measure
minimal   Least possible
minimax   A strategy in game theory
minimize   To depreciate
minimum, pl -**mums** or -**ma**   The lowest quantity
minion   A favorite
miniskirt   A short skirt
minister   A clergyman
ministry   The clergy
minitrack   A system to track the path of an artificial satellite

210

minium Red lead

miniver A white fur

mink A species of mammal

minnow A species of small fish

minor Under legal age

minorca A species of domestic fowl

minster A church

minstrel A performer

mint Candy

mintage The process of minting coins

minter One that mints

minty Having the flavor of mint

minuend A number from which another is to be subtracted

minuet A dance

minus Less

minuscule A lower-case letter

minute Sixty seconds

minutely At intervals of one minute

minuteman A soldier in the Revolutionary War

minutia, *pl* **-tiae** A small detail

minx, *pl* **minxes** A saucy girl

miosis, *pl* **-ses** Excessive contraction of the pupil of the eye

miotic An agent that causes miosis

mir, *pl* **mirs** or **miri** A Russian peasant commune

miracle An act of God

mirador A balcony that affords a fine view

mirage Something that is illusory

mire A bog

mirex An insecticide

mirk Variant of murk

mirror A surface that reflects the image

mirth Gaiety

miry Swampy

mirza A Persian title of honor

mis- Indicates error or wrongness; badness; failure. The following compounds are listed without definition (see Introduction):

misact	misagent	misapply
misadapt	misaim	misassay
misadd	misally	misate
misadvice	misalter	misatone

misaward	misgrow	misreckon
misbecome	misguess	misrefer
misbegin	misguide	misrely
misbehave	mishandle	misreport
misbelief	mishap	misrule
misbias	mishear	missay
misbill	mishit	misseat
misbind	misinfer	missend
misbrand	misinform	misshape
misbuild	misinter	misshod
miscall	misjoin	missort
miscarry	misjudge	missound
miscast	miskeep	misspaced
mischance	misknow	misspeak
miscite	mislabel	misspell
misclaim	mislabor	misspend
misclass	mislay	misspoke
miscoin	mislead	misstart
miscolor	mislearn	misstate
miscook	mislie	missteer
miscopy	mislight	misstep
miscount	mislit	misstop
miscreate	mislive	misstyle
miscue	mislodge	missuit
miscut	mismanage	misteach
misdate	mismark	mistend
misdeal	mismatch	misterm
misdeed	mismate	misthink
misdirect	mismove	misthrow
misdo	misname	mistime
misdoubt	misnomer	mistitle
misdraw	mispage	mistouch
misdrive	mispaint	mistrace
miseat	misparse	mistreat
misedit	mispart	mistrial
misemploy	mispatch	mistrust
misenroll	mispen	mistryst
misenter	misplace	mistune
misesteem	misplant	mistutor
misevent	misplay	mistype
misfield	misplead	misunion
misfile	mispoint	misusage
misfire	mispoise	misuse
misfit	misprint	misvalue
misform	misprize	misword
misframe	misquote	miswrite
misgauge	misraise	misyoke
misgovern	misrate	
misgraft	misread	

mischief An act that causes trouble

miscible Capable of being mixed
miscreant A villain
miser A greedy person
miserere Part of a church seat
misery Wretchedness
misgive To be suspicious
mishmash Hodgepodge
mislike To dislike
misogamy Hatred of marriage
misogyny Hatred of women
misology Hatred of reasoning
mispickel The mineral arsenopyrite
miss To let slip by
missal A prayer book
missel A thrush
missile A projectile
mission A diplomatic office
missis, missus One's wife
missive A message
missy A young girl
mist Condensed water vapor
mistake An error
mister A title
mistletoe A species of shrub
mistook Past tense of mistake
mistral A cold wind
mistress A skilled woman
mite A very small object
miter A headdress
miterwort A species of plants
mither Mother
mitigate To alleviate
mitosis A type of cell division
mitral Resembling a miter
mitre Variant of miter
mitt, mitten A hand covering
mittimus, *pl* **-muses** A legal writ
mitsvah Mitzvah
mitzvah, *pl* **mitzvoth** or **-vahs** A commandment
mix To combine
mixt Past tense of mix
mixture Something produced by mixing
mixup A state of confusion
mizzen, mizen A mizzenmast
mizzle A mistlike rain
mnemonic Assisting the memory
moa A species of bird

moan To lament
moat A ditch of water surrounding a castle
mob A disorderly crowd
mobcap A type of cap
mobile Moving quickly
mobster *Slang* A gangster
moccasin A soft slipper worn by American Indians
mocha An Arabian coffee
mochila A leather saddle covering
mock To ridicule
mockup A layout
mod A style of dress
modal Characteristic of a mode
mode The current fashion
model A design of an item
moderate Not extreme
moderato In moderate tempo
modern Contemporary
modest Reserved
modicum, *pl* **-cums** or **-ca** A small amount
modify To change
modiolus, *pl* **-li** The bony shaft of the cochlea
modish Stylish
modiste One who deals in ladies' fashions
modulate To regulate
module A unit of measurement
modulus, *pl* **-li** The absolute number of a complex number
modus A mode
mofette, moffette Volcanic activity emitting gases
mog To plod steadily
mogul A powerful person
mohair The hair of the Angora goat
mohur A gold coin
moidore A gold coin
moiety A half
moil Toil
moira Destiny
moire A fabric
moist Wet
moisture Dampness
mojarra A species of fish
moke *Slang* A donkey
mola A species of fish

molal   Relating to the mole
molality   The molal concentration of a solute
molar   A tooth
molasses   A thick syrup
mold   A matrix
mole   A species of burrowing mammal
molecular   Existing between molecules
molecule   A small particle
molehill   Earth dug up by a mole
moleskin   Fur of the mole
molest   To harass sexually
moll *Slang*   A gangster's mistress
mollah   Variant of mullah
mollify   To calm
molluscan, molluskan   Relating to the mollusks
mollusk   A species of marine invertebrate
molly   A species of fish
molt   To cast off
molto   Much
moly   The lily leek
molybdic   Pertaining to various metallic elements
mom, mommy   Mother
moment   A brief period of time
momus, *pl* **-muses** or **-mi**   One who criticizes
mon   Man
monachism   Monasticism
monad   A unit
monandry   Having one husband at a time
monarch   An absolute ruler
monarda   A species of plant
monas, *pl* **monades**   A single-celled organism
monastery   Residence of monks
monastic   A monk
monaural   Pertaining to sound reception
monaxial   Uniaxial
monazite   A mineral
monde   Society
monetary   Pertaining to money
monetize   To coin
money   Wealth

moneybag   A bag for holding money
moneyed, monied   Having much money
moneyer   A banker
monger   To peddle
mongoose   A species of mammal
mongrel   An animal of mixed breed
mongst   Amongst
monicker, moniker *Slang*   A person's name
monish   To admonish
monism   A doctrine
monition   A warning
monitor   To keep track of
monk   One who lives alone for religious reasons
monkery   A monastery
monkey   A species of long-tailed primate
monkfish   The goosefish
monkhood   Monasticism
monkish   Relating to monks
monoacid   A type of acid
monobasic   Designating a type of acid
monocarp   A monocarpic plant
monochord   An instrument used to study musical notes
monocle   An eyeglass
monocline   A geologic formation
monocrat   An autocrat
monocyte   A type of blood cell
monodrama   A drama written for one performer
monody   A verse for one voice
monogamy   Marriage with only one spouse at a time
monogram   Initials of a name
monogyny   The practice of having one wife at a time
monolith   A large block of stone
monologue, monolog   A soliloquy
monomer   A type of molecule
monomial   An expression having only one term
monoplane   An airplane with one pair of wings
monopode   A creature having only one foot
monopoly   Exclusive control**

monorail A single rail
monosome A type of chromosome
monostome Having one mouth
monotint A picture done in shades of one color
monotone A single tone
monotony Sameness
monotype Sole member of its group
monoxide A type of oxide
mons, *pl* **montes** A protuberance of the body
monsieur A man
monsoon A seasonal wind
monster An imaginary creature
montage A style of art
montane Growing in mountain areas
monte A card game
montero A type of cap
month A period of time
monument A memorial
monzonite An igneous rock
moo To low
mooch *Slang* To beg
mood A temporary feeling
moola, moolah *Slang* Money
moon A heavenly body that revolves around the earth
moonbeam A ray of moonlight
moonbow A rainbow formed by moonlight
mooncalf A freak
mooneye A freshwater fish
moonfish A marine fish
moonish Like the moon
moonlet A small moon
moonlit Lighted by the moon
moonport An installation for launching rockets to the moon
moonrise Rising of the moon
moonseed A species of vine
moonset Setting of the moon
moonshine Moonlight
moonshot Launching of a spacecraft to the moon
moonstone A mineral
moonwort A grape fern
moony Resembling the moon
moor To secure a vessel
moorage A place where a ship is moored

moorhen An aquatic bird
moorland A tract of moors
moorwort The bog rosemary plant
moose A hoofed mammal
moot To debate
mop To wash
mopboard The baseboard
mope To be gloomy
mopery *Slang* A trivial violation of law
moppet A child
moquette A fabric
mor Forest humus
mora, *pl* **morae** or **-ras** A unit of metrical time
moraine Debris deposited by a glacier
moral Concerned with the principles of right and wrong
morale Moral or mental condition
moralism A moral attitude
moralist A teacher of ethics
morality The quality of being moral
morass A bog
moratory Authorizing delay of payment
moray A species of marine eel
morbid Gruesome
morbific Causing disease
morceau, *pl* **-ceaux** A short literary piece
mordant Sarcastic
mordent A melodic ornament
more Greater
moreen A fabric
morel A species of mushroom
morello A variety of sour cherry
moreover Further
mores Manners
morgen A Dutch unit of land area
morgue A place where dead bodies are taken
moribund About to die
morion A type of helmet
morn Morning
morning Early part of the day
morocco A leather of goatskin
moron One who is mentally

retarded
morose Gloomy
morpheme A linguistic unit
morphia Morphine
morphic Pertaining to form
morphine A narcotic
morris A dance
morrow The next day
morsel A snack
mort A note sounded on a horn to announce a killing
mortal Causing death
mortar To plaster
mortgage To pledge
mortgagee The holder of a mortgage
mortgagor One who mortgages his property
mortician A funeral director
mortify To humiliate
mortise To join
mortmain Perpetual ownership of property
mortuary A place where dead bodies are kept prior to burial
morula, pl -**lae** A solid mass of cells
mosaic A decorative design made of small colored pieces
moschatel A plant
mosey Slang To get going
mosque A Moslem house of worship
mosquito A species of winged insect
moss A species of plant
mossback An old fish
mosso With animation
mossy Covered with moss
most The largest part
mostest Slang The most
mot A clever saying
mote A speck
motel A hotel for motorists
motet A musical composition
moth A species of insect
mothball A naphthalene ball which repels moths
mother A woman who has borne a child
motif A design in architecture

motile Capable of spontaneous motion
motion The ability to move
motivate To impel
motive A desire
motley Multicolored
motmot A species of bird
motor A device that produces motion
motorbus A bus
motorcar An automobile
motorman One who drives an electrically powered vehicle
motte, mott A small stand of trees
mottle To cover with spots
motto A short phrase
moue A pout
mouflon, moufflon A wild sheep
mouille To moisten
moulage A type of mold
moulin A vertical shaft through a glacier
mound A pile of earth
mount To climb
mountain A big quantity
mourn To feel sorrow
mouse A species of small rodent
mouser A cat that catches mice
mousse A variety of desserts
mousy Shyness
mouth The organ of chewing
mouton Processed sheepskin
move To change posture
movie A motion picture
moviedom Filmdom
moviegoer One who goes to movies
mow To cut
moxa A Chinese plant
moxie Slang Guts
mozetta A hooded cape
mozo A porter
mu The twelfth letter of the Greek alphabet
much A great degree
mucilage An adhesive
mucin A protein
muck Something regarded as filthy
muckamuck Slang An important person
muckrake To expose political

215

corruption
muckworm Worms found in mud
mucoid A protein
mucosa, pl **-sae** or **-sas** A mucous
membrane
mucous, mucose Secreting mucus
mucro, pl **mucrones** A sharp point
of certain plant and animal organs
mucus A bodily fluid
mud Soft, wet earth
mudcap To cover an explosive with
mud
mudcat A species of catfish
mudder A horse that runs well on a
muddy track
muddle To jumble
mudfish A species of fish
mudguard A fender
mudhole A hole full of mud
mudlark A street urchin
mudra Movements in East Indian
dancing
mudsill The lowest supporting
timber of a building
mudstone A type of rock
muezzin The crier who calls the
faithful to prayer
muff To bungle
muffin A cup-shaped bread
muffler A scarf
mufti Ordinary clothes
mug A container
mugger, muggar, muggur A
crocodile
muggy Humid
mugwort A species of plant
mugwump An independent person
mukluk A soft boot
mulatto A person of one white and
one Negro parent
mulberry A species of tree
mulch A protective covering
mulct A fine
mule A slipper
muleta A matador's red cape
muleteer A mule driver
muley Hornless
mulish Stubborn
mull To ponder
mullah, mulla A Moslem leader

mullein A species of plant
muller A device used for grinding
mullet A species of fish
mulligan A stew
mullion Dividing strip
multifid Cut into many lobes
multiped Having many feet
multiple More than one
multiplex Multiple
mum Not talking
mumble To utter indistinctly
mummer An actor
mummery A performance
mummify To embalm
mummy A preserved body
mumps A contagious disease
mun A man
munch To chew
munchies Snacks
munchkin A small imaginary being
mundane Worldly
mungo Reclaimed wool
municipal Pertaining to a city
muniment A means of defense
munition War materiel
munster, muenster A cheese
muntjac, muntjak A species of deer
muon An atomic particle
mural A large picture
murder The killing of a human
being
mure To confine
murex, pl **murices** or **-rexes** A species of marine gastropod
muricate Having a rough surface
murine A species of rodent
murk Gloom
murmur A mutter
murphy Slang A potato
murra, murrha A precious substance of ancient Rome
murrain An infectious disease
murre A species of sea bird
murrey A color
muscadine A woody vine
muscarine An organic compound
muscat A variety of white grapes
muscatel, muscadel A sweet wine
muscle A contractile organ
muscular Pertaining to muscles

muse To meditate
musette A dance
museum A building where art is exhibited
mush Boiled cornmeal
mushroom A species of fleshy fungi
music A musical composition
musician One skilled in music
musk An odorous substance secreted by certain animals
muskeg A swamp
musket A gun
musketeer A soldier
musketry Muskets
muskmelon A species of melon
muskrat An aquatic rodent
muslin A fabric
muspike A freshwater fish
musquash The muskrat
muss To make messy
mussel A bivalve mollusk
must Obligation
mustache Hair on the upper lip
mustachio A mustache
mustang A wild horse
mustard A species of plant
musteline Pertaining to furbearing mammals
muster To gather
musty Having a moldy odor
mutable Fickle
mutagen An agent that causes biological mutation
mutant Something that undergoes mutation
mutate To undergo alteration
mutatis The necessary changes having been made
mutchkin A unit of liquid measure
mute Unable to speak
mutele An ornamental block in architecture
mutilate To damage
mutineer One who takes part in a mutiny
mutiny Open rebellion
mutism The condition of being mute `
mutt *Slang* A mongrel dog

mutton Flesh of fully grown sheep
mutual Shared in common
mutuel A system of betting
muumuu A long, loose dress
muzhik A peasant
muzzle The barrel of a firearm
muzzy Blurred
my Used to indicate possession
myalgia Muscular pain
mycelium, *pl* **-lia** The vegetative part of a fungus
mycology A branch of botany
mycosis, *pl* **-ses** A disease
myelin, myeline A fatty material that encases certain nerve fibers
myelitis Inflammation of the spinal column
myeloid Pertaining to the spinal cord
myeloma, *pl* **-mas** or **-mata** A tumor of the bone marrow
myiasis Infestation of human tissue
mylonite A type of rock
myna, mynah A species of bird
mynheer A Dutchman
myogenic Of muscular origin
myograph An instrument for recording muscular contractions
myology The scientific study of muscles
myoma, *pl* **-mas** or **-mata** A tumor
myope One who has myopia
myopia A visual defect
myosin A protein
myosotis A species of plant
myotonia Tonic spasm
myriad A large number
myriapod A species of arthropod
myrmidon A faithful follower
myrrh A gum resin
myrtle A species of evergreen shrub
myself A form of the first person singular pronoun
mysost A cheese
mystery Something unexplained
mystic Mystical
mystical Spiritually symbolic
mystify To bewilder

mystique Mystical attitudes surrounding a person or thing
myth A traditional story
mythicize To turn into myth
mythos, *pl* **mythoi** Myth
myxedema A disease

myxocyte A large cell found in mucous tissue
myxoid Mucoid
myxoma, *pl* **-mas** or **-mata** A benign tumor

na No
nab To snatch
nabe A movie theater
nabis French artists
nabob A man of wealth
nacelle An enclosure on an aircraft
nacre Mother-of-pearl
nadir The lowest point
nae No
naevus Variant of nevus
nag To scold
nagana A disease of livestock
naiad A water nymph
nail A fingernail
nailhead The head of a nail
naive Unaffected
naked Nude
name A word by which a person is known
namesake A person named after another
nana A nurse
nandin An evergreen shrub
nankeen, nankin A fabric
nanny A child's nurse
naos An ancient temple
nap A brief sleep
napalm An incendiary bomb
nape The back of the neck
napery Table linen

naphtha A volatile liquid
naphthene A chemical compound
naphthol A chemical compound
napiform Shaped like a turnip
napkin A piece of material used while eating
napoleon A pastry
nappe Water flowing over a dam
nappy Hairy
narc *Slang* A narcotics' agent
narceine, narcein An opium derivative
narcissus, *pl* **-suses** or **-cissi** A species of plant
narcosis A stupor
narcotic A drug
narcotine An alkaloid
nard A species of plant
nares Nostrils
narghile, nargile, nargileh An Oriental pipe
narial, naric, narine Pertaining to the nostrils
nark *Slang* An informer
narrate To tell
narrow Lacking space
narthex A lobby of a church
narwhal, narwal, narwhale An arctic aquatic mammal
nary Not one

nasal Pertaining to the nose
nascent Coming into existence
nasberry A tropical tree
nastic Characterized by a response in plants
nasty Foul
natal Pertaining to birth
natant Swimming
nates The buttocks
natheless, nathless Nevertheless
nation A group of people organized under one government
native Inborn
natrolite A mineral
natron A mineral
natty Dapper
natural Produced by nature
nature The physical world
naught Nothing
nauplius, *pl* **-plii** A form of various crustaceans
nausea A stomach disturbance
nauseous Causing nausea
nautch A dance form
nautical Pertaining to navigation
nautilus, *pl* **-luses** or **-li** A species of mollusk
naval Having a navy
navar A method of air navigation
nave The central part of a church
navel A depression in the middle of the abdomen
navigate To control the course of a ship
navvy A laborer
navy A nation's warships
nawab A former ruler in India
nay A denial
nazi A fascist
nazify To cause to be a nazi
neap A wagon tongue
near Close in time
nearby Close
neat Tidy
neath Beneath
neb A beak of a bird
nebula, *pl* **-lae** or **-las** A mass of interstellar dust
necessary Essential
neck The part of the body joining the head to the trunk
neckband A band worn around the neck
necklace An ornament worn around the neck
neckline The edge of a garment near the neck
necktie A narrow strip of fabric worn around the neck
neckwear Items of dress worn around the neck
necrology A record of the deceased
necropsy An autopsy
necrose To affect with necrosis
necrosis, *pl* **-ses** The death of living tissue
nectar A drink
nectarine A variety of peach
nectary A glandlike organ that secretes nectar
nee Born with the name of
need Something wanted
neediness Poverty
needle A sewing implement
neep A turnip
negate To nullify
negative Indicating opposition
negatron An electron
neglect To disregard
negligee A woman's dressing gown
negligent Careless
negotiate To come to terms
negus A beverage
neigh The cry of a horse
neighbor A fellow man
neither Not either
nekton Aquatic, free-swimming animals
nelson A wrestling hold
nelumbo An aquatic plant
nematode A species of worm
nemesis, *pl* **-ses** An avenger
nene A Hawaiian goose
neolith A neolithic stone tool
neology A new word
neomorph A type of biological structure
neomycin An antibiotic drug
neon A gaseous element
neonate A newborn child

neophyte A new convert
neoplasm A tumor
neoprene A synthetic rubber
neoteric New
nepenthe A drug
nephew The son of one's brother or sister
nephrite A variety of jade
nepotism Favoritism shown to a relative
nerd *Slang* A dull person
nereis, *pl* **nereides** A species of marine worm
neritic Pertaining to shallow water
neroli An oil used in perfume
nervate Having veins
nerve Stamina
nervine Affecting the nerves
nervous Excitable
nervure A vascular ridge on a leaf
nervy Brazen
nescience Ignorance
nest A lair
nestle To draw close
net An openwork fabric
nether Located below
netlike Resembling a net
netop Companion
netsuke A Japanese ornamental figure
nettle A species of plant
network Netting
neuk A nook
neume, neum A sign used in music
neural Pertaining to the nerves
neuralgia Pain along a nerve
neuraxon A part of a nerve cell
neuritis Inflammation of a nerve
neurocyte Processes of a nerve cell
neurology Science of the nervous system
neuroma, *pl* **-mata** A tumor
neuron, neurone A nerve cell
neurosis, *pl* **-ses** A type of mental disturbance
neurotic Nervous
neuter Having no functional sexual organs
neutral Indifferent
neutrino An atomic particle

neutron An atomic particle
neve Granular snow
never Not ever
nevermore Never again
nevus, *pl* **-vi** A birthmark
new Recent
newborn Just born
newcomer One who just arrived
newel A staircase post
newfound Just found
newish Somewhat new
newlywed One just married
newmown Recently mown
newsboy A boy who sells newspapers
newscast A broadcast of news
newshawk A newspaper reporter
newspaper A publication containing news
newsprint Paper
newsreel A short movie that presents news
newsy Informative
newt A species of salamander
newton A unit of force
next Adjacent
nextdoor In the next building
nexus, *pl* **-uses** A connected series
ngwee Monetary unit of Zambia
niacin A B vitamin
nib The point of a pen
nibble To eat with small bites
niblick A golf club
niccolite A nickle ore
nice Pleasant
nicety Delicacy
niche A recess
nick An indentation
nickel A metallic element
nickelic Containing nickel
nicknack A trinket
nickname A shortened form of a proper name
nicotine A poisonous alkaloid
nictate, nictitate To wink
nide To nest
nidering A coward
nidify To make a nest
nidus, *pl* **-duses** or **-di** A nest
niece A daughter of one's brother or

220

sister
niello, *pl* **-elli** or **-los**   A metallic substance
nifty *Slang*   Stylish
niggard   A miser
niggle   To fret
nigh   Near
night   The period between sunset and sunrise
nightcap   A cap worn in bed
nightclub   A place of entertainment open at night
nightfall   Close of day
nightie, nighty   Nightgown
nightjar   A species of nocturnal bird
nightmare   Appalling
nightspot   A nightclub
nigrify   To make black
nigrosin   A color
nihil   Nothing
nil   Nothing
nill   To be unwilling
nim   To steal
nimble   Deft
nimbus, *pl* **-bi** or **-buses**   A luminous cloud
nimiety   Excess
nine   The cardinal number 9
ninebark   A flowering shrub
ninefold   Nine times
ninepin   A pin used in a game
nineteen   The cardinal number 19
ninny   A fool
ninon   A fabric
ninth   The ordinal number nine in a series
niobium   A metallic element
nip   To pinch
nipa   A palm tree
nipple   A protuberance on the breast
nippy   Biting
nirvana   Bliss
nisei   A native U.S. citizen born of immigrant Japanese parents
nisi   Not yet final
nisus   Exertion
nit   The egg of a parasitic insect
niter   A chemical salt
nitrate   To treat with nitric acid

nitric   Containing nitrogen
nitride   A compound containing nitrogen
nitrify   To oxidize into nitric acid
nitrile, nitril   A chemical compound
nitrite   Any salt of nitrous acid
nitrogen   A nonmetallic element
nitrous   Derived from nitrogen
nitty   Full of nits
nitwit   A silly person
nival   Growing under snow
niveous   Snowy
nix   A water sprite
nixie   A female nix
nizam   A Turkish soldier
no   Not so
nob *Slang*   A person of wealth
nobble   To cheat
nobby *Slang*   Stylish
nobelium   A radioactive element
nobility   The state of being a noble
noble   Showing greatness
nobleman   The nobility
noblesse   Noble birth
nobody   No one
nocent   Guilty
nock   To put a notch in
noctuid   A species of moth
noctule   A species of bat
nocturn   A religious service
nocturnal   Active at night
nocturne   A musical composition
nocuous   Poisonous
nod   To lower and raise the head
noddle   The head
noddy   A fool
node   A swelling
nodule   A node
nodus, *pl* **-di**   A complication
noel   A Christmas carol
noesis   Cognition
noetic   Of the intellect
nog   Eggnog
noggin   A small mug
noh   No
nohow   In no way
noil   A fiber
noir   Black
noise   A loud sound
noisome   Harmful

noisy   Making a loud noise
nolo   A legal plea
noma   An inflammation of the mouth
nomad   A wanderer
nomarch   The governor of a nomarchy
nomarchy   A province of modern Greece
nombril   The navel point
nome   A province in ancient Egypt
nominal   In name only
nominate   To appoint
nominee   One who is nominated
   non-   Indicates not. The following compounds are listed without definition (see Introduction):

nonacid	nonhardy	nonroyal
nonadult	nonhero	nonrural
nonage	nonhuman	nonsense
nonbank	nonideal	nonskid
nonbasic	nonionic	nonskier
nonbeing	nonjuror	nonslip
nonbook	nonlegal	nonsolar
noncash	nonlife	nonsolid
noncom	nonlocal	nonstick
nondairy	nonman	nonstop
nonego	nonmetal	nonsugar
nonelect	nonmodal	nontidal
nonempty	nonmoney	nontoxic
nonentity	nonmoral	nontrump
nonentry	nonnaval	nontruth
nonequal	nonobese	nonunion
nonevent	nonowner	nonurban
nonfarm	nonpagan	nonuser
nonfat	nonpapal	nonviable
nonfatal	nonpar	nonviral
nonfluid	nonparty	nonvocal
nonfocal	nonpolar	nonvoter
nonfood	nonprofit	nonwhite
nongame	nonquota	nonwoody
nongreen	nonrated	nonwoven
nonguilt	nonrigid	nonzero

nonagon   A polygon having nine sides
nonce   The present time
none   Not one
nones   A day in the ancient Roman calendar
nonesuch   A person without equal

nonillion   The cardinal number 1 followed by 30 zeros
nonpareil   Matchless
nonplus   A state of bafflement
nonpros   To enter a judgment
nonsked   An airline without schedules
nonsuit   To dismiss
nonuple   Ninefold
noo   Now
noodge   To nag
noodle   A strip of dry dough
nook   A corner
noon   Midday
noonday   Noon
noontide   Noon
noose   A loop in a lasso
nopal   A species of cactus
nope *Slang*   No
nor   And not
noria   A type of water wheel
norite   A mineral
norm   An average
normal   Typical
north   A cardinal point on the compass
norther   A cold wind from the north
northing   Progress toward the north
nose   The organ of smell
nosebag   A feedbag
noseband   A part of a bridle
nosegay   A bouquet
nosh   A snack
nosology   A classification of diseases
nostalgia   Homesickness
nostoc   A freshwater algae
nostril   Either of the external openings of the nose
nostrum   A quack medicine
nosy, nosey   Prying
not   In no way
notable   Remarkable
notarial   Pertaining to a notary
notary   A notary public
notation   A jotting
notch   A V-shaped cut
note   To write down
notebook   A book for notes
nothing   Not anything

notice Attention
notify To inform
notion A view
notional Imaginary
notochord The primitive backbone
notorious Infamous
notornis A flightless bird
notturno, *pl* **-ni** A nocturne
nougat A candy
noumenon, *pl* **-na** A perception reached by intellectual intuition
noun A word used to denote the name of something
nourish To provide with food
nous Reason
nova, *pl* **-vae** A type of star
novation Transference of a debt
novel A fictional prose narrative
novella, *pl* **-las** or **-le** A short novel
novelty Newness
novena, *pl* **-nas** or **-nae** A religious devotion
novercal Of a stepmother
novice A beginner
now At once
nowadays During the present time
noway, noways Nowise
nowhere Not anywhere
nowise Not at all
noxious Harmful
nozzle A spout
nth Most extreme
nu The thirteenth letter of the Greek alphabet
nuance A subtle variation
nub A knob
nubbin A stunted ear of corn
nubble A small lump
nubile Ready for marriage
nucellus, *pl* **-celli** Center of the ovule
nucha The nape of the neck
nuclear Relating to atomic nuclei
nuclease An enzyme
nucleate Having a nucleus
nucleon An atomic particle
nucleus, *pl* **-clei** Anything serving as a center of growth
nuclide A species of atom
nude Naked

nudge A gentle push
nudicaul Having no leaves on the stem
nudism The practice of living in the nude
nudnik *Slang* An annoying person
nugatory Worthless
nugget A small lump of gold
nuisance A bother
null Invalid
nullah A gully
nullify To annul
nullity The state of being null
numb Stunned
number To count
numbfish The electric ray
numen, *pl* **numina** A guardian deity
numeral A symbol used to denote a number
numerary Pertaining to a number
numerate To reckon
numerous Many
numinous Spiritually elevated
nummular Circular
numskull, numbskull A stupid person
nun A woman belonging to a religious order
nuncio An ambassador from the pope
nuncle An uncle
nunnery A house for nuns
nuptial A wedding
nurse One who cares for the ill
nursemaid One who cares for children
nursery A children's room
nursling An infant
nurture Food
nut A hard-shelled, one-celled fruit
nutation The act of nodding the head
nutgall A growth on a tree
nuthatch A species of bird
nutlet A small nut
nutmeat The kernel of a nut
nutmeg An evergreen tree
nutpick A tool for extracting kernels from nuts
nutria The coypu

nutrient   Something that nourishes
nutriment   Food
nutrition   The process of nourishing
nutritive   Nourishing
nutshell   The shell of a nut
nutty   Having a flavor of nuts
nuzzle   To cuddle together
nyala   A species of antelope

nyet   No
nylon   A synthetic material
nymph, nympha   A female spirit
nymphet   A young nymph
nympho *Slang*   A nymphomaniac
nystagmus   An involuntary movement of the eyeball

oaf   A clumsy person
oak   A species of tree
oaken   Of oak
oakmoss   A lichen that grows on oak trees
oakum   Hemp fiber used in caulking
oar   A pole used in rowing a boat
oarfish   A marine fish
oarlock   The device that holds the oar in place
oarman   One who rows
oasis, *pl* **-ses**   A fertile spot in a desert
oast   A kiln
oat   A species of grass
oatcake   A cake of baked oatmeal
oaten   Containing oats
oater *Slang*   A cowboy film
oath   That which is promised
oatmeal   Rolled oats
obdurate   Stubborn
obeah   A form of witchcraft
obedient   Dutiful
obelisk   A tall, four-sided stone with a pyramidal top
obelize   To mark with an obelus
obelus, *pl* **-li**   A symbol used in ancient writings

obese   Fat
obey   To carry out an order
obi   Part of a traditional Japanese dress
obiit   He (or she) died
obit   An obituary
obituary   A notice of a death
object   To raise an objection
oblast   An administrative division in the Soviet Union
oblate   Having the shape of a spheroid
obligate   To oblige
oblige   To make grateful
obligee   One who is under obligation to another
obligor   One who binds himself to another
oblique   Misleading
oblivion   The act of forgetting
oblong   Having a long dimension
obloquy   Abusive language
obnoxious   Offensive
oboe   A musical instrument
obolus, *pl* **-li**   A coin of ancient Greece
obovate   Egg-shaped, with the narrow end attached to the stalk

224

obovoid Egg-shaped with the narrow end attached to the stem
obscene Lewd
obscenity Lewdness
obscure Indistinct
obsequy A funeral
observant Alert
observe To perceive
obsess To preoccupy greatly
obsidian A volcanic glass
obsolete Outmoded
obstacle One that stands in the way
obstetric Pertaining to the practice of obstetrics
obstinate Stubborn
obstruct To impede
obtain To gain possession of
obtect Covered by a hardened secretion
obtest To entreat
obtrude To eject
obtund To make less intense
obturate To seal
obtuse Blunt
obverse A counterpart
obvert To turn
obviate To dispose of
obvious Quite apparent
obvolute Folded together with overlapping edges
ocarina A wind instrument
occasion A happening
occident The west
occiput, pl **occipita** or **-puts** The back of the skull
occlude To obstruct
occult Mysterious
occupant One who holds a place
occupy To fill up
occur To come about
ocean A large body of water
oceanic Pertaining to the ocean
ocellus, pl **-ocelli** A small simple eye
ocelot A wildcat
ocher, ochre An iron ore
ocotillo A cactuslike tree
ocrea, pl **-reae** A tubelike covering around certain stems
octad A group of eight
octagon A polygon with eight sides
octane A liquid hydrocarbon
octant A 45° arc
octave A series of tones
octavo A page size
octet, octette A group of eight
octillion The cardinal number represented by the figure 1 followed by 27 zeros
octonary Of the number eight
octopod Any animal with eight limbs
octopus, pl **octopi** A species of marine mollusk
octoroon One who is one-eighth Negro
octroi, pl **-trois** A tax
octuple Eightfold
ocular Visual
oculist An optometrist
od A hypothesized force in nature
odd Strange
oddball An eccentric person
oddish Peculiar
oddity Something that is odd
oddment An oddity
ode A lyrical poem
odeum, pl **odea** A concert hall
odious Offensive
odium Contempt
odograph A device for recording distance
odometer An instrument that indicates distance traveled
odontoid Resembling a tooth
odor A smell
odyssey An extended wandering
oedema Variant of edema
oedipal, oedipean Relating to the Oedipus complex
oenology The study of wines
oenomel A beverage
oersted A unit of magnetic intensity
oeuvre A work of art
of Coming from
off To go away
offal Rubbish

offbeat An unaccented beat
offcast Discarded
offend To be disagreeable
offense A crime
offer To propose
offertory A collection
offhand Impromptu
office A position of duty
officious Not official
offing Aloof
offish Aloof
offprint An excerpt of a printed article
offset A type of printing
offshoot A branch
offshore Away from the shore
offside A position in football
offspring Outcome
offstage Away from the stage
oft Often
often Many times
ofttimes Often
ogee A double-curved molding
ogham, ogam An early Irish alphabet
ogive A pointed arch
ogle To stare at
ogre A monster
ogress A female ogre
oh Used to express surprise
ohm A unit of electrical resistance
ohmage Resistance expressed in ohms
oho Used to express surprise
oil A liquid used for lubrication
oilbird The guacharo
oilcamp A place where oil workers live
oilcan A can for applying oil
oilcloth A fabric
oilpaper A type of paper
oilskin A waterproof cloth
oilstone A stone used for sharpening
oily Greasy
oink The grunt of a pig
ointment A medicine for the skin
oiticica A tree of the rose family
okapi A ruminant mammal
okay To approve
oke A unit of weight

okey Approval
okha A unit of weight
okra A tall plant
old Not new
olden Ancient
oldish Somewhat old
oldster An elderly person
oldwife, *pl* **-wives** A duck
ole A shout of approval
oleander A poisonous shrub
oleaster The Russian olive tree
oleate A chemical salt
olefin, olefine An alkene
oleic Derived from oil
olein, oleine The liquid part of fats
oleo Margarine
oleum, *pl* **-lea** or **-ums** Oil
olibanum Frankincense
oligarch A ruler of an oligarchy
oligarchy Government by the few
olio A spiced stew
olivary Shaped like an olive
olive The fruit of a Mediterranean tree
olivine A mineral
olla A wide-mouthed jar
ology A branch of learning
om A symbolic mystical utterance during meditation
omasum, *pl* **-sa** The third stomach of a ruminant animal
ombre, omber A card game
omega The 24th letter of the Greek alphabet
omelet A dish of eggs cooked with other foods
omen A prophetic sign
omentum, *pl* **-ta** A peritoneal fold
omer An ancient Hebrew unit of measure
omicron The fifteenth letter of the Greek alphabet
ominous Foreboding
omission The act of omitting
omit To leave out
omnibus Including many things
omnivore An omnivorous animal
omphalos, *pl* **-li** A center
on In contact with
onager A wild ass

onanism Coitus interruptus
once One time only
oncology The study of tumors
oncoming Approaching
one Single
oneness The state of being one
onerous Burdensome
oneself A person's self
ongoing Evolving
onion A plant
onionskin A translucent paper
onlooker A spectator
only Sole
onomastic Of names
onrush An assault
onset A start
onshore Toward the shore
onslaught An attack
onstage Being on stage
onto Upon
ontogeny The development of an individual organism
ontology Philosophy that deals with being
onus A burden
onward Forward
onyx A variety of agate
oocyte An egg that has not yet undergone maturation
oodles A lot
oogamous Pertaining to reproduction by oogamy
oogamy The fertilization of oogamous gametes
ooh Exclamation of delight
oolite, oolith A type of limestone
oology The branch of ornithology that deals with birds' eggs
oolong A Chinese tea
oompah A rhythmic tuba sound
oomph *Slang* Sex appeal
oophyte The stage in plants when sexual organs are developed
oops Whoops
oosperm A fertilized ovum
oosphere An egg ready for fertilization
oospore A thick-walled spore
ootheca The egg case of certain insects

ootid A section into which an ovum divides
ooze To ebb slowly
oozy Dripping
op A style of art
opacity Obscurity
opah A colorful marine fish
opal A mineral
opalesce To emit an iridescent shimmer of colors
opaque Impenetrable by light
open Exposed
openwork Ornamental work containing many openings
opera A dramatic performance set to music
operable Practicable
operand A quantity on which a mathematical operation is formed
operant Effective
operate To work
operatic Relating to an opera
operetta Light opera
operon A cluster of genes
operose Laborious
ophidian Snakelike
ophite An igneous rock
ophitic Of ophite
opiate A narcotic drug
opine To think
opinion A conclusion
opium An addictive narcotic
opossum A species of arboreal marsupial
opponent One that opposes another
opportune Occurring at the right time
oppose To resist
opposite Facing the other way
oppress To persecute
oppugn To oppose
opsin A type of protein
opsonic Having the effect of opsonin
opsonin An antibody of blood serum
opt To choose
optative Expressing a wish
optic Pertaining to vision

optimism Practice of looking at the bright side

optimist One who expects the best

optimize To make the most effective of

optimum, *pl* **-ma** or **-mums** Best

option Choice

optometry The profession of examining the eyes

opulent Affluent

opuntia A species of cactus

opus, *pl* **opera** or **opuses** A creative work

opuscule A minor work

oquassa A freshwater fish

or An alternative

ora Plural of os

orach, orache A species of plant

oracle A command from God

oracular Pertaining to an oracle

oral Spoken

orange A color

orangery A place where oranges are grown

orangutan An ape

orate To speak

orator One who speaks

oratorio A musical composition

oratory Rhetoric

orb A sphere

orbicular Orb-shaped

orbit The path of a celestial body

orc A sea animal

orchard An area where fruit trees are grown

orchestra A group of musicians who perform together

orchid A species of plant

orchil A species of lichen

orchis A species of orchid

orcinol A chemical compound

ordain To invest with ministerial duties

ordeal A painful experience

order To issue a command

ordinal Of a specified position in a numbered series

ordinary Commonplace

ordinate Arranged in regular rows

ordnance Artillery

ordo, *pl* **-dines** A religious calendar

ordure Filth

ore A mineral

oread A mountain nymph

oregano An herb used in seasoning

oreide Variant of oroide

orfray Variant of orphrey

organ A musical instrument

organdy A fabric

organelle A part of a cell

organic Relating to an organism

organize To arrange

organon, *pl* **-na** or **-nons** A set of rules for scientific investigation

organum, *pl* **-na** or **-nums** A type of vocal music

organza A fabric

organzine A raw-silk thread

orgasm Intense excitement

orgeat A flavoring

orgy Excessive indulgence

oribi An African antelope

oriel A bay window

orient The east

orifice A vent

origami A style of art

origin A source

original First

orinasal A sound produced with both nasal and oral passages open

oriole A species of bird

orison A prayer

orle A heraldic border

orlop The lowest deck of a ship

ormer An abalone shell

ormolu An alloy resembling gold

ornament An embellishment

ornate Flashy

ornery Stubborn

ornithic Relating to birds

orogeny The process of mountains being formed

oroide An alloy used in inexpensive jewelry

orology The study of mountains

orotund Soronous

orphan A child who has no parents

orphrey Elaborate embroidery

orpiment A yellow dye

orpine A species of plant

orrery A mechanical model of the solar system

orris A species of iris

orrisroot The roots of the orris

ort A scrap of food

orthicon A type of tube

ortho Correction of deformities

orthodox Adhering to a traditional practice

orthoepy The study of pronunciation

ortolan A species of bird

oryx, pl **oryxes** A species of antelope

os, pl **ora** An opening

oscillate To swing back and forth

oscine A species of songbird

osculant Embracing

osculate To kiss

osculum, pl **-la** Openings of a sponge

osier A species of willow

osmatic, osmic Having a sense of smell

osmium A metallic element

osmose To undergo osmosis

osmosis The diffusion of a fluid through a membrane

osmous Containing osmium

osmunda, osmund A species of fern

osnaburg A fabric

osprey A fish-eating hawk

ossein A protein substance in bone

osseous Bony

ossia Or else

ossicle A small bone

ossifrage A hawk

ossify To become bony

ossuary A container

osteal Bony

osteitis Inflammation of bone

ostensive Revealing

osteoid Resembling bone

osteoma, pl **-mas** or **-mata** A tumor

ostiary A church doorkeeper

ostinato A musical phrase

ostiole A small pore

ostium or **-tia** A small opening

ostmark A coin

ostracism Disgrace

ostracod A species of freshwater crustacean

ostrich A species of flightless bird

other Additional

otic Pertaining to the ear

otiose Lazy

otitis Inflammation of the ear

otocyst An organ of balance

otolith Particles found in the inner ear

otology The science of the ear

ottar Variant of attar

ottava A musical direction

otter A species of aquatic mammal

otto Perfume made from the petals of flowers

ottoman A type of couch

ouabain A heart stimulant

oubliette A dungeon

ouch A setting for a precious stone

oud A musical instrument

ought To be expected

ounce A unit of weight

our The possessive form of the pronoun we

ourself Myself: used in royal proclamations

ourselves A form of the first person plural pronoun

oust To force out

out Away from

out- Indicates to a surpassing or superior degree; located outside or externally. The following compounds are listed without definition (see Introduction):

outact	outbless	outcast
outadd	outbloom	outcaste
outargue	outbluff	outcatch
outask	outblush	outcavil
outate	outboast	outcharm
outback	outbox	outcheat
outbake	outbrag	outchide
outbark	outbrave	outclass
outbawl	outbribe	outclimb
outbeam	outbuild	outcook
outbeg	outbully	outcrawl
outbid	outburn	outcrow
outblaze	outburst	outcry
outbleat	outcaper	outcurse

outdance	outguide	outrival
outdare	outgun	outroar
outdo	outhear	outrock
outdodge	outhit	outrode
outdoer	outhowl	outrun
outdone	outhumor	outrung
outdoor	outjinx	outsail
outdoors	outjump	outsang
outdrank	outkeep	outsat
outdraw	outkick	outsavor
outdream	outkiss	outscold
outdress	outlast	outscore
outdrew	outlaugh	outscorn
outdrink	outleap	outsell
outdrive	outlearn	outserve
outdrop	outlive	outshame
outdrunk	outlove	outshine
outeat	outman	outshoot
outecho	outmarch	outshout
outer	outmatch	outsin
outermost	outmove	outsing
outfable	outpace	outsit
outface	outpaint	outsleep
outfast	outpass	outsmart
outfawn	outpitch	outsmile
outfeast	outpity	outsmoke
outfeel	outplan	outsnore
outfield	outplay	outsoar
outfight	outplod	outsold
outfind	outpoint	outspeak
outfire	outpoll	outspell
outflank	outpray	outspend
outfly	outpreen	outspoke
outfool	outpress	outspoken
outfoot	outprice	outstand
outfought	outpull	outstare
outfound	outpush	outstart
outfox	outquote	outstate
outfrown	outrace	outstay
outgain	outrage	outsteer
outgive	outraise	outstood
outglare	outran	outstrip
outglow	outrang	outstudy
outgnaw	outrange	outstunt
outgo	outrank	outsulk
outgoing	outrave	outsung
outgrew	outreach	outswear
outgrin	outread	outswim
outgrow	outride	outtalk
outguess	outring	outtask

outtell	outvoice	outwhirl
outthank	outvote	outwile
outthink	outwait	outwill
outthrob	outwalk	outwind
outthrow	outwar	outwish
outtold	outwarred	outwit
outtower	outwaste	outwore
outtrade	outwatch	outwork
outtrick	outwear	outworn
outtrot	outweary	outwrite
outtrump	outweep	outyell
outvalue	outweigh	outyelp
outvaunt	outwept	outyield

outbound Headed away

outbreed To subject to outbreeding

outcrop To protrude above the ground

outcross An individual produced by crossbreeding

outfall A place where a stream discharges

outfit To equip

outflow To flow out

outgas To remove gas from

outhaul A rope on a ship

outhouse An outside toilet

outland A foreign land

outlaw A criminal

outlawry Defiance of the law

outlay Money spent

outlet A vent

outline An abstract

outlook An attitude

outlying Remote

outmoded Obsolete

outmost Outermost

outpost An outlying settlement

outpour An outpouring

output Production

outre Bizarre

outrigger A type of canoe

outright Openly

outset Start

outside Exterior

outsize An unusual size

outskirts Outlying areas

outspread To stretch

outstroke An outward stroke

outturn Yield

outward Outer

ouzel A species of bird
ouzo A greek liqueur
ova Plural of ovum
oval Egg-shaped
ovaritis Inflammation of an ovary
ovary A female reproductive gland
ovate Oval
ovation Applause
oven A place for baking
ovenbird A species of bird
over On the other side of

over- Indicates location or position; excess. The following compounds are listed without definition (see Introduction):

overable
overact
overage
overall
overalls
overapt
overarch
overarm
overate
overawe
overbake
overbear
overbet
overbid
overbig
overbite
overblow
overboard
overbold
overbook
overbore
overborn
overborne
overbred
overbuild
overbusy
overbuy
overcall
overcast
overcloud
overcoat
overcold
overcome
overcook
overcool

overcoy
overcram
overcrop
overdare
overdear
overdeck
overdo
overdoer
overdose
overdraft
overdraw
overdress
overdrive
overdry
overdue
overdye
overeager
overeasy
overeat
overexert
overfar
overfast
overfat
overfear
overfeed
overfill
overfish
overflow
overfly
overfond
overfoul
overfree
overfull
overgild
overgird

overglad
overglaze
overgoad
overgrow
overhand
overhang
overhard
overhate
overhead
overheap
overhear
overheat
overhigh
overhold
overholy
overhope
overhot
overhung
overhunt
overidle
overjoyed
overjust
overkeen
overkill
overkind
overlade
overladen
overlaid
overlain
overland
overlap
overlate
overlax
overlay
overleaf

overleap
overlet
overlewd
overlie
overlive
overload
overlong
overlook
overlord
overloud
overlove
overly
overman
overmany
overmatch
overmeek
overmelt
overmen
overmild
overmix
overmuch
overnear
overneat
overnew
overnice
overnight
overpass
overpay
overpert
overplay
overplus
overply
overpower
overprice
overprint
overprize
overproof
overran
overrank
overrash
overrate
overreach
overrich
override

overrife
overripe
overrode
overrude
overruff
overrule
overrun
oversad
oversale
oversalt
oversave
oversaw
overscore
overseas
oversee
overseed
overseer
oversell
overset
oversew
oversexed
overshoe
overshoot
overshot
oversick
overside
oversight
oversize
overskirt
oversleep
overslip
overslow
oversoak
oversoft
oversold
oversoon
overspend
overspin
overstake
overstate
overstay
overstir
overstock
overstuff

oversup
oversure
overtake
overtame
overtart
overtask
overtax
overthin
overthrow
overtime
overtire
overtoil
overtone
overtook
overtop
overtrick
overtrim
overtrump
overturn
overurge
overuse
overvalue
overview
overvote
overwarm
overwary
overweak
overwear
overween
overweigh
overwet
overwhelm
overwide
overwily
overwind
overwise
overword
overwore
overwork
overworn
overwound
overwrite
overzeal

overhaul To fix
oversoul The spirit which inspires all living things
overstep To go beyond
overt Not hidden
overture A musical composition

overturn To upset
ovibos The musk ox
ovicidal Capable of killing eggs
oviduct A tube through which ova travel from an ovary
oviform Egg-shaped
ovine Sheeplike
oviposit To lay eggs
ovisac An egg receptacle
ovoid, ovoidal Egg-shaped
ovolo, *pl* **-li** A convex molding
ovonic Relating to electronics
ovulate To produce ova
ovule An immature ovum
ovum, *pl* **ova** An egg
ow Used to express pain
owe To be in debt to
owl A species of nocturnal bird
owlet A young owl
owlish Resembling an owl
own Individual
owner One that owns
ownership The fact of being an owner
ox, *pl* **oxen** A bovine mammal
oxalate A chemical salt
oxalis A species of plant
oxazine A chemical compound

oxblood A deep red color
oxbow A part of an ox yoke
oxeye A species of plant
oxford A fabric
oxheart A variety of cherry
oxidant An oxidizing agent
oxidase An oxidizing enzyme
oxide A binary compound of oxygen with another element
oxime A chemical compound
oxlip A primrose plant
oxpecker An African bird
oxtail The tail of an ox
oxtongue A species of plant
oxygen A gaseous element
oxymoron A figure of speech in which opposite ideas are combined
oxytocic A drug
oxytocin A pituitary hormone
oxytone A word with an acute accent on the last syllable
oy Exclamation of worry
oyer A copy of a bond
oyez, oyes Used to introduce the opening of court
oyster A species of edible mollusk
ozone A form of oxygen
ozonide An explosive chemical

pa Father
pabulum Food
pac A type of shoe
paca A rodent
pace A stride
pacemaker A runner that sets the pace
pacha Variant of pasha

pachisi An ancient game
pachuco One of a Mexican-American gang
pachyderm A species of large mammal
pacific Tranquil
pack A bundle
package A wrapped object

packet A boat
packsack A bag
pact An agreement
pad One's apartment
padauk A species of tree
paddle A tool for stirring
paddock A fenced area for horses
paddy A rice field
padlock A type of lock
padre Father
padrone A master
paduasoy A fabric
paean An expression of joy
paella A Spanish food fish
paeon A metrical foot
pagan A heathen
page A boy who runs errands
pageant An elaborate presentation
pageboy A hairstyle
paginal Consisting of pages
paginate To number the pages of
pagoda A Hindu temple
pah An exclamation of disgust
pahlavi A gold coin
pail A bucket
paillasse A mattress
paillette A spangle
pain Suffering
paint A coloring substance
pair Two corresponding items
paisa, *pl* **paise** A unit of money
paisano Countryman
paisley A fabric
pajama A garment for sleeping
pal A chum
palace The residence of a royal
  person
paladin A heroic champion
palanquin A covered litter
palatal Of the palate
palate The sense of taste
palatial Spacious
palatine A soldier
palaver Idle talk
pale Pallid
palea, *pl* **-leae** A small bract
paleface A white person
paleolith An ancient stone
  implement
palestra, *pl* **-trae** A school in

ancient Greece
palette An artist's board
palfrey A riding horse
palikar A Greek soldier
paling A fence made of pickets
palinode A poem
palisade Steep cliffs
pall A gloomy effect
palladic Pertaining to palladium
palladium A metallic element
pallet A type of bed
pallette A part of armor
palliate To make an excuse
pallid Dull
pallium, *pl* **-ums** or **-lia** A cloak
pallor Paleness
palm The inner surface of the hand
palmar Pertaining to the palm
palmary Superior
palmate Having webbed toes
palmette A palm-leaf design
palmetto A species of tropical palm
palmist One who practices
  palmistry
palmistry The art of telling
  fortunes
palmitin A chemical compound
palomino A type of horse
palooka *Slang* An inept boxer
palp A sensory organ
palpate To examine by touching
palpus, *pl* **-pi** A palp
palsgrave A titled palatine
palsy Paralysis
palter To quibble
paltry Petty
paludal Marshy
pam The jack of clubs in various
  games
pampa A grassland area in South
  America
pampean Pertaining to the pampas
pamper To coddle
pampero A wind of the pampas
pamphlet A small printed work
pan A container
panacea A cure-all
panache Dash
panada A thick sauce
panama A hat

panatela A cigar
pancake A griddle cake
panchax A species of fish
pancreas A gland lying behind the stomach
panda A bearlike mammal
pandanus A species of palmlike tree
pandect A legal code
pandemic General
pander, panderer A procurer
pandore A musical instrument
pandowdy A deep-dish apple pie
pandy A slap on the palm of the hand
pane A division of a window
panel A sheet of material
pang A sudden pain
pangolin A species of mammal
panhandle To beg
panic A sudden terror
panicky Tending to panic
panicle A flower cluster
panne A finish for certain fabrics
pannier A wicker basket
pannikin A small pan
panocha, panoche A type of candy
panoply A suit of armor
panoptic Including everything visible in one view
panorama An unlimited view
panpipe A wind instrument
pansy A color
pant To breathe rapidly
pantalets Bloomers
pantaloon Trousers
pantheon A Roman temple
panther A black leopard
pantie, panty Women's underpants
pantile An S-curved roofing tile
pantoffle A slipper
pantomime Acting with gestures
pantoum A verse form
pantry A small room
pantsuit A woman's outfit
pantun A Malayan verse
panzer Armored
pap A soft food
papa Father
papacy The office of the pope

papain An enzyme
papal Pertaining to the papacy
papaw A tree
papaya An evergreen tree
paper Material made from cellulose pulp
paperback A book having a flexible cover
paperwork Work involving written papers
papery Resembling paper
papilla, *pl* **-pillae** A nipple-like projection
papillon A breed of dog
papoose A young child
pappus, *pl* **pappi** A tuft of bristles surmounting the achene
pappy Father
paprika A seasoning
papule, papula A congested spot
papyrus, *pl* **-ruses** A kind of paper
par Average
para Monetary unit of Yugoslavia
parablast The food yolk of a meroblastic egg
parable A story with a moral lesson
parabola A conic section
parachute A device used to retard the falling speed
parade A public procession
paradigm An example
paradise Heaven
paradox A statement contrary to received opinion
paradrop A delivery by parachute
paraffin A waxy substance
paragon A pattern of excellence
paragraph A division of a written work
parakeet A species of small parrot
parallax The apparent change in position
parallel Having comparable parts
paralysis, *pl* **-ses** Loss of the ability to move
paralyze To affect with paralysis
parament Ecclesiastical vestments
paramo A treeless plain
paramount Primary
paramour A lover

parang   A heavy knife
paranoia   A mental disorder
paranoid   Afflicted with paranoia
parapet   A protective wall
paraph   A flourish below a signature
parasang   A Persian unit of distance
parasite   An organism that feeds on another
parasol   A small umbrella
paratroop   A soldier trained to parachute
paravane   A device to cut cables
parboil   To cook partially by boiling
parcel   A package
parcener   A joint heir
parch   To make dry
parchment   A skin prepared for writing
pard   A leopard
pardon   To forgive
pare   To remove the outer skin
paregoric   Camphorated tincture of opium
parent   A mother or father
paresis   Partial paralysis
pareu   A Polynesian garment
pareve   Made without meat or milk
parfait   A dessert
parget   Plaster
parhelia   Spots appearing on a solar halo
pariah   A social outcast
paries, *pl* **parietes**   The wall of an organ
parietal   Dwelling within
parish   A civil district
parity   Equality
park   To place
parka   A jacket
parkway   A highway
parlance   A manner of speaking
parlando   Sung in a manner of speech
parlay   To bet
parley   A discussion
parlor, parlour   A room for entertainment
parlous   Perilous

parochial   Located in a parish
parody   A travesty
parol   An utterance
parole   The release of a prisoner
parolee   One who is released
paronym   A word having the same root as another
paroxysm   A sudden attack
parquet   Main floor of a theater
parr   A young salmon
parrel   A sliding loop of rope
parricide   One who murders a near relative
parrot   A species of bird
parry   To turn aside
parse   To analyze a word
parsec   A unit of astronomical distance
parsimony   Stinginess
parsley   A cultivated herb
parsnip   A cultivated plant
parson   A clergyman
parsonage   Residence of a parson
part   A piece
partake   To participate
parterre   A flower garden
partial   Incomplete
partible   Divisible
particle   A small piece
partisan   A guerrilla
partita   Instrumental pieces
partite   Divided into parts
partition   A section
partlet   A woman's garment
partner   A spouse
partridge   A species of game bird
party   A social gathering for pleasure
parure   A set of matched jewelry
parvenu   One who has risen above his social class
parvis   A portico in front of a church
pas   A dance step
paschal   Pertaining to Easter
pase   A movement of a matador's cape
paseo   A leisurely walk
pash   To smash
pasha   A title of honor

pass To proceed
passage Transit
passant A heraldic design
passbook A bankbook
passe Out-of-date
passel A big quantity
passenger One who travels
passible Sensitive
passim Here and there
passion An intense love
passive Submissive
passkey A type of key
passport A document permitting travel to other countries
password A secret word
past Gone by
pasta Food made of dough
paste An adhesive
pastel A soft hue
pastern Part of a horse's foot
pasticcio, pl -ci A musical work
pastiche A type of artistic work
pastille, pastil A lozenge
pastime A recreational activity
pastina Small pieces of macaroni
pastor A minister
pastoral A country scene
pastorale An opera based on a rural theme
pastrami Smoked beef
pastry Baked foods
pasture To herd animals
pasty Pale
pat To tap gently
patagium, pl -gia A wing membrane of a bird
patch A small part
patchy Made up of patches
pate The head
patella, pl -tellae The kneecap
paten A plate
patency The state of being obvious
patent A grant protecting an inventor
patentee One who is granted a patent
patentor One that grants a patent
pater Father
paternal Fatherly
path A course of action

pathetic Inadequate
pathogen An agent that causes disease
pathology The study of disease
pathos A feeling of pity
pathway A path
patience Understanding
patient One under medical care
patina A filmy coating
patine To form a patina
patio An outer dining area
patois A dialect
patriarch A paternal leader
patricide One who murders his father
patriot One who defends his country
patristic Relating to early leaders of the Christian church
patrol A person who moves about and observes for security reasons
patron A benefactor
patroness A female patron
patroon One who held an estate under an early Dutch grant
patsy Slang One who is cheated
patten A type of shoe
patter To chatter rapidly
pattern A model
patty A small cake of chopped food
patulous Open
paucity Smallness of number
paunch The belly
pauper One who is very poor
pause To tarry
pavan, pavane A dance
pave To cover
pavement A paved surface
pavid Timid
pavilion A summerhouse
pavior, paviour One who paves
pavis, pavise A medieval shield
pavonine Like a peacock
paw The foot of an animal
pawl A hinged mechanical device
pawn Guaranty
pawnshop The business of a pawnbroker
pawpaw Variant of papaw
pax A religious tablet

pay To give
payday The day wages are paid
payee One to whom money is paid
payload Cargo
paymaster One in charge of paying wages
payment The act of paying
paynim A pagan
payoff Full payment
payola *Slang* Bribery
payroll Money paid out to employees
pe The seventeenth letter of the Hebrew alphabet
pea A species of plant
peace The absence of war
peach A tree of the rose family
peacock The male peafowl
peafowl A large pheasant
peag, peage Variant of wampum
peahen The female peafowl
peak A mountain
peal A chime
peanut A nutlike, oily seed of an annual vine
pear A cultivated tree
pearl To cover with pearls
pearlite A cast-iron alloy
pearly Resembling pearls
pearmain A variety of apple
peasant A countryman
pease, *pl* **peasen** A pea
peasecod, peascod The pod of the pea
peat Decayed plant matter used as a plant covering
peavey, peavy A device used to move logs
pebble A small stone
pecan A tree
peccable Liable to sin
peccant Sinful
peccary A hoofed mammal
peccavi A confession of sin
peck To strike with the beak
pectase An enzyme
pectate A chemical salt
pecten, *pl* **-tines** An organ resembling a comb
pectin A colloidal substance
pectoral A chest muscle

peculate To steal
peculiar Strange
pedagogue A teacher
pedagogy Teaching
pedal A device operated by the foot
pedalfer A rich soil
pedant One who exhibits his knowledge
pedate Having feet
peddle To sell
peddler One who sells
pederast A man who practices pederasty
pederasty Sexual relations between a man and a boy
pedes Plural of pes
pedestal A base for a column
pedicel, pedicle An organ serving as a support
pedicular Caused by lice
pedicure Care of the feet
pediform Shaped like a foot
pedigree Ancestry
pediment An architectural part
pedlar, pedler Variants of peddler
pedocal A rich soil
pedology The study of the behavior of children
pedometer An instrument that measures distance traveled on foot
pedro A card game
peduncle A flower stalk
pee The letter p
peek To glance
peekaboo A game
peel The skin of certain fruits
peen A ball-shaped hammer
peep The sound of a young bird
peephole A small hole through which one may look
peepshow An exhibition viewed through a peephole
peepul A fig tree
peer A nobleman
peerage The title of a peer
peeress The wife of a peer
peerless Without equal
peetweet The spotted sandpiper
peeve To annoy
peevish Fretful

peewee A small thing

peg A tapered pin used to plug a hole

pegboard A board with holes

pegbox A part of a stringed instrument

peh Variant of feh

peignoir A woman's dressing gown

pekan A carnivorous mammal

pekin A fabric

pekoe A type of black tea

pelage The coat of a mammal

pelagic Living in ocean waters

pelerine A woman's cape

pelf Wealth

pelican A species of web-footed bird

pelisse A long, outer garment

pelite A type of rock

pellagra A chronic disease

pellagrin One afflicted with pellagra

pellet A bullet

pellicle A thin film

pellmell In wild haste

pellucid Transparent

peloria Unusual regularity of a flower form

pelorus, *pl* **-ruses** A type of compass

pelota Jai Alai

pelt An animal hide

peltate Shield-shaped

peltry Animal skin

pelvic Of the pelvis

pelvis, *pl* **-vises** or **-ves** A basin-shaped part of the skeleton

pemmican A food prepared by North American Indians

pen An instrument for writing

penal Subject to punishment

penalty A punishment

penance The confession of sin

penates Roman gods of the household

pence Plural of penny

pencel A flag

penchant A strong liking

pencil An instrument for writing

pendant A necklace

pendent Dangling

pendragon Supreme leader

pendular Swinging back and forth

pendulous Wavering

pendulum A device used in clocks

penetrant Piercing

penetrate To pierce

penguin A species of flightless marine birds

penis, *pl* **-nises** or **-nes** A male sex organ

penitent Feeling remorse

penknife, *pl* **-knives** A pocketknife

penman A writer

penna, *pl* **pennae** Any of the feathers forming the contour of a bird

pennant A small triangular flag

pennate Feathered

penni, *pl* **-nis** or **pennia** A Finnish coin

penniless Very poor

pennon A banner

pennoncel A small banner

penny A cent

pennywort A species of plant

penology The practice of criminal rehabilitation

pensile Suspended

pension A retirement benefit

pensive Engaged in deep thought

penstock A gate used to control water

pent Shut up

pentacle A five-pointed star

pentad The number five

pentagon A polygon having five sides

pentane A volatile liquid

pentarchy Government by five rulers

pentosan a complex carbohydrate

pentose A sugar

pentyl Amyl

penuche, penuchi A candy

penult The next to the last syllable in a word

penumbra A partial shadow

penurious Stingy

penury Extreme poverty

peon, *pl* **peons** or **peones** An

unskilled laborer

peonage The condition of being a peon

peony A species of garden plant

people A body of persons

pep High spirits

peperoni A sausage

peplos, *pl* **-loses** A garment of ancient Greece

peplum A flounce attached to the waist of a dress

pepo The fruit of various related plants

pepper A woody vine

peppery Fiery

peppy Full of pep

pepsin, pepsine A digestive enzyme

peptic Assisting digestion

peptide, peptid A substance that promotes digestion

peptone A protein compound

per Through

peracid A type of acid

percale A fabric

percaline A fabric

perceive To become aware of

percept Something perceived

perch A place for sitting

perchance Perhaps

percoid A species of fish

percolate To filter

percuss To strike firmly

perdition The loss of one's soul

perdu, perdue A soldier sent on a dangerous mission

peregrine Alien

perennial Lasting a long time

perfect Without defect

perfecto A cigar

perfervid Zealous

perfidy Deliberate breach of faith

perforate To penetrate

perforce By necessity

perform To enact a role

perfume A pleasing scent

perfumer One who sells perfume

perfuse To spread over

pergola A passageway

perhaps Maybe

perianth The outer envelope of a flower

periapt An amulet

pericarp The wall of a ripened fruit

periclase A mineral form of magnesium oxide

pericline A mineral

periderm An outer layer of tissue in plants

peridot A mineral

perigee The point nearest the earth in the orbit of the moon

peril Serious danger

perineum, *pl* **-nea** A region of the body

period A unit of time

periotic Situated around the ear

perique A type of tobacco

perisarc A horny external covering

periscope A type of optical instrument

perish To die

peristyle Columns surrounding a temple

periwig A wig

perjure To testify falsely

perk To rise up

perky Cheerful

perlite A volcanic glass

permanent Lasting

permeate To pervade

permit To tolerate

permute To change the order of

peroneal Pertaining to the fibula

perorate To speak

peroxide A bleaching agent

perpend To ponder

perpetual Lasting for a long time

perplex To bewilder

perry A beverage

persecute To harass

persevere To persist

persimmon A species of tree

persist To be insistent

person A human being

persona, *pl* **-nae** or **-nas** The characters of a novel

personify To represent

personnel Persons employed

perspire To give off perspiration

persuade To convince
pert Saucy
pertain To have reference
pertinent Relating to a specific matter
perturb To upset
pertussis Whooping cough
peruke A wig
peruse To examine
pervade To permeate
perverse Perverted
pervert To corrupt
pervious Open to ideas
pes, *pl* **pedes** A foot
pesade The position of a horse when rearing
peseta Monetary unit of Spain
pesewa Monetary unit of Ghana
pesky Annoying
peso Monetary unit of numerous countries
pessary A contraceptive device
pessimism The practice of looking on the dark side of things
pest A nuisance
pesthole A place infested with disease
pesticide A chemical used to kill pests
pestle To grind
pesto A pasta sauce
pet An animal kept for companionship
petal A segment of a corolla
petaline Of a petal
petaloid Petallike
petalous Petaled
petard A firecracker
petcock A faucet
petechia, *pl* **-chiae** A small spot on a body surface
peter To diminish gradually
petiolar Pertaining to a petiole
petiole A leafstalk
petit Minor
petite Small and trim
petition A formal request
petrel A species of sea bird
petrify To deaden
petrol Gasoline

petroleum Fuel
petrosal Located near the temporal bone
petrous Resembling rock
petticoat A woman's slip
pettifog To act like a petty lawyer
pettish Peevish
petty Trivial
petulant Peevish
petunia A species of plant
petuntze, petuntse A variety of feldspar
pew A church bench
pewee, peewee A species of bird
pewit The lapwing
pewter A tin alloy
peyote, peyotl A cactus
pfennig, pfennige Monetary unit of Germany
phaeton A carriage
phage An organism that destroys bacteria
phalange A phalanx
phalanx, *pl* **-lanxes** or **phalanges** A compact body of people
phallic Resembling a phallus
phallus, *pl* **phalli** or **-luses** The penis
phantasm A phantom
phantom A ghost
pharisee A member of an ancient Jewish sect
pharmacy A drugstore
pharos A lighthouse
pharynx, *pl* **pharynges** or **pharynxes** A section of the digestive tract
phase A distinct stage of development
pheasant A species of bird
phenol A caustic compound
phenolic Derived from phenol
phenology The study of biological phenomena
phenyl A univalent chemical radical
phew Used to express relief
phi The 21st letter of the Greek alphabet
phial A small bottle
philander To flirt

philately The study of postage stamps
philology The love of learning
philomel A nightingale
philter A love potion
phiz *Slang* A facial expression
phlebitis Inflammation of a vein
phlegm Mucus secreted by the glands of the respiratory tract
phloem A plant tissue
phlox, *pl* **phloxes** A species of plant
phobia An intense fear
phoebe A species of bird
phoenix A mythical bird
phon Acoustical measurements
phonate To vocalize
phone A telephone
phoneme A unit of speech
phonemic Pertaining to phonemes
phonetic Pertaining to speech sounds
phonic Having the nature of sound
phonolite A volcanic rock
phonon A quantum of sound energy
phonotype A phonetic symbol used in print
phony, phoney Fake
phooey Used as an exclamation of contempt
phosgene A poisonous gas
phosphate A carbonated beverage
phosphor A substance that emits light
phot A unit of illumination
photic Pertaining to light
photo A photograph
photomap A map made from aerial photos
photon A quantum of radiant energy
photopia Daylight vision
photoplay A motion picture
photoset To set by photocomposition
phrasal Like phrases
phrase A sequence of words with a meaning
phratry A tribal unit
phreatic Of ground water

phrenic Of the mind
pht Used as an expression of mild anger
phthalic Derived from naphthalene
phthalin A chemical compound
phthisic, phthisis A disease of the lungs
phycology The study of seaweeds and algae
phylaxis Inhibiting of infection by the body
phyle, *pl* **-lae** Political subdivision in ancient Athens
phyletic Pertaining to a phylum
phyllite A foliated rock
phyllode A leafstalk that functions as a leaf
phylloid Leaflike
phyllome A plant structure that functions as a leaf
phylum, *pl* **-la** A taxonomic division
physic A medicine
physical Of the body
physician A medical doctor
physicist A scientist
physics The science of matter and energy
physique The body
phytolite A fossil plant
phyton A unit of plant structure
pi, *pl* **pis** The sixteenth letter of the Greek alphabet
pia Spinal membrane
piacular Wicked
piaffe To perform the piaffer
piaffer A movement in horsemanship
pianism The technique of piano playing
piano A musical instrument
piassava, piassaba A palm tree
piaster, piastre Monetary unit of several countries
piazza A verandah
pibroch A musical piece for the bagpipe
pic A photograph
pica A unit of type size
picador A horseman in a bullfight

picara   A female picaro
picaro   An adventurer
picaroon   A pirate
picayune   Anything trivial
piccolo   A small flute
pice   A monetary unit of Pakistan and Nepal
piceous   Black as pitch
pick   To select
pickax, pickaxe   A type of pick
pickerel   A species of freshwater game fish
picket   A person who protests
pickle   To preserve
picklock   A thief
pickup   The act of picking up
picky   Fussy
picnic   An outdoor excursion with food
picoline   A chemical compound
picot   Ornamental edging
picotee   A variety of carnation
picquet   Variant of piquet
picrate   A chemical salt
picture   A visual image
picul   A unit of weight
piddle   To squander
piddock   A species of mollusk
pidgin   A mixed language
pie   A baked food eaten for dessert
piebald   Spotted
piece   A portion
piecemeal   Piece by piece
pied   Covered with two or more colors
piedmont   Lying at the foot of a mountain
pieplant   Rhubarb
pier   A platform over water used to secure ships
pierce   To penetrate
pieta   A representation of Mary grieving over the body of Jesus
pietism   Exaggerated pious feeling
piety   Religious devotion
piffle   To babble
pig   A species of mammal
pigboat   *Slang*   A submarine
pigeon   A species of bird
pigfish   A marine fish

piggery   A place where pigs are kept
piggin   A wooden bucket
piggish   Greedy
piggy   A small pig
piggyback   On the shoulders
piglet   A young pig
pigment   A substance used as coloring
pigmy   Variant of pygmy
pignut   A tree
pigpen   A place where pigs are kept
pigskin   The skin of a pig
pigsney   A darling
pigsty   A pigpen
pigtail   A plait of braided hair
pigweed   A wild plant
pika   A species of small mammal
pike   A species of freshwater game fish
piker *Slang*   A person who does things in a petty way
pilaf, pilaff   A rice dish
pilar   Covered with hair
pilaster   A rectangular column
pilchard   A species of small marine fish
pile   A stack of objects
pileate   Having a pileus
pileum, *pl* pilea   The top of a bird's head
pileus, *pl* pilei   The cap of a mushroom
pilewort   A species of plant
pilfer   To steal
pilgrim   A traveler
pill   A tablet of medicine
pillage   To plunder
pillar   A column
pillbox   A box for pills
pillion   A cushion behind a saddle
pillory   Exposure to public scorn
pillow   A cushion
pilose   Covered with hair
pilot   To control the course of
pilotage   The fee paid to a pilot
pilule   A pill
pima   A fabric
pimento   The allspice tree
pimiento   A garden pepper
pimp   A procurer

pimpernel A species of plant
pimple A swelling of the skin
pimply Having pimples
pin A slender, pointed piece of metal
pinafore A child's apron
pinaster A pine tree
pinata A paper-mache container
pinball An electronic game
pincer Something that resembles one of the grasping parts of pincers
pincers A grasping tool
pinch To squeeze
pine A species of evergreen tree
pineal Having the form of a pine cone
pineapple A tropical plant
pinedrops A parasitic plant
pinene A main element in turpentine
pinery A forest of pine trees
pinesap A plant growing on tree roots
pinetum, *pl* **-ta** A pine tree plantation
piney Variant of piny
pinfish A spiny-finned fish
pinfold A place for stray animals
ping A high-pitched sound
pinhead The head of a pin
pinhole A tiny puncture
pinion A bird's wing
pinite A mineral
pink A color
pinkeye An inflammation of the eye
pinkie, pinky The little finger
pinkish Fairly pink
pinko *Slang* A political radical
pinkroot A disease of plants
pinna, *pl* **pinnae** or **-nas** A feather
pinnace A small boat
pinnacle A small spire on a roof
pinnate Resembling a feather
pinniped A species of aquatic mammal
pinnule, pinnula A featherlike part
pinochle, pinocle A card game
pinole Flour of ground corn and mesquite beans

pinon, *pl* **pinons** or **pinones** A species of pine tree
pinpoint A tiny spot
pinprick A slight wound
pinscher A breed of dog
pinsetter A device that sets up pins
pinstripe A thin stripe on fabrics
pint A unit of measure
pinta A skin disease
pintado The cero fish
pintail A duck
pintle A pin used as a pivot
pinto A spotted horse
pintsize Small
pinup A picture that may be pinned on a wall
pinwale A fabric
pinweed A species of plant
pinwork A type of needlepoint
pinworm A parasitic worm
pinxit Part of an artist's signature
piny Covered with pines
pinyon Variant of pinon
piolet An ice ax
pion An atomic particle
pioneer To explore
piosity Excessively pious
pious Devout
pip A small seed
pipage Pipes
pipe A hollow cylinder
pipefish A species of freshwater fish
pipeline A line of pipe
piperine A chemical compound
piperonal A powder having a floral odor
pipette, pipet A type of glass tube
pipit A species of songbird
pipkin A small pot
pippin A variety of apple
pipsqueak Insignificant
pipy A pipelike sound
piquant Spicy
pique To injure the feelings of
piquet A card game
piracy The act of pirating
piragua A dugout canoe
piranha, pirana A species of voracious fish

pirarucu The arapaima fish
pirate A robber of ships
pirog, *pl* **-rogen** or **-roghi** or **-rogi** A Russian pastry
pirogue A canoe
pirouette A dance turn
pirozhki, piroshki, pirojki Russian pastries
piscary A place for fishing
pisciform Having the shape of fish
piscina, *pl* **-nae** A basin used in churches
piscine Pertaining to fish
pish Used to express contempt
pisiform Pealike
pismire An ant
pisolite Limestone
pissoir A public urinal
pistachio, pistache A tree
pistareen A silver coin
pistil The seed-bearing organ of flowers
pistol A gun
pistole An obsolete gold coin
pistoleer One armed with a gun
piston A part of an engine
pit A deep hole
pita A species of plant
pitapat To make a repeated tapping sound
pitch To toss
pitchfork A tool for pitching hay
pitchman A peddler
pitchout A pitch in baseball
pitchy Full of pitch
piteous Pathetic
pitfall A hidden danger
pith The substance
pithy Meaningful
pitman A mine worker
piton A tool used in mountain climbing
pitsaw A type of saw
pittance A meager allowance
pituitary The pituitary gland
pity A sorrow
piu More
pivot To turn on a shaft
pix *Slang* Photographs
pixy, pixie An elflike creature

pizza An Italian baked dish
pizzazz, pizazz *Slang* Flamboyance
pizzeria A place where pizzas are made
pizzicato Played by plucking
pizzle The penis of an animal
placable Tolerant
placard A poster
placate To appease
place A definite location
placebo A substance with no medication given to humor a patient
placenta, *pl* **-tas** or **-tae** A vascular organ
placid Composed
placket A slit in a garment
placoid Platelike
plagal Designating a medieval musical mode
plagiary Plagiarism
plague A pestilence
plaguy, plaguey Bothersome
plaice A species of fish
plaid A tartan pattern
plain Simple
plaint A complaint
plaintiff One who institutes a suit
plaintive Mournful
plait A braid
plan A program
planar Flat
planarian A species of flatworm
planation Erosion
planch A plank
planchet A disk of metal
plane A flat surface
planet A celestial body
planetoid An asteroid
plangent Resounding loudly
plank A piece of thick lumber
plankter Organisms that constitute plankton
plankton Organisms found in water
plant An organism of the vegetable kingdom
plantain A species of plant
plantar Pertaining to the sole of the feet
planula, *pl* **-lae** Free-swimming

larva of various organisms
plaque An engraved plate
plash To splash
plasma, plasm The liquid part of blood
plasmin An enzyme
plaster A mixture of lime, sand and water
plastic A synthetic material
plastid A structure occurring in plant cells
plastron A protective breastplate
plat To braid
plate A dish
plateau, *pl* **-teaus** or **-teaux** A tableland
platelet A protoplasmic disk
platen The roller on a typewriter
platform A raised floor
platina Platinum
platinic Pertaining to platinum
platinize To coat with platinum
platinoid Any metal associated with platinum
platinum A metallic element
platitude A trite remark
platoon A military unit
platter A large dish
platy A species of fish
platypus, *pl* **-puses** An aquatic mammal
plaudit An expression of praise
plausible Valid
plausive Applauding
play To engage oneself in amusement
playa The bank of a river
playact To perform in a play
playback The act of replaying a newly made record
playbill A program for a play
playboy A wealthy man devoted to pleasurable activities
playgoer One who goes to the theater
playmate A companion in play
playpen An enclosure for a baby
plaza A public square
plea An appeal
pleach To interlace

plead To implore
pleasance A pleasure garden
pleasant Agreeable
please To give pleasure
pleasure A delight
pleat A fold in cloth
pleb A plebeian
plebe A freshman at a naval or military academy
plebeian A coarse person
plectrum, *pl* **-trums** or **-tra** Something used to pluck the strings of an instrument
pled Past tense of plead
pledge A promise
pledgee One to whom something is pledged
pledgor One who pledges
plenary Full
plenitude Abundance
plenteous Abundant
plentiful Having plenty
plenty Abundance
plenum, *pl* **-nums** or **plena** Fullness
pleonasm Redundancy
pleopod An appendage of crustaceans
plethora Excess
pleura, *pl* **pleurae** A membrane that envelops the lung
pleurisy Inflammation of the pleura
pleuron, *pl* **pleura** A lateral plate on the body segments of arthropods
pleuston A species of plant
plexor A medical instrument
plexus, *pl* **-uses** Any interlacing of parts
pliant Easily bent
plica, *pl* **plicae** A fold of skin
plicate Pleated
pliers A tool
plight To betroth
plimsoll, plimsol, plimsole A sneaker
plinth A slab upon which a statue is placed
plisse A fabric
plod To trudge
plop To drop heavily

plosion The articulation of a plosive sound
plot A small lot
plough Variant of plow
plover A species of wading bird
plow A farm tool
plowboy A boy who plows
plowhead Part of a plow
plowland Land under cultivation
plowman A farmer
ploy A maneuver
pluck To pick
plug A cork
plum A species of tree
plumage The feathers of a bird
plumate Resembling a feather
plumb A device used to establish a vertical line
plumbago Graphite
plumber One who installs plumbing
plumbery A plumber's shop
plumbism Lead poisoning
plume A feather
plumelet A small plume
plummet To plunge
plumose Feathery
plump Chubby
plumule A down feather
plumy Covered with feathers
plunder To pillage
plunge To throw oneself into something
plunk To plump
plural Composed of more than one
plus Added to
plush A material having a deep pile
plutocrat A person of great influence
pluton Igneous rock
pluvial, pluvian Rainy
ply To join together
plywood A material of layers of wood glued together
pneuma The spirit
pneumonia A chronic disease
poach A method of cooking
pochard A species of duck
pock A pockmark
pocket A pouch sewed onto a garment
pockmark A scar
pocky Having pocks
poco A little
pocosin An upland swamp
pod A seed vessel
podagra Gout
podesta A magistrate of medieval Italy
podiatry The study of foot ailments
podium, pl -**dia** or -**ums** A dais
podzol, podsol A type of soil
poem A composition in verse
poesy Poetry
poet One who writes poems
poetaster A would-be poet
poetess A female poet
poetize To write poetry
pogonia A species of orchid
pogonip A dense fog
pogrom An organized massacre
pogy A marine fish
poi Hawaiian food
poignant Touching
poilu Slang A French soldier
poinciana A species of tropical tree
point The sharp end of a knife
poise Balance
poison A substance that causes injury
poke To jab
pokeweed A tall plant
poky, pokey Slow
polar Pertaining to a pole
polder An area of low-lying land
pole A long, rounded piece of material
poleax, poleaxe A battle-ax
polecat A species of mammal
polemic An argument
polestar The star Polaris
police A force maintained to keep order
policy A procedure
polis, pl -**leis** A city-state of ancient Greece
polish To make shiny
politburo The executive committee of the Communist Party
polite Courteous

politesse Politeness
politic Shrewd
politick To talk politics
politico A politician
polity A form of government
polka A dance
poll The place where votes are cast
pollard An animal that no longer has its horns
polled Hornless
pollen Material produced by the anthers of flowering plants
pollex, *pl* **pollices** The thumb
polliwog, pollywog An immature frog
pollock, pollack A marine food fish
pollster A poller
pollute To corrupt
polo An equestrian game
polonaise A dance
polonium A radioactive element
poltroon A base coward
polyester A synthetic resin
polygala A species of plant
polygamy The practice of having more than one mate at a time
polygene A type of gene
polyglot One with a knowledge of several languages
polygon A closed plane figure bounded by straight line segments
polygyny The practice of having two or more wives at the same time
polymath One with varied learning
polymer A chemical compound
polynya Area of open water surrounded by sea ice
polyp Any of various coelenterates
polypary The common framework of a polyp colony
polypnea Panting
polypod Having numerous feet
polypody A species of fern
polypore A type of fungus
polyuria Excessive urination
polyzoic Consisting of a colony of zooids
pomace Pulpy residue remaining from squeezed fruit
pomade Hair ointment

pomander A mixture of aromatic substances
pome Fruit with no stones but having seeds
pomelo The grapefruit
pommel To beat with one's fists
pomology The study of fruit
pomp Splendor
pompadour A hair style
pompano A species of fish
pompon, pompom A decoration
poncho A blanketlike cloak with a hole for the head
pond A small body of water
ponder To consider
pondweed A species of aquatic plant
pone Corn pone
pongee A fabric
poniard A dagger
pons, *pl* **pontes** A tissue joining two parts of an organ
pontifex A priest of ancient Rome
pontiff The pope
pontil A glassmaker's tool
pontine Pertaining to bridges
pontoon A floating structure
pony A small breed of horses
ponytail A hair style
pooch *Slang* A dog
pood A Russian unit of weight
poodle A breed of dogs
poof An exclamation used to express disappearance
pooh An exclamation of disdain
pool A swimming pool
poolroom A place for the playing of pool
poon A species of tree
poop The stern of a ship
poor Having no wealth
poorhouse Formerly, a house for paupers
poori A flat wheat cake
pop A sudden sound
popcorn A variety of corn
pope The head of the Roman Catholic Church
popedom The papacy
popery The doctrines of the Roman

Catholic Church
popeyed Amazed
popgun A toy gun
popinjay A vain person
popish Pertaining to the popes
poplar A species of tree
poplin A fabric
popover A type of muffin
poppet A valve
popple Choppy water
poppy A species of plant
poppycock Humbug
populace The masses
popular Well liked
populate To people
porcelain A type of ceramic
porch A covered structure at the entrance to a house
porcine Pertaining to pigs
porcupine A species of rodent
pore To gaze
porgy A species of fish
poriferan A sponge
pork Flesh of a hog used as food
porker A fattened pig
porkpie A pie with pork
porky Fat
porno, porn *Slang* Pornography
porosity The state of being porous
porous Full of pores
porphyrin A nitrogen-containing organic compound
porphyry An igneous rock
porpoise A species of aquatic mammal
porridge Boiled oatmeal
porringer A bowl for porridge
port A waterfront district
portend To serve as a warning
portent An omen
porter A doorman
porteress Variant of portress
portfolio A briefcase
porthole A ship's window
portico A type of porch
portiere A curtain
portion Part of a whole
portly Stout
portrait A likeness of a person
portray To represent in a play

portress A female porter
pose To sit for a portrait
poseur An insincere person
posh Exclusive
posit To place
position A place
positive No doubt
positron An atomic particle
posse A body of men with legal authority
possess To own
posset A drink
possible Potential
possum Variant of opossum
post The starting gate
postage The charge for mailing
postaxial Situated behind the axis of the body
postbox A mailbox
postcava The posterior vena cava
postdate To put on a later date
posterior Following
postern A rear gate
postfix To affix
postiche False
postlude A concluding piece of music
postman A mail man
postmark The mark that cancels the stamp
postnasal Posterior to the nose
postnatal Occurring immediately after the birth
postobit Happening after one's death
postpone To put off
postulate To demand
posture A bodily position
posy A flower
pot A cooking vessel
potable Fit to drink
potage A soup
potash An alkaline compound
potassium A metallic element
potation The act of drinking
potato A plant having edible tubers
potatory Pertaining to drinking
potbelly A protruding belly
potboiler An uninspired piece of writing

potboy A boy who works in a tavern

poteen Irish whiskey

potent Powerful

potentate A monarch

pother A fuss

potherb A species of plant

pothole A hole in a roadway

pothook A hook for hanging a pot

pothouse A tavern

potiche A type of jar

potion A medicinal drink

potlatch A feast among Indians

potluck Food readily available

potpie A meat pie

potpourri A combination of various elements

potsherd, potshard Broken pottery

potstone A variety of steatite

pottage A stew

pottery Wares shaped from moist clay

pottle A drinking vessel

potto A species of primate

potty A child's toilet

pouch A bag

pouf A hair style

poulard, poularde A spayed hen

poult A young fowl

poultice Something applied to a sore

poultry Domestic fowls

pounce To attack suddenly

pound A unit of weight

poundal A unit of force

pour To rain hard

pout To sulk

poverty The condition of being poor

pow The sound of a shot

powder Finely dispersed solid particles

power Force

powwow A North American Indian ceremony

pox Syphilis

praam A type of boat

practical Capable of being put into effect

practice To make a habit of

praedial Pertaining to land

praetor An ancient Roman magistrate

pragmatic Practical

prairie An area of rolling grassland

praise An expression of approval

praline A candy

pram A perambulator

prance To strut

prandial Pertaining to dinner

prank A practical joke

prat *Slang* The buttocks

prate To chatter

pratfall *Slang* A comic fall in burlesque

pratique Clearance granted a ship by health authorities

prattle Babble

prau Variant of proa

prawn A species of edible crustacean

praxis, *pl* **-es** Practical exercise of a branch of learning

pray To say a prayer

prayer A fervent request

pre- Indicates an earlier time; beforehand. The following compounds are listed without definition (see Introduction):

preact	precited	preheat
preadapt	preclean	prehuman
preadmit	precook	prejudge
preadopt	precool	prelegal
preadult	precure	prelim
preaged	predate	prelimit
preallot	predawn	preman
prearm	predigest	premature
preatomic	predusk	premed
preaver	preelect	premedic
prebill	preenact	premen
prebind	preexist	premix
prebless	prefab	prename
preboil	prefigure	prenatal
prebound	prefix	preoccupy
precancel	prefixal	preordain
precast	preflight	prepack
precede	prefocus	prepaid
precensor	preform	prepare
precheck	prefrank	prepay
prechill	pregame	preplace

preplan preshrunk preunion
preplant presift preunite
preprint presoak prevent
prepunch presold preview
preschool prestamp previous
prescore pretaste prevue
preserve pretax prewar
preset preteen prewarn
preshape pretest prewash
preshow pretreat prewrap

preacher A minister
preachy Inclined to preach
preamble Preliminary
preaxial Positioned in front of a body axis
prebend A clergyman's stipend
precedent An act used as an example
precept A writ
precess To go before
precinct A police station
precious Valuable
precipice The face of a cliff
precis An abstract
precise Definite
preclude To prevent
precursor A harbinger
predator One who plunders
predicate To assert
predict To foretell
preemie, premie An infant born prematurely
preen To take pride in oneself
preface An introduction
prefect An administrative official
prefer To like better
pregnant Mentally fertile
prejudice Bias
prelacy The office of a prelate
prelate A high-ranking clergyman
prelect To lecture
prelude A piece of music
premier Supreme
premiere The first performance
premise To state in advance
premium Something offered free
premolar A tooth
premorse Ending abruptly
prep Preparatory
prepense Premeditated

prepotent Predominant
prepuce A fold of skin covering the uncircumcised penis
presage An omen
presbyter A priest
prescind To consider individually
prescribe To recommend
prescript Set down
presence A person who is present
present To introduce
preside To act as chairman
president One appointed to preside over an organized body of people
presidio A military post
presidium A high-ranking body in the Soviet Union
press To bear down on
pressman One who operates a printing press
pressmark A notation in a book
pressor Causing an increase in blood pressure
pressrun Number of copies printed
pressure Harassment
prestige Coveted status
presto In rapid tempo
presume To take for granted
pretend To make believe
pretense The act of pretending
pretext Pretense
prettify To make pretty
pretty Attractive
pretzel A type of biscuit baked in the form of a loose knot or stick
prevail To triumph
prevalent Generally practiced
previse To foresee
prexy *Slang* A president
prey A victim
priapic, preapean Phallic
priapism A lascivious attitude
priapus A Greco-Roman god
price The cost of something purchased
prick The act of piercing
pricket A spike for holding a candle
prickle A pricking sensation
prickly Tingling
pride Self-respect
priedieu, *pl* **dieus** or **-dieux** A foot-

stool for kneeling on
priest A minister
priestess A female priest
prig A person who acts smug
prim Neat
primacy The state of being first
primal First in time
primary Being first
primate A bishop of highest rank
prime First in quality
primero A card game
primeval Pertaining to the earliest ages
primitive Archetypal
primo In the first place
primp To preen
primrose A species of plant
primus, *pl* **-muses** The head bishop in Scotland
prince A hereditary ruler
princess A hereditary female ruler
principal The head of a school
principle Moral standards
prink To primp
print An impression made upon a surface
prior Preceding in order
prioress The head of a priory of nuns
priority Something given prior attention
priory A monastery governed by a prior
prism A cut-glass object
prismatic Multicolored
prismoid A geometric solid
prison A penitentiary
prisoner One serving a prison sentence
prissy Fussy
pristine Uncorrupted
prithee I pray thee
privacy Secrecy
private Secluded
privateer A crew member of a privateer
privation Lacking the comforts of life
privet A species of plant
privilege A special right

privily Privately
privity Secret knowledge
privy One who is in privity with another
prize An award
pro Affirmative vote
proa A Malayan boat
probable Likely to happen
probang A surgical rod
probate Establishment of legal validity
probe To explore
probity Uprightness
problem A situation that is difficult
proboscis A prominent nose
procarp A female sex organ in certain algae
proceed To go forward
process Passage of time
proclaim To declare
proclitic A word having no independent accent
proconsul A governing official
procreate To originate
proctor To supervise
procure To acquire
prod To poke
prodigal Lavish
prodigy A person with exceptional talents
prodrome The sign of the onset of a disease
produce To yield
product Something produced
proem A preface
profane Blasphemous
profess To declare
proffer To tender
profile A side view
profit The return on an investment
profiteer One who makes great profits
profound Far-reaching
profuse Plentiful
progeny Offspring
prognosis A prediction
program A list of the events in a public presentation
progress To move forward

prohibit To prevent
project A plan
prolan A sex hormone
prolapse To slip out of place
prolate Elongated
proleg A limb attached to the abdomens of certain insect larvae
prolific Producing works in great numbers
proline An amino acid
prolix Tedious and wordy
prologue An introductory act
prolong To lengthen in duration
prom A formal school dance
promenade A leisurely walk
prominent Eminent
promise A vow
promisee One to whom a promise is made
promisor One who makes a promise
promote To further
prompt Punctual
pronate To turn the palm downward or backward
prone Tending
prong A sharply pointed part of a tool
pronghorn A small deer
pronoun A word that may be used in place of a noun
pronounce To declare
pronto Quickly
proof Validation
proofread To check copy for corrections
prop To support
propagate To multiply
propane A flammable gas
propel To cause to move
propend To have a tendency toward
propene Propylene
proper Fitting
property Ownership
prophase The first stage in mitosis
prophecy A prediction
prophesy To predict
prophet One who predicts
propolis A waxy substance collected by bees
proponent An advocate
propose To suggest
propound To propose
propriety The quality of being proper
propyl A univalent radical
prorate To distribute proportionally
prorogue To discontinue a session of
prosaic Not poetic
proscribe To denounce
prose Commonplace
prosecute To carry on
prosit To your health
proso Variety of millet
prosodic According to the principles of prosody
prosodist A person skilled in prosody
prosody The art of versification
prospect Possibility
prosper To thrive
prostate A gland in male mammals
prostrate To be overcome
prostyle Having a row of columns across the front
prosy Prosaic
protasis The introduction of a classical drama
protean Readily adaptable
protease An enzyme
protect To guard
protege One whose career is promoted by an influential person
protegee A female protege
protein A nitrogenous organic compound
proteose A protein
protest To object to
protist Any of the unicellular organisms
protium An isotope of hydrogen
protocol Etiquette observed by heads of state
proton An atomic particle
protract To prolong
protrude To project
proud Gratifying

prove To establish the truth
proverb An adage
provide To prepare
provident Providing for future needs
province An administrative area of a country
proviso A clause in a document
provoke To arouse
provost An official in certain colleges
prow The ship's bow
prowess Superior ability
prowl To roam in search of prey
proximal Proximate
proximate Nearest
proximo In the following month
proxy A substitute
prude One who is prudish
prudence The state of being prudent
prudery Prudish behavior
pruinose Having a powdery covering
prune A variety of dried plum
prunella, prunello A fabric
prunelle A liqueur
prurient Interested in sexual matters
prurigo A skin disease
pruritus Severe itching
pruta Monetary unit of Israel
pry To snoop
psalm A hymn
psalmody The singing of psalms
psaltery, psaltry A musical instrument
pseudo Fake
pseudonym A pen name
pshaw An exclamation of disgust
psi The 23rd letter of the Greek alphabet
psilocin A hallucinogenic drug
psych *Slang* To lose one's nerve
psyche The human soul
psychic Pertaining to the human mind
psycho Psychotic
psylla, psyllid A species of plant lice

ptarmigan A species of bird
pteropod A species of mollusk
ptisan A medicinal infusion
ptomaine, ptomain An alkaloid substance
ptosis Drooping of the upper eyelid
ptyalin An enzyme
pub A tavern
puberty Period approaching maturity
pubes Hair appearing at puberty
pubic Pertaining to pubes
pubis, *pl* **-bes** The forward portion of either of the hipbones
public Of the community
publican A tavernkeeper
publicity Information for public interest
publish To issue a publication
puccoon A species of plant
puce A color
puck A disk used in ice hockey
puckish Impish
pudding A sweet dessert
puddle A small pool of liquid
puddler One who puddles
pudency Shame
pudendum, *pl* **-da** External genitals
pudgy Chubby
pueblo An American Indian village
puerile Childish
puff A sudden gust of wind
puffball A species of white-fleshed, round fungi
puffin A species of sea bird
pug A small dog
puggree, pugree, puggaree, pugaree A cloth band wrapped around a hat
pugilist A boxer
puisne One of lower rank
puissant Powerful
puja A Hindu prayer
puke Variant of vomit
pukka Genuine
pul, *pl* **puls** or **puli** Monetary unit of Afghanistan
pule To whine
puli, *pl* **-lis** or **pulik** A long-haired sheep dog

pull To tug at
pullet A young hen
pulley A device used to raise weight
pullout A withdrawal
pullover A garment put on over the head
pulmonic Pertaining to the lungs
pulp A soft, moist mass
pulpit A raised platform in church
pulpwood Soft wood
pulque A Mexican beverage
pulsar A celestial object that emits radio pulses
pulsate To quiver
pulse A regular beating
pulsejet A type of jet engine
pulverize To grind
pulvinus, *pl* **-ni** A swelling at the base of a leafstalk
puma The mountain lion
pumice Volcanic rock
pummel To pommel
pump To drive air into
pumpkin A large fruit
pun A play on words
punch A drink of fruit juices
puncheon A supporting timber
punctate Marked with tiny spots
punctual Prompt
puncture To make a hole
pundit A scholar
pung A horse-drawn sleigh
pungent Biting
punish To give punishment
punk Chinese incense
punka, punkah A ceiling fan
punkie, punky A species of insect
punkin Variant of pumpkin
punster One who makes puns
punt A kicking play in football
punty An iron rod used in glassmaking
puny Weak
pup A puppy
pupa, *pl* **-pae** or **-pas** An insect in the nonfeeding stage of development
pupil A student
pupilage The state of being a pupil

pupillary Of the pupil of the eye
puppet A doll
puppetry The art of making puppets
puppy A young dog
purblind Partly blind
purchase To buy
purdah A curtain used to screen women in India
pure Free from impurities
purebred An animal of unmixed stock
puree A smooth-textured form of cooked foods
purfle To decorate the edge of
purgatory A place of temporary punishment
purge To purify
purine A chemical compound
purism Strict adherence to traditional correctness
purist One who practices purism
purl To knit with a purl stitch
purlieu An outlying area
purlin A supporting timber
purloin To steal
purple A color
purplish Having a purple tint
purport To profess
purpose A goal
purr Sound made by a cat
purse A small bag
purser One in charge of money on board a ship
purslane A trailing weed
pursuant In accordance with
pursue To chase
pursuit The act of chasing
purulent Secreting pus
purvey To furnish
purview Outlook
pus A fluid formed in infected tissue
push To shove
pushball A game
pushcart A cart pushed by hand
pushover Something easily accomplished
pushpin A game
pushrod A rod in an engine

puss A cat
pussley, pusley The purslane plant
pussy A cat
pussyfoot To shy away from
pussytoes A species of plant
pustular Having pustules
pustule A swelling filled with pus
put To set
putamen, *pl* **-tamina** A shell-like covering
putative Generally regarded as such
putlog A supporting timber
putoff An excuse
putout A play in baseball
putrefy To cause to decay
putrid Rotten
putsch A sudden attempt to overthrow a government
putt A light golf stroke
puttee A strip of cloth wound around the leg
putto A male cupid
putty A type of cement
puzzle To cause uncertainty
pya Monetary unit of Burma
pyelitis Inflammation of the kidney
pyemia The presence of pus in the blood
pygidium, *pl* **-ia** The posterior body area of certain arthropods
pygmy Unusually small
pyknic Designating a fleshy physique
pylon A gateway
pylorus The passage between the stomach and the duodenum

pyoderma A skin disease
pyosis The formation of pus
pyralid A species of moth
pyramid An Egyptian royal tomb
pyre A funeral pile of combustible wood
pyrene The stone of various fruits
pyrenoid A protein granule of certain algae
pyretic Feverish
pyrexia Fever
pyric Pertaining to burning
pyridine A flammable liquid
pyriform Pear-shaped
pyrite A metallic sulfide
pyrogen A substance that produces fever
pyrone A chemical compound
pyronine A dye
pyrope A variety of garnet
pyrosis Heartburn
pyrostat A thermostat
pyroxene A crystalline mineral silicate
pyrrhic A Greek metrical foot
pyrrole A chemical compound
python A species of snake
pythoness A prophetess
pyuria The presence of pus in the urine
pyx The container in which the wafer of the Eucharist is kept
pyxidium, *pl* **-ia** A pyxis
pyxie An evergreen shrub
pyxis, *pl* **pyxides** A dehiscent, dry fruit

qabbala   A secret doctrine

qadarite   A member of an early Moslem philosophical school

qadi   A Moslem judge

qaf   The 21st letter of the Arabic alphabet

qaid   A Moslem leader

qaimaqam   A Turkish official during the Ottoman Empire

qantar   Unit of weight measurement

qarmatian   A Moslem sect of the Middle Ages

qashqai   A member of the qashqai people

qasida   An Arabic poem

qat   An evergreen shrub of Arabia and Africa

qazaq   A member of the Kirghiz tribe

qere, qeri   Marginal annotations in the Hebrew bible

qibla   Direction toward which Moslems pray

qinah   A Hebrew elegy

qindar, qintar   Monetary unit of Albania

qiviut   The hair of the musk ox

qiyas   Islamic judgment of a belief by application of established principles governing some analogous belief

qoph   The 19th letter of the Hebrew alphabet

qoran   The sacred text of Islam, the Koran

qua   In the capacity of

quack   Sound uttered by a duck

quackery   The methods of a charlatan

quad   A quadrangle

quadrant   A quarter section of a circle

quadrat   A piece of type metal

quadrate   A square

quadric   Pertaining to geometric surfaces

quadrille   A dance

quadroon   A person having one-quarter Negro ancestry

quadruped   A four-footed animal

quadruple   Having four parts

quaere   A question

quaestor   An ancient Roman official

quaff   To drink heartily

quag   A marsh

quagga   An extinct zebralike mammal

quaggy   Like a marsh

quagmire   Wet, boggy ground

quahog, quahaug   An edible clam

quaich, quaigh   A drinking cup

quail   A species of bird

quaint   Old-fashioned in a pleasing way

quake   To shiver

qualify   To moderate

quality   A feature

qualm   Faintness

quandary   A dilemma

quantic   An algebraic function

quantify   To determine the quantity of

quantity   The exact amount

quantize   To express in multiples of a basic unit

quantum, pl -ta   A specified quantity

quark   A hypothetical atomic particle

quarrel   A disagreement

quarry   Prey

quart A liquid measure of capacity
quartan A recurrent fever
quarte A position in fencing
quarter One-fourth
quartern A fourth part
quartet, quartette A group of four musicians
quartic A quantic of the fourth degree
quartile Part of a frequency distribution
quarto Having four leaves to the sheet
quartz A mineral
quartzite A metamorphic rock
quasar A distant celestial object that emits light or radio waves
quash To annul
quasi Seemingly
quassia A tropical tree
quassin A medicinal compound
quatrain A stanza of four lines
quaver To tremble
quay A wharf
quayage A charge for the use of a quay
quean An unmarried woman
queasy Nauseated
quebracho A species of tree
queen A female ruler
queenly Resembling a queen
queer Strange
quell To suppress
quench To satisfy
quenelle A type of dumpling
querist An inquirer
quern A hand-turned grain mill
querulous Peevish
query A question
quest A search
question Uncertainty
questzal, quezal A Central American bird
queue A line of people
quibble A petty objection
quiche A custard-filled pastry
quick Speedy
quickie *Slang* Something done quickly
quicklime Calcium oxide

quicksand A wet sand deposit in which a person may easily be engulfed
quickset A plant suitable for hedges
quickstep A step used when marching in quick time
quid Something to be chewed
quiddity The real nature of something
quidnunc A busybody
quiescent Dormant
quiet Silent
quietude A state of tranquillity
quietus Death
quill A writing pen made from a feather
quillback A species of fish
quillet A quibble
quillwort A species of aquatic plant
quilt A type of bed cover
quinate Arranged in groups of five
quince An applelike fruit
quincunx An arrangement of five objects
quinine A medicinal alkaloid
quinoid A chemical compound
quinone A chemical compound
quinsy An inflammation of the tonsils
quint A group of five
quintain An object used by knights as a target
quintal A unit of weight
quintar Variant of qintar
quintet A group of five
quintile A portion of frequency distribution
quintuple Consisting of five parts
quip A gibe
quipster One who makes quips
quipu, quippu A device used by the ancient Peruvians to record events
quire A set of 24 or 25 sheets of paper
quirk A peculiarity
quirt A riding whip
quisling A traitor
quit To give up

quite Completely
quitrent Rent paid in lieu of services
quitter One who quits
quittor An inflammation of an animal's hoof
quiver To tremble
quixotic Romantically idealistic
quiz, *pl* **quizzes** To interrogate
quizzical Questioning
quod *Slang* Jail
quoin The external corner of a building

quoit A game
quondam Former
quorum A select group
quota An allotment
quotation A passage that is quoted
quote To repeat
quoth Said
quotha Used to express surprise
quotient The result when one number is divided by another
qursh, qurush Monetary unit of Saudi Arabia

rabat A clerical collar
rabbet A groove
rabbi, rabbin A Jewish spiritual leader
rabbit A species of mammal
rabble A mob
rabid Fanatical
rabies An infectious disease
raccoon, racoon A species of mammal
race Mankind
raceme An arrangement of flowers
racemic A type of chemical compound
racemose Growing in a raceme
raceway A racetrack
rachis, *pl* **-chides** or **-chises** The spinal column
rachitis An infant's disease
rack A stand in which to hold various articles
racketeer A gangster
rackety Noisy

raconteur One skilled at telling stories
racy Risque
rad A unit of energy
radar An electronic detecting method
raddle To interweave
radial Moving along a radius
radian A unit of measure
radiance The state of being radiant
radiant Emitting light
radical Basic
radicand A quantity
radicle A part of a plant embryo
radio Wireless communication
radioman A radio technician
radish A species of plant
radium A radioactive element
radius, *pl* **-dii** or **-uses** A measure of circular area
radix, *pl* **radices** or **-dixes** A point of origin
radome A domelike housing for a

radar antenna
radon A radioactive element
radula, *pl* **-lae** In mollusks, a tonguelike organ
raffia A palm tree
raffish Vulgar
raffle A lottery
raft A lot
rag A piece of cloth
raga A form in Hindu music
ragbag A bag for rags
rage Anger
ragi A cereal grass
raglan A type of coat
ragman A man who sells rags
ragout A stew
ragtag Riffraff
ragtime A style of music
ragweed A species of weed
ragwort A species of plant
rah Hurrah
raid A surprise attack
rail A species of marsh bird
railhead The farthest point of a railroad line
raillery Banter
railroad To push through quickly
railway A railroad
raiment Garments
rain To fall like rain
rainbow An arc of colors in the sky
raincoat A water-resistant coat
raindrop A drop of rain
rainfall A fall of rain
rainspout A roof gutter spout
rainwear Waterproof clothing
raise To cause to rise
raisin A variety of grape dried for eating
raj Sovereignty
rajah, raja A ruler in India
rake To gather
rakehell A roue
raki, rakee A brandy
rakish Smart
rale A respiratory sound
ralliform Pertaining to rails
rally To assemble
ram A male sheep
ramate Branched

ramble To roam
rambutan An Asian tree
ramekin, ramequin A cheese dish
ramie A woody plant
ramiform Branchlike
ramify To branch out
ramjet A type of jet engine
ramose Having many branches
ramp To rage
rampage Frenzied action
rampant Unrestrained
rampart A fortification
rampike A tree stump
rampion A species of plant
ramrod A rod for cleaning guns
ramson A broad-leaved garlic
ramtil An African plant
ramulose Having small branches
ramus, *pl* **-mi** A branchlike part of a structure
ran Past tense of run
ranch A large farm
rancheria An Indian village
ranchero A rancher
ranchman One who runs a ranch
rancho A ranch
rancid Sour
rancor, rancour Ill will
rand Monetary unit of South Africa
randan A boat rowed by three persons
random Haphazard
randy Bawdy
rang Past tense of ring
range Tones within the capacity of a voice
rangy Roomy
rani, *pl* **-nis** The wife of a rajah
rank An official position
rankle To cause irritation
ransack To search
ransom To obtain the release of
rant To rave
rap To strike
rape An outrageous assault
rapeseed The seed of the rape plant
raphe, *pl* **-phae** A seamlike line between two halves of an organ
raphide, raphis A bundle of needle-shaped crystals

rapid   Swift
rapier   A sword
rapine   Plunder
rapparee   A bandit
rappee   Snuff
rappel   A method of descending from a mountainside
rappen   A Swiss coin
rapport   Relationship
rapt   Engrossed
raptor   A bird of prey
rapture   Ecstasy
rare   Uncommon
rarebit   A cheese dish
rarefy   To refine
rareripe   Ripening early
rasbora   A species of tropical fish
rascal   A scoundrel
rase   Variant of raze
rash   Impetuous
rasorial   Scratching the ground for food
rasp   To file
raspberry   A species of plant
rat   A species of rodent
ratafia, ratafee   A cordial
rataplan   The beating of a drum
ratatat   A sharp rapping sound
ratchet   A mechanism permitting motion in one direction only
rate   A price
ratel   The honey badger
ratfink *Slang*   A contemptible person
ratfish   A marine fish
rathe   Eager
rather   Preferably
ratify   To approve
ratine   A fabric
ratio   The relative size of two quantities
ration   A fixed portion
ratite   A flightless bird
ratline, ratlin   A rope on a ship
ratoon, rattoon   A shoot growing from the root of a plant
ratsbane   Rat poison
rattail   A file
rattan   A species of palm
ratteen   A fabric

ratter   An animal skilled at killing rats
rattle   To talk rapidly
rattlebox   A species of plant
rattler   A rattlesnake
rattly   Clattering
rattrap   A dilapidated place
raucous   Loud and rowdy
raunchy *Slang*   Smutty
ravage   To devastate
rave   To rage
ravel   To unravel
ravelin   A fortification
raven   A large bird
ravenous   Voracious
ravigote   A spicy vinegar sauce
ravin   Voracity
ravine   A deep gorge
ravioli   A pasta dish
raw   Uncooked
rawboned   Having a lean frame
rawhide   Untanned hide of animals
ray   A narrow beam of light
rayon   A synthetic material
raze   To demolish
razor   A sharp cutting instrument
razorback   A hog
razz *Slang*   To tease
re   The second tone of the diatonic scale

re-   Indicates again or anew. The following compounds are listed without definition (see Introduction):

reabsorb	reallot	reassess
reaccede	realter	reassign
reaccent	reanalyze	reassort
reaccept	reannex	reassume
reaccuse	reanoint	reassure
reacquire	reappear	reattach
readapt	reapply	reattack
readd	reappoint	reattain
readdict	reargue	reattempt
readjust	rearm	reavail
readmit	rearouse	reavow
readopt	rearrange	reawake
readorn	rearrest	rebait
reaffirm	reascend	rebid
reaffix	reassail	rebill
realign	reassert	rebind

rebirth	reconvene	reemploy	refurnish	reinjure	remet
rebloom	recook	reenact	regain	reinsert	remigrate
reboard	recopy	reendow	regather	reinspect	remix
reboil	recount	reengage	regauge	reinstall	remixture
reborn	recouple	reenjoy	regave	reinsure	remodel
rebound	recover	reenlist	regear	reinter	remodify
rebuild	recrate	reenter	regild	reinvent	remold
reburial	recross	reequip	regive	reinvest	remount
rebury	recrown	reerect	reglaze	reinvite	rename
rebutton	recur	reevoke	regloss	reinvoke	renew
recall	recurrent	reexhibit	reglow	reinvolve	renotify
recane	recut	reexpel	reglue	reissue	renumber
recap	redamage	reexport	regrade	reiterate	reobject
recapture	redate	refall	regraft	rejoin	reobserve
recarry	redecide	refashion	regrant	rejudge	reobtain
recast	redefeat	refasten	regrate	rekey	reoccupy
recatalog	redefine	refeed	regrew	rekindle	reoccur
recertify	redefy	refell	regrind	reknit	reoil
rechange	redeliver	refight	regroove	relabel	reopen
rechannel	redemand	refigure	regroup	relace	reoppose
recharge	redeny	refile	regrow	relaunch	reordain
rechart	redeploy	refill	rehammer	relaunder	reorder
recheck	redeposit	refilm	rehandle	relay	reorient
rechew	redescend	refilter	rehang	relearn	reoutfit
rechoose	redesign	refind	reharden	relend	repacify
recircle	redevelop	refinish	rehash	relet	repack
recite	redid	refire	rehear	reletter	repackage
reclad	redigest	refit	reheat	relight	repaint
reclaim	redip	refix	reheel	reline	repanel
reclasp	redispose	reflew	rehem	relist	repaper
reclean	redistill	reflies	rehinge	relit	repass
reclothe	redivide	refloat	rehire	relive	repave
recoal	redo	reflood	rehouse	reload	repay
recock	redock	reflow	rehung	reloan	repeat
recode	redraw	reflower	reignite	relocate	repeople
recodify	redried	refly	reimage	relock	reperk
recoin	redrill	refocus	reimplant	relume	rephrase
recolor	redrive	refold	reimport	remail	repigment
recomb	redry	reforge	reimpose	remake	repin
recombine	redye	reformat	reincite	reman	replace
recommit	reearn	refortify	reincur	remap	replan
recompose	reecho	refought	reindex	remark	replant
recompute	reedit	refound	reinduce	remarry	replaster
reconduct	reeject	reframe	reinduct	remaster	replate
reconfine	reelect	refreeze	reinfect	rematch	replay
reconfirm	reembark	refresh	reinflate	remeasure	replead
reconquer	reembody	refront	reinforce	remeet	repledge
reconsign	reembrace	refry	reinform	remelt	replenish
reconsole	reemerge	refuel	reinfuse	remend	replunge
reconsult	reemit	refurbish	reinhabit	remerge	repolish

repot
repour
repower
repress
reprice
reprint
reprobe
reprocess
reproduce
reproof
republish
repurify
repursue
requalify
reradiate
reread
rerecord
rerise
reroll
reroute
rerun
resaddle
resaid
resail
resale
resalute
resample
resaw
resay
rescore
rescreen
reseal
research
reseat
resee
reseed
reseek
reseen
reseize
reseizure
resell
resend
resent
reset
resettle
resew
reshape
resharpen
reshine
reship

reshoe
reshoot
reshow
resift
resilver
resituate
resize
resketch
resmelt
resmooth
resold
resolder
resole
resorb
resort
resought
resow
respace
respade
respeak
respecify
respell
resplice
resplit
respread
respring
restack
restaff
restage
restamp
restart
restate
restitch
restock
restore
restretch
restrike
restring
restrive
restruck
restrung
restudy
restuff
restyle
resubject
resubmit
resume
resummon
resupply
resurge

resurgent
resurvey
retack
retailor
retake
retape
retaste
retax
reteach
retear
retell
retemper
retest
retestify
rethink
rethread
retie
retime
retint
retitle
retold
retool
retouch
retrace
retrack
retrain
retread
retrial
retrieve
retrim
retry
retune
return
retwist
retying
retype
reunify
reunite
reusable
reuse
reutilize
reutter
revalue
revarnish
reverify
revest
revibrate
revictual
review
revisit

revoice
revote
rewake
rewaken
rewan
rewarm
rewash
rewax
reweave
reach To arrive at
react To be affected
reactor A circuit element
read To make a study of
real Actual
realgar A mineral
really In reality
realm A kingdom
realty Real estate
ream A quantity of paper
reap To harvest
rear The hind part
rearward Directed toward the rear
reason Intelligence
reave To plunder
reb A confederate soldier
rebate To return part of
rebato A collar
rebec, rebeck A musical instrument
rebel One who is in rebellion
rebozo A scarf
rebuff To reject
rebuke To criticize
rebus, *pl* **-buses** A puzzle
rebut To refute
rebuttal The act of rebutting
recant To make a formal retraction
recede To withdraw
receipt To mark as having been
  paid
receive To get
recent New
recept A mental image
receptor A nerve ending specialized to receive stimuli
recess An alcove
rechauffe Heated leftover food
recherche Rare
recipe A formula
recipient One who receives
recision The act of rescinding

reweigh
reweld
rewiden
rewin
rewind
rewire
rewoke
rewoken
rewon

reword
rework
rewound
rewove
rewoven
rewrap
rewrite
rewrought
rezone

262

recital   A performance
reck   To be concerned about
reckless   Careless
reckon   To regard as
reclame   Publicity
recline   To lie down
recluse   A hermit
recognize   To acknowledge
recoil   To draw back
recommend   To advise
reconcile   To resolve a dispute
recondite   Concealed
reconvey   To convey back to a previous owner
record   Data on a particular topic
recoup   To make up for
recourse   Turning to someone for help
recreant   Cowardly
recreate   To refresh
recrement   Refuse
recruit   To engage for military duty
rectal   Pertaining to the rectum
rectangle   A parallelogram with a right angle
rectify   To correct
rectitude   Rightness
recto   The right-hand page of a book
rector   A clergyman in charge of a parish
rectory   The house in which a rector lives
rectrix, *pl* **rectrices**   A feather of a bird's tail
rectum, *pl* **-tums** or **-ta**   The terminal portion of the large intestine
rectus, *pl* **-ti**   A straight muscle
recumbent   Resting
recur   To happen again
recurrent   Returning regularly
recurvate   Curved backward
recurve   To curve backward
recusant   A dissenter
red   A color
redact   To revise
redan   A fortification
redbait   To denounce as Communist
redbird   A species of bird
redbreast   A robin
redbrick   Pertaining to various British universities
redbud   A species of tree
redbug   A chigger
redcap   A porter
redcoat   A British soldier during the American Revolution
redd   To put in order
rede   To counsel
redear   A sunfish
redeem   To fulfill
redeye   A danger signal
redfin   A species of minnow
redfish   A species of fish
redhead   A person with red hair
redia   A larval stage of many trematodes
redneck *Slang*   A poor white Southerner
redolent   Fragrant
redouble   To repeat
redoubt   A fortification
redound   To recoil
redox   A chemical reaction
redpoll   A species of bird
redress   To remedy
redroot   A species of plant
redshank   A wading bird
redshirt *Slang*   An inactive roster player
redstart   A species of bird
redtop   A type of grass
reduce   To diminish
reductase   An enzyme
redundant   Superfluous
redux   That has been revived
redwing   A species of bird
redwood   A tall evergreen tree
reed   A species of tall grass
reedbird   The bobolink
reedbuck   An African antelope
reedling   A marsh bird
reef   To reduce the size of a sail
reek   To give off an unpleasant odor
reel   To stagger
reeve   To fasten by passing through something
ref   Referee
refect   To refresh
refer   To direct
referee   To supervise

reference Connection
referent Something referred to
refine To purify
reflect To throw back from a surface
reflex Turned backward
refluent Flowing back
reflux A flowing back
reforest To replant
reform To improve·
refract To deflect
refrain To hold back
refuge Shelter
refugee One seeking refuge
refulgent Brilliant
refund To give back
refuse To decline
refute To prove to be wrong
regal Royal
regale To delight
regalia Rights and privileges belonging to a king
regard To have affection for
regardant Looking backward, with the head in profile
regatta A boat race
regelate To freeze ice after a pressure has been removed
regency The office of a regent
regent One who rules in the place of a sovereign
reges Plural of rex
regicide The killing of a king
regime A system of government
regimen A regulated system
regiment A military unit
regina, pl **-nae** or **-nas** Queen
reginal Queenly
region An area
regisseur The director of a ballet
register To enroll
registrar One who keeps records in a college
registry Registration
reglet A narrow, flat molding
regnal Of a king
regnant Ruling
regolith A layer of loose rock
regorge To disgorge
regress To go back

regret To feel sorry
regular Normal
regulate To control
regulus, pl **-li** Metal that sinks to the bottom of a furnace
rehearse To practice
reify To regard as real
reign To exercise sovereign power
reimburse To repay
rein A part of a bridle
reindeer A large deer
reject To repudiate
rejoice To fill with joy
relapse To fall back
relate To tell
relation A relative
relative Related
relaxant A drug
relaxin A female hormone
release To set free
relegate To assign
relent To become gentler
relevant Pertinent
reliant Having reliance
relic A keepsake
relict A plant species surviving in a changed environment
relief Ease from pain
relieve To ease
relievo The projection of figures from a flat background
religion Belief in a divine power
relish Pleasure
relucent Shining
reluct To show resistance
rely To depend upon
rem A quantity of ionizing radiation
remain To stay
remand To send back
remarque A mark on an engraved plate
remedial Intended to correct something
remedy To cure
remember To think of again
remex, pl **remiges** A flight feather of a bird's wing
remind To cause to remember
reminisce To recollect

remise To give up a claim to
remiss Negligent
remit To transmit
remnant A remainder
remora A species of fish
remorse Regret
remote Slight
remove To take away
remuda A herd of horses
renal Pertaining to the kidneys
renascent Showing renewed vigor
rend To split
renegade An outlaw
renege To fail to carry out a promise
reniform Kidney-shaped
renin An enzyme
renitent Resisting pressure
rennet The membrane lining the stomach of unweaned animals
rennin An enzyme
renounce To give up
renovate To make new again
renown Celebrity
rent Payment for the right to occupy property
rente Annual income
rentier One who has fixed income from rents
rep, repp A fabric
repair To fix
repand Having a wavy margin
repartee A witty reply
repast A meal
repeal To withdraw
repel To reject
repent To feel remorse
repertory A repertoire
repetend A refrain
repine To be discontented
replete Gorged
replevin, replevy To regain possession of
replica A copy
reply To give an answer
report To give an account of
repose Relaxation
reposit To store
repossess To take back
repousse A raised design

reprehend To reprove
represent To symbolize
reprieve To give temporary relief
reprimand A severe rebuke
reprise Repetition
reproach To rebuke
reprobate To condemn
reprove To scold
reptant Creeping or crawling
reptile A species of cold-blooded vertebrate
republic A type of government
repudiate To disown
repugn To resist
repulse To repel
repute Reputation
request To ask
requiem A musical composition
require To need
requisite Essential
requite To make return for
reredos A screen behind an altar
rescind To void
rescript An official decree
rescue An act of saving
reseau, *pl* **-seaus** or **-seaux** A screen used in photography
resect To cut away
reseda A species of plant
resemble To be similar
reserve To retain
reservoir A body of water
resh The 20th letter of the Hebrew alphabet
reside To exist
resident One who lives in a place
residual The remainder
residue The remainder of something
residuum Residue
resign To quit
resile To spring back
resin To rub with resin
resinoid Pertaining to resin
resist To oppose
resistor An element in an electric circuit
resolute Unwavering
resolve To make a firm decision about

resonant Pertaining to resonance
resonate To resound
resound To reverberate
resource An available supply
respect A feeling of honor
respire To breathe
respite A rest
respond To answer
response An answer
rest Sleep
rester One who rests
restitute To restore
restive Restless
restore To re-establish
restrain To repress
restrict To hold back
result To occur as a consequence
resume To begin again
resupine Lying on the back
resurrect To raise from the dead
ret To dampen
retable A raised shelf above an
   altar
retail To sell in small quantities
retain To remember
retard To delay
retch To vomit
rete, *pl* **retia** An anatomical mesh
retene A chemical compound
retiary Resembling a web
reticent Reserved
reticle A network of fine lines in an
   optical instrument
reticule A woman's bag
retiform Arranged like a net
retina, *pl* **-nas** or **retinae** A membrane of the eye
retinene A retinal pigment
retinue A group of assistants
retire To retreat
retiree A retired person
retort To reply
retract To take back
retral Reverse
retreat A refuge
retrench To cut down
retroact To react
retrocede To recede
retrofire To ignite
retrofit A change in design

retroflex Turned backward
retrorse Bent backward
retsina A Greek wine
returnee One who returns
retuse Having a rounded apex with
   a small notch
reunion A reuniting
rev To increase the speed of
revamp To renovate
reveal To make known
reveille A signal on a bugle
revel To make merry
revenge Retaliation
revenue Income
revere To regard with respect
reverend Clerical
reverie A daydream
revers A part of a garment
reverse Opposite
revert To return to a former state
revet To protect with a revetment
revetment A facing of masonry
revile To rail against
revise To modify
revive To bring back to life
revoke To cancel
revolt To rebel
revolve To rotate
revolver A gun
revue A musical show
revulsion A feeling of disgust
reward A gift for a special service
rex, *pl* **reges** A king
reynard A fox
rhamnose A methyl pentose
rhapsody A musical composition
rhatany A shrub
rhea A species of flightless bird
rhematic Pertaining to a verb
rhenium A metallic element
rheology The study of the flow of
   matter
rheostat An electrical resistor
rhesus A monkey
rhetor A teacher of rhetoric
rhetoric The study of speech
rheum A discharge from the eye or
   nose
rheumatic Pertaining to
   rheumatism

rhinal   Nasal
rhinitis   Inflammation of the nasal mucous membranes
rhino   A rhinoceros
rhizoid   A rootlike structure
rhizome   A rootlike stem growing underground
rhizopod   A protozoan
rhizopus   A species of fungus
rho   The seventeenth letter of the Greek alphabet
rhodium   A metallic element
rhodora   A shrub of the heath family
rhombic   Having a shape of a rhombus
rhomboid   A geometric shape
rhombus, *pl* **-buses** or **-bi**   A geometric shape
rhonchus, *pl* **-chi**   A rattling, snoring sound
rhubarb   A species of plant
rhumb   A point on a mariner's compass
rhumba   Variant of rumba
rhyme   To compose verse
rhyolite   A volcanic rock
rhythm   A flow with regular recurring elements
rhythmist   One who has a keen sense of rhythm
ria   An inlet
rial   Monetary unit of Iran
riata   A lasso
rib   A curved piece in an arch
ribald   Pertaining to lewd humor
riband   A ribbon
ribband   A part used in ship building
ribbon   A narrow strip of fabric
ribgrass   A weedy plant
ribose   A pentose sugar
ribosome   A spherical particle
ribwort   Variant of ribgrass
rice   A cereal grass
ricebird   A species of bird
rich   Possessing wealth
richen   To make rich
richweed   A plant
ricin   A poisonous protein

rick   A stack of hay
rickets   A disease
rickety   Shaky
rickey   A drink
rickrack   A flat braid used in trimming
richshaw, ricksha   A two-wheeled vehicle
ricochet   To rebound
ricotta   A cottage cheese
rictus   The expanse of the open mouth
rid   To free from something objectionable
riddance   A removal of
riddle   An enigma
ride   To be conveyed in a vehicle
ridge   A long hill
ridicule   To make fun of
ridley   A marine turtle
ridotto   A social gathering in early England
riel   Monetary unit of Cambodia
rife   Prevalent
riff   A repeated musical phrase
riffle   A reef in a stream
riffler   A filing tool
riffraff   Rabble
rifle   A firearm
rift   A cleft
rig   To equip
rigadoon   A dance
rigatoni   A pasta dish
right   Proper
rightism   A conservative political philosophy
rightist   A member of the right
rigid   Stiff
rigmarole   Nonsense
rigor   Hardship
rigorism   Strictness in conduct
rile   To anger
riley   Upset
rill   A small brook
rillet   A small rill
rim   The outer part of a wheel
rime   Hoarfrost
rimose   Full of cracks
rimple   To wrinkle
rind   Outer covering of fruits

ring To encircle

ringbolt An eyebolt with a ring at the head

ringbone A growth on a horse's hoof

ringdove A pigeon

ringent Gaping

ringhals An African snake

ringlet A small circle

ringside A place that provides a close view

ringtail A ring-tailed monkey

ringworm A skin disease

rink An area for skating

rinse To wash lightly

riot An outbreak

rip To slash

riparian Pertaining to the bank of a river

ripcord A cord pulled to release something

ripe Mature

riposte, ripost A quick thrust

ripple A slight wave

ripplet A small ripple

ripply Sounding like ripples

riprap A foundation of stones

ripsaw A type of saw

riptide Opposing tides

rise To get up

risible Inclined to laugh

risk Danger

risotto A rice dish

risque Bordering on indecency

rissole A pastry

rite A ceremonial act

ritter A knight

ritual The form of a ceremony

ritzy *Slang* Elegant

rivage A coast

rival A competitor

rive To tear apart

river A flowing stream of water

riverine Pertaining to a river

riverweed A plant

rivet To fasten

riviere A necklace

rivulet A small stream

riyal Monetary unit of Saudi Arabia

roach A species of fish

road A passageway

roadbed The foundation of a road

roadshow A show by a touring company

roadstead An anchorage place for ships

roadster A type of auto

roadway A road

roam To wander

roan A color

roar To laugh loudly

roast To cook in an oven

rob To steal

robalo A species of marine food fish

robe An outer garment

robin A species of bird

roble An oak

roborant A tonic

robot A humanoid mechanical device

robust Hardy

roc A legendary bird

rochet A linen vestment

rock A stone

rockaby, rockabye Used to lull a baby to sleep

rockaway A carriage

rockery A rock garden

rocket To rise rapidly

rocketeer One who designs rockets

rockfish A species of fish

rockling A species of fish

rockrose A species of plant

rockweed A species of seaweed

rockwork A natural mass of rocks

rococo A style of art

rod A straight, slender piece of some material

rode Past tense of ride

rodent A species of mammal

rodeo An exhibition of cowboy skills

roe Fish eggs

roebuck A male roe deer

roentgen The unit of quantity in measuring radiation

rogation A prayer

rogatory Requesting information

roger The pirate flag
rogue A rascal
roguery Trickery
roguish Mischievous
roil To stir up
roister To swagger
role A part played by an actor
roll To move by turning over and over
rollaway A type of bed
rollback A reduction of prices
rollick To frolic
rollmop A fillet of herring
rollway A chute for rolling logs
romaine A variety of lettuce
roman A style of type
romance A love affair
romaunt A romantic poem
romp To play
rondeau, pl **-deaux** A poem
rondel A rondeau of 14 lines
rondelet A short rondeau
rondo A musical composition
rondure A circle
rood A crucifix
roof The exterior surface covering a building
rooftree A roof beam
rook A dishonest gamester
rookery A breeding place for birds
rookie Slang An inexperienced person
room Living quarters
roomette A compartment in a railroad car
roorback, roorbach A false story devised for political effect
roost A perch on which birds sleep
root The underground part of a plant
rootlet A small root
rootstalk A plant part
rootstock A rootlike stem
rooty Full of roots
rope A lasso
ropewalk The place where ropes are made
ropy Resembling ropes
roque A form of croquet

rorqual A species of whale
rosary A series of prayers
rose A species of shrub
roseate Rose-colored
rosebay A species of shrub
rosebud The bud of a rose
rosebush A shrub that bears roses
rosefish A food fish
roselle A tropical plant
rosemary An evergreen shrub
roseola A skin rash
rosette An ornament made to resemble a rose
rosewood A species of tree
rosin A pine-tree resin
rostellum, pl **-tella** A small beak-like part
roster A list of names
rostrate Having a beaklike part
rostrum, pl **-trums** or **-tra** A place for public speaking
rot To decay
rota A roster
rotary A rotating device
rotate To turn on an axis
rotche, rotch A seabird
rote A musical instrument
rotenone An insecticide
rotgut Slang Low-grade whiskey
rotifer A species of aquatic organism
rotiform Shaped like a wheel
rotl A unit of weight
roto A printing process
rotor A rotating part
rotten Decomposed
rotund Rounded
rotunda A round building
roturier A commoner
rouble Variant of ruble
rouche Variant of ruche
roue A lecherous man
rouge A cosmetic
rough Having an uneven surface
roughcast A coarse plaster
roughdry To dry without ironing
roughhew To shape roughly
roughneck A rowdy person
roughshod Shod with horseshoes that have metal points

roulade   A musical embellishment
rouleau, pl -**leaux** or -**leaus**   A small roll of something
roulette   A gambling game
round   Shaped like a ball
roundel   A curved form
roundelay   A dance
roundlet   A small circle
roundsman   One who makes rounds
roundup   The herding of cattle
roup   A disease of poultry
rouse   To stir up
roust   To rout
rout   A defeat
route   A salesman's territory
router   One that routes
routine   A standard procedure
roux   A mixture of flour and butter
rove   To roam
row   To propel a boat
rowan   The mountain ash
rowboat   A boat propelled by oars
rowdy   Disorderly
rowel   To spur
rowen   A second crop
rowlock   An oarlock
royal   Of a kingdom
royalism   Support of a monarch
rozzer Slang   A policeman
rub   To move over something with pressure and friction
rubasse   A variety of quartz
rubato   Deviating from a strict tempo
rubber   An elastic substance
rubbish   Trash
rubble   Broken pieces of rock
rubdown   A massage
rube Slang   An unsophisticated person
rubella   A disease
rubeola   Measles
rubescent   Reddening
rubicund   Ruddy
rubious   Red
ruble   Russian currency
rubric   A part of a book that appears in red
ruby   A color
ruche   A pleated strip of fine fabric

ruck   To crease
rucksack   A type of knapsack
ruckus   A commotion
ruction   A ruckus
rudd   A freshwater fish
rudder   A blade used to direct a boat
ruddle   Iron ore
ruddock   The robin
ruddy   Rosy
rude   Discourteous
ruderal   A plant growing in poor ground
rudesby   A rude person
rudiment   A basic element
rue   To regret
ruff   A collar
ruffian   A rowdy person
rufous   Reddish
rug   A floor covering
ruga   A fold in the lining of the stomach
rugger   Rugby
rugose   Full of wrinkles
ruin   Total destruction
ruinate   Ruined
ruinous   Destructive
rule   A regulation
rum   An alcoholic liquor
rumba   A dance
rumble   To make a deep, reverberating sound
rumen, pl -**mina** or -**mens**   The first stomach of a ruminant
ruminant   A species of mammal
rummage   To search through
rummer   A large drinking glass
rummy   A card game
rumor, rumour   Hearsay
rump   The hindquarters of an animal
rumple   To wrinkle
rumrunner   One engaged in smuggling liquor
run   To move swiftly
runabout   A small boat
runagate   A vagabond
runaway   One that runs away
runback   A play in football
rune   A mystical poem
rung   Past tense of ring

runlet A rivulet
runnel A brook
runny Tending to flow
runt A small animal
runway An extension of a stage
rupee A monetary unit of India
rupiah A monetary unit of Indonesia
rupture To burst
rural Rustic
rurality The state of being rural
ruse A deception
rush To dash
rushee A college student rushed by a fraternity
rusk A sweetened biscuit

russet A color
rust A coating formed by corrosion
rustic Country life
rustle To make soft sounds
rut To make grooves
rutabaga A plant with an edible root
ruth Compassion
rutilant To have a reddish glow
rutile A mineral
ruttish Lustful
rye A cereal grass
ryegrass A species of grass
rynd An iron support
ryot A tenant farmer

sab To sob
sabbat The witches' Sabbath
saber, sabre A sword
sabin The unit for absorption of sound
sable A carnivorous mammal
sabot A wooden shoe
sabotage Intentional destruction
saboteur One who commits sabotage
sabra A native-born Israeli
sabulous, sabulose Sandy
sac A pouchlike structure
sacaton A native grass
saccade A rapid movement of the eye
saccate Having a pouch
saccharin A sweetener
saccule A small sac
sacculus, *pl* **-li** Saccule

sachem A North American Indian chief
sachet A small bag of perfumed powder
sack A large bag
sackbut A musical instrument
sackcloth A fabric
sacral Pertaining to the sacrum
sacrament A religious rite
sacred Made holy
sacrifice The act of giving up something of value
sacrilege The desecration of something held sacred
sacring Consecration of the bread and wine of the Eucharist
sacristan, sacrist A sexton
sacristy A vestry
sacrum, *pl* **-cra** A bone of the pelvis
sad Unhappy

271

saddle A leather seat for a rider
saddlebow Part of a saddle
saddler One who works with saddles
saddlery Tack
sade, sadhe The eighteenth letter of the Hebrew alphabet
sadhu, saddhu A Hindu holy man
sadiron A flatiron
sadism Getting pleasure from inflicting pain
sadist One marked by sadism
safari An expedition
safe Secure
safeguard A precaution
safelight A type of lamp
saffron A color
safranine, safranin A dye
safrole A liquid used in making soap
sag To droop
saga A long narrative
sagacity Shrewdness
sagamore A North American Indian chief
sage A wise, elderly person
sagebrush A species of aromatic plant
sagger, saggar A clay casing
sagittal Resembling an arrowhead
sago An edible starch
saguaro, sahuaro A cactus
sahib A title of respect in colonial India
said Past tense of say
saiga An antelope
sail To travel by water in a sailboat
sailboat A boat propelled by sail
sailcloth Fabric for making sails
sailfish A species of fish
sailor One who serves in the navy
sailplane A light glider
saimin A soup
sain To make the sign of the cross
sainfoin A perennial plant
saint A very holy person
saintdom The condition of being a saint
sainthood The condition of being a saint

saith Third person singular present indicative of say
sake Purpose
saker A falcon
sal Salt
salaam A Moslem greeting
salacious Bawdy
salad A dish of fruits or raw vegetables
salami A spiced sausage
salary Compensation for services
sale A selling of property
salep A meal ground from orchid roots
saleratus Baking soda
salic Pertaining to igneous rocks
salicin A chemical compound
salient Prominent
salify To make salty
salina A salt marsh
saline Salty
saliva Fluid secreted by the salivary glands
sallet A medieval helmet
sallow Of a pale complexion
sally A sudden rush
salmi, salmis A spiced food dish
salmon A species of food fish
salol A chemical compound
salon A drawing room for entertaining
saloon A tavern
saloop A hot drink
salp, salpa A species of tunicate
salpinx The Fallopian tube
salsa Latin American dance music
salsify A plant
salt Sodium chloride
saltant Jumping or dancing
saltbox A type of house design
saltbush A species of plant
saltern A saltworks
saltine A cracker
saltire A heraldic design
saltpeter, saltpetre Potassium nitrate
saltwort A species of plant
salud A toast
saluki A breed of dog
salutary Remedial

salute To greet
salvage To save
salvation Being saved from danger
salve A medicinal ointment
salver A serving platter
salvia A species of plant
salvo A concerted discharge of firearms
salvor A salvager
samara A dry, one-seeded fruit
samarium A metallic element
samba A dance
sambar, sambur An Asian deer
same Identical
samekh, samech, samek The fifteenth letter of the Hebrew alphabet
samiel Variant of simoom
samisen A Japanese musical instrument
samite A fabric
samlet A young salmon
samovar A metal urn
samp A porridge
sampan A flat-bottomed skiff
samphire A species of plant
sample A specimen
samsara A continuing cycle in which the same soul is reborn over and over
samurai A Japanese warrior
sanctify To consecrate
sanction A decree
sanctity Godliness
sanctuary A sacred place
sanctum, pl **-tums** or **-ta** A holy place
sand Loose, granular particles of disintegrated rock

The following words are listed without definition (see Introduction):

sandbag	sandhog	sandpile
sandbank	sandier	sandpiper
sandbar	sandiest	sandpit
sandblast	sandlike	sandstone
sandbox	sandman	sandworm
sander	sandpaper	sandy

sandal A type of shoe
sandarac A North African tree

sandblind Partially blind
sandbur A species of grass
sandhi Sound modification
sandwich To place in layers
sandwort A species of plant
sane Rational
sangaree A beverage
sangh An association in India
sangria An alcoholic beverage
sanguine A red color
sanicle A species of plant
sanies A discharge from a wound
sanitary Clean
sanity Saneness
sannup A married male American Indian
sans Without
santonin A chemical compound
sap Plant juice
sapajou A monkey
saphead *Slang* A stupid person
saphena, pl **-nae** A vein of the leg
sapid Savory
sapient Wise
sapling A young tree
sapodilla An evergreen tree
saponify To convert into soap
saponin A soapy solution from plants
saponite A mineral
sapor, sapour Flavor
sapphire A gemstone
saprobe An organism that gets its nourishment from decaying organic matter
sapropel Aquatic sludge
sapsago A variety of cheese
sapsucker A woodpecker
sapwood Newly formed outer wood
saraband A dance
saran A resin used in making wrapping material
sarape Variant of serape
sarcasm A contemptuous remark
sarcenet A fabric
sarcoid Pertaining to flesh
sarcoma, pl **-mata** or **-mas** A malignant tumor
sarcous Consisting of flesh

sard, sardius A variety of quartz
sardine A species of herring
sardonic Cynical
sardonyx A variety of onyx
sargasso A seaweed
sarge Sergeant
sari An outer garment of India
sarong A garment worn in the Pacific islands
sartorial Relating to a tailor
sartorius A muscle of the thigh
sash A frame in which glass is set
sashay To strut
saskatoon A shrub
sass Back talk
sassaby An African antelope
sassafras A tree
sassy Impudent
sastruga, *pl* **-gi** A ridge of snow
satang Monetary unit of Thailand
satanic Wicked
satchel A small bag
sate To indulge
sateen A fabric
satellite A moon
satem Pertaining to a group of Indo-European languages
satiable Capable of being satiated
satiate To satisfy fully
satiety The state of being satiated
satin A fabric
satinet A fabric
satinpod A plant
satire A type of literary work
satisfy To assure
satori Spiritual enlightenment sought by Zen Buddhists
satrap A subordinate ruler
satrapy The territory under the rule of a satrap
saturant Impregnating
saturate To soak
saturnine Gloomy
satyr A lecher
sauce Anything that adds flavor
saucebox An impertinent child
saucepan A cooking pot
sauger A freshwater fish
saul Soul
sauna A Finnish bath

saunter To stroll
saurel A marine fish
saurian A species of reptile
sauropod A species of dinosaur
saury A species of fish
sausage Seasoned meat in a casing
saute To fry lightly in fat
sauterne A dessert wine
savage Barbaric
savagery The act of being savage
savanna, savannah A treeless plain
savant A wise man
save To store
saveloy A highly seasoned sausage
savin, savine A species of shrub
savior, saviour A person that saves
savor, savour To taste
savvy *Slang* To understand
saw To cut
sawbones *Slang* A surgeon
sawbuck A sawhorse
sawdust Particles of wood produced in sawing
sawfish A species of fish
sawfly A species of insect
sawhorse A rack supporting a piece of wood
sawmill A lumber mill
sawn Past participle of saw
sawyer A person employed at sawing wood
sax Saxophone
saxatile Living among rocks
saxhorn A brass wind instrument
saxifrage A species of plant
saxony A fabric
saxophone A wind instrument
saxtuba A bass saxhorn
say To speak
sayonara Farewell
sayyid, sayid A Moslem title of respect
scab A crust covering a healing wound
scabbard A sheath for a sword
scabble To dress stone
scabies A skin disease
scabrous Scaly
scad A species of marine fish
scaffold A platform used in

construction

scagliola An imitation marble

scalade, scalado Variants of escalade

scalage The estimate of lumber in a log

scalar Involving a scale

scalare The anglefish

scalawag A rascal

scald To burn with hot liquid or steam

scale An instrument for weighing

scalene Having three unequal sides

scall A scaly eruption of the skin

scallion A green onion

scallop To bake in a casserole with milk and bread crumbs

scalp The skin covering the head

scalpel A knife

scammony A plant

scamp A rascal

scampi Large shrimp

scan To scrutinize

scandal A disgrace

scandent Climbing

scandia Scandium oxide

scandium A metallic element

scansion The analysis of verse into metrical feet and rhythm patterns

scant Meager

scape The shaft of a column

scapegoat A person bearing blame for others

scaphoid Boat-shaped

scapose Consisting of a scape

scapula, *pl* **-las** or **-lae** A shoulder bone

scapular A garment worn by monks

scar A mark left by a wound

scarab A beetle

scarce Not plentiful

scarcity Shortage

scare To frighten

scarecrow A figure used to scare birds

scarf, *pl* **scarfs** or **scarves** A piece of cloth worn around the neck

scarfskin The outermost layer of skin

scarify To criticize

scarious, scariose Thin, dry and membranous

scarlet A color

scarp A cliff

scat To go away fast

scatback *Slang* A small, fast running back

scathe Harm

scatter To disperse

scaup A diving duck

scavenge To collect

scenario An outline of a dramatic work

scenarist A writer of screenplays

scend To be heaved upward

scene The scenery for a play

scenery Stage backdrops

scent A perfume

scepter, sceptre A staff held by rulers

schatchen A Jewish matchmaker

schav A chilled soup

schedule A timetable

scheelite A mineral

schema, *pl* **-mata** An outline

schematic A procedural diagram

scheme A plot

scherzo, *pl* **-zos** or **-zi** A lively musical movement

schiller A bronzelike luster in certain minerals

schilling Monetary unit of Austria

schism A split in an organized group

schist A type of rock

schizoid Having schizophrenia

schizont A cell that multiplies by fission

schizopod A species of shrimplike crustacean

schlemiel *Slang* A bungling person

schlep, schlepp *Slang* A clumsy person

schlieren Small streaks in igneous rocks

schlock *Slang* Trash

schmaltz, schmalz *Slang* Highly sentimental

schmeer, schmear *Slang* A bribe

schmo, schmoe *Slang* A dolt
schmoose, schmooze *Slang* To gossip
schmuck *Slang* A jerk
schnapps A strong alcoholic liquo
schnauzer A breed of dog
schnitzel A veal cutlet
schnook *Slang* One easily cheated
schnorrer *Slang* One who lives by sponging off others
schnozzle *Slang* The nose
scholar A learned person
scholium, *pl* **-ums** or **-lia** An explanatory note
school A place of learning
schoolman A scholar
schooner A ship
schorl A mineral
schtick, schtik Variants of shtick
schuss To make a fast straight run in skiing
schwa A vowel sound
sciatic Pertaining to sciatica
sciatica Neuralgic pain in the hip
science A branch of study
sciential Skillful
scilicet Namely
scimitar, scimiter A sword
scintilla A particle
sciolism Superficial knowledge
scion A descendant
scirrhus, *pl* **scirrhi** or **-huses** A cancerous growth
scissile Capable of being cut easily
scission The act of cutting
scissor To cut with scissors
sciuroid Resembling a squirrel
sclaff To scrape the ground before hitting the golf ball
sclera The outer coating of the eyeball
sclerite An outer plate of an arthropod
scleritis Inflammation of the sclera
scleroid Hardened
scleroma, *pl* **-mata** A hardened patch of bodily tissue
sclerosis, *pl* **-ses** A hardening of a body part
sclerous Hardened

scoff To laugh at
scofflaw One who habitually breaks the law
scold To reprimand
scolex, *pl* **-leces** or **-lices** Part of a tapeworm
scollop Varient of scallop
sconce A decorative bracket for candles
scone A pastry
scoop To dip
scoot To hurry
scop A minstrel
scope Extent
scopula, *pl* **-lae** A tuft of hairs
scorch To char
score To gain a point
scoria, *pl* **scoriae** Slag
scorn Contempt
scorpion A species of arachnid
scotch To stifle
scoter A species of diving duck
scotoma A blind area within the visual field
scotopia Ability to see in dim light
scoundrel A villain
scour To clean
scourge To punish
scouse A stew
scout A member of the Boy Scouts
scow A flat-bottomed boat
scowl To look angry
scrabble To struggle
scrag A stunted tree
scraggly Ragged
scram *Slang* Get out in a hurry
scramble To throw together
scrap A fragment
scrapbook A book for pictures
scrape To rub
scrapple A mush
scratch To rub
scrawl To write hastily
scrawny Skinny
screak To shriek
scream To utter a piercing cry
scree A slope of loose rock
screech A high-pitched piercing cry
screed A tiresome speech

screen A room divider
screw A metal fastener
screwball A type of pitch
screwy Slang Crazy
scribble To write hastily
scribe A copyist
scrim A fabric
scrimp To economize
scrimshaw A carved piece of ivory
scrip A small scrap of paper
scripsit He (or she) wrote it
script A style of writing
scripture A sacred writing
scrivener A scribe
scrod A young cod or haddock
scrofula A disease of the lymphatic glands
scroll A roll of parchment
scrollwork Ornamental work with a scroff motif
scrooch, scrootch To crouch
scrotum, pl -**ta** or -**tums** The pouch of skin holding the testicles
scrounge To forage
scrub To rub hard
scruff The back of the neck
scruffy Shabby
scrum, scrummage A play formation in Rugby
scrunch To crunch
scruple Principle
scrutable Open to being understood
scrutiny A critical look
scuba Equipment worn by divers
scud To move swiftly
scudo, pl -**di** A former Italian monetary unit
scuff To shuffle
scull A type of oar
scullery A room joining the kitchen
scullion A kitchen servant
sculpin A species of fish
sculpsit He (or she) sculptured it
sculpt To sculpture
sculptor One who sculptures
sculpture The art of shaping figures
scum Impure matter
scunner A strong aversion

scup A food fish
scurf Dry skin
scurrile, scurril Scurrilous
scurry To hurry
scurvy A disease
scut A stubby tail
scutage A tax
scutate Shaped like a shield
scutch To separate the fibers
scute A horny plate
scutter To scuttle
scutum, pl -**ta** A scute
scythe A mowing implement
sea A large body of salt water
seaboard The seacoast
seaborne Afloat
seacoast Land bordering the sea
seadog A fogbow
seafarer A sailor
seafood Fish
seafowl A sea bird
seagirt Surrounded by the sea
seagoing Seafaring
seal An emblem
sealant A sealing agent
sealery The occupation of hunting seals
sealskin The fur of a seal
seam A line formed by sewing two fabrics together
seaman A sailor
seamark A guide in navigation
seamount An underwater mountain
seamster A tailor
seamy Sordid
seance A spiritualist meeting
seaplant An airplane with floats
seaport A harbor
seaquake An undersea earthquake
sear To char
search To explore
seascape A picture of the sea
seashell The shell of a marine mollusk
seashore Land by the sea
seaside The seashore
season A period of time
seat A chair
seaward Toward the sea
seaware Seaweed used as fertilizer

seaway A sea route
seaweed A species of marine algae
sebum Secretion of the sebaceous glands
sec, secant A straight line intersecting a curve at two or more points
secco The art of painting on dry plaster
secede To withdraw
secern To discriminate
secession The act of seceding
seclude To make private
second A unit of time
secondo, pl -**di** The lower part in a piano duet
secret Kept hidden
secrete To conceal
secretin A hormone
sect A group united by common beliefs
sectary A member of a sect
sectile Capable of being cut smoothly
section A portion
sector A division of something
secular A layman
secund Arranged on one side of an axis
secure Safe
sedan A type of auto
sedate Composed
sedge A species of plant
sedile, pl **sedilia** A church seat
sediment Matter that settles to the bottom
sedition The stirring up of rebellion against a government
seduce To entice
sedulous Diligent
sedum A species of plant
see To visualize
seecatch An adult male fur seal
seed A beginning
seek To search for
seel To stitch closed the eyes of
seem To appear
seep To ooze
seepage The act of seeping
seer A prophet

seeress A female seer
seesaw An up-and-down movement
seethe To be excited
segment To divide
segno, pl -**gni** A musical sign
sego A plant
segregate To separate
seicento The 17th century
seiche An oscillation of water
seidel A beer mug
seignior, seigneur A feudal lord
seine A fishing net
seism An earthquake
seismic Caused by an earthquake
seismism The phenomena involved in earthquakes
seize To grab
seizin, seisin Legal possession
selah A word of unknown meaning, signifying pause
seldom Rarely
select To pick out
selectee One who is selected
selectman A town official
selector The person who selects
selenate A chemical salt
selenite A variety of gypsum
selenium A nonmetallic element
self The individual
selfhood Individuality
selfish Egotistic
selfsame The very same
selfward Toward oneself
sell To offer for sale
sellout An event for which all seats have been sold
selsyn A remote-control device
seltzer Carbonated mineral water
selvage, selvedge The edge of a fabric woven so that the edge will not ravel
semantic Pertaining to meaning
semaphore A system of flag signaling
sematic Serving as a warning of danger
semblance A resemblance
seme A Heraldic design
sememe The meaning of a

278

morpheme

semen Secretion of the male reproductive system

semester A division of an academic year

semi A large freight trailer truck

semiarid Characterized by little rainfall

semicolon A punctuation mark

semifit Relating to the condition of the body

semihard Partly hard

semimat Having a slighter luster

seminal Containing seed

seminar A course of advanced study

seminary A theological school

semiology The science of sign language

semiotic Relating to semantics

semipro Semiprofessional

semiraw Partly raw

semisoft Soft but firm

semitone A half tone

semolina A product of wheat used for pasta

semplice Plainly, in music

sempre A music direction

sen The 100th part of a yen

senarius, *pl* **-narii** A verse containing six metrical feet

senary Having six parts

senate The upper house of Congress

senator A member of the senate

send To dispatch

sendal A fabric

sendoff A celebration for someone leaving

senega A medicinal root

senescent Elderly

senile Exhibiting infirmities of old age

senility The state of being senile

senior A student in his fourth year

senna A species of plant

sennet A call on a trumpet signaling actors

sennight A week

sennit Plaited material for making hats

senopia Improvement of near vision

senor, *pl* **senores** A Spanish title of courtesy

senora The Spanish title of courtesy for a married woman

senorita A Spanish title of courtesy for an unmarried woman

sensate To sense

sensation The faculty of perception

sense A capacity to understand

senseless Meaningless

sensible Aware

sensor A device that responds to a stimulus

sensual Suggesting sexuality

sentence To pass sentence upon

sentient The mind

sentiment A view

sentinel A sentry

sentry A guard

sepal Any of the leaflike parts of the calyx

sepaloid, sepaline Resembling a sepal

separate To divide

sepia A dark brown pigment

sepoy A native soldier

seppuku A form of Japanese suicide

sepsis A poisoned state caused by bacteria in the body

sept A clan

septal Pertaining to a septum

septate Having a septum

septenary Pertaining to the number seven

septet A group of seven

septic Causing sepsis

septum, *pl* **-ta** A partition

septuple Containing seven

sepulcher, sepulchre A burial vault

sepulture A sepulcher

sequel A continuation

sequela, *pl* **-lae** Something that follows

sequence A succession

sequent Subsequent

sequester To segregate

sequin A spangle

sequoia A large evergreen tree

sera Plural of serum

serac A mass broken off of a glacier

seraglio A sultan's palace

serape A poncho

seraph, pl **-aphs** or **aphim** or **-aphin** A celestial being

sere Dry

serenade A musical composition

serene Tranquil

serf A person in servitude

serge A fabric

sergeant, serjeant A rank

serial Arranged in a series

seriate Arranged in rows

seriatim In a series

sericeous Like silk

sericin A type of protein

seriema A cranelike bird

series An arrangement of events

serif A fine line finishing off the main stroke of a letter

serigraph A type of print

serin A species of bird

serine An amino acid

serious Done in earnest

sermon A religious discourse

serology The study of serum

serosa, pl **-sas** or **-sae** A serous membrane

serous Containing serum

serow A species of antelope

serpent A snake

serpigo A spreading skin eruption

serranid A species of fish

serrate Having toothlike projections

serried Crowded

serrulate Having notches along the edge

serum, pl **-rums** or **sera** Blood and other vital bodily fluids, and their constituent parts

serval A wild cat

servant One who performs domestic services

serve To work for

service A religious rite

servile Submissive

servitor An attendant

sesame A plant

sesamoid Of a small bone

sessile Not free-moving

session A meeting of a judicial body

sesterce A coin of ancient Rome

sestet A stanza of six lines

sestina A verse form

set To place

seta, pl **setae** A stiff hair

setback A defeat

setiform Having the form of a bristle

setline A type of fishing line

setoff A counterclaim

setose Setaceous

setscrew A regulating screw

settee A sofa

settle To establish

settlings Sediment

setup Bearing

seven The cardinal number 7

sevenfold Consisting of seven parts

seventeen The cardinal number 17

seventh The ordinal number seven in a series

sever To dissolve

severe Strict

sew To fashion with a needle and thread

sewage Waste matter

sewer A conduit for carrying off sewage

sewerage A system of sewers

sewn Past participle of sew

sex The character of being male or female

sexennial Of six years

sexily In a sexy manner

sexiness The state of being sexy

sexism Exploitation of one sex by the other

sexology The study of sexual behavior

sexpot *Slang* A woman who has great sex appeal

sext The fourth of the canonical hours

280

sextan Occurring every six days
sextant A navigational instrument
sextet A musical composition for six performers
sextile The position of two heavenly bodies sixty degrees apart
sexton A maintenance man in a church
sextuple To multiply by six
sexy Erotic
sferics The study of atmospherics
sforzando Strongly accented
sgraffito, pl **-fiti** A method of producing a design on ceramics
sh Used to urge silence
shabby Worn-out
shack A shanty
shackle A manacle
shacko Variant of shako
shad A species of fish
shadbush A species of shrub
shaddock A tropical tree
shade To screen from light
shadfly The mayfly
shadow A phantom
shadowbox To spar with an imaginary opponent
shady Shaded
shaft A spear
shag To make shaggy
shagbark A hickory tree
shagreen A variety of leather
shah The former ruler of Iran
shaitan An evil being
shake To vibrate
shakedown Blackmail
shakeup A reorganization
shako A military hat
shale A fissile rock
shall To express futurity
shalloon A fabric
shallop A boat
shallot A plant
shallow Not deep
shalom Peace
shalt Second person singular present tense of shall
sham Empty pretense
shaman A medicine man among certain North American Indians

shamas, shammes, shammas The candle used to light the other candles in a Hanuka menorah
shamble To walk awkwardly
shame Disgrace
shammer One who shams
shammy Variant of chamois
shampoo To wash
shamrock A species of plant
shamus Slang A policeman
shanghai To kidnap
shank A part of the human leg
shantung A fabric
shanty A shack
shape A contour
shapeup A method of selecting a work crew
shard A piece of broken pottery
share A portion
sharif Variant of sherif
shark A species of marine fish
sharkskin A fabric
sharp Distinct
sharpie A fishing boat
shatter To ruin
shave To remove hair from
shavetail Slang A second lieutenant
shaw A thicket
shawl A cloth worn over the head and shoulders
shawm A double-reed wind instrument
shay A chaise
shazam An exclamation used to accompany the sudden appearance or disappearance of something
she A female
shea An African tree
sheaf, pl **sheaves** An archer's quiver of arrows
shear To remove the fleece from
shearling A young sheep
sheatfish A catfish
sheath A case for a knife
sheathe To put into a sheath
sheave To gather
shebang A situation
shebeen A place where liquor is sold without a license

shed   A small building
sheen   Shininess
sheep   A species of horned ruminant mammal
sheepcote   A sheepfold
sheepfold   A pen for sheep
sheepish   Embarrassed
sheer   Transparent
sheet   Material used on a bed
sheik, sheikh   An Arab chief
sheikdom   The area ruled by a sheik
shekel   An ancient unit of weight
sheldrake   A species of duck
shelf   A flat structure used to hold objects
shell   The outer covering of various organisms
shellac, shellack   A thin varnish
shellback   An experienced sailor
shellbark   The shagbark
shellfire   Artillery fire
shellfish   A species of aquatic animals having a shell
shelta   An esoteric jargon
shelter   A refuge
sheltie   A Shetland pony
shelve   To postpone
sheol   Hell
shepherd   One who herds sheep
sherbet   A frozen dessert
sherd   Variant of shard
sherif   An Arab prince
sheriff   A law-enforcement officer
sheroot   Variant of cheroot
sherry   A wine
shew   Show
shield   Protective armor
shieling   A pasture
shift   To switch
shifty   Crafty
shikar   To hunt
shikaree, shikarree, shikari   A big game hunter
shill *Slang*   A gambler's confederate
shim   To level
shimmer   To glimmer
shimmy   A dance
shin   The tibia
shinbone   The tibia
shindig   A celebration

shindy   A commotion
shine   To glisten
shingle   A small signboard
shinleaf   A woodland plant
shinny   A form of hockey
ship   A vessel of considerable size
shipload   Cargo for a ship
shipman   A sailor
shipmate   A fellow sailor
shipment   Cargo
shipshape   Orderly
shipway   A ship canal
shipworm   A species of wormlike marine mollusk
shire   A county of Great Britain
shirk   To put off
shirr   To gather cloth into rows
shirt   A garment
shitah   A hardwood tree
shittim   The wood of the shittah
shiv *Slang*   A knife
shiva   A period of mourning
shivaree   Variant of charivari
shive   A shallow cork
shiver   To shudder
shmo   Variant of schmo
shoal   A place where water is shallow
shoat   A young pig
shock   A heavy blow
shoddy   Cheap material
shoe   A covering for the foot
shoebill   A wading bird
shoehorn   A device to help slip on a shoe
shoelace   A cord used for lacing shoes
shoetree   A form inserted into a shoe
shofar, *pl* **-fars** or **shofroth**   A trumpet made from a ram's horn
shogun   A former Japanese military leader
shoji   A Japanese paper screen
shone   Past tense of shine
shoo   To drive away
shoofly   A child's rocker
shooin   One who is expected to win easily
shook   Past tense of shake

282

shoon   Plural of shoe
shoot   To fire a weapon
shop, shoppe   A small store
shophar   Variant of shofar
shoptalk   Talk concerning one's business
shopworn   Frayed
shoran   A navigational system
shore   A coast
shorn   Alternate past participle of shear
short   Not long
shortage   Deficit
shortcake   A dessert
shorthand   A system of speed writing
shorthorn   A breed of cattle
shortia   A species of plant
shortstop   A player in baseball
shot   The firing of a gun
shote   Variant of shoat
shotgun   A type of gun
shott   A closed basin
shotten   Having recently spawned
should   Duty
shoulder   The part of the body between the neck and the upper arm
shouldst   Second person singular past tense of shall
shout   A loud cry
shove   To push rudely
shovel   A tool for digging
shoveler   One who shovels
show   To point out
showboat   A boat containing a theater
showbread   The twelve loaves of bread placed at the altar in the Temple as a token offering every Sabbath
showcase   A display case
showdown   An event that forces a conclusion
shower   A brief rain
showgirl   A chorus girl
showoff   An exhibitionist
shrapnel   Shell fragments
shred   To cut into shreds
shrew   A species of mammal

shrewd   Astute
shriek   An outcry
shrieval   Pertaining to a sheriff
shrift   The act of shriving
shrike   A species of bird
shrill   To scream
shrimp   A species of marine decapod crustacean
shrine   A hallowed place
shrink   To contract
shrive   To confess
shrivel   To shrink
shroud   A cloth used in burial
shrub   A woody plant
shrug   To make a gesture of doubt
shrunk   Past tense of shrink
shtetl, *pl* **shtetlach**   A Jewish community
shtick *Slang*   A special talent
shuck   The outer covering
shudder   To tremble
shuffle   To scuffle
shul   Variant of synagogue
shun   To keep away from
shunpike   A side road
shunt   To turn aside
shush   To demand silence
shut   To close
shutdown   A temporary closing
shuteye *Slang*   Sleep
shutoff   A device that shuts off something else
shutout   A game in which one team fails to score points
shuttle   A vehicle making frequent stops
shy   Bashful
shylock   An exacting creditor
shyster *Slang*   An unscrupulous person
si   Yes
sial   A type of rock formation
siamang   A gibbon
siamese   A water pipe with a double connection
sib   A kinsman
sibilant   Making a hissing sound
sibilate   To hiss
sibling   A brother or sister
sibyl   A prophetess

sibylline, sibylic, sibyllic Prophetic
sic Thus
sick Ill
sickbay Hospital of a ship
sickbed A sick person's room and bed
sickle An implement for cutting
siddur A Jewish prayer book
side One of the opponents in a contest
sidearm Thrown with a sideways sweep
sideband A radio frequency band
sidekick *Slang* A partner
sideling Sloping
sidelong Sideways
sideman A musician
sidereal Stellar
siderite A mineral
sideshow A small show offered in addition to the main attraction
sideslip To slip to one side
sidespin A rotary motion that spins a ball
sideward Directed toward one side
sidle To move sideways
siege To try to capture
sienna A type of clay
sierra A mountain range
siesta A rest
sieve To sift
sift To put through a sieve
sigh To mourn
sight The fact of seeing
sigil A seal
sigma The eighteenth letter of the Greek alphabet
sigmoid Having the shape of the letter S
sign An indicator
signal A message
signature The act of signing one's name
signet A seal
signify To denote
signor, *pl* **signori** or **-gnors** Italian title of courtesy
signora, *pl* **sognore** or **-ras** Italian title of courtesy for a married woman
signore, *pl* **signori** Signor
silage Fodder
silence Stillness
silent Quiet
silenus, *pl* **-ni** A woodland deity
silesia A fabric
silex Silica
silica The dioxide of silicon
silicic Derived from silica
silicide A silicon compound
silicle A short, fat silique
silicon A nonmetallic element
silicone A silicon compound
silique A type of seed pod
silk Fiber produced by silkworms
silkweed Milkweed
silkworm A species of caterpillar
sill The base of a window
silly Foolish
silo A structure for storing fodder
siloxane A chemical compound
silt Sedimentary material
silurid A species of catfish
silva Variant of sylva
silvan Variant of sylvan
silver A metallic element
silverfish A species of fish
silverly With a silvery appearance
silvern Silvery
silverrod A plant
silvics The study of forests
sima Rock material of the earth's inner crust
simian An ape
similar Related in appearance
simile A figure of speech
simitar Variant of scimitar
simlin Variant of cymling
simmer To cook below the boiling point
simnel A bread
simoleon *Slang* A dollar
simoniac One who practices simony
simonize To clean and wax
simony The buying or selling of sacred things
simoom, simoon A wind of the Sahara

simp *Slang* A simpleton
simpatico Compatible
simper A silly smile
simple Easy
simpleton A fool
simplex Not complex
simplist Given to simplistic theories
simular, simulant Simulating
simulate To imitate
simulcast To broadcast over TV and radio at the same time
sin A transgression of moral law
sinapism A mustard plaster
since Between then and now
sincere Honest
sinciput, *pl* **-puts** or **sincipita** The forehead
sine The function of an acute angle in a right angle
sinecure An office that requires little work
sinew A tendon
sinewy Vigorous
sing To produce musical sounds
singe To scorch
single Solitary
singlet A man's undershirt
singleton Something existing singly
singsong A monotonous rhythm
singular Being only one
sinister Ominous
sinistral Left-handed
sink To go down slowly
sinkhole A depression
sinter To weld together
sinuate Having a wavy margin
sinuous Winding
sinus A cavity
sinusoid A sine curve
sip The act of sipping
siphon A type of tube
sippet Any small piece
sir A form of address
sirdar A person of rank
sire To beget
siren A temptress
sirenian A species of aquatic mammal

sirloin A cut of meat
sirocco A hot, humid wind
sirrah, sirra A contemptuous form of address
sirree, siree Used for emphasis after *yes* or *no*
sirup Variant of syrup
sirvente A lyric verse
sis Sister
sisal A plant
siskin A species of bird
sissy An effeminate boy or man
sister A female having the same mother and father as another
sit To rest
sitar A Hindu stringed instrument
site The place of an event
sith Since
sitology The science of diet and nutrition
situate To locate
situs Location
six The cardinal number 6
sixfold Having six parts
sixpence A coin worth six pennies
sixpenny Worth sixpence
sixteen The cardinal number 16
sixth The ordinal number six in a series
sixtieth The ordinal number 60 in a series
size The physical extent of something
sizzle To seethe with anger
skald An ancient Scandinavian poet
skat A card game
skate To glide along
skatole, skatol A chemical compound
skean A dagger
skedaddle To run away
skee Variant of ski
skeet A variety of trapshooting
skeg The afterpart of the keel
skein A coil of yarn
skeletal Pertaining to the skeleton
skeleton The framework of a human body
skep A beehive

skeptic One who doubts
sketch To outline
skew To turn at an angle
skewback A supporting abutment
skewbald A brown-and-white patchwork horse
skewer A spit
ski A runner for gliding over snow
skiagram A picture made up of shadows
skid The act of sliding
skiddoo *Slang* To go away
skiff A flat-bottomed boat
skijoring A skiing sport
skill Expertness
skillet A frying pan
skim To pass over lightly
skimp To be thrifty
skin The membranous tissue covering the body
skinflint *Slang* A miser
skink A species of lizard
skintight Fitting closely to the skin
skip To hop and step
skipjack A species of fish
skirl To play on the bagpipe
skirmish A minor conflict
skirret A plant
skirt A woman's garment
skit A short theatrical sketch
skitter To flit
skittish Nervous
skittles A bowling game
skive To pare
skivvy *Slang* A man's underwear
skoal Used as a drinking toast
skua A sea bird
skulk To lurk
skull The framwork of the head
skull The framework of the head
skullcap A type of cap
skunk A species of mammal
sky The upper atmosphere
skyborne Airborne
skycoach An airliner
skydive The sport of jumping from an airplane
skyey From the skies
skylark To frolic
skylight An overhead window
skyline The horizon

skysail A type of sail
skyway An air lane
slab A thick piece of something
slack Not busy
slag Residue from the smelting of metallic ore
slain Past participle of slay
slake To satisfy
slalom Skiing in a zigzag course
slam To shut forcefully
slander A malicious statement
slang A specialized vocabulary
slant A sloping direction
slap A smacking blow
slapdash In a reckless manner
slaphappy *Slang* Giddy
slapjack Variant of flapjack
slapstick Crude comedy
slash To cut
slat A narrow strip
slatch A calm between breaking waves
slate A roofing material
slather To spread thickly with
slattern An untidy woman
slaughter Massacre
slave A human being who is owned by another
slavish Servile
slaw Coleslaw
slay To kill
sleave To separate
sleazy Cheap
sled A vehicle for snow
sledge A type of vehicle
sleek Well-groomed
sleep A state of rest
sleet A mixture of rain and hail or snow
sleeve The part of a garment that covers the arm
sleigh A vehicle on runners for snow
sleight Dexterity
slender Slim
slept Past tense of sleep
sleuth A detective
slew A lot
slice A portion
slick Shrewd

slide To glide
slight Meager
slim Slender
slime Viscous mud
slimsy, slimpsy Flimsy
slimy Filthy
sling A slingshot
slingshot A device used for hurling small stones
slink To sneak
slip To lose one's balance
slipcase A box for a book
slipknot A type of knot
slipover A slipover garment
slidshod Careless
slipslop Watery food
slipt Past tense of slip
slipway The area sloping toward the water
slit A narrow cut
slither To slip and slide
sliver A splinter
slob A crude person
sloe A shrub
slog To plod along
slogan A catchphrase
sloop A sailing boat
slop Watery food
slope An inclined position
slopwork Inferior workmanship
slosh To splash
slot A narrow groove
sloth A species of arboreal mammal
slouch To assume an awkward position
slough A stagnant marsh
sloven A sloppy, careless person
slow Not moving quickly
slowdown A slackening
slowpoke *Slang* One who moves slowly
slowworm A lizard
sloyd A Swedish system of manual training
slub To draw out and twist
sludge A muddy deposit
slue To twist
slug A piece of type metal
slugabed A lazy person

slugfest A fight
sluggard An idler
sluice An artificial channel for water
slum Poor housing
slumber To sleep deeply
slumlord A landlord of slum property
slump To collapse
slung Past tense of sling
slunk Past tense of slink
slur To pronounce indistinctly
slurp To eat or drink noisily
slurry A watery mixture
slush Partly melted snow
slut A slovenly woman
sly Cunning
slyboots A clever person
slype A covered passageway in a cathedral
smack To kiss noisily
small Little
smallish Somewhat small
smallpox A disease
smalltime Unimportant
smalt A color
smaltite, smaltine A mineral
smart Bright
smarten To improve
smarty Cocky
smash To shatter
smashup A car wreck
smatter To prattle
smaze A mixture of smoke and haze
smear To spread
smearcase Cottage cheese
smell To detect the scent of
smelt To melt or fuse
smelter An apparatus for smelting
smew A duck
smidgen, smidgeon, smidgin A small quantity
smilax A species of plant
smile To look with a pleasant expression
smirch To soil
smirk A simpering smile
smite To afflict
smith A metalworker
smithery A smithy

287

smithy A forge
smock An outer garment
smog Pollution
smoke A cloud of fine particles
smokejack A device which turns a spit
smoky Emitting smoke
smolder, smoulder To burn with no flame
smolt A young salmon
smooch *Slang* To kiss
smooth Having an even surface
smoothen To smooth
smote Past tense and alternate past participle of smite
smother To suffocate
smudge To make dirty
smug Self-satisfied
smuggle To bring in illicitly
smut A particle of sooty matter
smutch To stain
snack A light meal
snaffle A horse bit
snafu *Slang* To mix up
snag A tear in a fabric
snail A species of mollusk
snake A species of legless reptile
snakebird A species of bird
snakebite The bite of a snake
snakehead The turtlehead plant
snakeroot A species of plant
snakeskin The skin of a snake
snakeweed A species of plant
snaky Sly
snap A type of fastener
snappish Curt
snapshot A photograph
snare To trap
snarl To growl
snatch To grasp
snazzy *Slang* Flashy
sneak To slink
sneer A contemptuous facial expression
sneeze To exhale in a sudden, explosive action
snell A line used to attach a fishhook to a fish line
snib To latch
snicker A snide laugh

snide Sarcastic
sniff To smell
sniffy Haughty
snifter A pear-shaped glass
snip To cut
snipe A species of wading bird
snippet A small piece
snippy Impertinent
snit A fit of anger
snitch *Slang* To tattle
snivel To run at the nose
snob An arrogant person
snobbish Pretentious
snood A netlike cap
snook A species of marine fish
snooker Pocket billiards
snoop To pry
snooty Snobbish
snooze To doze
snore To make noises while sleeping
snorkel A breathing apparatus
snort To express ridicule
snot *Slang* An impudent youngster
snout A facial part of an animal's muzzle
snow Precipitation in the form of white or translucent ice crystals

The following words are listed without definition (see Introduction):

snowball	snowflake	snowplow
snowbound	snowland	snowshed
snowbroth	snowless	snowshoe
snowcap	snowlike	snowslide
snowdrift	snowman	snowstorm
snowfall	snowmelt	snowsuit
snowfield	snowpack	snowy

snowbell A shrub
snowberry A species of shrub
snowbird A species of bird
snowblink A glow in the sky
snowbush A shrub
snowdrop A species of plant
snub To treat with contempt
snuck Past tense of sneak
snuff To sniff
snuffbox A box for carrying snuff
snuffle To sniffle
snug Cozy

snuggery A cozy place
so In the manner shown
soak To make completely wet
soap A cleansing agent
soapbark A tropical tree
soapbox A box used as a platform
soapstone A type of rock
soapsuds Suds from soapy water
soapwort A plant
soar To glide
soave A wine
sob To cry
sobeit Provided that
sober Serious
sobriety Solemnity
sobriquet A nickname
socage A medieval system of land tenure
soccer A type of ball game
social Getting along well with others
societal Social
society The rich social class
sock, *pl* **sox** A short stocking
socket An opening
socko *Slang* Very popular
socle A block serving as a base for a pedestal
sod Turf
soda A soft drink
sodalist A member of a sodality
sodalite A mineral
sodality A society
sodamide Sodium amide
sodden Saturated
soddy A house built of sod
sodium A metallic element
sodomite One who practices sodomy
sodomy Abnormal sexual intercourse
soever In any way
sofa A couch
sofar A system for locating an underwater explosion
soffit The underside of an architectural structure
soft Not hard
softball A type of baseball
software Material for a computer

softwood The wood of a coniferous tree
softy, softie One who is overly sentimental
soggy Soaked
soigne, soignee Elegant
soil The surface layer of earth
soilage Green crops for feeding livestock
soilure A smudge
soiree A party
sojourn A brief residence
soke The area under a court's jurisdiction
sol The fifth tone of the diatonic scale
solace Consolation
solan A gannet
solander A box to protect books
solanine A poisonous alkaloid
solar Pertaining to the sun
solarium, *pl* **-laria** or **-iums** A glassed-in porch
solatium, *pl* **-tia** Compensation for damage to the feelings
soldan A sultan
solder A metal alloy used for joining metal parts
soldier One who serves in the army
soldiery A body of soldiers
soldo Former coin of Italy
sole Only
solecism Breach of etiquette
solemn Serious
solenoid A type of electric coil
solicit To entreat
solid Having definite shape and volume
solidus, *pl* **-di** An ancient Roman coin
soliloquy A dramatic discourse
solitaire A card game played by one person
solitary Alone
solitude Isolation
solleret A shoe worn with armor
solo To perform alone
solstice A turning point
soluble Easily dissolved
solum, *pl* **-la** or **-lums** A soil layer

solus, sola Alone

solute Substance dissolved in a solution

solution The state of being dissolved

solve To explain

solvent Able to pay one's debts

soma, pl **-mata** or **-mas** The body of a plant

somatic Pertaining to the body

somber, sombre, sombrous Gloomy

sombrero A Mexican hat

some An indefinite number

somite A body segment

somnolent Sleepy

son A male offspring

sonance Sound

sonant Voiced

sonar A detecting system

sonata A musical composition

sonatina, pl **-nas** or **-ne** A short sonata

sone A unit of loudness

song A musical composition for singing

songster One who sings

sonic Relating to sound

sonnet A 14-line poetic form

sonneteer One who writes sonnets

sonny A little boy

sonorant A voiced sound

sonority A sound

sonship The state of being a son

sonsy, sonsie Handsome

sook Variant of souk

soon In the near future

soot A dispersion of black particles

sooth Soothing

soothe To calm

soothfast Loyal

soothsay To predict

sop To soak

sophism A plausible but fallacious argument

sophist A scholar

sophomore A second-year student

sopor A stupor

soprano, pl **-os** or **-prani** The highest melodic line in a harmony

sora A marsh bird

sorb To take up and hold

sorbet Sherbet

sorbose A type of sugar

sorcerer A wizard

sorceress A female sorcerer

sorcery Witchcraft

sord A flight of mallards

sordid Foul

sordino, pl **-ni** A mute for an instrument

sore Painful to the touch

sorehead A person who is angry

sorel Variant of sorrel

sorghum A species of grass

sorgo, sorgho A variety of sorghum

soricine Shrewlike

sorites A form of argument

sororal Sisterly

sororate The marriage of a man to his deceased wife's sister

sorority A college organization for women

sorosis, pl **-ses** A woman's club

sorption The process of sorbing

sorrel A color

sorrow Sadness

sorry Feeling sympathy

sort To arrange

sortie A quick raid

sorus, pl **-sori** A cluster of fungus spores

sot A drunkard

sotol A species of woody plant

sottish Drunken

sou A former French coin

soubrette A frivolous young woman in a play

souchong A variety of Chinese black tea

souffle A baked food dish

sough A soft, murmuring sound

sought Past tense of seek

souk An open-air marketplace

soul The spirit of the dead

sound A wide body of water

soundman One in charge of sound effects

soup A liquid food

soupcon A tiny amount

sour Sharp and tangy

sourball A hard candy
source A point of origin
sourdine a trumpet mute
sourdough a prospector
sourpuss *Slang* One who has a gloomy expression
soursop A tropical tree
sourwood A tree
souse To drench
soutache A narrow braid
soutane A cassock
south A cardinal point on the compass
souther A wind from the south
southern Pertaining to the South
southing Toward the south
southpaw *Slang* A left-handed baseball pitcher
southron A southerner
souvenir A memento
sovereign Supreme
soviet A legislative assembly in the Soviet Union
sow An adult female hog
sowbelly Salt pork
sowbread A plant
sowens A porridge
sox Plural of sock
soy The soybean
soybean The seed of a cultivated plant
sozzle To mix in a sloppy manner
spa A mineral spring
space An interval of time
spaceman An astronaut
spaceport A center for spacecraft
spaceship A rocket-propelled vehicle for space travel
spacesuit A suit for space flights
spacewalk The act of moving about in space
spacey *Slang* Under the influence of a drug
spacious Extensive
spade A tool for digging
spadefish A species of fish
spadix, *pl* **spadices** A flower cluster
spaghetti A pasta dish
spagyric Alchemical

spake Past tense of speak
spall To break up into fragments
span A period of time
spandrel, spandril The space between two arches
spang Precisely
spangle A small decorative object
spaniel A breed of dog
spank To slap on the buttocks
spanworm A measuring worm
spar To box
spare To do without
sparerib A cut of pork
sparge To sprinkle
sparid A species of marine fish
spark A particle resulting from friction
sparkler A firework
sparling A young herring
sparrow A species of bird
sparse Not dense
spasm A sudden contraction of a muscle
spasmodic Convulsive
spastic A person who suffers from spasms
spat A petty quarrel
spate, spait A sudden outpouring
spathe A leaflike organ
spathic Sparry
spatial Having the nature of space
spatter To scatter in drops
spatula A knifelike implement
spavin A disease of horses
spawn The eggs of aquatic animals
spay To excise the ovaries of
speak To talk
speakeasy *Slang* A place where illegal drinks are sold
spear A weapon
spearfish A marine game fish
spearhead To be the leader of
spearman A soldier armed with a spear
spearmint An aromatic plant
spearwort A species of plant
special Exceptional
specie In kind
species A distinct kind
specify To state

specimen A sample
specious Deceptive
speck A small spot
specs, specks Spectacles
spectacle An unusual display
spectator One who attends an event
specter, spectre An apparition
spectral Ghostly
spectrum, *pl* -**tra** or -**trums** A continuous range
specular Like a spectrum
speculum, *pl* -**la** or -**lums** A mirror used as a reflector in a telescope
sped Past tense of speed
speech The faculty of speaking
speed To accelerate
speedboat A motorboat
speedster A fast auto
speedup An increase in speed
speedway A track for racing autos
speedwell A species of plant
speiss A metallic mixture
spell To form a word
spellbind To enchant
spelldown A spelling bee
spelt A variety of wheat
spelter Crude zinc
spelunker One who explores caves
spencer A trysail
spend To pay out
spent Consumed
sperm The male gamete
spermary An organ in which gametes are formed
spermine A chemical compound
spew To eject
sphagnum A species of moss
sphene A titanium ore
sphenic Shaped like a wedge
sphenoid A bone of the skull
spheral Globe-shaped
sphere A planet
spheroid An ellipsoid
spherule A small sphere
sphery Starlike
sphinx, *pl* **sphinxes** or **sphinges** The monumental sphinx at Giza
sphygmic Of the pulse
spica, *pl* -**cae** A bandage

spicate Arranged in a spike
spiccato A musical bowing technique
spice Something that adds zest and flavor
spicebush An aromatic shrub
spicery Spices
spicule, spicula, *pl* -**lae** A small spike
spiculum, *pl* -**la** A spicule
spider A species of arachnid
spiel *Slang* A harangue
spiff, spiffy To make stylish
spigot A faucet
spike A flower cluster
spikelet A small spike
spikenard An aromatic plant
spiky Long and pointed
spile A plug
spilikin A game
spill To cause to fall
spillage The amount spilled
spillway A channel in a reservoir
split Past tense of spill
spilth The act of spilling
spin To draw out and twist
spinach A cultivated plant
spinal Having to do with the spine
spindle A slender pin used in spinning
spindly Tall and slender
spindrift Spray from a rough sea
spine The spinal column
spinel A mineral
spinet A small piano
spinifex A species of grass
spinney, spinny A thicket
spinoff A secondary product
spinose Spiny
spinous Spiny
spinster A woman who spins thread
spinule A small thorn
spiracle A respiratory aperture
spiral A spiral curve
spirant Fricative
spire A pinnacle
spirea, spiraea A species of plant
spireme, spirem The filaments that appear at the beginning of mitosis

spirit A supernatural being
spiroid Resembling a spiral
spirula, *pl* **-lae** A species of cephalopod mollusk
spit A rod on which meat is cooked
spital A hospital
spitball A type of pitch in baseball
spite Regardless of
spitfire One who is easily aroused
to anger
spittle Saliva
spittoon A cuspidor
spitz A breed of dog
spiv One engaged in shady
dealings
splash To splash liquid
splat A piece of wood
splatter To spatter
splay An expansion
spleen Bad temper
splendent Brilliant
splendid Magnificent
splendor Grandeur
splenic Pertaining to the spleen
splenius, *pl* **-nii** A muscle of the
neck
splice To join at the ends
spline A pliable strip of material
splint A splinter
split To divide into two parts
splotch A discolored area
splurge To spend wastefully
splutter To speak incoherently
spode Fine chinaware
spoil To damage
spoke A rod that connects the hub
and the rim of a wheel
spondaic Consisting of spondees
spondee A metrical foot
sponge A species of marine animal
spongin A fibrous material
spongy Like a sponge
sponson A structure projecting
over the side of a ship
sponsor A godfather or godmother
spontoon A spear-like weapon of
the 18th century
spoof A hoax
spook A ghost

spool A cylinder upon which
thread is wound
spoon An eating utensil
spoonbill A species of wading bird
spoony, spooney Foolishly
sentimental
spoor The trail of an animal
sporadic At irregular intervals
spore A bacterium in a dormant
spore A bacterium in a dormant
stage
sporran A pouch worn by Scottish
Highlanders
sport A recreation
sporty Carefree
spot A position
spotty Spotted
spousal Pertaining to marriage
spouse One's married partner
spout To gush forth in a rapid
stream
sprag A device for preventing a
vehicle from rolling backward
sprain A wrenching of the liga-
ments of a joint
sprang Past tense of spring
sprat A species of fish
sprawl To spread out awkwardly
spray To disperse a liquid
spread To stretch
spree A lively frolic
sprig A small twig
spring To leap
springbok A gazelle
springe A type of snare
springy Elastic
sprinkle To release drops of water
sprint A short race
sprit A bowsprit
sprite, spright An elf
sprocket Toothlike projections on a
wheel rim
sprout To begin to grow
spruce A species of evergreen tree
sprue A tropical disease
sprung Past tense of spring
spry Lively
spud A type of tool
spue Variant of spew
spume Foam

spumoni An Italian ice cream
spun Past tense of spin
spunk Pluck
spunky Spirited
spur A climbing iron
spurge A species of plant
spurious False
spurn To scorn
spurrier A maker of spurs
spurry A species of weedy plant
spurt A sudden gush
sputnik An artificial satellite of the earth
sputter To stammer
sputum, *pl* **-ta** Spit
spy To watch secretly
spyglass A telescope
squab A young pigeon
squabble To bicker
squabby Short and stout
squad A small group of soldiers
squadron Any organized body or group
squalene A chemical compound
squalid Miserable
squall To scream loudly
squalor The state of being squalid
squama, *pl* **-mae** A scale
squamous, squamose Scaly
squander To spend wastefully
square A rectangle having four equal sides
squarish More square than round
squash A species of plant
squat To sit on one's heels
squaw A North American Indian woman
squawfish A species of fish
squawk To screech
squawroot A plant
squeak To make a shrill, high-pitched sound
squeal To produce a loud, shrill sound
squeamish Nauseated
squeegee An implement for removing water
squeeze To compress
squelch To squash
squib A firecracker

squid A species of cephalopod mollusk
squiggle A small wiggly mark
squill A species of plant
squilla, *pl* **-las** or **squillae** A species of marine crustacean
squinch To squint the eyes
squint To peer with the eyes partly closed
squire A country gentleman
squirm To writhe
squirrel A species of arboreal rodent
squirt To eject in a thin swift stream
squish To squash
squoosh To squeeze into a soft, liquid mass
sri A Hindu title of address
stab To pierce with a pointed weapon
stabile A stationary abstract sculpture
stable Enduring
staccato Made up of abrupt sounds
stack A chimney
stacte A spice
staddle A supporting framework
stadia A method of surveying
stadium, *pl* **-dia** or **-diums** A structure in which athletic events are held
staff A rod
stag The adult male deer
stage A raised platform
stagehand One who works backstage
staggard A full-grown male red deer
staghound A breed of dog
stagnant Stale
stagnate To become stagnant
stagy Having a theatrical quality
staid Sober
stain A blemish
stair A staircase
staircase A flight of steps
stake A pointed piece of wood
stalag A German prisoner-of-war camp

stale Dry

stalemate A deadlock

stalk A stem that supports a plant

stall To come to a standstill

stallion An adult male horse that has not been gelded

stalwart Sturdy

stamen, pl **-mens** or **stamina** The pollen-producing organ of flowers

stamina Endurance

stammel A fabric

stammer To falter in speech

stamp To impress

stampede A sudden mass movement

stance A manner of standing

stanch Variant of staunch

stanchion A support

stand To maintain an upright position

standard Criterion

standby One kept in readiness

standee One using standing room

standout An outstanding person

standstill A halt

standup Upright

stang Past tense of sting

stanhope A carriage

stank Past tense of stink

stannary A tin-producing region

stannic Pertaining to tin

stannite A mineral

stanza A division of a poem

stapes, pl **stapedes** A bone of the inner ear

staple A major feature

star A luminous body seen in the night sky

starboard The right side of a ship

starch A substance used to stiffen fabrics

stardom The status of a very successful entertainer

stare To fix with a steady gaze

starets, pl **startsy** A spiritual advisor

starfish A species of marine echinoderm

stargaze To daydream

stark Bare

starlet A young motion picture actress

starlight Starlit

starling A species of bird

starlit Lighted by stars

start To begin

starve To be hungry

starwort A species of plant

stash To hide

stasis, pl **-ses** Stoppage of body fluids

state An emotional condition

statehood The status of being a state

stateroom A private compartment

stateside Toward the continental United States

static Quiescent

station A depot

stationer One who deals in stationery

statistic Numerical datum

stative A verb which expresses a condition

stator Part of a motor

statuary A sculptor

statue A sculpted work of art

statuette A small statue

stature Caliber

status A standing

statute A law

staunch True

stave A rung of a chair

stay To remain

staysail A type of sail

stead Advantage

steadfast Steady

steak A cut of meat

steal To commit theft

stealth Furtiveness

steam Energy

steamboat A steamship

steamy Emitting steam

steapsin An enzyme

stearate A chemical salt

stearic Derived from fat

stearin The solid form of fat

steatite A variety of talc

steed A horse

steel An iron alloy

295

steelhead   Rainbow trout

steelwork   A plant where steel is produced

steelyard   A type of weighing machine

steenbok   An African antelope

steep   Precipitous

steepen   To make steeper

steeple   A tall tower

steer   To maneuver

steerage   A section of a passenger ship

steeve   To stow in the hold

stegodon   A species of extinct mammal

stegosaur   A species of dinosaur

stein   A mug

steinbok   Variant of steenbok

stela, pl -**lae**   Stele

stele, pl -**les** or -**lae**   A grave marker

stellar   Consisting of stars

stellate   Shaped like a star

stellify   To transform into a star

stem   The main axis of a plant

stemma, pl **stemmata** or -**mas**   A family tree

stemmer   One that removes stems

stemson   A supporting timber on a ship

stemware   Glassware with a stem

stench   A stink

stencil   A pattern made by stenciling

step   A manner of walking

stepchild   The child of one's spouse by a former marriage

steppe   A large grass-covered plain

stepson   The son of one's spouse by a former marriage

stepwise   Like a series of steps

stere   A unit of volume

stereo   Stereophonic sound

steric   Having to do with the spatial arrangement of the atoms in a molecule

sterile   Barren

sterlet   A sturgeon

sterling   English money

stern   Firm

sternal   Pertaining to the sternum

sternmost   Farthest astern

sternpost   The main, upright piece at the stern of a ship

sternson   A connecting piece on a ship

sternum, pl -**na** or -**nums**   The breastbone

sternward   Astern

sternway   The backward movement of a vessel

steroid   A chemical compound

sterol   A solid alcohol

stertor   A snoring sound

stet   A printer's term

stevedore   One hired to load or unload ships

stew   A dish cooked by stewing

steward   A supervisor

stibine   A poisonous gas

stibnite   A mineral

stich   A line of verse

stick   A long piece of wood

stickball   A form of baseball

stickle   To argue

stickpin   A pin worn on a necktie

stickum   An adhesive substance

stickup Slang   A holdup

stiff   Rigid

stifle   To smother

stigma, pl **stigmata** or -**mas**   A shameful brand

stilbene   A chemical compound

stilbite   A mineral

stile   A turnstile

stiletto   A dagger

still   Silent

stillman   One who owns a still

stilly   Calm

stilt   A wading bird

stimulus, pl -**li**   Something that incites to action

sting   To feel a sharp pain

stingray   A species of ray

stingy   Meager

stink   To emit a foul odor

stinkbug   A species of insect

stinkhorn   A species of foul-smelling fungus

stinkpot   A jar containing combustibles

stinkweed A species of plant
stinkwood A species of tree
stint To be sparing with
stipe A supporting part of a plant
stipel A secondary stipule
stipend A salary
stipple To produce artwork by means of dots or small dabs of color
stipular Pertaining to a stipule
stipule An appendage at the base of leaves in various plants
stir To provoke
stirk A heifer
stirps, *pl* **stirpes** A branch of a family
stirrup Part of a horse's saddle
stitch A single movement of a threaded needle
stithy An anvil
stiver A former Dutch coin
stoa, *pl* **stoae** or **-as** An ancient Greek colonnade
stoat The ermine
stock Livestock
stockade An enclosed area
stockinet A fabric
stockman A rancher
stockpile A supply of material
stodgy Stuffy
stogy, stogie, stogey A cigar
stoic One unaffected by pleasure or pain
stoke To tend the fire
stokehold A room in which boilers are stoked on a ship
stokehole The opening in a furnace
stole A woman's scarf or fur
stolid Showing little emotion
stollen A rich yeast bread
stolon A plant stem
stoma, *pl* **-mata** or **-mas** A mouth-like opening
stomach The abdomen
stomp To trample
stone Rock
stonechat A species of bird
stonecrop A species of plant
stonefish A species of fish
stonefly A species of insect

stoneware Pottery
stood Past tense of stand
stooge A puppet
stool A footstool
stoop To bend
stop To cease moving
stopcock A faucet
stope To remove ore
stopgap A substitute
stopover A brief stop
stopple A stopper
storage A place for storing goods
storax A species of tree
store A shop
storey A floor of a tall building
stork A species of wading bird
storm A heavy fall of snow, rain or hail
story A fictitious literary composition
stoss Facing the direction from which a glacier moves
stotinka, *pl* **-ki** Monetary unit of Bulgaria
stound An ache
stoup A bucket
stout Sturdy
stove An apparatus for heating
stovepipe A tall man's hat
stow To store away
stowage The state of being stowed
stowaway One who hides aboard ship
straddle To sit astride of
strafe To attack
straggle To fall behind
straight Erect
strain To exert
strait A passage of water joining two larger bodies
strake A planking on a ship
strand To run aground
strange Unfamiliar
strangle To smother
strangury Painful urination
strap A narrow piece of leather
strass Glass used in making artificial gems
strata Plural of stratum
strategy A plan of action

strath A wide river valley
stratify To become layered
stratum, *pl* **-ta** A layer of material
stratus, *pl* **-ti** A cloud
straw Threshed grain
stray To wander about
streak A trait
stream Running water
street A public thoroughfare
strega An Italian liqueur
strength Physical power
strenuous Energetic
stress Emphasis placed upon something
stretch To distend
stretto, *pl* **-ti** or **-tos** A final musical section performed at a faster tempo
streusel A topping for coffee cakes
strew To scatter
stria, *pl* **striae** A thin, narrow channel
striate Grooved
stricken Wounded
strickle A foundry tool
strict Accurate
stride To walk with long steps
strident Shrill
stridor A strident sound
strife A conflict
strigil A scraping tool
strigose Having stiff bristles
strike To hit sharply
strikeout Striking out
string A slender cord
stringent Severe
strip To remove
stripe A distinct band
striper *Slang* An enlisted man who wears stripes
stripling A grown boy
stript Past tense of strip
strive To struggle
strobe A strobe light
strobila, *pl* **-lae** The body of a tapeworm
strobile, strobilus, *pl* **-bili** A pine cone
strode Past tense of stride
stroke A blow

stroll A leisurely walk
stroma, *pl* **-mata** The tissue framework of an organ
strong Robust
strongbox A box for valuables
strongyle, strongyl A species of worm
strop To sharpen
strophe A stanza
stroud A fabric
strove Past tense of strive
struck Past tense of strike
structure A building
strudel A pastry
struggle To grapple
strum To play casually
struma, *pl* **-mae** or **-mas** Scrofula
strumpet A harlot
strung Past tense of string
strut To swagger
stub Anything that has been physically shortened
stubborn Obstinate
stucco A type of plaster
stuck Past tense of stick
stud A horse used for breeding
studbook A register for pedigreed animals
student One who attends school
studfish A freshwater fish
studhorse A stallion
studio An artist's workroom
studious Devoted to study
study The process of studying
stuff Junk
stull A supporting timber
stultify To make ridiculous
stum Grape juice
stumble To flounder
stump Part of a tree trunk
stumpage Standing timber
stun To overwhelm
stung Past tense of sting
stunk Pat tense of stink
stunt To hinder the growth
stupa A Buddhist shrine
stupe A compress
stupid Dull
stupor Daze
sturdy Strong

sturgeon A species of fish
stutter To stammer
sty A pen for swine
stylar Like a stylus
style The current way of dressing
stylet A surgical probe
stylite An early Christian ascetic
styloid Slender and pointed
stylus, *pl* **-luses** or **-li** A phonograph needle
stymie, stymy An impasse
stypsis The use of a styptic
styptic Astringent
styrax Storax
styrene A chemical staple for plastics
suable Capable of being sued
suasion Variant of persuasion
suave Smoothly gracious
sub To act as a substitute
sub- Indicates below; under; to a lesser degree. The following compounds are listed without definition (see Introduction):

subabbot	subclimax	subitem
subacid	subcool	subjacent
subacrid	subcortex	subjugate
subacute	subcutis	sublease
subadult	subdeacon	sublet
subaerial	subdean	sublevel
subagent	subdeb	sublunary
subalar	subdepot	submarine
subalpine	subdivide	submerge
subaltern	subecho	submerse
subapical	subedit	submiss
subarctic	subentry	submit
subarea	subepoch	subnasal
subarid	suberect	subnodal
subatom	subfamily	subnormal
subatomic	subfield	suboptic
subaxial	subfix	suboral
subbase	subfloor	suborder
subbass	subfluid	suboval
subbreed	subgrade	subovate
subcause	subgroup	subpar
subcell	subhead	subpart
subchief	subhuman	subplot
subclan	subhumid	subpolar
subclass	subidea	subpubic
subclerk	subindex	subrace

subregion	subsoil	subtorrid
subrent	subsolar	subtotal
subring	subsonic	subtract
subrule	subspace	subtribe
subsale	substage	subtunic
subscribe	subteen	subtype
subscript	subtenant	subunit
subsect	subtext	subvicar
subset	subtitle	subviral
subshaft	subtone	subvocal
subshrub	subtonic	subway
subside	subtopic	subzone

subchaser A submarine chaser
subdue To put down
suberin A substance found in cell walls of cork
suberize To form a corklike substance
suberose Corky
subgenus, *pl* **-genera** Subdivision of a genus
subito Quickly
subject Disposed to
subjoin To annex
sublimate To modify
sublime Majestic
suborn To induce to commit a wrong act
suboxide An oxide containing little oxygen
subpoena, subpena A legal writ
subserve To further
subsidy A grant
subsist To exist
substance Matter
substrate Material upon which an enzyme acts
subsume To include within a larger class
subtend To be opposite to
subtile Subtle
subtle Elusive
subulate Tapering to a point
suburb A residential area
subvert To ruin
succeed To follow after
success One that is successful
succinct Concise
succor, succour Relief
succotash Corn and lima beans

together
succuba, pl **-bae** Succubus
succubus, pl **-buses** or **-bi** A female demon
succulent Juicy
succumb To give in
such Of this or that kind
suchlike Like
suck To draw liquid into
suckle To nurse
sucrase An enzyme
sucre Monetary unit of Ecuador
sucrose Sugar
suction A vacuum
sudatory A sweat bath
sudd Floating masses of weeds
sudden Abrupt
suds Soapy water
sue To appeal to
suede A fabric
suet Hard, fatty tissue
suffer To feel pain
suffice To be adequate
suffix Something added to the end
suffocate To choke
suffrage The right to vote
suffuse To spread over
sugar A sweet carbohydrate
suggest To propose
suicide The act of killing oneself
suint A natural grease in the fleece of sheep
suit A garment
suitcase Luggage
suite A retinue
suitor One who is courting a woman
sukiyaki A Japanese dish
sulcate Grooved
sulcus, pl **-ci** A deep groove
sulfate A chemical compound
sulfide A sulphur compound
sulfinyl Thionyl
sulfite A chemical salt
sulfone A sulphur compound
sulfonyl Sulfuryl
sulfur A nonmetallic element
sulfuret A sulfide
sulfuryl Sulfonyl
sulk To sullenly withdraw

sullage Sewage
sullen Morose
sully To stain
sulphur Variant of sulfur
sultan A Moslem ruler
sultana The wife of a sultan
sultry Hot and humid
sum An amount of money
sumac, sumach A species of shrub
summary Concise
summer The season between spring and autumn
summery Like summer
summit The top
summon To convene
sump A cesspool
sumpter A pack animal
sun The star about which the earth revolves

The following words are listed without definition (see Introduction):

sunback	sunglass	sunroom
sunbaked	sunglow	sunscald
sunbath	sunlamp	sunset
sunbathe	sunland	sunshade
sunbeam	sunless	sunshine
sunbonnet	sunlight	sunspot
sunbow	sunlike	sunstroke
sunburn	sunlit	sunsuit
sunburst	sunny	suntan
suncured	sunproof	sunup
sundial	sunrise	sunward
sundown	sunroof	sunwise

sunbird A species of bird
sundae Ice cream with toppings
sunder To divide
sundew A species of plant
sundog A small rainbow
sundrops A species of plant
sundry Various
sunfish A species of fish
sunflower A species of plant
sung Past tense of sing
sunk Past participle of sink
sunn A tough fiber
sunstone A variety of feldspar
sup To dine
super An extra actor
superb Luxurious

superego A division of the psyche
superior Above average
superman A man with superhuman powers
supernal Heavenly
superpose To place over something else
supersede To replace
supervene To ensue
supervise To oversee
supinate To turn so that the palm is upward
supine Passive
supper The evening meal
supplant To take the place of
supple Pliant
supply To satisfy
support To bear the weight of
suppose To assume
suppress To subdue
supreme Greatest in importance
surah A fabric
sural Of the calf of the leg
surbase A type of molding
surcease To stop
surcharge An additional sum
surcoat A garment
surd A voiceless sound
sure True
surety Self-assurance
surf Wave action
surface The outermost part
surfbird A shore bird
surfboard A board used for riding waves
surfboat A strong boat
surfeit To supply to excess
surge To be tossed about on waves
surgeon A physician who performs operations
surgery A treatment by operation
surgical Used in surgery
suricate A species of mammal
surly Gruff
surmise To make a conjecture
surmount To overcome
surname One's family name
surpass To go beyond
surplice An outer vestment
surplus An amount in excess of what is needed
surprint To overprint
surprise To catch unawares
surreal Fantastic
surrender To give up
surrey A carriage
surrogate A substitute
surround To encircle
surtax An additional tax
survey To scrutinize
survive To exist
suspect To imagine
suspend To interrupt
suspense The state of being uncertain
suspicion A hint
suspire To sigh
sustain To maintain
sutler A camp follower who peddles to soldiers
sutra, sutta A scriptural narrative
suttee A Hindu custom of cremation
suture The process of joining two surfaces together
suzerain A feudal lord
svelte Graceful
swab A mop
swaddle To swathe
swag To sway
swage To shape
swagman A migrant worker
swain A lover
swale, swail A wet, marshy area
swallow To ingest
swam Past tense of swim
swami, swamy A Hindu title of respect
swamp A marsh
swan A species of aquatic bird
swang Past tense of swing
swank Elegant
swannery A place where swans are raised
swanskin A fabric
swap To trade
sward, swarth A meadow
sware Past tense of swear
swarf Metallic shavings
swarm A group of bees

swart Swarthy

swarthy Having a dark complexion

swash To swagger

swastika, swastica The emblem of Nazi Germany

swat To slap

swatch A sample piece

swath A strip

swathe To wrap in bandages

sway To move back and forth

swayback An abnormal sagging of the spine

swear To vow

swearword An obscene word

sweat To perspire

sweatbox A place in which one sweats

sweater An outer garment

sweatshop A shop where employees are underpaid

swede A rutabaga

sweep To clean

sweet Having a taste like sugar

sweetie Sweetheart

sweetmeat A delicacy

sweetsop A tropical tree

swell To expand

swellfish The puffer fish

swelter To feel very hot

swerve To veer

swift Fast

swig A gulp

swill To feed with slop

swim To move through water

swimsuit A garment for swimming

swindle To defraud

swine A species of ungulate mammal

swing To oscillate

swinge To whip

swinish Filthy

swipe To strike

swirl To move with a whirling motion

swish To rustle

swiss A fabric

switch To divert

swive To copulate with

swivel To turn

swizzle A mixed drink

swob Variant of swab

swollen Past participle of swell

swoon To faint

swoop To scoop

swop Variant of swap

sword A weapon

swordbill A hummingbird

swordfish A game and food fish

swordplay Fencing

swordsman One skilled in the use of a sword

swordtail A species of fish

swore Past tense of swear

sworn Past participle of swear

swot To study hard

swum Past participle of swim

swung Past tense of swing

sybarite One devoted to pleasure and luxury

sycamine The black mulberry

sycamore A species of tree

syce A groom for horses

sycee Fine silk

syconium, pl **-nia** A fleshy fruit

sycosis A disease of the hair

syenite An igneous rock

syllable A unit of spoken language

syllabub A dessert

syllabus, pl **-bi** A course outline

sylph A graceful woman

sylphid A young sylph

sylva The forests of a region

sylvan Living in the forest

sylvite, sylvin, sylvine Potassium chloride

symbiont, symbiote An organism living closely with another

symbol Something that represents something else

symmetry Condition of being symmetrical

sympathy The capacity for understanding

symphony A long musical composition

symposium, pl **-sia** A conference

symptom An indication

synagogue, synagog A place for Jewish worship

synapse, synapsis, pl **-ses** The

point at which a nerve impulse passes from one neuron to another

sync To synchronize

syncarp A fleshy fruit

synchro A remote-control device

syncline A rock formation

syncom A communications satellite

syncopate To modify a musical rhythm

syncope The dropping of letters from the middle of a word

syndetic Serving to connect

syndic A business agent

syndicate A group transacting business

syndrome Symptoms that indicate a disorder

synesis A grammatical construction

syngamy The fusion of two gametes

synod An assembly of churches

synonym A word having the same meaning as another

synopsis, *pl* **-ses** A brief outline

synoptic Presenting a summary

synovia A lubricating fluid secreted by membranes

syntax The way in which words are put together to form phrases and sentences

synthesis, *pl* **-ses** The combining of separate elements to form a whole

synthetic Artificial

sypher To overlap to form a flush surface

syphilis A venereal disease

syringa A shrub

syringe A medical instrument

syrinx, *pl* **syringes** or **syrinxes** The vocal organ of songbirds

syrphid A species of fly

syrup, sirup A thick, sweet liquid

system A set of things so related as to form a unity

systemic Pertaining to a system

systole The rhythmic contraction of the heart

syzygy A pair of opposites

ta Thank you

tab A flap

tabanid A species of fly

tabard A garment

tabaret A fabric

tabbis A silk fabric

tabby A cat

tabes A disease

tabla A drum

tablature A form of musical notation

table A piece of furniture

tableau, *pl* **tableaux** A scene

tableland A plateau

tablet A pad of writing paper

tabloid A newspaper

taboo, tabu A ban against something

tabor, tabour A small drum

taboret, tabouret A stool

tabular Flat

tabulate To arrange

tacet Be silent
tache A buckle
tachylyte A basaltic rock
tacit Unspoken
taciturn Silent
tack A short nail
tackling Gear
tacky Shabby
taco A tortilla folded around a filling
taconite An iron-ore
tact Diplomacy
tactic A maneuver
tactile Pertaining to the sense of touch
taction Contact
tad A small boy
tadpole The larva of certain amphibians
tael A unit of weight
taenia, pl **-niae** A headband
taffeta A fabric
taffrail The rail around the stern of a ship
taffy Candy
tafia, taffia A cheap rum
tag A children's game
tagalong One that follows another
tagboard A cardboard
tagmeme A unit of grammatical form
tahini A spicy sauce
tahr A species of goatlike mammal
taiga A subarctic evergreen forest
taiglach Variant of teiglach
tail The rear part of an animal's body
tailback A backfield position on a football team
tailfan The fanlike structure at the rear of a lobster
tailgate The tailboard of a vehicle
taille A French feudal tax
tailor One who makes clothes
tailpiece An appendage
tailrace A part of a millrace
tailskid A skid on an airplane
tailspin The spiral descent of a plane
tain A tin plate

taint To stain the honor of something
taj A Moslem cap
takahe A flightless bird
take To seize
takedown The process of taking down
takeoff The act of leaving the ground
takeout The act of taking out
takeover Assuming control
takeup The act of making tight
takin A goatlike mammal
tala Monetary unit of Western Samoa
talapoin A monkey
talaria Winged sandals
talc A mineral used in talcum
talcose, talcous, talcky Containing talc
talcum Talcum powder
tale A lie
talent Ability
taler A former German coin
talesman An alternate juror
tali Plural of talus
talion A punishment
taliped Clubfooted
talipes A deformity of the foot
talipot A palm tree
talisman Something having magic power
talk To speak
talkathon A prolonged period of talking
talkie A film with sound
tall Having great height
tallage To tax
tallboy A highboy
tallith, pl **tallithim** A prayer shawl
tallow A mixture of fats
tally To record
tallyho A hunting cry
tallyman A scorekeeper
talon The claw of a bird of prey
talus, pl **-li** The ankle
tam A cap
tamale A Mexican food dish
tamandua An anteater
tamarack A species of tree

tamarau, tamarao A short-horned buffalo
tamarin A species of monkey
tamarind A tropical tree
tamarisk A species of shrub
tambac Variant of tombac
tambour A drum
tame Docile
tammy A fabric
tamp To pack down
tampion A cannon cover
tampon A plug of cotton
tan A color
tanager A species of bird
tanbark The bark of various trees
tandem A carriage
tang A sharp taste
tangelo A citrus tree
tangent Irrelevant
tangerine A citrus tree
tangible Real
tangle To snarl
tango A dance
tangram A Chinese puzzle
tanist The heir apparent
tank A container
tanka A Japanese verse form
tankard A large drinking cup
tannic Obtained from tannin
tannin A chemical compound
tansy A species of plant
tantalite A mineral
tantalum A metallic element
tantalus A wine stand
tantara A trumpet fanfare
tantivy At top speed
tantra Hindu religious writings
tantrum A fit of rage
tanyard A section of a tannery
tap To strike lightly
tapa A cloth made from tree bark
tapadera, tapadero Part of a saddle
tape To bind together
tapestry A textile wall hanging
tapetum, pl **-ta** A layer of cells
tapeworm A species of flatworm
tapioca A pudding
tapir A species of ungulate mammal
tappet A moving lever

taproom A bar
taproot The main root of plants
tapster A bartender
tar A black viscid mixture
tarantula A species of spider
tarboosh, tarbush A type of Moslem cap
tardy Late
tare A species of weedy plant
targe A small shield
target An object of attack
tariff A schedule of fees
tarlatan, tarletan A fabric
tarmac A paved road
tarn A small mountain lake
tarnal Damned
tarnish To discolor
taro A tropical plant
tarok, taroc A card game
tarot A card used in fortunetelling
tarp Tarpaulin
tarpaper A paper used as a roofing base
tarpaulin Waterproof canvas
tarpon A species of fish
tarragon An aromatic herb
tarry To linger
tarsal Pertaining to the tarsus of the foot
tarsier A species of primate
tarsus, pl **-si** Part of the foot
tart Sour
tartan A textile pattern
tartar A deposit on the teeth
tartrate A chemical salt
tartuffe, tartufe A hypocrite
tarweed A species of plant
task An objective
tass A drinking cup
tasse, tasset A part of armor
tassel A dangling ornament
taste To partake
tasty Savory
tat To make tatting
tater A potato
tatter A shred
tatting Lace
tattle To tell
tattoo A design made on the skin
tau The 19th letter of the Greek alphabet

taught Past tense of teach
taunt To mock
taupe A color
taurine Like a bull
taut Tense
tauten To stretch tight
tautog, tautaug A marine fish
tautonym A taxonomic designation
tav The 23rd letter of the Hebrew alphabet
tavern A saloon
taw A marble
tawdry Gaudy
tawny A color
tax A strain
taxeme A minimal feature in grammatical construction
taxi To travel in a taxi
taxicab An auto for hire
taxidermy The art of stuffing animals
taximeter A device to compute the fare in a taxi
taxis A unit of troops
taxiway A strip for aircraft
taxon, pl **taxa** A taxonomic unit
taxonomy The science of classification
taxpayer One who pays taxes
taxus An evergreen tree
tea A beverage
teaberry The wintergreen plant
teach To give instruction to
teacup A small cup
teahouse A place where tea is served
teak A tall evergreen tree
teakettle A kettle used for making tea
teal A species of duck
team A group of players
teammate A member of a team
teamster A Truck driver
teamwork Cooperative effort
teapot A pot in which tea is steeped
teapoy A small table
tear To pull apart
teardrop A single tear
tearoom A teashop
tease To make fun of

teasel, teazel, teazle A species of plant
teashop A tearoom
teaspoon A small spoon
teat A nipple
technic Variant of technique
technique A procedure of using basic skills
tectonic Pertaining to construction
tectrix, pl **-trices** A feather of a bird's wing
ted To spread
teddy A woman's undergarment
tedious Tiresome
tedium Boredom
tee The letter t
teem To abound
teen, teenage The years from thirteen through nineteen
teeny Tiny
teepee Variant of tepee
teeter To totter
teeth Plural of tooth
teethe To grow teeth
teetotum A spinning top
tegmen, pl **-mina** A covering
tegua A moccasin
tegular Overlapping
tegument An outer covering
teiglach A confection
tektite A meteorlike, small glass object
tela, pl **-lae** A weblike membrane
telamon, pl **telamones** A male figure used as a supporting pillar
telecast To broadcast
teledu A mammal of East Indies
telega A cart
telegenic Looking attractive on television
telegony The predominant genetic influence of one sire over other sires by the same female
telegram A wire
telegraph A communications system
telemark A turn in skiing
teleost A species of fish
telepathy Communication by unknown means

telephone A system for conveying speech

telephoto Pertaining to a lens that produces an enlarged image

teleplay A play written for television

telescope To slide inward or outward

telesis Planned progress

telethon A lengthy telecast

televise To broadcast by television

telic Purposeful

telium, *pl* **-lia** A structure formed on a plant infected by a rust fungus

tell To narrate

telltale One who tells

tellurian An earth-dweller

telluride A tellurium compound

tellurium A metallic element

telly Television

telome The terminal branchlet of a primitive vascular plant

telpher An overhead cable car

telson A terminal segment of certain arthropods

temblor An earthquake

temerity Rashness

temper To harden

tempera A painting medium

temperate Moderate

tempest A violent storm

template A pattern

temple A house of worship

tempo, *pl* **-pos** or **-pi** A rate of rhythm

temporal Short-lived

temporary Transient

tempt To entice

tempura A Japanese food dish

ten The cardinal number 10

tenable Logical

tenace A combination of two high cards

tenacious Stubborn

tenancy The period of a tenant's occupancy

tenant One who occupies a building

tenantry Tenancy

tench A freshwater fish

tend To be inclined

tendency An inclination to think in a certain way

tender Fragile

tendon A band of fibrous tissue

tendril An organ of attachment for climbing plants

tenement A residence

tenesmus An ineffectual attempt to urinate or defecate

tenet An opinion

tenfold Ten times

teniasis Infestation with tapeworms

tennis A game

tenon A projection on the end of a piece of wood

tenor A high male voice

tenotomy The surgical division of a tendon

tenpence Ten pennies

tenpenny Costing tenpence

tenpin A bowling pin

tenrec A species of mammal

tense Taut

tensile Pertaining to tension

tension A mental strain

tensor A muscle that tenses

tent A canvas shelter

tentacle A flexible protrusion on certain animals

tentage Tent equipment

tentative Provisional

tenter To stretch cloth

tenth The ordinal number ten in a series

tenuis, *pl* **-ues** A voiceless series

tenuity Lack of firmness

tenure Occupation

tenuto Sustained

teocalli, *pl* **-lis** An ancient temple

teosinte A grass

tepal A division of the perianth

tepee A tent of skins

tepefy To become tepid

tepid Lukewarm

tequila A liquor

terahertz One trillion hertzes

teraohm One trillion ohms

teraphim Small idols

307

teratoid Monstrous

teratoma, *pl* **-mas** or **-mata** A tumor

terbium A metallic element

tercel A male hawk

tercet A group of three lines that rhyme with one another

terebene A mixture of terpenes

teredo A marine mollusk

terete Cylindrical and tapered

tergal Dorsal

tergum, *pl* **-ga** The dorsal surface

teriyaki A Japanese food dish

term A period of time

terminal Extremity

terminus, *pl* **-nuses** or **-ni** The end of something

termite A species of insects

termor One that holds an estate for life

tern A species of sea bird

ternary Arranged in threes

terpene A chemical compound

terrace A porch

terrain, terrane Ground

terrapin A species of turtle

terrarium, *pl* **-ia** An enclosure for small plants

terrazzo A flooring material

terrene Earthly

terret A metal ring on a harness

terrible Dreadful

terrier A breed of dog

terrific Magnificent

territory A region

terror Fear

terry A fabric

terse Concise

tertian Every third day

tesla A unit of measure

tessera, *pl* **tesserae** Small squares used in mosaic patterns

test A criterion

testa, *pl* **-tae** The hard outer coating of a seed

testament A will

testate Having made a will before death

testator One who has made a will

testatrix A woman who has made a will

testicle A testis

testify To talk under oath

testimony Proof

testis, *pl* **-tes** The male reproductive gland

teston, testoon A variety of coins

testudo A protection used by Roman soldiers

testy Touchy

tetanus An infectious disease

tetany A condition characterized by muscular spasms

tetched Slightly demented

tetchy Peevish

teth The ninth letter of the Hebrew alphabet

tether A rope fastened to an animal

tetra A species of fish

tetracid A type of acid

tetrad A set of four

tetragon A four-sided polygon

tetrapod Having four feet

tetrarch A subordinate governor

tetrode An electron tube

tetryl A chemical compound

tetter A skin disease

texas A structure on a river steamboat

text The body of a written work

textbook A book for study

textile Fabric

texture The composition of a substance

thalamus, *pl* **-mi** A part of the brain

thaler Variant of taler

thallic Pertaining to thallium

thallium A metallic element

thalloid Resembling a thallus

thallus, *pl* **thalli** or **-luses** A stemless plant body

than Used to express exception

thanage The rank of a thane

thane In early England, one who held land in return for military services

thaneship The office of a thane

thank To give thanks to

that, *pl* **those** The one indicated

thatch Plant stalks used for roofing

thaw To melt

the Used to refer to a particular person or thing

thearchy Theocracy

theater, theatre A building used for various presentations

thebaine A poisonous alkaloid

theca, *pl* **-cae** An anatomical covering

thecate Encased

thee The objective case of the pronoun thou

theelin Estrone

theft Larceny

their A possessive form of the pronoun they

theism Belief in the existence of a god

them The objective case of the pronoun they

thematic Relating to a theme

theme A topic of discussion

then At that time

thenar The palm of the hand

thence Therefrom

theocrat A ruler of a theocracy

theodicy A defense seeking to vindicate a divine justice which allows evil to exist

theology The study of religion

theorbo A 17th century lute

theorem An idea assumed to be true

theory A plan as to how something might be done

therapist A specialist in therapy

therapy The treatment of illness

there In that place

thereat There

thereby As a result

therefor For that

therefore As a result

therefrom From that

therein In that place

thereof Concerning this

thereon Thereupon

thereto Thereunto

thereunto To that

thereupon Upon this

therewith With that

therm, therme A unit of heat

thermal, thermic Caused by heat

thermion An electrically charged ion

theropod A species of dinosaur

thesaurus, *pl* **-sauri** A book of synonyms and antonyms

thesis, *pl* **-ses** A dissertation

theta The eighth letter of the Greek alphabet

thetic Prescribed

theurgy Supernatural intervention

thew A muscle

they The third person plural pronoun in the nominative case

thiamine, thiamin A B vitamin

thiazine A chemical compound

thiazole A chemical compound

thick Not thin

thickhead A blockhead

thickset Stout

thief, *pl* **thieves** One who steals

thieve To steal

thigh A part of the leg

thill A shaft on a wagon

thimble A small cup worn on the finger

thin Not thick

thine Belonging to thee

thing An object

think To form in the mind

thiol Mercaptan

thionic Containing sulfur

thionyl Sulfinyl

thiourea A chemical compound

thiram A disinfectant

third The ordinal number three in a series

thirl To pierce

thirst A craving for liquid

thirteen The cardinal number 13

thirtieth The ordinal number 30 in a series

thirty The cardinal number 30

this, *pl* **these** The person or thing mentioned

thistle A species of weedy plant

thither In that direction

tho Though

thole To endure

thong A narrow strip of leather

thoracic Near the thorax

thorax, *pl* **-raxes** or **thoraces** The part of the body between the neck and the abdomen

thoria Thorium dioxide

thorite A thorium ore

thorium A metallic element

thorn A prickle

thornback A spider crab

thoron A radioactive isotope of radon

thorough Absolute

thorp A hamlet

thou The second person singular pronoun in the nominative case

though Although

thought The process of thinking

thousand The cardinal number 1,000

thrall Slavery

thrash To flog

thread A fine string of material

threadfin A species of fish

threat A menace

three The cardinal number 3

threefold Three times as many

threesome A group of three

threnody A song of lamentation

thresh To separate seeds from the plants

threshold A doorsill

threw Past tense of throw

thrice Three times

thrift Frugality

thrill To excite

thrips A species of insect

thrive To prosper

thro Through

throat The front part of the neck

throaty Hoarse

throb To pound

throe A violent pang of pain

thrombin An enzyme

thrombus, *pl* **-bi** A clot occluding a blood vessel

throne The chair occupied by a king

throng A multitude

throstle A species of thrush

throttle To regulate the speed of

through In the midst of

throve Past tense of thrive

throw To hurl

throwaway Something that is thrown out

throwback An atavistic example of reversion

thrown Past participle of throw

thru Through

thrum To strum

thrush A species of songbird

thrust To push

thruway An expressway

thud A dull sound

thug A hoodlum

thuggee Murder formerly practiced by the thugs in India

thulium A metallic element

thumb The first digit of the hand

thumbhole The hole on a wind instrument

thumbnail The nail of the thumb

thumbnut A wing nut

thumbtack A wide, flat head tack

thump To beat soundly

thunder The sound that follows a flash of lightning

thurible A censer

thurifer An alter boy who carries a thurible

thus In this manner

thwack To whack

thwart To block

thy The possessive form of the pronoun thou

thylacine A wolflike marsupial

thyme A species of aromatic herb

thymic Pertaining to thyme

thymol A chemical compound

thymus A ductless glandlike structure

thyroid The thyroid gland

thyroxin, thyroxine The active hormone of the thyroid gland

thyrse, thyrsus, *pl* **-si** A type of flower cluster

thyrsoid Similar to a thyrse

thyself Yourself

ti The seventh tone of the diatonic scale

tiara The Pope's triple crown

tibia, *pl* **-iae** or **-ias** The shinbone

tic A muscular contraction
tick A moment
ticket A label
tickle To titillate
ticklish Sensitive to tickling
tickseed The coreopsis plant
ticktack To ticktock
ticktock Sound made by a clock
tidal Having tides
tidbit A choice bit
tide The rise and fall of the ocean
tideland Land under water during high tide
tidemark An indicator
tiderip A riptide
tideway A tidal channel
tidings News
tidy Neat
tidytips A California wildflower
tie To fasten
tieback A loop for holding drapes back
tier Rows placed one above another
tierce The third of the seven canonical hours
tiff A huff
tiffany A fabric
tiffin Lunch
tiger A feline mammal
tigerish Resembling a tiger
tight Close together
tightrope A rope on which acrobats perform
tightwad *Slang* A miser
tiglon, tigon The offspring of a male tiger and a female lion
tigress A fierce, sensuous woman
tike Variant of tyke
tiki A Polynesian god
til The sesame plant
tilbury A carriage
tilde A diacritical mark
tile A piece of baked clay
tilefish A species of fish
till Until
tillage The tilling of land
tilt To tip
tiltyard A yard for tilting contests
timbal A kettledrum
timbale A pastry shell filled with

cooked food
timber A dressed piece of wood
timbre The quality of sound
timbrel A percussion instrument
time The period between two events
timecard An employee's card, recording arrival and depature
timeous Timely
timepiece A watch
timework Piecework
timeworn Trite
timid Shy
timorous Timid
timothy A grass
timpani A set of kettledrums
timpanum Variant of tympanum
tin A metallic element
tinamou A species of quaillike bird
tincal Crude borax
tinct A color or tint
tincture A pigment
tinder Combustible material
tinderbox A box for holding tinder
tine A prong on a fork
tinea A skin disease
tinfoil A thin sheet of tin
ting The sound of a small bell
tinge To tint
tinhorn *Slang* One who pretends to have money
tinker One who mends pots and pans
tinkle To make light metallic sounds
tinnitus A ringing in the ear
tinny Tasting of tin
tinsel A decoration
tinsmith One who works with tin
tinstone A mineral
tint To color
tintype A type of photograph
tinwork Work in tin
tiny Very small
tip The end of something
tipcart A cart that can be tilted
tipcat A game
tipi Variant of tepee
tippet A scarflike garment
tipple To drink habitually

311

tipstaff, *pl* **-staves**   A staff with a metal tip

tipster   One who sells tips

tipsy   Slightly drunk

tiptoe   To walk quietly

tiptop   The very top

tirade   A long violent speech

tire   To lose interest

tiresome   Wearisome

tiro   Variant of tyro

tisane   Herbal tea

tissue   Soft, absorbent paper

tit   A species of bird

titan   One of great size

titanate   A chemical salt

titanic   Colossal

titanite   A mineral

titanium   A metallic element

titanous   Containing titanium

titbit   Variant of tidbit

titer, titre   The strength of a solution

tithe   A tax of one tenth

titi   A species of shrub

titian   A color

titillate   To excite

titivate   To dress up

titlark   A songbird

title   A name given to a book

titlist   A titleholder

titman   The smallest in a litter of pigs

titmouse, *pl* **-mice**   A species of bird

titrate   To test by titration

titter   A giggle

tittie   A sister

tittle   A jot

tittup   A caper

titty   A teat

titular   Bearing a title

tizzy   A state of frenzied excitement

tmesis   The separation of the parts of a compound word

to   In the direction of

toad   A species of tailless amphibian

toadeater   Variant of toady

toadfish   A species of fish

toadflax   A species of plant

toadstool   An inedible fungus

toady   A servile flatterer

toast   To warm

tobacco   A species of plant

toboggan   A long, narrow sled

toby   A drinking mug

toccata   A freestyle composition

tocology   The practice of obstetrics

tocsin   An omen

tod   A unit of weight

today   During the present day

toddle   To walk with unsteady steps

toddler   A child learning to walk

toddy   A drink

tody   A species of bird

toe   One of the digits of the foot

toecap   A covering for the tip of a shoe

toehold   An advantage

toenail   The nail on a toe

toff *Slang*   A dandy

toffee, toffy   A candy

toft   A hillock

tog   A coat

toga, *pl* **-gas** or **-gae**   An outer garment

together   In a group

toggery   Clothing

toggle   A device used to hold something

togue   The lake trout

toil   To labor

toile   A fabric

toilet   To groom oneself

toiletry   An article used in grooming oneself

toilette   Grooming

toilsome   Laborious

token   A sign

tola   A unit of weight

tolan   A chemical compound

tolbooth   A prison

told   Past tense of tell

tole   Enameled metalware

tolerant   Forbearing

tolerate   To permit

tolidine   A chemical compound

toll   A charge for services

tollbooth   A booth at a tollgate

tollgate A gate where a toll is collected

tollhouse A tollbooth

tolu A resin

toluene, toluol A flammable liquid

tolyl A univalent organic radical

tom A male cat

tomahawk A weapon

tomalley The liver of a lobster

tomato A cultivated plant

tomb A place of burial

tombac, tomback, tombak An alloy of copper and zinc

tomboy A young girl who behaves like a boy

tombstone A gravestone

tomcat A male cat

tomcod A marine fish

tome A large book

tomentum, *pl* **-ta** A network of small blood vessels

tomfool A foolish person

tommy A loaf of bread

tommyrot *Slang* Nonsense

tomorrow The day following today

tomtit A small bird

ton A unit of weight

tonal Pertaining to tones

tonality A system of tones

tone A musical sound

tong A Chinese association

tongue The fleshy organ of the mouth

tonguing The use of the tongue in playing wind instruments

tonic A medicine

tonight This night

tonneau A cover for a small open sports car

tonsil A lymphoid organ

tonsorial Pertaining to barbering

tonsure The act of shaving the head

tontine A form of insurance

tonus Contraction characteristics of a muscle in a state of rest

tony *Slang* Stylish

too In addition

took Past tense of take

tool An instrument worked by hand

toolbox A case for carrying tools

toolmaker A machinist

toon A tall tree

toot To sound a whistle in short blasts

tooth, *pl* **teeth** One of a bonelike structure in the jaw

toothache An aching pain near the tooth

toothpick A small piece of wood

toothsome Savory

toothwort A species of plant

toothy Having prominent teeth

tootle To toot softly

toots *Slang* Darling

tootsy, toosie *Slang* A girl

top The highest part

topaz A mineral

topcoat A lightweight overcoat

tope To drink

topee, topi A sun helmet

topflight First-rate

topfull, topful Filled to the top

tophus, *pl* **-phi** Urate deposit in tissue

topiary The art of trimming shrubs

topic A theme

topknot A headdress

toplofty Pretentious

topmast A mast on a ship

topminnow A species of fish

topmost The highest

topnotch Excellent

topology A topographical study of a specific land area

toponym A name derived from a place

toponymy The study of place names

topotype An organism taken from the area typical of that species

topper A topcoat

topple To overturn

topsail A sail of a ship

topside The upper part of a ship

topsoil The surface layer of soil

topspin A spin given to a struck ball

toque A woman's hat

tor A crag

torah, tora The body of Jewish religious literature

torch A flambeau

tore Past tense of tear

toreador A bullfighter

torero A matador

toric Pertaining to a torus

torii The gateway of a Shinto temple

torment Mental anguish

tormentil A Eurasian plant

torn Past tense of tear

tornado A violent windstorm

tornillo A lathe

toroid A doughnut-shaped coil

torose Bulging

torpedo A self-propelled underwater projectile

torpid Dormant

torpor Mental inactivity

torquate Having a ringlike band about the neck

torque A twisting effect

torques A band of feathers around the neck

torr A unit of pressure

torrent A deluge

torrid Scorching

torsade A twisted cord

torsion The act of twisting

torso, *pl* **-sos** or **-si** The trunk of the human body

tort A wrongful act

torte A layer cake

tortilla A Mexican-type pancake

tortoise A species of turtle

torture The infliction of severe pain

torus, *pl* **tori** A type of molding

tosh Nonsense

toss To throw

tosspot A drunkard

tossup An even chance

tost Past tense of toss

tostada A fried tortilla

tot A little child

total The whole quantity

tote To haul

totem A symbol

totemism Belief in totems

tother The other

toucan A species of bird

touch To bring into contact with something else

touchback A play in football

touchdown A scoring play in football

touche Used to express concession to an opponent

touchhole In early firearms, the hole through which the charge was touched off

touchline A sideline bordering the field

touchup The act of improving

tough Rugged

toupee A hair piece

tour A trip to various places

touraco A species of bird

tournedos A beefsteak

tourney To compete in a tournament

tousle To dishevel

tout To praise

tow To pull along

towage A charge for towing

toward In the direction of

towboat A tugboat

towel A cloth used for drying

tower A tall building

towhead A head of pale yellow hair

towhee A species of bird

towline A line used in towing a vessel

town A city

townie A resident of a town

township A division of a county

townsman A town resident

towpath A path alongside a canal

towrope A towline

toxemia A condition of toxins in the blood

toxic Poisonous

toxicant A poisonous agent

toxin, toxine A poisonous substance

toxoid A form of toxin

toy A plaything for children

toyon A shrub

toyshop A shop where toys are sold

trabeate Constructed with lintels

trace A touch
trachea, *pl* **-cheae** or **-as** The tube carrying air to the lungs
tracheid A cell in woody tissue
trachoma A viral disease
trachyte An igneous rock
track A trail
trackage Railway tracks
trackman One who inspects railroad tracks
tract An expanse of land
tractate An essay
tractile Ductile
tractor A farming vehicle
trade A craft
trademark A symbol identifying a product
tradesman A dealer
tradition Customs handed down
traditor, *pl* **-es** A traitor
traduce To slander
traffic Vehicles in transit
tragedy A disastrous event
tragic Pertaining to tragedy
tragopan A species of pheasant
tragus, *pl* **-gi** Hairy part of the ear
trail Leave a track
train Connected railroad cars
trainband A militia
trainee One who is being trained
trainload The capacity of a freight train
trainman A brakeman
traipse To walk about
trait A distinguishing feature
traitor One who commits treason
traitress A female traitor
traject To transmit
tram A cable car
tramcar A streetcar
trammel A shackle for a horse
tramp To trudge
tramway A streetcar line
trance A hypnotic state
tranquil Serene
transact To negotiate
transcend To be superior to
transect To divide
transept A part of a church building

transfer To shift from one place to another
transfix To fix fast
transform To change
transfuse To instill
transient Transitory
transit Passage
translate To explain
transmit To convey
transmute To transform
transom A small window above a door
transonic Moving at a speed from subsonic to supersonic
transpire To become known
transport To carry away
transpose To interchange
tranship To transfer cargo
transude To pass through pores
trap A device for capturing
trapan Variant of trepan
trapeze A bar used by gymnasts
trapezoid A bone of the wrist
trappean, trappous Consisting of luggage
trapunto A type of quilting
trash Garbage
trass A volcanic rock
trauma, *pl* **-mas** or **-mata** An emotional shock
travail Hard work
trave A crossbeam
travel To journey
traverse To cross
travesty A burlesque
travois, travoise A sledge used by Plains Indians
trawl A fishing line
tray A shallow receptacle
treachery Treason
treacle Molasses
tread To subdue
treadle A lever operated by the foot
treadmill A monotonous job
treason Violation of allegiance toward one's country
treasure Something considered valuable
treat To entertain at one's own expense

treatise An account of some subject
treble Triple
trebuchet, trebucket A medieval catapult
trecento The 14th century
tree A tall, woody plant
treenail, trenail A wooden peg used to fasten timbers
tref Unfit for consumption according to Jewish law
trefoil A species of plant
trehala An edible substance obtained from beetles
treillage Latticework
trek A journey
trellis A frame used for climbing plants
trematode A species of flatworm
tremble To shiver
tremolo A tremulous musical effect
tremor A vibrating movement
tremulous Trembling
trench A ditch
trenchant Penetrating
trend A course
trepan A boring tool
trepang A species of sea cucumber
trephine A surgical instrument
trepid Timid
trespass To transgress
tress A lock of hair
trestle A framework supporting a bridge
tret An allowance paid for deterioration of goods in transit
trews Close-fitting trousers
trey A playing card with three spots
triable Capable of being tried
triacid A type of acid
triad A group of three
trial An effort
triangle A three-sided polygon
triarchy A triumvirate
triaxial Having three axes
triazine A chemical compound
triazole A chemical compound
tribade A lesbian
tribasic Containing three replaceable hydrogen atoms

tribe A division of ancient cultures
tribesman A member of a tribe
tribrach A type of metrical foot
tribune A protector of the people
tributary A stream flowing into a river
tribute A gift of respect
trice To hoist with a rope
triceps An arm muscle
trichina, *pl* **-nae** or **-nas** A parasitic worm
trichite Crystallite occurring in volcanic rock
trichoid Hairlike
trichome A hairlike outgrowth
trick A practical joke
trickish Tending to use tricks
trickle To drip
trickster A person who tricks
triclinic A system of three unequal axes
tricolor Having three colors
tricorn, tricorne A cocked hat
tricot A fabric
tricuspid Having three points
tricycle A vehicle with three wheels
tridactyl Having three parts
trident A three-pronged spear
triennial Lasting three years
triennium, *pl* **-ennia** A period of three years
trierarch The commander of a trireme
trifid Divided into three parts
trifle A little
trifocal Eyeglasses with trifocal lenses
trifold Triple
trig Neat
triglyph An ornament in a Doric frieze
trigon A Roman harp
trihedral Having three sides
trill A warble
trillion The cardinal number represented by 1 followed by 12 zeros
trillium A species of plant
trilogy A group of three dramatic

316

works

trim To make neat

trimester A term of three months

trimeter A verse line of three metrical feet

trimetric Having three metrical feet

trimorph A substance existing in three forms

trinal Threefold

trinary Ternary

trine Threefold

trinity A triad

trinket A small ornament

trio A composition for three performers

triode A type of electron tube

triolet A poem

trioxide A chemical compound

trip A journey

tripe Rubbish

tripedal Having three feet

triplane An airplane with three sets of wings

triple Threefold

triplet A group of three

triplex Triple

triploid A triploid cell

tripod A three-legged stool

tripoli Siliceous rock

tripos A tripod

trippet A mechanical part

triptane A chemical compound

triptych An ancient writing tablet

trireme A Roman galley

trisect To divide into three parts

trismus Lockjaw

trisomic A trisomic cell

triste Sad

tristesse Sadness

tristeza A disease of citrus trees

tristful Gloomy

tristich A triplet

trite Commonplace

tritheism Belief in three gods

tritium A radioactive hydrogen isotope

triton A species of marine gastropod mollusk

tritone A musical interval of three

tones

triumph To prevail

triumvir, *pl* **-virs** or **-viri** Any of three associated in office

triune A trinity

trivalent Having a valence of three

trivalve Having three valves

trivet A small three-legged stand

trivia Unimportant matters

trivium, *pl* **-ia** The division of the seven liberal arts

triweekly Three times a week

trocar A surgical instrument

trochaic A trochee

trochal Shaped like a wheel

troche A medicinal lozenge

trochee A metrical foot

trochlea, *pl* **-leae** An anatomical structure that resembles a pulley

trochoid Having a rotary motion

trodden Past participle of tread

trode Past tense of tread

troffer A fixture for flourescent lighting

trogon A species of bird

troika A carriage

troll To sing heartily

trolley A streetcar

trollop A slovenly woman

trombone A musical instrument

trommel A sieve for sifting rock and ore

tromp To tramp

trompe A device for producing a blast

trona A mineral

troop A group of soldiers

troopship A ship for carrying troops

troostite A mineral

trope A figure of speech

trophic Pertaining to nutrition

trophy A symbol of victory

tropic Either of two circles of the celestial sphere parallel to the equator

tropine A poisonous alkaloid

tropism The growth of an organism toward an external stimulus

trot A race for trotting horses

troth Fidelity
trotline A fishing line
trouble A state of danger
troublous Troubled
trough A gutter
trounce To beat
troupe A company of touring actors
troupial A species of bird
trousers Pants
trousseau A bride's wardrobe
trout A species of fish
trouvere, trouveur A school of poets
trove A find
trow To suppose
trowel A tool used in cement work
troy Expressed in troy weight
truancy Absenteeism
truce An armistice
truck A heavy vehicle
truckage Goods hauled by truck
truckle A caster
truckload The quantity a truck carries
truckman A truck driver
truculent Savage
trudge To plod
trudgen A swimming stroke
true Reliable
trueblue One of unswerving loyalty
trueborn Genuinely such by birth
truelove A sweetheart
truepenny A trusty person
truffle A species of subterranean fungus
truism A statement of a truth
trull A harlot
truly Sincerely
trump To take a card
trumpet A wind instrument
truncate To shorten
truncheon A club
trundle To propel on wheels
trunk A large case
trunkfish A species of fish
trunnion A pin
truss A supporting beam
trust Faith
trustee An agent who administers property
truth Reality
try To make an effort
tryma, pl **-mata** A type of nut
tryout A performance before the official opening
trypsin An enzyme
trysail A type of sail
tryst A meeting between lovers
tsadi Hebrew letter
tsar Variant of czar
tsimmes A stew
tsk Exclamation of disapproval
tsoris Trouble
tsunami A huge ocean wave
tsuris A series of misfortunes
tuatara, tuatera A reptile
tub A bathtub
tuba A wind instrument
tubal Pertaining to a tube
tubate Forming a tube
tubby Short and fat
tube A hollow cylinder
tubercle A swelling
tuberose A tuberous plant
tubifex, pl **-fexes** A species of worm
tubule A small tube
tubulous Tubular
tuchun A Chinese military governor
tuck To gather and fold
tuckahoe A species of plant
tucket A trumpet fanfare
tufa A kind of porous stone
tuff A porous rock
tuffet A tuft of grass
tuft A clump of trees
tug To strain at
tugboat A boat built for towing larger boats
tuille A part of armor
tuition A fee for schooling
tule A species of bulrush
tulip A flowering plant
tulle Netting used for veils
tumble To roll end over end
tumbrel, tumbril A cart
tumefy To swell
tumescent Swelling

tumid Swollen
tummy The stomach
tumor A swelling
tump A small mound
tumpline A band used to support a pack on the back
tumular Pertaining to a tumulus
tumulose Full of mounds
tumult The din of a great crowd
tumulus, *pl* **-li** An ancient burial mound
tun A large cask
tuna A species of food fish
tundra A treeless plain of the arctic region
tune A melody
tungstate A chemical compound
tungsten A metallic element
tungstic A chemical compound
tunic A loose-fitting garment
tunnel An underground passage
tunny Variant of tuna
tup A ram
tupelo A species of tree
tuppence Variant of twopence
tuppenny Variant of twopenny
tuque A woolen cap
turban A Moslem headdress
turbary A peat bog
turbid Muddy
turbine A type of motor
turbit A domestic pigeon
turbofan A turbojet engine
turbojet A jet engine
turbot A species of fish
turbulent Unruly
tureen A deep dish
turf Sod
turgid Swollen
turgor The state of being turgid
turion A scaly stem that rises from the ground
turkey A large American bird
turmeric A species of plant
turmoil Confusion
turn To revolve
turnabout The act of turning about
turncoat A traitor
turnery The workshop of a lathe operator

turnhall A gymnasium
turnip A plant of the mustard family
turnkey A jailer
turnover A pastry
turnpike A highway
turnsole A species of plant
turnspit One who turns a spit
turnstile A mechanical device used to admit people one at a time
turnup Something turned up
turpeth A plant root used in medicine
turpitude Depravity
turps Turpentine
turquoise A color
turret A gunner's enclosure
turtle A species of reptile
tusche A substance used in lithography
tush An exclamation expressing disapproval
tusk A long, pointed tooth
tussah, tussore An Asian silkworm
tussis A cough
tussle To scuffle
tussock, tussuck A clump of grass
tut Used to express impatience
tutelage Guardianship
tutor A private teacher
tutoyer To speak to familiarly
tutti All
tutty An impure zinc oxide
tutu A ballet skirt
tuxedo A man's semiformal dinner jacket
tuyere A pipe through which air is forced
twaddle Idle talk
twain Two
twang To cause to make a sharp sound
twayblade A species of orchid
tweak To pinch
tweed A fabric
tweet A chirping sound
tweeze To extract with tweezers
twelfth The ordinal number 12 in a series
twelve The cardinal number 12

twentieth   The ordinal number 20 in a series

twenty   The cardinal number 20

twerp *Slang*   A person regarded as insignificant

twibil, twibill   A battle-ax

twice   Two times

twiddle   To fiddle with

twig   A small branch

twiggen   Made of twigs

twiggy   Twiglike

twilight   The subdued light after sunset

twill   A fabric

twin   One of two offspring born at the same birth

twine   To twist together

twinge   A sudden pain

twinight   Designating a baseball doubleheader that begins in late afternoon

twinkle   To flicker

twinning   The bearing of twins

twirl   To spin

twirp   Variant of twerp

twist   To wind

twit   To ridicule

twitch   To jerk

twixt   Betwixt

two   The cardinal number 2

twofold   Double

twopence   Two pennies

twopenny   Cheap

twosome   A duo

tycoon   A magnate

tyke   A small child

tympan   A membranelike part

tympani   Variant of timpani

tympanist   One who plays percussion instruments

tympanum, *pl* **-na** or **-nums**   The middle ear

tympany   Pomposity

typal   Typical

type   A perfect example

typebar   Part of a typewriter

typecast   To cast in an acting role similar to one's real-life character

typeface   The face of printing type

typeset   To set in type

typhoid   Typhoid fever

typhoon   A tropical cyclone

typhus   An infectious disease

typical, typic   Having the nature of a representative kind

typo   A typographical error

typology   The study of classifications

tyramine   A chemical compound

tyranny   Unjust government

tyrant   An absolute ruler

tyre   Variant of tire

tyro   A novice

tyrosine   An amino acid

tzar   Variant of czar

tzuris   Variant of tsuris

ubiety   The condition of being in a particular place

ubiquity   Omnipresence

udder   A mammary gland

udo   A Japanese plant

ugh   An exclamation of disgust

ugli   A citrus fruit

ugly   Unsightly

320

ugsome Disgusting
uh Variant of huh
uhlan, ulan A mounted Prussian lancer
uitlander An outlander
ukase An edict
uke, ukulele A small guitar
ulcer A skin lesion
ulema A Moslem scholar
ulna, *pl* **-nae** or **-nas** A bone of the forearm
ulster An overcoat
ulterior Subsequent
ultima The last syllable of a word
ultimate Final
ultimo Of the preceding month
ultra Extreme
ultraism Extremism
ulu An Eskimo knife
ululate To howl
umbel A type of flower cluster
umber A color
umbilicus, *pl* **-ci** The navel
umbo, *pl* **umbones** or **-bos** The knob at the center of a shield
umbra, *pl* **-brae** A dark area
umbrage A shadow
umbrella A protective cover from the rain
umiak An Eskimo boat
umlaut A change in the sound of a vowel
umpire, ump One who administers the rules in games
umpteen A large number
un One

un- Indicates not or reversal; renewal; or deprivation. The following compounds are listed without definition (see Introduction):

unabashed	unaided	unargue
unabated	unaimed	unarm
unabetted	unaired	unarmored
unable	unalike	unartful
unabused	unallied	unashamed
unacted	unalloyed	unasked
unadorned	unamused	unassured
unafraid	unaneled	unatoned
unaged	unapt	unattired
unagile	unaptly	unavenged
unavowed	uncertain	undaring
unawaked	unchain	undated
unaware	unchanged	undaunted
unawed	uncharged	undecayed
unbacked	uncharted	undeceive
unbaked	unchary	undecided
unbar	unchaste	undecked
unbarbed	unchecked	undefaced
unbased	unchewed	undefiled
unbathed	unchic	undefined
unbeaten	unchilled	undenied
unbelt	unchosen	undesired
unbenign	unchurch	undevout
unbiased	uncivil	undiluted
unbidden	unclad	undimmed
unbind	unclaimed	undivided
unbitted	unclasp	undo
unblamed	unclean	undrained
unblest	unclear	undrape
unbloody	unclipped	undreamt
unbolt	uncloak	undress
unboned	unclog	undried
unborn	unclothe	undulled
unbought	unclouded	undutiful
unbound	uncloyed	undyed
unbowed	uncoated	uneager
unbrace	uncocked	unearned
unbraid	uncoined	uneasy
unbranded	uncolored	uneatable
unbred	uncombed	uneaten
unbridled	uncomely	unedible
unbroke	uncomic	unedited
unbruised	uncommon	uneffaced
unbrushed	uncooked	unended
unbuckle	uncool	unending
unburden	uncork	unengaged
unburied	uncounted	unentered
unburned	uncouth	unenvied
unburnt	uncover	unenvious
unbutton	uncrate	unequal
uncaged	uncreated	unerased
uncalled	uncropped	unerring
uncandid	uncrowded	unethical
uncap	uncurable	unevaded
uncaring	uncurbed	uneven
uncashed	uncured	unevenly
uncasked	uncurl	unexalted
uncaught	uncursed	unexcited
uncaused	uncut	unexcused
unceasing	undamped	unexotic

321

unexpert	ungodly	uninvoked	unloving	unoffered	unpriced
unexpired	ungot	unironed	unlucky	unoiled	unprimed
unexposed	ungotten	unissued	unmake	unopen	unprinted
unfaded	ungowned	unjaded	unman	unopposed	unprized
unfading	ungraced	unjoined	unmanful	unornate	unprobed
unfair	ungraded	unjoyful	unmanly	unowned	unproved
unfairly	ungreased	unjudged	unmannish	unpack	unproven
unfallen	ungreedy	unjust	unmapped	unpaged	unpruned
unfancy	unguided	unjustly	unmarked	unpaid	unpure
unfasten	unhailed	unkempt	unmarred	unpainful	unpurged
unfazed	unhalved	unkept	unmarried	unpainted	unquaking
unfeared	unhandled	unkind	unmask	unpaired	unquelled
unfearful	unhandy	unkindly	unmatched	unparted	unquiet
unfed	unhanged	unkingly	unmated	unpatched	unquoted
unfeigned	unhappy	unkissed	unmatted	unpaved	unraised
unfelling	unharmed	unknit	unmatured	unpaying	unraked
unfelt	unharmful	unknown	unmeant	unpeg	unranked
unfenced	unharness	unkosher	unmellow	unpen	unrated
unfertile	unhasty	unlabeled	unmelted	unperfect	unravaged
unfilial	unhatched	unlabored	unmended	unpick	unrazed
unfilled	unhealed	unlace	unmerited	unpierce	unread
unfilmed	unhealthy	unlade ,	unmesh	unpile	unready
unfired	unheard	unlaid '	unmet	unpin	unreal
unfished	unheated	unlash	unmilled	unpitied	unrebuked
unfit	unheeded	unlatch	unmingled	unpitying	unrefined
unflexed	unhelped	unlawful	unmixed	unplaced	unrelated
unfoiled	unhelpful	unleased	unmixt	unplanned	unrelaxed
unfond	unheroic	unleash	unmodish	unplanted	unrenewed
unforced	unhewn	unled	unmold	unplayable	unrented
unforged	unhinge	unlethal	unmolten	unplayed	unrepaid
unforked	unhip	unletted	unmoral	unpleased	unrested
unformed	unhired	unlevel	unmounted	unpledged	unrestful
unfought	unhitch	unlevied	unmourned	unpliable	unrevised
unfound	unholily	unlicked	unmovable	unpliant	unrevoked
unframed	unholy	unlighted	unmoved	unplowed	unrhyme
unfree	unhonored	unlikable	unmoving	unplucked	unrifled
unfrock	unhook	unlike	unmown	unplug	unrimed
unfunded	unhoped	unlikely	unmuffle	unplumbed	unrinsed
unfunny	unhostile	unlined	unmusical	unpoetic	unripe
unfused	unhoused	unlisted	unnail	unpointed	unrisen
unfussy	unhuman	unlit	unnamable	unpoised	unroasted
ungalled	unhung	unlive	unnamed	unpolite	unrobe
ungenial	unhurt	unlively	unnatural	unpolitic	unroped
ungentle	unhusk	unload	unneeded	unpalled	unrough
ungently	unideal	unlobed	unneedful	unpopular	unruffled
ungenuine	unimbued	unlocated	unnerve	unposed	unruled
ungifted	unimpeded	unlock	unnoisy	unposted	unruly
unglassed	uninjured	unlovable	unnoted	unpotted	unrumpled
unglazed	uninsured	unloved	unnoticed	unpressed	unrushed
ungloved	uninvited	unlovely	unobliged	unpretty	unrusted

unsaddle
unsafe
unsafely
unsaintly
unsalable
unsalted
unsampled
unsated
unsaved
unsavory
unsawed
unsawn
unsayable
unscaled
unscanned
unscarred
unscented
unscrew
unseal
unseared
unseat
unseeded
unseeing
unseemly
unseen
unseized
unselfish
unsent
unserved
unsew
unsex
unsexual
unshackle
unshaded
unshaken
unshamed
unshaped
unshapely
unshapen
unshared
unsharpen
unshaved
unshaven
unshed
unshell
unship
unshod
unshorn
unshrunk
unshut

unsifted
unsighted
unsigned
unsilent
unsimilar
unsinful
unsized
unskilled
unslaked
unsliced
unsling
unsmoked
unsnagged
unsoaked
unsober
unsocial
unsoiled
unsold
unsolid
unsolved
unsoothed
unsorted
unsought
unsound
unsoured
unsowed
unsown
unspent
unsphere
unspilled
unspilt
unsplit
unspoiled
unspoken
unspotted
unsprung
unspun
unsquared
unstable
unstack
unstained
unstalked
unstamped
unstarred
unstated
unsteady
unstep
unstinted
unstocked
unstop

unstrap
unstring
unstriped
unstrung
unstudied
unstuffed
unstung
unstylish
unsubdued
unsubtle
unsuited
unsullied
unsung
unsunk
unsure
unsurely
unswathe
unswayed
unswept
unswollen
untack
untactful
untagged
untainted
untaken
untamable
untame
untanned
untapped
untasted
untaught
untaxed
untenable
untended
untested
unthanked
unthawed
unthrifty
untidily
untidy
untilled
untilted
untimely
untinged
untipped
untired
untiring
untitled
untold
untorn

untouched
untraced
untrained
untrapped
untreated
untried
untrimmed
untrod
untrue
untruly
untrusty
untruth
untufted
untunable
untuned
untuneful
unturn
untutored
untwilled
untypical
ununited
unurged
unusable
unused
unusual
unuttered
unvalued
unvaried
unvarying
unveil
unveined

unversed
unvexed
unvext
unviable
unvisited
unvocal
unwalled
unwanted
unwarier
unwariest
unwarily
unwarlike
unwarmed
unwarned
unwarped
unwary
unwashed
unwasted
unwatched
unwatered
unwax
unwean
unweary
unweave
unwed
unwedded
unweeded
unweighed
unwelcome
unwelded
unwell

unwept
unwetted
unwhipped
unwieldy
unwifely
unwilled
unwinking
unwise
unwisely
unwished
unwitting
unwomanly
unwon
unwonted
unwooded
unwooed
unworked
unworldly
unworn
unworried
unworthy
unwounded
unwoven
unwrap
unwrinkle
unwritten
unwrung
unyoke
unzip
unzoned

unai, unau A sloth
unanimous Being in complete harmony
unbelief Lack of belief
unbend To relax
unbodied Without body
unbosom To confide one's feelings
uncanny Strange
uncial Pertaining to a style of letters
unciform Hook-shaped
uncinate Hooked at the tip
uncius, *pl* **-ni** A hooklike structure
uncle The brother of one's mother or father
unclench To relax
unclose To open
unco A stranger
uncoil To unwind

unconcern Lack of interest
uncouple To disconnect
uncross To move from a crossed position
unction An ointment
uncus, *pl* **-unci** A hook-shaped part
under In a lower place

under- Indicates below or under; inferiority; lower quality. The following compounds are listed without definition (see Introduction):

underact	undergird	underpin
underage	undergo	underplay
underarm	undergod	underprop
underate	underhand	underrate
underbid	underhung	underrun
underbud	underjaw	undersea
underbuy	underlaid	undersell
undercoat	underlap	underside
undercool	underlay	undersign
undercut	underlet	undersoil
underdo	underlie	undertax
underdog	underline	undertone
underdress	underlip	undertow
undereat	underlit	undervest
underfeed	undermine	underwear
underfoot	underpass	underwing
underfur	underpay	underwood

underset A current below the ocean
undertake To take upon oneself
undies Underwear
undine A female water spirit
undraw To draw to one side
undue Excessive
undulant Resembling waves
undulate To move in waves
unduly Excessively
undying Endless
unearth To dig up
unfailing Constant
unfix To unfasten
unfledged Immature
unfold To open
unfurl To unroll
ungainly Clumsy
ungird To remove
ungirt Loose
ungual Having a hoof
unguent A salve
unguis, *pl* **-gues** A clawlike

structure
ungulate Having hoofs
unhallow To profane
uniaxial Having only one axis
unicolor One color
unicorn A mythical creature
unicycle A one-wheeled bicycle
unifilar Having one thread
uniform Unchanging
unify To consolidate
union Marriage
unipolar Produced by a single pole
unique Unparalleled
unisex Involving a fashion that is undifferentiated for the sexes
unison Complete agreement
unit Any fixed amount
unite To join
univalent Single
univalve A one-piece shell
universe All mankind
univocal Having only one meaning
unkennel To uncover
unlearn To forget
unless Except on the condition that
unlimber To prepare for action
unlimited Without limits
unlink To unfasten
unloose To set free
unmeet Improper
unmindful Careless
unmoor To become unmoored
unpeople To depopulate
unquote To close a quotation
unravel To separate
unreason Nonsense
unreel To unwind
unreeve To withdraw a rope
unreserve Candor
unrest Uneasiness
unriddle To solve
unrig To strip of rigging
unrip To rip open
unrivaled Unequaled
unroll To unwind
unroot To uproot
unround To pronounce without rounding of the lips
unsay To retract
unseam To undo the seams of

unset Unmounted
unsettle To disrupt
unsnap To unfasten
unsnarl To disentangle
unspeak To retract
unsteel To make soft
unstick To free
unswear To retract an oath
untangle To resolve
unteach To cause to unlearn something
unthink To disregard
unthread To draw out the thread
untie To straighten out
until Up to the time of
unto To
untoward Not favorable
untread To retrace
untruss To undo
untwine To disentangle
untwist To unwind
unvoice To make voiceless
unwind To uncoil
unwish To cease to wish for
up To a higher station

up- Indicates up; upper; upward. The following compounds are listed without definition (see Introduction):

upbear	upfling	upmost
upbeat	upflow	upper
upboil	upfold	uppercut
upbore	upgather	uppermost
upborne	upgaze	uppile
upbuild	upgoing	upprop
upcast	upgrade	upraise
upchuck	upgrow	upreach
(slang)	upgrowth	uprear
upclimb	upheap	upright
upcoil	upheaval	uprise
upcountry	upheave	uprising
upcurl	upheld	upriver
upcurve	uphill	uproot
updart	uphoard	uprouse
update	uphold	uprush
updive	upkeep	upsend
updo	upland	upset
updraft	upleap	upshift
upend	uplife	upshoot
upfield	uplight	upside

upsoar	upstream	uptilt
upspring	upstroke	uptoss
upstage	upsurge	uptown
upstairs	upsweep	uptowner
upstand	upswell	uptrend
upstare	upswing	upturn
upstart	uptake	upwaft
upstate	uptear	upward
upstep	upthrow	upwell
upstir	upthrust	upwind

upas A tree
upbraid To censure
upholster To cover furniture
upon On
uppity, uppish Inclined to be snobbish
uproar A tumult
upshot The outcome
upsilon The 20th letter of the Greek alphabet
uracil A chemical compound
uraeus A figure on an ancient headdress
uranic Celestial
uranium A radioactive element
uranous Pertaining to uranium
uranyl A bivalent radical
urate A salt of uric acid
urb An urban area
urban Pertaining to a city
urbane Elegant
urbia Cities
urchin A small boy
urea A chemical compound
urease, urase An enzyme
uredo A burning itch
ureide A chemical compound
uremia An abnormal condition of the blood
ureter The duct that conveys urine from the kidney to the bladder
urethane A chemical compound
urethra, pl **-thras** or **-thrae** The canal through which urine is discharged
uretic Urinary
urge To impel
urgent The state of being urgent
uric Pertaining to urine
uridine A chemical compound

urinal A fixture in a men's restroom
urine Fluid secreted by the kidneys
urn A vase
urochord Variant of tunicate
urodele A species of amphibian
urolith Urinary calculus
urology The study of the urinary tract
uropod Abdominal appendages of certain crustaceans
uroscopy The examination of urine
ursine Pertaining to a bear
urticant Causing itching
urticate To sting with nettles
urus An extinct wild ox
urushiol A toxic substance
us The objective case of the pronoun we
usable Capable of being used
usance Usage
use To consume
usher One who escorts people to their seats
usherette A female usher
usual Ordinary
usufruct The right to use another's

property as long as it is not damaged
usurer One who lends money at high interest
usurp To seize without right
usury The practice of lending money at high interest
ut The musical tone C
utensil An implement
uterine Pertaining to the uterus
uterus An organ of female mammals
utile Useful
utility Usefulness
utilize To put to use
utmost Maximum
utopia An idealized situation
utricle A membranous sac of the inner ear
utter To speak
uvea A layer of the eye
uveitis Inflammation of the uvea
uvula, *pl* **-las** or **-lae** The mass suspended from the soft palate above the back of the tongue
uxorial Characteristic of a wife

vacant Empty
vacate To give up
vacation A period of relaxation
vaccinal Relating to vaccination
vaccinate To inoculate
vaccine A substance that produces immunity to disease
vacillate To fluctuate
vacuity An empty space
vacuole A small cavity

vacuum, *pl* **-ums** or **vacua** A void
vadose A shallow place
vagabond A wanderer
vagal Pertaining to the vagus nerve
vagary A whimsical idea
vagility Freedom of movement
vagina, *pl* **-nas** or **-nae** The canal leading from the vulva to the uterus
vagotomy Surgical division of the

vagus nerve
vagrant A tramp
vague Not clear
vagus, *pl* **-gi** A cranial nerve
vahine Variant of wahine
vail To lower
vain Futile
vainglory Boastfulness
vair A fur
valance An ornamental drapery
vale A valley
valence, valency The capacity of an element to combine with another
valerian A species of plant
valet A man's personal servant
valgus, *pl* **-guses** An abnormal twist outward
valiant Showing valor
valid Binding
valine An amino acid
valise A small bag
valley A stretch of low-lying land
valonia A substance from the dried acorn cups of oak trees
valor, valour Bravery
valuable Something of value
valuator An appraiser
value The worth of a thing
valvate Having valvelike parts
valve A device that regulates liquid flow
valvular Pertaining to valves
valvule, valvula, *pl* **-lae** A small valve
vambrace Part of armor
vamoose *Slang* Go away
vamp A seductive woman
vampire A figure in folklore who sucks the blood of sleeping victims
van A covered truck
vanadium A metallic element
vanda A species of orchid
vandal One who destroys
vane A weather vane
vang A guy rope on a ship
vanguard A leading position
vanilla A flavoring extract
vanillic Derived from vanilla
vanillin A chemical compound
vanish To disappear

vanity The condition of being vain
vanquish To defeat
vantage Superiority
vanward Advanced
vapid Stale
vapor Visible particles of moisture
vaporish Like vapor
vaquero A cowboy
vara A unit of length
varia Literary works
variant Differing
variate Something that varies
varicella Chicken pox
varicose Abnormally swollen
variegate To make varied
varietal Of a variety
variety Diversity
variform Having many forms
variola Smallpox
variorum A literary work containing various scholarly versions
various Different
varix, *pl* **-ices** A varicose vein
varlet An attendant
varmint, varment A troublesome animal
varnish A smooth coating
varsity A college team
varus, *pl* **-uses** Abnormally bent
varve A layer of sediment
vary To modify
vas, *pl* **vasa** A vessel or duct
vascular Of the vessels that convey blood
vasculum, *pl* **-la** A box for plant specimens
vase A decorative container
vasectomy Surgical resection of the vas deferens
vassal A servant
vast Great in area
vasty Vast
vat A large vessel
vatic Pertaining to a prophet
vault An arched structure
vaunt To brag about
vav, vau The sixth letter of the Hebrew alphabet
vavasor, vavasour, vavassor A feudal vassal

vaward Variant of vanguard
veal Meat of a young calf
vealer A calf intended for food
vector An insect that produces a disease-producing organism
vedette A small scouting boat
vee The letter v
veep A vice president
veer To swerve
vegetable A species of plant
vegetal Vegetative
vegetate To grow
vehement Emphatic
vehicle A device for carrying passengers
veil A piece of transparent fabric
vein A vessel that transports blood
veinlet A small vein
velamen, pl **velamina** A velum
velar Of a velum
velate Having a velum
veldt, veld Grazing area of South Africa
velleity The weakest kind of desire
vellum A parchment
veloce Rapidly
velocity Speed
velours, velour A fabric
veloute A sauce
velum, pl **-la** A thin membranous tissue
velure A fabric
velvet A fabric
vena, pl **venae** A vein
venal Open to bribery
venatic Pertaining to hunting
vend To sell
vendee A buyer
vender, vendor One who sells
vendetta A feud between two families
vendue A public sale
veneer A thin surface layer
venerate To regard with respect
venereal Having to do with sexual love
venery The pursuit of sexual activity
venge To avenge
venial Pardonable

venire A writ
venison The meat of a deer
venom A poisonous secretion
venose Venous
venous Pertaining to veins
vent An exit
ventail Part of a medieval helmet
ventral Abdominal
venture A dangerous undertaking
venturi A device used to measure the flow of a liquid
venue The locality of an event
venule A small vein
vera Very
veracity Accuracy
verandah, veranda A balcony
verb A word that expresses action
verbatim Word for word
verbena A species of plant
verbiage Wordiness
verbose Wordy
verboten Forbidden
verdant Green with vegetation
verderer, verderor The official in charge of royal forests
verdict The decision reached by the jury
verdin A small bird
verditer A carbonate of copper
verdure Greenness
verge The brink
verify To substantiate
verily In fact
verism Realism in art
veritas Truth
verity Truth
verjuice The juice of unripe fruit
vermeil Vermilion
vermicide A substance used to kill worms
vermilion A color
vermin A species of animal
vermouth A white wine
vernacular The native speech of a country
vernal Occurring in the spring
vernier A device for measuring instruments
veronica A species of plant
verruca, pl **-cae** A wart

versant The slope of a mountain

versatile Competent in many things

verse Poetry

versicle A short verse

versine A trigonometric function

version A translation

verso Any left-hand page of a book

verst A unit of linear measure

versus Against

vert The green growth of a forest

vertebra, *pl* **-brae** or **-bras** Any one of the bones of the spinal column

vertex, *pl* **-texes** or **-tices** The summit

vertical Upright

verticil A circular arrangement

vertigo The feeling of dizziness

vertu Variant of virtu

vervain A species of plant

verve Vitality

vervet A monkey

very Complete

vesica, *pl* **-cae** A bladder

vesicant A blistering substance

vesicate To blister

vesicle A small bladder

vesper An evening service

vesperal A book used at vespers

vespiary A nest of hornets

vespid A species of insect

vespine Resembling a wasp

vessel A container

vest A sleeveless garment

vesta A short friction match

vestal Pure

vestee A woman's garment

vestiary Of clothes

vestibule An entrance hall

vestige A trace of something that once existed

vestment A garment

vestry A room in a church

vesture Apparel

vesuvian A mineral

vet A veterinarian

vetch A species of plant

veteran A former member of the armed forces

vetiver A grass

veto A rejection of a proposal

vex To annoy

vexillum, *pl* **vexilla** A flag

via By way of

viable Practicable

viaduct A bridge

vial A small container

viand An article of food

viatic, viatical Pertaining to traveling

viaticum, *pl* **-ca** or **-cums** The Eucharist given to a dying person

viator, *pl* **viatores** A traveler

vibrant Full of energy

vibrate To move back and forth rapidly

vibrato A tremulous effect

vibrio A comma-shaped microorganism

vibrissa, *pl* **-brissae** A whisker of a cat

viburnum A species of shrub

vicar A church official

vicarship The office of a vicar

vice An evil action

vicenary Pertaining to 20

vicennial Happening every 20 years

viceregal Pertaining to a viceroy

vicereine The wife of a viceroy

viceroy A ruler

vicinage The vicinity

vicinal Nearby

vicinity A nearby area

vicious Evil

victim One who suffers injury or loss

victor The winner

victoria A carriage

victory Winning outcome

victress A female victor

victual Food

vicuna A llamalike mammal

vide See

video The picture portion of a telecast

vidette Variant of vedette

vidicon A television camera tube

vie   To compete
view   A picture
viewpoint   A point of view
viewy   Showy
viga   A ceiling beam
vigil   A watch kept during regular sleeping hours
vigilante   A member of an unauthorized vigilance committee
vignette   A short literary sketch
vigor, vigour   Active strength
vigoroso   Vigorous
viking   A Scandinavian mariner
vilayet   An administrative division of Turkey
vile   Wretched
vilify   To defame
vilipend   To despise
villa   A country residence
village   A rural town
villain   A scoundrel
villatic   Rural
villein   A feudal serf
villous, villose   Covered with villi
villus, pl **villi**   Soft, fine hairs on certain plants
vim   Vitality
vin   Wine
vina   A musical instrument
vinasse   Residue left in a still
vincible   Capable of being defeated
vinculum, pl **-la**   A connecting fold
vindicate   To clear of blame
vine   A climbing plant
vinegar   A sour liquid
vineyard   Land planted with grapevines
vinic   Derived from wine
vino   Wine
vinous   Pertaining to wine
vintage   The year of origin
vintner   A wine merchant
viny   Like vines
vinyl   A plastic
viol   A stringed musical instrument
viola   A stringed musical instrument
violate   To break a law
violent   Extreme
violet   A species of plant

violin   A musical instrument
violone   A musical instrument
viper   A species of snake
viperine   Resembling a viper
virago   A quarrelsome woman
viral   Caused by a virus
virelay, virelai   A verse form
vireo   A species of bird
virga   Falling precipitation that evaporates before reaching the ground
virgate   Rod-shaped
virgin   A maiden
virgule   A printing mark
virid   Verdant
virile   Having masculine vigor
virology   The study of viruses
virtu   A love for fine arts
virtue   Goodness
virtuoso, pl **-sos** or **-si**   A brilliant performer
virulent   Extremely poisonous
virus, pl **-uses**   A submicroscopic pathogen
vis   Strength
visa   An endorsement on a passport
visage   Countenance
visard   Variant of vizard
viscacha   A species of rodent
viscera   The internal organs of the body
viscid   Viscous
viscose   Viscous
viscount   A British nobleman
viscous   Having a sticky fluid consistency
viscus   Singular of viscera
vise   A clamping device
visible   Capable of being seen
vision   The sense of sight
visit   To call on
visitant   A visitor
visitor   A guest
visor, vizor   The brim of a cap
vista   An avenue
visual   Visible
vita   A brief biography
vital   Vigorous
vitamer   A chemical compound
vitamin, vitamine   Organic sub-

stances necessary for proper nutrition

vitascope A motion-picture projector

vitellin A protein found in egg yolk

vitellus The yolk of an egg

vitiate To spoil

vitiligo A skin disease

vitreous Glassy

vitrify To change into glass

vitriol Sulfuric acid

vitta, *pl* **vitae** A streak of color

vittle Variant of victual

viva A shout of approval

vivace Lively

vivarium, *pl* **-ums** or **-ia** A place for keeping animals

vive An exclamation of acclaim

vivid Brilliant

vivify To animate

vivisect To perform vivisection

vixen A female fox

vizard A mask

vizier, vizir A Moslem official

vocable A word

vocal Having a voice

vocalic Consisting of a vowel

vocation An occupation

vocative A grammatical case

vodka An alcoholic liquor

vogue The prevailing style

voice The sounds produced by the vocal organs

void Empty

voidance The act of voiding

voila There it is

voile A fabric

volant Agile

volar Palm of the hand

volatile Explosive

volcano A mountain of volcanic materials

vole A species of rodent

volitant Capable of flying

volition A deliberate decision

volley A tennis shot

volplane The glide of an airplane

volt A unit of electromotive force

voltaic Galvanic

voluble Fluent

volume A book

voluntary Intentional

volunteer One who offers his services

volute A scroll-like ornament

volva A mushroom covering

volvox A species of flagellate protozoan

volvulus Intestinal obstruction

vomer A skull bone

vomica, *pl* **-cae** A pus-containing cavity

vomit To spew forth

vomitus Vomited matter

von Of

voodoo A belief in sorcery

voracious Ravenous

vorlage A position in skiing

vortex, *pl* **-texes** or **-tices** A whirlwind

vortical Whirling

votary A devout worshiper

vote A written ballot, an expression of opinion

votive Toward fulfillment of a vow

vouch To verify

voussoir A wedge-shaped stone in an arch

vow A pledge

vowel A speech sound

vox Voice

voyage A journey

voyageur A boatman

voyeur One who derives pleasure from viewing sexual objects

vroom Sound made by a motor vehicle

vug, vugg, vugh A hollow in a rock

vulcanite A hard rubber

vulgar boorish

vulgate The common speech of a people

vulpine Clever like a fox

vulture A species of large bird

vulva, *pl* **-vae** The external genital organs of the female

vulvitis Inflammation of the vulva

vying Contending

wab A web
wabble Variant of wobble
wacko *Slang* A person who is wacky
wacky *Slang* Silly
wad A lump of something
waddy A cowboy
wade To walk in water
wadi A riverbed
wafer A cookie
waff To flutter
waffle A batter cake
waft To propel through the air
waftage The state of being wafted
wafture The act of wafting
wag To waddle
wage Salary
waggery Waggish behavior
waggish Playfully humorous
waggle To wobble
wagon A vehicle
wagoner A wagon driver
wagonette A carriage
wagtail A species of bird
wahine A woman
wahoo A shout of enthusiasm
waif An orphaned child
wail To lament
wain A farm wagon
wainscot A wall paneling
waist A blouse
waistband A sash
waistcoat A vest
waister A seaman
waistline The line of the waist
wait To tarry
waitress A female waiter
waive To give up
wake To cease to sleep
wale A welt
walk To move by steps

walkaway A victory easily won
walkout A strike
walkover A walkaway
walkup A building with no elevator
wall An upright structure
wallaby A species of marsupial
wallah, walla One employed in a particular occupation
wallaroo A kangaroo
wallet A billfold
walleye A food and game fish
wallop To thrash
wallow To revel
wally Pleasing
walnut A species of tree
walrus, *pl* **-ruses** A large marine mammal
waltz A dance
wamble To stagger
wame The belly
wampum Beads
wan Pale
wand A scepter
wander To roam
wanderoo A monkey
wane To dwindle
wangle To manipulate
wanigan, wannigan, wangan A supply chest used in a logging camp
want To lack
wanton Lewd
wapiti A large deer
war A state of armed conflict
warble To sing with melodic embellishments
ward A large room in a hospital
warden The head of a prison
wardenry The duties of a warden
wardress A prison matron

wardrobe Garments
wardroom Officers' mess on a warship
wardship Custody
ware A piece of goods
warfarin A chemical compound
warhead Part of a missile
warlock A wizard
warlord A military leader
warm Moderately hot
warmth Ardor
warn To caution
warp To twist out of shape
warpath A hostile course
warrant To guarantee
warrantee One to whom a warranty is made
warrantor One who gives a warranty
warren A colony of rabbits
warrener One who keeps a warren
warrior One engaged in battle
warsaw A marine fish
wart A growth on the skin
warty Covered with warts
wary Cautious
was First and third person singular past indicative of be
wash To cleanse
washcloth A face cloth
washday A day set aside for washing clothes
washout A failure
washy Watery
wasp A species of insect
waspish Snappish
wassail A toast
wast Second person singular past tense of be
wastage Gradual process of wasting
waste To squander
wastrel One who wastes
wat A Buddhist temple
watap, watape A type of thread
watch To look for
watchcase The casing for a watch
watchdog A guard dog
watchword A password
water A clear, tasteless, colorless liquid

waterage The movement of goods by water
waterbuck A species of antelope
watercress A plant
waterish Watery
waterleaf A species of plant
waterlog To soak with water
watt A unit of power
wattle Supports of a thatched roof
wave To move back and forth
waveband Radio frequencies
waveform A mathematical graph
wavelet A small wave
waw Variant of vav
wax A substance secreted by bees
waxberry Waxy fruit
waxbill A species of bird
waxen Covered with wax
waxwing A species of bird
waxwork Figures made of wax
waxy Resembling wax
way The manner of doing something
waybill A list of goods
wayfarer One who travels
waylay To ambush
wayworn Wearied
we The persons speaking
weak Lacking energy
weakfish A species of fish
weal A welt
weald A woodland
wealth Riches
wean To withhold mother's milk from the young
weapon Any instrument used in combat
weaponry Weapons
wear To have on
wearisome Causing mental fatigue
weasand The throat
weasel A species of mammal
weather Condition of the atmosphere
weave To make a fabric on a loom
web A complex network
webby Resembling a web
weber A unit of magnetic flux
webster A weaver

webworm A species of caterpillar
wed To marry
wedge A tapered piece of something
wedgie A woman's shoe
wedlock The state of being married
wee Tiny
weed An undesired plant
week A period of seven days
ween To think
weenie, weeny Variants of wiener
weep To lament
weepy Tearful
weever A species of fish
weevil A species of beetle
weft A woven fabric
weigela A species of shrub
weigh To determine the weight of
weight A unit of measure
weir A fence placed in a stream to catch fish
weird Eerie
weirdie, weirdy, weirdo *Slang* A weird person
weka A species of flightless bird
welch Variant of welsh
welcome A cordial greeting
weld To join by applying heat
weldment A unit of welded pieces
welfare Public relief
welfarism The policies of a welfare state
welkin The vault of heaven
well Satisfactorily
wellaway, welladay Woe is me
wellhead The source of a well
welsh *Slang* To evade debt payment
welt A bump on the skin
welter To roll about
wen A benign skin tumor
wench A loose woman
wend To go
went Past tense of go
wept Past tense of weep
were Past subjunctive of be
werewolf, *pl* **-wolves** A person changed into a wolf
wergeld, werglid, wereglid A price set upon a man's life

wert Second person singular past indicative of be
weskit A vest
west A cardinal point on the compass
wester A storm coming from the west
westerner A native of the west
westing A westward direction
wet Damp
wetback A Mexican laborer who illegally comes into the U.S.
wether A gelded male sheep
wetland Marshes
wettish Somewhat wet
whack To slap
whacky Variant of wacky
whale A species of marine mammal
whaleback A type of steamship
whaleboat A boat used by whalers
whalebone The hornlike material in the upper jaw of certain whales
whaler A whaling ship
wham, whammo A heavy blow
whammy *Slang* A jinx
whang A thong of leather
whangee A species of grass
whap Variant of whop
wharf A landing dock
wharfage The use of a wharf
what Which thing
whatever No matter what
whatnot A trivial thing
wheal A small bite on the skin
wheat A species of cereal grass
wheatear A small bird
wheaten Derived from wheat
wheatworm A nematode worm
wheedle To cajole
wheel A circular frame turning on a single axis
wheelbase The distance from the front to rear axle
wheelie A stunt performed on a vehicle
wheelman A helmsman
wheelwork An arrangement of wheels in a machine
wheen A few
wheeze To breathe hard

wheezy Producing a wheezing sound

whelk A species of snail

whelm To submerge

whelp A puppy

when At what time

whenas Whereas

whence From where

whenever When

where In what place

whereas Inasmuch as

whereat At what

whereby By what

wherefore For what

wherefrom From what

wherein In what

whereinto Into what

whereof Of what

whereon On what

whereto To what

whereupon Upon what

wherever Where

wherewith With what

wherry A racing scull

whet To sharpen

whether In case

whetstone A stone for sharpening knives

whew Used to express relief

whey The watery part of milk

which What particular one

whichever Any one

whicker To whinny

whiff A waft

whiffet A little puff

whiffle To blow fitfully

while A period of time

whilom Former

whilst While

whim A passing fancy

whimbrel A wading bird

whimper To whine

whimsical Playful

whimsy Idle fancy

whin Coarse grass

whinchat A songbird

whine To utter a high-pitched nasal sound

whinny To neigh

whinstone A dark-colored rock

whiny Given to whining

whip To lash

whipcord A fabric

whiplash The lash of a whip

whippet A breed of dog

whipsaw A crosscut saw

whipstall A stunt in flying

whipstock The handle of a whip

whipt Past tense of whip

whipworm A species of roundworm

whir, whirr To move quickly so as to produce a whizzing sound

whirl To spin rapidly

whirligig A toy

whirlpool An eddy

whirlwind A whirling air current

whisk To whip

whiskey Alcoholic liquor

whisper To speak softly

whist A card game

whistle To make a clear, shrill sound

whistler One who whistles

whit A particle

white Having the color of milk

whitebait A species of small edible fish

whitecap A wave with a crest of foam

whitefish A species of food fish

whitefly A species of insect

whitehead A species of bird

whiteout An optical phenomenon occurring in polar regions

whitewash A mixture of lime and water

whitewood Light-colored wood of various trees

whitey *Slang* A blond man or boy

whither To what place

whitlow Inflammation of the finger

whittle To cut small bits from

whiz, whizz To rush about

who What or which person

whoa Stop

whodunit A mystery story

whoever No matter who

whole Complete

wholism Variant of holism

wholly Entirely

335

whom Objective case of who

whomever Objective case of whoever

whomp To hit

whoof A deep breathy sound

whoop A loud shout

whoopee An exclamation of joy

whoopla Variant of hoopla

whoosh To make a rushing sound

whop To thrash

whore A prostitute

whoredom Prostitution

whoreson Son of a whore

whorish Lewd

whorl A flywheel

whort, whortle The whortleberry

whose The possessive case of who

whoso Who

why The reason for something

whydah, whidah A species of African bird

wick The fibers in a candle

wicket A small gate

wickiup An Indian hut

wicopy A species of tree

wide Broad

widgeon A freshwater duck

widget A gadget

widow A woman whose husband has died

width The quality of being wide

widthwise From side to side

wield To exert influence

wiener A frankfurter

wife, *pl* **wives** A married woman

wig A headpiece of false hair

wigan A fabric

wigeon Variant of widgeon

wiggery Wigs

wiggle To twist from side to side

wight A living being

wiglet A small wig

wigwag To move back and forth

wigwam A North American Indian dwelling

wilco I will comply with your request

wild Not tamed

wildcat A species of wild feline

wildfire A raging fire

wildfowl A wild bird

wildling A wild plant

wildwood A natural forest

wile Cunning

will To decide upon

willet A shore bird

willies *Slang* Uneasy feeling

williwaw, willywaw A sudden cold wind

willow A species of tree

willy To clean textile fibers

wilt To droop

wily Crafty

wimble A hand tool

wimp *Slang* A weak person

wimple A woman's head covering

win To achieve victory

wince To flinch

winch A hoisting device

wind Air in motion

windage The part of the ship exposed to the wind

windbag A talkative person

windburn Reddened skin

windfall A sudden good fortune

windflaw A sudden blast of wind

windgall A swelling on a horse's leg

windlass A hoisting device

windmill A mill that runs by wind power

window An opening to admit light

windpipe The trachea

windrow A row of hay

windsock A device that indicates the direction of the wind

windward The direction from which the wind blows

wine Fermented juice of grapes

winery A place for making wine

wineskin A goatskin bag

wing Organs of flight

wingback A backfield position in football

wingding *Slang* A festive celebration

winglet A small wing

wingover An aerial maneuver

wink To blink

winkle To rout

winnow To scatter
wino *Slang* An alcoholic
winsome Charming
winter The coldest season
winterly Wintry
wintry Cold
winy Heady
winze A mine shaft
wipe To brush
wire To send a telegram
wireman A lineman
wiretap A listening device
wirework Products made of wire
wireworm A species of millipede
wirra Used to express sorrow
wiry Of wire
wisdom Good judgment
wise Having good judgment
wiseacre One who thinks he knows it all
wisecrack *Slang* A flippant remark
wisent The European bison
wish A desire
wishbone The forked bone in the breastbone of most birds
wisp A bundle of twigs
wist To know
wisteria, wistaria A species of woody plant
wit Good sense
witan A wise man
witch One who practices sorcery
witchery Sorcery
wite To blame
with Next to
withal In addition
withe A willow twig
wither To droop
withy Tough
witloof A salad plant
witness A person who gives evidence
witticism A witty remark
witting Knowledge
wittol A man who tolerates his wife's infidelity
wive To marry a woman
wivern, wiver A two-legged dragon
wiz A clever person

wizard A sorcerer
wizardry Sorcery
wizen To dry up
woad A plant
wobble To move from side to side
woe Grief
woebegone, wobegone Woeful
woke Past tense of wake
wold A high plain
wolf, *pl* **wolves** A carnivorous mammal
wolfram Tungsten
wolfsbane A plant
wolverine A carnivorous mammal
woman An adult female
womb The uterus
wombat A nocturnal mammal
womenfolk Women
won To dwell
wonder A feeling of puzzlement
wonk *Slang* A student who studies too hard
wonky *Slang* Feeble
wont Accustomed to
woo To make love to
wood A growth of trees
woodbin A box for storing firewood
woodbine A species of vine
woodblock A woodcut
woodchat A species of bird
woodcock A game bird
woodcut A print made from wood
woodlark A songbird
woodnote A song of a forest bird
woodpile A pile of wood
woodruff A species of plant
woodshed A shed for storing wood
woodsman A forester
woodsy Suggestive of the woods
woodwind A musical instrument
woodworm A wood-boring worm
woof The texture of a fabric
wool The hair of sheep
woolly, wooly Pertaining to wool
woolpack A bale of wool
woolsack A sack for wool
woolskin A sheepskin
woops Variant of oops
woosh Variant of whoosh

woozy Dizzy
word A comment
wordage Wording
wordbook A dictionary
wore Past tense of wear
work Labor
workaday Everyday
workbag A bag for holding work materials
workbox A box for materials used in work
workfolk Laborers
workload The amount of work done
workout A period of exercise
workweek The number of hours worked
world The earth
worm A species of invertebrate
wormhole A hole made by a worm
wormseed A species of plant
wormwood A species of aromatic plant
worn Affected by wear
worriment Worry
worrisome Anxious
worry To be troubled
worrywart One who tends to worry
worse Less good
worship Religious homage
worst Unfavorable
worsted A fabric
wort A plant
worth Wealth
wost Present second person singular of wit
wot To know
would Past tense of will
wouldst, wouldest Second person singular past tense of will
wound An injury
wove Past tense of weave
wow An exclamation of surprise

wrack Wreckage
wraith A ghost
wrangle To bicker
wrangler A cowboy
wrap A cloak
wrapt Past tense of wrap
wrasse A species of fish
wrastle to wrestle
wrath Rage
wreak To inflict
wreath A ring of flowers
wreathe To make into a wreath
wreck Destruction
wren A species of bird
wrench A sudden twist
wrest To take away
wrestle To struggle
wretch A mean person
wriggle To squirm
wright One who constructs
wring To squeeze
wrinkle A crease on an otherwise smooth surface
wrist The junction between the hand and the forearm
wristlet A bracelet
writ An order issued by a court
write To inscribe
writhe To squirm
written Past participle of write
wrong Not correct
wrongdoer One who does wrong
wrote Past tense of write
wroth Angry
wrought Formed
wrung Past tense of wring
wry Twisted
wryneck A species of bird
wunderbar Wonderful
wurst Sausage
wye The letter y
wynd A narrow lane
wyvern A two-legged dragon

xanthan A gum produced by bacteria fermentation
xanthate A chemical salt
xanthin A yellow pigment
xanthine A chemical compound
xanthoma A skin disease
xanthone A chemical compound
xanthous Yellow
xebec A three-masted sailing vessel
xenia The effect of pollen on plants
xenolith A rock fragment foreign to the rock in which it is found
xenon A gaseous element
xerarch Developing in desert areas
xeric Having a dry condition
xerosere A climatic cycle beginning in a dry area

xerosis Abnormal dryness
xi The fourteenth letter of the Greek alphabet
xiphoid Shaped like a sword
xu Monetary unit of Vietnam
xylan A gummy substance found in woody tissues
xylem A plant tissue
xylene A flammable hydrocarbon
xylidine A chemical compound
xylograph A wood engraving
xyloid Woody
xylol Xylene
xylophone A musical instrument
xylose A type of sugar
xylotomy The preparation of sections of wood for inspection
xyster A surgical instrument

ya You
yabber Talk
yacht A pleasure boat
yack *Slang* To talk
yagi A directional antenna
yah Yes
yahoo A crude person
yahrzeit A Jewish ceremony
yak A bovine mammal

yam A species of vine
yamen The residence of a Chinese official
yammer To whine
yang The masculine force in Chinese philosophy
yank To jerk
yap To yelp
yapok, yapock An aquatic marsup-

339

ial mammal

yard A unit of length

yardage Cloth

yardarm Either end of a yard supporting a square sail

yardman One employed in a railroad yard

yare Lively

yarmulke, yarmelke A skullcap worn by male Jews

yarn A story

yarrow A species of plant

yashmak, yashmac, yasmak A veil worn by Moslem women

yataghan, yatagan A Turkish sword

yatter *Slang* To chatter foolishly

yaupon An evergreen holly

yaw To deviate from the course

yawl A sailing vessel

yawn To open wide

yawp To yelp

yaws A skin disease

yclept, ycleped Known as

ye You

yea Yes

yeah, yeh Yes

yean To bear young

yeanling Newly born

year A period of time

yearbook A school year book

yearling Being one year old

yearn To have a deep desire

yeast Leaven

yeasty Restless

yech A gagging sound

yegg *Slang* A burglar

yell To cry out

yellow A color

yellowy Somewhat yellow

yelp To utter a sharp cry

yen To yearn

yenta, yente A busybody

yeoman A naval clerk

yeomanry Yeomen

yep *Slang* Yes

yes Used to express agreement

yesterday The day before the present day

yet Now

yeti The abominable snowman

yew A species of evergreen tree

yield To surrender

yin The female force in Chinese philosophy

yip A yelp

yipe Used to express surprise

yippee Used to express joy

yod, yodh The tenth letter of the Hebrew alphabet

yodel To sing with a fluctuating voice sound

yoga A mystic and ascetic discipline

yogh A Middle English letter

yogi, yogin One who practices yoga

yogurt, yoghurt, yoghourt A custardlike food

yohimbine A poisonous alkaloid

yoicks A cry used in fox hunting

yok Variant of yak

yoke A device that encircles the necks of a pair of oxen

yokel A country bumpkin

yolk The yellow part of an egg

yonder, yon, yond Over there

yoni A representation of the vulva

yore Time past

you The person to whom one is speaking

young Not old

youngish Somewhat young

youngster A child

younker A young man

your Belonging to you

yourself, *pl* **-selves** A form of the pronoun you

youth The state of being young

yow An exclamation of pain

yowl To howl

ytterbia A chemical compound

ytterbic Containing ytterbium

yttria Yttrium oxide

yttric Derived from yttrium

yttrium A metallic element

yuan Monetary unit of China

yucca A species of plant

yuck, yucky *Slang* Something disgusting

yuk *Slang* A loud laugh

yulan A Chinese tree
yule The Christmas season
yum, yummy Delicious

yup *Slang* Yes
yurt A circular tent
ywis Certainly

zacaton A species of grass
zaddick A righteous man
zaffer, zaffre An oxide of cobalt
zaftig *Slang* Having a voluptuous
figure
zag A sharp turn
zaibatsu Japanese families that
dominate finance
zaire Monetary unit of Zaire
zamia A species of cycad
zamindar A landowner
zanana Variant of zenana
zany A foolish person
zap *Slang* Energy
zapateado A flamenco dance
zareba, zareeba A camping place
zarf A holder for a hot coffee cup
zax A cutting tool
zayin The seventh letter of the
Hebrew alphabet
zeal Fervor
zealot One who is zealous
zealotry Excessive zeal
zebec, zebeck Variants of xebec
zebra A species of African mammal
zebu An oxlike animal
zecchino, *pl* **-ni** A coin
zechin Variant of sequin
zedoary A plant with a medicinal
stem
zee, zed The letter z
zein A protein
zemstvo An administrative body in

Czarist Russia
zenana The part of the house
reserved for women
zenith The upper portion of the sky
zeolite A mineral
zephyr The west wind
zeppelin A rigid airship
zero The symbol O
zest Gusto
zeta The sixth letter of the Greek
alphabet
zeugma A figure of speech
zibeline, zibelline A fabric
zibet, zibeth A civet cat
zig A sharp turn
ziggurat, zikkurat A temple tower
zigzag A course having sharp turns
zilch *Slang* Nothing
zillah An administrative district
zillion A very large number
zinc A metallic element
zincate A chemical compound
zincite A zinc ore
zineb An insecticide
zinfandel A red wine
zing A high-pitched humming
sound
zingara, *pl* **-re** A female Gypsy
zingaro, *pl* **-ni** A Gypsy
zinger *Slang* A punch line
zinnia A species of plant
zip Vim
zipper A fastening device

ziram A chemical salt
zircon A mineral
zirconia Zirconium oxide
zither A musical instrument
ziti Tubular pasta
zizith The tassels on prayer shawls
zloty Monetary unit of Poland
zodiac An imaginary band in the heavens
zoea The larval stage of various crabs
zoisite A mineral
zombie, zombi A voodoo snake deity
zone A region separate from others
zonetime A time used at sea
zonked *Slang* Intoxicated
zonule A small zone
zoo A collection of animals
zoochore A plant
zoogenic Caused by animals
zoogloea A mass of bacteria
zoography The description of animals
zooid A cell that has independent movement
zooks Used as a mild oath
zoolatry The worship of animals
zoology The science of animals
zoom To swoop
zoometry The measurement of animals
zoon, *pl* **-ons** or **zoa** An animal developed from a fertilized egg
zoonosis, *pl* **-ses** A disease that can be transmitted from animals to man
zoophile A lover of animals
zoophyte An invertebrate animal
zoosperm A spermatozoon
zoospore An asexual sporangial spore
zootomy The anatomy of animals other than man
zori A Japanese sandal
zorille, zoril An African mammal
zoster A belt
zounds A mild oath
zowie An exclamation of enthusiasm
zoysia A species of grass
zucchini A variety of squash
zwieback A type of bread
zygoid Pertaining to a zygote
zygoma, *pl* **-mata** or **-mas** The zygomatic bone
zygosis, *pl* **-ses** The union of two gametes
zygote The cell formed by two gametes
zymase, zyme An enzyme
zymogen, zymogene The inactive protein that develops into an enzyme
zymology The science of fermentation
zymosis Fermentation
zymurgy The branch of chemistry dealing with fermentation
zyzzyva A species of weevil

Appendix 1

Have a Word Game Party

"A rhapsody of words."
Hamlet, Act III, Scene IV
Shakespeare
(1564–1616)

The Original Word Game Dictionary

Now that you've improved your vocabulary and word game skills you're probably anxious to play word games with your family or friends. What better way to spend an evening than bantering words back and forth—especially since you're virtually a pro now, anxious to show how clever you are. But you want to make it a fun party; after all, did you really buy those word games *just* to enrich your mind?

Here, then, are a few words (all found in the dictionary) about how to plan and prepare for your word game party.

THE INVITATION

It's fun when friends drop in for a game or two, but if you're going to throw a real word game party you must plan and prepare for it.

The first detail is the invitations. They must be ultra-special and should convey the theme of your party. Let your imagination run wild. Here are a few suggestions.

Create your own crossword sheet to be filled out by the invitee, or fill in the blank spaces with your party information.

P	arty featuring word games
A	t 828 Banklick Street, etc.
R	eply: RSVP 234-6477
T	ime: 7:00 PM, October 17
Y	ou, we look forward to!

PARLOR WORD GAMES

A good way for your guests to relax and become better acquainted—especially if they're a large group—is to engage them in parlor games before beginning the more serious word games.

Parlor games that employ words have been played for countless years. They're imaginative and require no specialized knowledge and, best of all, they're fun. A selection of some of the more interesting and better-known ones can be found in Appendix 2 of this book.

One enjoyable activity is to invite your guests to work on a giant crossword puzzle on the floor. Depending on the sensabilities of your guests, an amusing gimmick can be crossword toilet paper.

What an outrageous prize for game winners! You may want to put a roll in the bathroom and include a felt-tip marker. These and similar items are available in most novelty shops.

MAKE 'EM EAT THEIR WORDS

You can put words *into* your guests' mouths, too. As poetess Emily Dickinson said, "He ate and drank the precious words."

Here's a hearty dinner menu:

WORD EDIBLES

Perquackey® Punch
Addiction Antipasto Platter
Dig-It® Dip
Alphabet Soup (add alphabet noodles to any recipe)
Scrabble® Salad
Royalty® Roast
PROBE® Potatoes
CROZZLE® Cream with Catchword™ Cookies

Serve your guests these zany goodies and snacks:

THAT'S INCREDIBLE® Ice Cream Sundaes—*Pile it on!*
RAZZLE™ Raisin Pie—*Words can't describe it.*
HANGMAN™ Hamburgers—*Serve with onion rings.*
Scrabble® Eggs—*Scrambled eggs with assorted garnishes*
BOGGLE® Bagels—*Bagel halves with cream cheese and assorted toppings.*
DIXIT Dip—*Your favorite recipe.*
CROSS CUBES™ Crackers—*Assorted crackers.*
Upper Hand™ Sandwiches—*Open-face creations.*
Crossword Dominoes™ Dainties—*Go wild!*
Alphabet Popcorn Balls—*Add Alpha-Bits® cereal.*

It's easy to apply the name of your favorite word games to your own recipes. Whether you serve a full-course dinner or just fun-time snacks, your guests will delight in these unique creations of your imagination. A few quick and easy recipes are listed which you and your guests may enjoy.

Perquackey® Punch

cranberry juice
  (or fruit drink)
ginger ale
raspberry or lemon sherbet

Mix any amount of cranberry juice or fruit drink with an equal amount of ginger ale. Put a small scoop of sherbet into each glass and fill with the punch mixture.

CROZZLE® Cream

strawberries, raspberries or blueberries
  (frozen or fresh)
whipped cream
sugar sprinkles

Stir berries into a sweetened whip cream. Garnish with sugar sprinkles. Or for a quickie cream, add a jar of strained baby food fruit (apricots, plums, or the like) to an appropriate amount of whipped cream for a delightful cream fluff.

Alphabet Yummies

¼ cup butter or oleomargarine
40 regular marshmallows (or 4 cups miniatures)
4 cups of Alpha-Bits® cereal
nuts, raisins, candies (optional)

Melt butter in a large saucepan. Add marshmallows, letting them melt in butter. Pour mixture over Alpha-Bits®. Add nuts, raisins, or candies. Press mixture into a 9″ x 13″ x 2″ pan and allow to cool. Cut into squares or alphabet shapes. (Alphabet-shaped cookie cutters are fun to use.) If you wish to add color to your Yummies, add a few drops of food coloring into the hot mixture before pouring. Or you can add a small amount of another cereal for color, such as Strawberry Shortcake™.

GAME ACCESSORIES

There's nothing worse than settling down to play a game and realizing that everything's not ready. If your game needs pads and pencils, have them handy on the table. Prepare a checklist of things you need for the party and *use it*.

LIGHTING AND TABLE COVERING

Lighting is important, so be sure your light is spread evenly; no shadows and no glare. Even if a special friend is invited for a "party for two," save the candlelight 'til later!

A green cloth is the ideal table covering; green is easy on the eyes and makes a neutral background for most games. If you're thinking of purchasing a special cover for your game table, we suggest you buy a piece of green felt at a fabric store. It comes in large widths so that it can be easily cut into any shape.

BACKGROUND MUSIC

Background music is fine for your game-playing, but only if it isn't distracting. Don't turn on the radio—even FM—because an announcer can interfere with the words you're trying to make. Tapes or records are the only answer; however, don't play songs, either vocal or instrumental. If a person knows the lyrics, he'll often find himself singing under his breath.

Light classical music is recommended. Symphonic tone poems are perfect . . . by composers like Frederick Dulius, John Ireland, Richard Strauss, or Arnold Bax. Also, some orchestral works by composers like Rachmaninoff, Ravel, Grieg, Debussy, or Tchaikovsky are excellent. Background music should be soft and hardly noticeable—just loud enough to give your party that special touch of class.

CLOTHING

Naturally, if you're having friends or family over, you want to look your best—but when you're playing games you want to be relaxed, so dress casually. For dry humor, how about a skirt or blouse bearing your initials?

Some people feel that a card dealer's visor (preferably green) is a fun item to wear when you're playing games. You can bring it out when you're ready to sit down to play; then slip it on without fanfare. See what a rise that'll get out of your guests!

One note of advice: shirts or blouses with full droopy sleeves are unhandy in many games. Baggy sleeves can really interfere with the action in games like CATCHWORD™, Scrabble® Brand Scoring Anagrams, and Dig-It!™.

PRIZES FOR WINNERS

Prizes can be either elaborate awards or novelty items. One award that will be appreciated is the *Original Word Game Dictionary* in either hardcover or quality paperback. Other items to consider are word games and books (but be sure to pen something personal into them). Inexpensive party favors can include initial monograms, crossword puzzle booklets, and card dealer's visors. If you're clever with crafts there are many things you can make and personalize with monograms.

AWARD CERTIFICATES

Attractive certificates can easily be made, as fancy or as simple as you care to make them, and either serious or humorous.

The winner might like the other players to autograph the certificate, too. Then it becomes a nice remembrance of all one's friends at your word-game party. Whatever you give as prizes, make them keepsakes of a happy get-together.

A FEW FINAL WORDS . . .

When you're playing word games remember to *always* make it a fun time, whether it's a big party or one of your regular weekly get-togethers with old friends or kin. You never want a guest to quote Eliza Doolittle's famous line: "Words, words, words, I'm so sick of words!"

A word of caution about prematurely challenging an opponent and saying, "That's not a word!" *Make sure* you know you're right. It's rather embarrassing when a competitor shows you the word in the *Original Word Game Dictionary*. If you *must* challenge a word, do it in a friendly yet matter-of-fact tone, such as, "I really don't think that's a word."

And if your guests stay too late, you can always show how clever you are and quote Homer,who said, more than two thousand years ago, "There is a time for many words, and there is also a time for sleep."

Appendix 2

Popular Parlor Word Games

"Large divine and comfortable words."
Alfred, Lord Tennyson
English Poet
(1809–1892)

Parlor games go back to the ancient Greeks. One simple and rather simple-minded pastime the Romans played required one player to challenge another to guess whether he held an odd or an even number of nuts in his fist.

Today's parlor games may not be as old but most of them were handed down, origins unknown, from one generation to another. The names and rules change with use and vary with every family and community who play them; so *you* can feel entirely free to improvise. Young folks addicted to today's electronic entertainment marvels are often surprised to learn how exciting parlor games can be.

The following games are fun to play and require little skill; the more participants, the more excitement.

OLD-TIME SPELLING BEE
Any number of players
All ages
Competitive

One person is chosen as the teacher and the other players are the pupils. The teacher prepares a list of words taken from the *Original Word Game Dictionary*. Some people find it fun to nickname each pupil, thereby helping create an atmosphere of schooldays gone by.

The teacher reads aloud a word and the first pupil tries to spell it out loud. If he or she spells it correctly the teacher then reads the next word for the second pupil. When a pupil fails to correctly spell a word, he or she drops out of the game and the misspelled word is then passed on to the next pupil. The pupil who spells the most words right wins the game.

"A" TO "Z"
Any number of players
All ages
Mildly competitive

The players decide on a specific category such as animals, cities, flowers, food, or the like. The first player starts by saying any word in the chosen category. The next player follows with another word in the same category, but his or her word must begin with the *last* letter of the previous word.

For example, if the category is "animals" the words might progress like this: "cow, weasel, leopard, deer," etc.

Players should be allowed only five seconds to think of a word and anyone who calls out an incorrect word, or fails to think of a word, drops out of that round. The player who stays in the longest wins the game.

THE MINISTER'S CAT
Any number of players
All ages
Fast and fun

A version of the pre-Victorian parlor game featured in the movie, *Scrooge,* this game is sometimes known as *I Love My Love, The Duchess' Dog,* or *Hiram's Old Pet Pig.* It can often produce a lot of laughs.

The first player starts by saying, "The minister's cat," adding a word beginning with "A" to complete the statement. Example: "The minister's cat is aristocratic." The next player repeats the title but adds a word beginning with "B." Example: "The minister's cat is beautiful."

The game progresses through the alphabet as each player makes a statement about *The Minister's Cat.* If a player hesitates or gives an incorrect word, he or she drops out of that round. The player who stays in the longest wins the game.

FLASH WORD
Any number of players
All ages
Energetic fun

This is a vigorous parlor word game, requiring fast thinking. The first player says a word (nouns work best) and, without hesitating, the next player says the first word that flashes into his or her mind. It must be a word that has been suggested by or is associated with the first player's word. If a player hesitates before saying his or her *Flash Word,* he or she drops out. The player who stays in the longest wins the game.

ANIMAL, VEGETABLE OR MINERAL
or
TWENTY QUESTIONS
Any number of players
All ages
Competitive but light-hearted

This is one of the most versatile and enduring parlor games. It can be played at any age level with any degree of complexity.

One player is chosen as "It" and leaves the room. The other players choose a word, quotation, famous name, animal, or some such. The "It" person returns and tries to guess the secret subject by asking no more than *Twenty Questions*. The moderator tells him if the subject is animal, vegetable, or mineral." Then the other players must answer truthfully the next twenty questions, "Yes" or No," except when the query can be truthfully answered, "partly correct." If the "It" person guesses the secret word or phrase within *Twenty Questions*, he or she sits down and another player becomes the guesser.

COFFEEPOT
Any number of players
All ages
Fun rather than competitive

Folks played this game around the turn of the century, and it continues to delight players even today. The object is for players to guess an activity.

To start the game, one player is chosen to leave the room. The rest of the players choose a verb or participle describing an activity. Example: cry, crying; dance, dancing; laugh, laughing, etc. The player who's chosen "It" returns to the room and asks each player a question substituting the word *Coffeepot* for the missing word. Example: "Do you have fun when you coffeepot?" The other players must always answer truthfully, "Yes" or "No," or reply with statements like, "Whenever I stub my toe," etc. Since the guesser does not know the activity, the answers can be very funny.

When the guesser realizes the *Coffeepot* word, the player who triggered the clue is the next guesser. If the guesser fails to guess the correct activity after a predetermined number of rounds, the *Coffeepot* is declared empty and another guesser is chosen.

TEAPOT
Any number of players
All ages
Fun rather than competitive

A variation of the old *Coffeepot* game, this is sometimes called *Tea Party*. One player is chosen to leave the room. The other players choose a word for him or her to guess, preferably a homonym—a word with the same pronunciation as another but with a different meaning. Examples: air, err, heir; boar, bore; dew, do, due; hair, hare; dear, deer; etc.

When the guesser returns to the room, the other players converse substituting the word *Teapot* for the chosen word (the guesser may join in if he or she likes). Example: For the word, "deer," a player may say, "I hear the Smiths saw a *Teapot* last night." After the guesser discovers the mysterious *Teapot* word, a new guesser is chosen.

FAMOUS PERSONALITY
Any number of players
All ages—best for adults
Requires diversified knowledge

Any category of famous people, living or dead, fictitious or real, may be used in this game, e.g. singers, artists, composers, movie stars, cartoon characters, or television personalities.

The first participant to play the "personality" chooses the person he or she is going to "be" and tells the other players the initial of his or her fanciful last name. Example: "G" (for Betty Grable). The next player then thinks of a famous personality whose name begins with that particular letter and asks a question that might describe the person about whom he or she is thinking. The questioner is not to name the celebrity whom he has in mind.

For example, if someone is thinking of George Gershwin, he or she may ask, "Did you write a famous jazz composition?" If the "personality" believes he or she is referring to Gershwin, the answer would be, "No, I am not George Gershwin."

If the "personality" fails to recognize a description, the player who gave it may then ask one general question, such as "Are you living?" or "Are you a fictional character?" or "Are you an actor?" The "personality" must always give a truthful "Yes" or "No" reply.

A player who cannot think of someone with a name beginning with the chosen letter, can pass to the next player. The person who guesses the name of the "personality" wins the round and becomes the next "personality." However, if no one can guess the "personality" correctly after a few rounds, the "personality" tells them *whom* he or she is and someone else is chosen as the next *Famous Personality*.

HIDDEN WORDS
Any number of players
All ages
Requires concentration

This game requires paper and pencils for each player. It's an entertaining way to vastly improve your word-game skills.

A main entry word is chosen and each player writes it down. The object is to see how many *Hidden Words* can be found in the main entry word within a certain time limit. The usual limit for each round is three minutes.

The player with the most correctly spelled words wins the round.

Example: *thoroughfare*

age	fore	heat	rag	rug
are	fought	hog	rage	rut
argue	four	hoof	rare	tag
ate	fraught	hoot	rat	tar
ear	gat	hot	rate	tare
eat	gate	hough	rear	tau
era	gear	hour	rogue	tea
far	go	hug	roof	tear
fare	goat	huge	root	thorough
fag	goof	oaf	rot	through
fat	got	oar	rote	to
fear	hag	oat	rotor	too
foot	hare	or	rouge	tor
footage	hat	ought	rough	tough
for	hear	our	route	tour